butter's going up

MARK. I see that butter's going up.
LEN. I'm prepared to believe it, but
    it doesn't answer my question.

The Dwarfs

butter's going up

A critical analysis of Harold Pinter's work

by Steven H. Gale

Duke University Press • Durham, North Carolina • 1977

© 1977, Duke University Press
L.C.C. card no. 74–78833
I.S.B.N. 0–8223–0339–6
Printed in the United States of
America by Heritage Printers, Inc.

Contents

Acknowledgments

No study of this length can be written without the help and good wishes of many people over a long period of time. The love and interest of my family, from my grandparents to my nephew and niece (cats included), gave me the strength I needed. Former professors taught me how to approach a work of literature critically: Leon Howard showed me where to look, William Templeman showed me what to look for, and Emil Roy introduced me to Pinter's writing and its intricacies; Katherine Bull Stanton's understanding and encouragement were invaluable; and my wife Kathy's time-consuming aid and advice deserve more thanks than it is possible to express.

I would also like to express my gratitude to the editor of Duke University Press, Ashbel G. Brice, and to Kimball King and Kenneth R. R. Gros Louis for their sensitive reading and useful suggestions along the way. Additional technical help came from Alan Clugston, and the University of Puerto Rico provided a research grant. Many of those I contacted in the course of my investigations were friendly, understanding, and helpful, including Harold Pinter, who freely answered my questions, Sue Rolfe of the Royal Shakespeare Company, those who have worked with Pinter, such as Peter Hall, John Bury, Donald Pleasence, Julie Christie, and Alan Bates, and the staffs at *London Magazine*, Methuen, and Grove Press (in particular Fred Jordan), as well as those in various theatres, film companies, museums, libraries, and photographers' studios. Jim Goldsmith's help in locating early reviews of *No Man's Land* was invaluable.

Finally, I would like to acknowledge my indebtedness to the writings of Lawrence M. Bensky, John Russell Taylor, Henry Hewes, Martin Esslin, Arnold P. Hinchcliffe, and George Wellwarth, and to my students and colleagues whose discussions have led me to a fuller understanding and appreciation of the works of Harold Pinter.

butter's going up

Introduction

. . . the most original,
disturbing, and arresting talent
in theatrical London . . .

When Harold Pinter wrote his first play, *The Room,* in 1957 he was a repertory actor who had previously published a few poems and started an autobiographical novel. A mere ten years later he was being widely acclaimed by the most important critics of the modern theatre. In J. L. Styan's words he was one of the "two most exciting playwrights in England,"[1] and according to Charles Marowitz he was the "most important dramatist in the New Wave."[2] Joseph Chiari found that the playwright's ability to create intricately fused rhythmical structures made Pinter "the most gifted and versatile of the contemporary dramatists,"[3] while F. J. Bernhard was discussing the "dramatic poetry" of his plays and Harold Hobson in the London *Sunday Times* had

1. Styan, "The Published Play," pp. 601–5. Full citations of works referred to will be found in the Annotated Bibliography that precedes the index.
2. Charles Marowitz, "New Wave in a Dead Sea," p. 270.
3. Joseph Chiari, *Landmarks.*

called him "the most original, disturbing, and arresting talent in theatrical London."[4]

And critical estimation of the author's talents is still rising. Martin Esslin, who devoted little space to Pinter in the first edition of his seminal work *The Theatre of the Absurd* in 1961, expanded his section on Pinter eight years later in the revised edition of 1969 and has written two book-length studies of the artist (one in German) as "indisputably one of the most exciting and original dramatists to have emerged since World War II."[5] Arnold Hinchcliffe has devoted a monograph to demonstrating that Pinter is the only "confident and successful exponent" of Absurd drama on the British scene, a "playwright particularly of our time."[6] In another volume on Pinter, Walter Kerr claims that Pinter is "the only man working in the theatre today who writes existential plays existentially. . . . He remakes the play altogether so that it will function according to existential principles."[7] John Russell Taylor, like Esslin, found the need to expand his section on Pinter in the 1969 revision of his important examination of England's "Angry" theatre, *Anger and After*, originally published in 1962. Like Esslin, too, he has written a book exclusively about Pinter, whom he now considers the "most consistently successful serious dramatist of his generation."[8]

The stature that Pinter has attained as a playwright is astounding, given the relatively short time he has been writing. It is even more astounding when the critical reaction to the first performances of his works is considered. Milton Shulman reviewed the first London performance of *The Birthday Party* and came to the conclusion that "it will be best enjoyed by those who believe that obscurity is its own reward," for "Mr. Pinter just isn't funny enough."[9] Other reviewers also harped on the obscurity of the drama. On May 20, 1958, the *Times* noted: "The first act sounds an offbeat note of madness; in the second the note has risen to a sort of delirium; and the third act studiously refrains from the slightest hint of what the other two may have been about," while on the same day the *Manchester Guardian* lamented, "What all this means, only Mr. Pinter knows, for as his characters speak in *non-sequiturs*, half-gibberish and lunatic ravings, they are unable to explain their actions, thoughts, or feelings. If the author can forget Beckett, Ionesco and Simpson, he may do much better next time." Pinter has personally answered some of these charges in his explanations of his concepts of verification and the use of language, but for such a radical change in critical acceptance to have occurred, there must be more reason than simply a dramatist's defense of his own works.

The change in the general public's reactions to the plays of Harold Pinter

4. Harold Hobson, in *Sunday Times* (London), 25 May 1958.
5. Martin Esslin, *The Peopled Wound*, cover note.
6. Arnold P. Hinchcliffe, *Harold Pinter*, inside jacket note.
7. Walter Kerr, *Harold Pinter*, p. 3.
8. John Russell Taylor, *Harold Pinter*, inside cover note.
9. Milton Shulman, in *Evening Standard* (London), 20 May 1958.

closely parallels and is just as dramatic as the reversal in critical opinion. *The Birthday Party* was forced off the London stage after one week, having earned £260 11s. 8d. There were six people at the Thursday afternoon matinee (representing a take of £2 9s.). Within the next few years, however, Pinter's dramas *The Caretaker, The Lover,* and *The Homecoming* were being cited as "best play of the year," there was standing room only for audiences in London and New York, the author had been honored with the award of C.B.E. (Commander of the Order of the British Empire) in the Queen's Birthday Honours List (1966), and his popularity had reached international proportions with a commission from sixteen member nations of the European Broadcasting Union and premieres of his dramas being presented in Germany, Ireland, and America.

What is responsible for the increasing interest and acceptance of the work of this young playwright is the plays themselves. As Martin Gottfried points out in *A Theatre Divided,* the dramatist's popularity stems from his ability to present ideas in acceptable and successful dramatic modes, for he is certainly "a man of the theatre" in every sense of the word, combining the avant-garde and the traditional, utilizing "outer realism with bizarre plotting for the purposes of mood, audience manipulation and theatre magic"[10] to deal with subjective contents—menace, truth, love, memory.

Pinter's success has also been attributed to his "originality," to his "suprarealistic language," and to the fact that he is a member of the "Angry Theatre," the "Theatre of the Absurd," the "Drama of Menace," the "Kitchen Sink School," "Existential Drama," or "Hyperrealistic Theatre." In the face of these multitudinous and contradictory claims, only by turning to the works themselves can we legitimately evaluate each play and the playwright.

A careful analysis of the Pinter canon will demonstrate that his continual development as a dramatist is an important factor in his increasing popularity. Interestingly, this element of his writing has been neglected by the critics in spite of the fact that it is still happening: technically Pinter continues to improve, but more important, he does not belabor any single topic. Rather, he continues to explore new themes. Indeed, there is a distinct pattern of thematic development which may be traced as his interest moves from subject to subject in an organic manner. That is, each play grows out of what he has written before. Moreover, it becomes clear that there is a definite progression, especially in his major dramas, as he examines a subject through a series of plays, each examination studying another aspect of a problem or approaching the topic from a different angle. Once this exploration has been completed the playwright moves on to look at a new problem, one which has somehow grown out of his examination of the preceding topic.

As will also be seen, this approach forms an interesting pattern of creativity. In essence the author explores the various aspects of a question

10. Martin Gottfried, *A Theatre Divided,* p. 8.

through a series of minor works and then writes a major play which sums up his thematic conclusion. He then begins another set of plays, which will in turn lead to another major drama. The procedure of this study, then, will be to determine the meaning and techniques of Pinter's dramas by assuming that the texts are understandable without dependence on philosophies, traditions, rituals, or psychoanalysis. This will in turn help explain why he is popular, what appeals to his audiences, why he can be considered an influential force working in the British theatre, and why he is validly called the most important dramatist writing today and possibly of our generation.

Chapter I. Biography

. . . there was a good deal of violence there, in those days . . .

Pinter's early life shows its influence on the subject matter of his first three plays and suggests why, thematically, he begins where he does.

Harold Pinter was born on October 10, 1930, in Hackney, a working-class section in the East End of London, the only child of a Jewish ladies' tailor, Hyman (Jack) Pinter, and his wife Frances (nee Mann). There is a family tradition that the family arrived in England from Portugal (where their name was originally Pinto, da Pinto, or da Pinta) by way of Hungary sometime early in this century.

In an interview in the "Talk of the Town" section of the 25 February 1967 issue of the *New Yorker* Pinter remembers that he lived in a brick house on Thistlewaite Road, near Clapton Pond, until the outbreak of the war in 1939. The area was generally run down, filled with railway yards, shops, and a smelly soap factory. The River Lea, a tributary of the Thames, ran nearby, and there was also a canal, but both were fairly polluted from surrounding factories. He mentions that his mother is a "marvellous cook" and that his father worked very hard, as much as twelve hours a day. Eventually the elder Pinter lost his own shop and had to go to work for someone else.

When World War II broke out, Pinter was sent to Cornwall. There he and twenty-four other boys were under the care of a Mrs. Williams, who lived in a castle with nice grounds overlooking the English Channel. Pinter was a "morose little boy," though, and did not enjoy himself in spite of his surroundings and the fact that his father (who was an air-raid warden during the war) and his mother occasionally traveled the four-hundred-mile round trip from London to visit him.

Money was a problem, and after about a year he had to return home. He moved again, this time with his mother, to a place nearer London, and then in 1944 he returned to London: "On the day I got back to London . . . I saw the first flying bomb. I was in the street and I saw it come over. . . . There were times when I would open our back door and find our garden in flames. Our house never burned, but we had to evacuate several times."

Pinter won a scholarship to the local grammar school, Hackney Downs, where he studied until 1947. At the all-boys school (about 600 enrollment), which was a ten-minute walk from his home, he acted the part of Macbeth in 1946 and then Romeo under the fondly remembered direction of Joseph Brearley, his English master. The only scholastic subject to interest the otherwise restless teen-ager was English language and literature. He played football and cricket and ran the hundred-yard dash in ten point two, a school record at the time. At thirteen he had also had his first love affair and had begun writing poetry.

After leaving Hackney Downs Grammar School, Pinter thought about going to a university, but the only two he was really interested in were Oxford and Cambridge, neither of which he was eligible for, since he did not know Latin. Instead he applied for a grant to study acting at the Royal Academy of Dramatic Art. On the recommendation of R. D. (Reggie) Smith, a producer, he was given a London County Council grant.

After about two terms he found that he "didn't care for it very much,"[1] possibly because he "hadn't the sophistication to cope with the other students," according to an anonymously written "Profile" in the *Observer* of 15 September 1963. He faked a nervous breakdown in order to escape and spent the next several months roaming the streets without his parents' knowledge while continuing to draw his grant. He tried the Central School of Speech and Drama, too, but he did not study seriously because he was "mostly in love at the time and tied up with that," he remarks in an interview with Lawrence Bensky.[2]

1. As Martin Esslin reports him mentioning in a conversation in 1967. *The Peopled Wound*, p. 3.
2. Bensky, "Harold Pinter: An Interview," p. 17.

When Bensky asked whether the drama schools were of any use to him as a playwright, Pinter answered simply, "None whatsoever."

During these years after the war, Pinter reports that he encountered violence in the East End when Fascism began to be revived in England. "I got into quite a few fights down there. If you looked remotely like a Jew you might be in trouble. Also, I went to a Jewish club, by an old railway arch, and there were quite a lot of people often waiting with broken milk bottles in a particular alley we used to walk through. There were one or two ways of getting out of it—one was a purely physical way, of course, but you couldn't do anything about the milk bottles—*we* didn't have any milk bottles. The best way was to talk to them, you know, sort of 'Are you all right?' 'Yes, I'm all right.' 'Well, that's all right then, isn't it?' And all the time keep walking toward the lights of the main road" (Bensky, p. 30).

There were other times when trouble would arise merely because he happened to be passing a Fascist street meeting in Ridley Road market, near Dalston Junction: "They'd interpret your very being, especially if you had books under your arms, as evidence of your being a communist. There was a good deal of violence there, in those days."

Having grown up listening to horrible tales about the treatment of Jews in Hitler's Germany and then having to fight his way through street gangs, Pinter was disenchanted with violence and war. When he turned eighteen he became liable for the National Service, but "couldn't see any point in it at all," and declared himself a conscientious objector (Bensky, p. 31). After all, he "was aware of the suffering and of the horror of war, and by no means was I going to subscribe to keeping it going."[3] He refused to go. As a result, he was taken to the medical examination in a police car and had two tribunals and two trials. The first tribunal denied his application. At his second tribunal, he reports in the *New Yorker* interview, "I took one of my close friends, Morris Wernick, to speak for me. The others took reverends. But I had no religious beliefs by then. There were a lot of colonels with mustaches at the tribunal. It was very, very stuffy. I took Wernick, and he made an immortal speech on my behalf. He said, 'Now I *am* going into the Army, so I am not a conscientious objector, but I can assure you, that you will never change *him*. It's a waste of time to try to persuade him to change his mind.'" Again his application was rejected and he had to stand trial before a magistrate. He expected to go to prison—"I took my tooth brush to the trials"—but he was still under twenty-one, it was a civil offense, and he appeared before a "slightly sympathetic" magistrate (the same one both times) who fined him ten pounds at the first trial and twenty pounds at the second trial (Bensky, p. 32). His parents paid the fine each time.

In 1950 Pinter's first publications appeared. In the August issue of *Poetry London* (No. 19) his two poems "New Year in the Midlands" and "Chandeliers

3. "Talk of the Town," *New Yorker*, 25 Feb. 1967.

and Shadows" were published. "New Year in the Midlands" was reprinted with two new poems, "Rural Idyll" and "European Revels," in the next issue the following November, this time attributed to "Harold Pinta." This does not seem to be a printing error, since Pinter was signing letters using this spelling at the time.

About this time, too, he began to act professionally, although he continued to write: "Not plays. Hundreds of Poems—about a dozen are worth republishing," he recalls in "Writing for Myself." Several of these were in dialogue, and some later appeared in an altered form as revue sketches. He also wrote some unpublished prose pieces and started an autobiographical novel, *The Dwarfs*, which has been abandoned, though certain strains of it have appeared in his plays (including, of course, one titled *The Dwarfs*). Most of his time, however, was involved with acting.

The first theatre-going experience Pinter had was seeing Sir Donald Wolfit playing King Lear. He returned five times and later acted the part of one of the king's knights in a production of *King Lear* with Wolfit.

Reggie Smith, who had helped Pinter with his Royal Academy of Dramatic Art grant, helped Pinter as an actor, giving him small parts on the radio, the first professional role being in the BBC Home Service Broadcast, "Focus on Football Pools," on September 19, 1950. On October 31 Pinter, now twenty, took part in "Focus on Libraries."

The following year saw Pinter beginning his acting career in earnest. On January 14 he appeared in the part of Abergavenny in Smith's BBC Third Programme production of Shakespeare's *Henry VIII*. Then he answered Anew McMaster's advertisement in the *Stage* for actors for a Shakespearean tour of Ireland. "He offered me six pounds a week, said I could get digs for twenty-five shillings at the most, told me how cheap cigarettes were and that I could play Horatio, Bassanio and Cassio. It was my first job proper on the stage," Pinter says in *Mac*, a fond remembrance of the eighteen-month period of one-night stands which began that September. Although it was sometimes rustic and disorganized, Pinter generally enjoyed touring with a company which included among others Alun Owen, Patrick Magee, and Barry Foster: "Ireland wasn't golden always, but it was golden sometimes and in 1950 it was, all in all, a golden age for me and for others."[4]

In 1953 Pinter acted in Wolfit's classical season at King's Theatre in Hammersmith, where he met Vivien Merchant (the stage name of Ada Thomson), both playing small parts in *As You Like It*. In 1954 he assumed the stage name David Baron and began touring provincial England in repertory, appearing in such places as Huddersfield, Torquay, Bournemouth, Whitby, Colchester, Birmingham, Chesterfield, Worthing, Palmers Green, and Richmond. At Bournemouth in 1956 Pinter met Vivien Merchant again when they played leads opposite each other and they were married.

4. Harold Pinter, *Mac*, p. 16.

Writing the Plays

In 1957 Henry Woolf, a friend of Pinter's, telephoned the actor during a repertory stand in Torquay, Devon, and asked him if he would write a play for production by the Drama Department at Bristol University six days later. Pinter said no, but he began writing a play based on an image of two men he had seen in a small room at a London party. It took him four days, working in the afternoons between morning rehearsals of one play and evening performances of another, and *The Room* was first acted in the old Drama Studio, a converted squash court in the Wills Memorial Building which has since served the university as a furniture storeroom.

The play, directed by Woolf, was so successful that a new production was entered in the *Sunday Times* student drama festival, where critic Harold Hobson, sitting as one of the judges, was so impressed by the work that he wrote a review of it. The review attracted the attention of Michael Codron, who wrote to Pinter immediately to ask if he had a full-length play. He had just finished *The Birthday Party.*

Near the end of January 1958 Pinter's son Daniel was born and Codron took an option on *The Birthday Party.* Pinter and his wife had both been offered jobs at the Alexandria Theatre in Birmingham, but decided to stay in London and took a flat in Chiswick. The first performance of *The Birthday Party* was at the Arts Theatre, Cambridge, on April 28, 1958, Pinter helping in the directing. Three weeks later, May 19, it opened at the Lyric Theatre, Hammersmith, for its first London presentation—to be met by overwhelming criticism in the daily press. After a run of one week the play was taken off the stage, though, ironically, Harold Hobson defended it vigorously in the London *Sunday Times* the next day (May 25), showing great insight into the work and praising Pinter's ability highly.

Pinter continued writing. *Something in Common*, which was an unperformed radio play, and *A Slight Ache* were both completed that year. In 1959 *The Dumb Waiter* was performed for the first time, in German, at the Frankfurt Municipal Theatre, and a semi-amateur production of *The Birthday Party* at the Tower Theatre in Canonbury, Islington, brought some favorable reviews. Disley Jones' *One to Another*, a musical revue at the Lyric Theatre in Hammersmith, included two sketches written by Pinter at Jones' request, "Trouble in the Works" and "The Black and White," when it was produced in July; and later that month *A Slight Ache* was broadcast on the BBC Third Programme, with Vivien Merchant playing Flora. "Getting Acquainted," "Last to Go," "Request Stop," and "Special Offer" appeared in another musical revue, *Pieces of Eight*, in September.

The year 1960 marks the beginning of Pinter's rise to success. *The Room*, directed by Pinter, and *The Dumb Waiter* were put on together at the Hampstead Theatre Club in January, the role of Rose being acted by Vivien Merchant and that of Mr. Kidd by Henry Woolf, for whom the play was originally written. That March the BBC Third Programme broadcast *A Night Out*, Harold Pinter taking the part of Seeley and Vivien Merchant that of The Girl. *The Birthday Party* and *Night School*, with Vivien Merchant as Sally, were telecast by Associated Rediffusion Television later that year; and *A Night Out*, Pinter and Vivien Merchant recreating their roles of Seeley and The Girl, was televised by ABC-TV.

The Birthday Party also became the first Pinter play to be performed professionally in America when the Actors' Workshop production in San Francisco opened on July 27; and Pinter took over the role of Goldberg briefly during a run of the drama at Cheltenham. In December *The Dwarfs* was broadcast on the BBC's Third Programme.

The most important event to take place in 1960 was the opening of *The Caretaker* at the Arts Theatre Club in London on April 27 (on May 30 it moved to the Duchess Theatre in London's fashionable West End). The play won critical acclaim from critics such as Kenneth Tynan, who admittedly had earlier castigated Pinter's work, and traditionalists like Noël Coward similarly praised both the work and its author. Soon the first awards began coming in as the *Evening Standard* cited the play as the best of 1960 and the Newspaper Guild of New York gave its Page 1 Award to *The Caretaker*, also recognizing it as the best play of 1960.

In 1961 *The Collection* was televised by Associated Rediffusion Television, with Vivien Merchant in the part of Stella. Pinter briefly replaced Alan Bates as Mick in *The Caretaker* before it closed at the Duchess Theatre after a run of 425 performances.

In February 1962 Pinter codirected *The Collection* with Peter Hall at the Aldwych Theatre, London (Michael Horden giving a fine performance as Harry), and then read "The Examination" on the BBC Third Programme in September.

The years 1963 to 1967 have been Pinter's most impressive to date. First, *The Lover*, directed by Joan Kemp-Welch, was telecast by Associated Rediffusion Television on March 28, 1963, in a production which was to bring Guild of British Television Producers and Directors Awards to Alan Badel and Vivien Merchant for their leading performances, as well as awards for best script to Pinter from the Guild and the Prix Italia for Television Drama at Naples. Pinter also directed the first stage presentation of the play, with Vivien Merchant as Sarah, when it opened with *The Dwarfs* at the Arts Theatre Club in London. He directed both plays with Guy Vaesen's assistance. Joseph Losey's film *The Servant*, from Pinter's first screenplay, based on a novel by Robin Maugham, was released in November, Pinter playing a "society man" in it. Meanwhile a group of movie and theatre personalities, including Richard Burton and Elizabeth Taylor, Noël Coward, Peter Sellers, and Leslie Caron, created Caretaker Films Ltd. to finance a film version of *The Caretaker*, directed by Clive Donner and starring Alan Bates as Mick, Robert Shaw as Aston, and Donald Pleasence as Davies. The first public showing was at the Berlin Film Festival that year, where it was awarded a Silver Bear. The film also received a Certificate of Merit at the Edinburgh Festival.

The following year Pinter received both the British Screenwriters Guild and the New York Film Critics awards for his screenplay adaptation of *The Servant*, the official British entry at the Venice Film Festival and the first New York Film Festival; five previously unperformed revue sketches were broadcast on the BBC Third Programme ("Applicant," "Dialogue for Three," "Interview," "That's All," and "That's Your Trouble"); the author read the prose version of *Tea Party* on the BBC Third Programme; and he directed a revival of *The Birthday Party* at the Aldwych.

Nineteen sixty-five was the year of *The Homecoming*. In March Pinter won the British Film Academy Award for best screenplay of the preceding year for his scenario of Penelope Mortimer's *The Pumpkin Eater*. *Tea Party*, in its television-play form, with Vivien Merchant in the role of Wendy, was televised in England by the BBC-1 and throughout Europe as part of the European Broadcasting Union's "The Largest Theatre in the World" series, appearing in eleven countries within a week. Also that month *The Homecoming* began its pre-London tour.

On June 3, 1965, *The Homecoming* opened at the Aldwych. Vivien Merchant played the part of Ruth in Peter Hall's production, which was immediately applauded by critics like Hobson as the dramatist's masterpiece, though reviewers like Robert Brustein, head of the Yale Drama School, were openly puzzled. To close out the year Pinter took the role of García in Sartre's *No Exit* in a BBC Television presentation.

Pinter neither acted nor directed in 1966, though he was awarded the C.B.E. in the Queen's Birthday List—"the year *after* the Beatles," he emphasizes.[5] *The Quiller Memorandum*, for which he wrote the scenario, was released in November.

In January 1967 *The Homecoming* opened in New York, to mixed reviews. Walter Kerr damned with faint praise, while expressing a higher opinion than the British critics had of the work—it went on to win the Antoinette Perry (Tony) Award for the best play on Broadway, the New York Drama Critics Circle Award for the best play on Broadway, and the Whitbread Anglo-American Award for the best British play on Broadway. Back to acting and directing, Pinter was seen as Stott on the BBC-TV telecast of *The Basement* in February of that year and then directed Robert Shaw's *The Man in the Glass Booth* in London in July. Another Losey film with a screenplay by Pinter, *Accident*, also opened in February, with Vivien Merchant cast in a major supporting role and featuring Pinter in a bit part as a television producer. The film was proclaimed one of the year's ten best by the National Board of Review. In

5. Bensky, p. 14.

August Pinter read a poem he had written to eulogize Joe Orton at Orton's funeral.

The year 1968 was a fairly quiet one in terms of production, though interesting because of Pinter's battle with the Lord Chamberlain, who objected to several four-letter words in *Landscape*. Since radio is not subject to the Lord Chamberlain's censorship, however, the play was performed uncut on the BBC Third Programme. Other than that, the only thing of interest was the release of the film version of *The Birthday Party*.

In 1969 Pinter completed the screenplay version of L. P. Hartley's *The Go-Between*, and he appeared with Donald Pleasence on the award-winning NBC Experiment in Television production, *Pinter People*, which showed the two men creating cartoon versions of several of the author's revue sketches. *Night*, with Vivien Merchant as The Woman, opened at the Comedy Theatre in London as one of several one-act plays about marriage under the common title *Mixed Doubles*; and *Landscape* and *Silence* were given their world premieres by the Royal Shakespeare Company at the Aldwych.

The next year, 1970, was superficially unproductive, with only the screenplay of *The Homecoming* appearing, but Pinter was at work on a new play, *Old Times*. He also directed Simon Gray's *Butley* in London in August and James Joyce's *Exiles*, again in London, in November of the same year. In addition, the poem "All of That" saw publication in 1970, and Pinter was elected honorary fellow by the Modern Language Association of America. He was also awarded Hamburg University's Shakespeare Prize.

Old Times opened under Peter Hall's direction at the Aldwych Theatre on June 1, 1971, starring Vivien Merchant, and moved to New York six months later. *The Go-Between* also appeared publicly in 1971, winning Golden Palm honors at the Cannes Film Festival as best picture, and in December Pinter reported that he had adapted Aidan Higgins' novel *Langrishe, Go Down* for the screen. His seven-line "poem" was included in an interview in the *New York Times Magazine*, and his twenty-minute-long *Monologue* was performed on British television.

In 1972 Pinter wrote an adaptation of Marcel Proust's *A la recherche du temps perdu*, which was to be filmed by Losey. The film version of *The Homecoming*, directed by Peter Hall, was released in the autumn of 1973; and Pinter became an associate director of the National Theatre and also directed his first film in the same year, an adaptation of Gray's *Butley* starring Alan Bates, who was featured in the stage version which Pinter had directed some three years earlier. The following year he began writing again, though he also took time to direct John Hopkins' comic observation of life in the suburbs, *Next of Kin*, at the Old Vic.

No Man's Land, directed by Peter Hall and featuring masterful performances by John Gielgud and Ralph Richardson, opened at the Old Vic on April 23, 1975, and in July Pinter himself directed Gray's *Otherwise Engaged* (starring Alan Bates) in London. Pinter's film adaptation of F. Scott Fitz-gerald's *The Last Tycoon* was shot under the direction of Elia Kazan.

Harold Pinter the Man

During the years that Pinter was in an unconscious apprenticeship for his career as a playwright, screen writer, and sometimes director/actor, he wrote poems and prose and acted. He also held a number of odd jobs, including doorman, snow shoveler, street salesman, and dance-hall bouncer. His pro-cession of living quarters reflects his increasing prosperity: when his wife be-came pregnant, they took a basement room in the run-down Notting Hill Gate section of London, where Pinter held still another position—caretaker of their building. They moved to Chiswick when *The Birthday Party* was to open, and then to the middle-class district of Kew with the more successful production of *The Caretaker*. A bow-fronted Regency house in the south-coast town of Worthing was the next move, but the long drive to London proved too incon-venient, so the family rented a flat in Kensington. Finally he has arrived in a five-story house in the exclusive Regent's Park section of London.

Pinter has had a passion for cricket since he was a child and always took his cricket bat with him when the house had to be evacuated during German bombing attacks. In fact, he has said that his three main interests (in "equal thirds") are his family, working in the theatre (and in films), and cricket. He also enjoys reading, drinking, and sex—thinking about sex, too, for that matter. The importance of his family to him and their closeness is stressed by the fact that he does not like to be away from them even for a short while. Since his son Daniel is now in his teens and cannot leave school in London, Pinter re-fuses to travel to New York, for example, to direct a play because his family cannot go with him.[6] He admits that music is important to him, both jazz and classical, and Boulez and Webern are among his favorite composers. He has mentioned a fondness for Berg, Bach, and the Beatles, too. He also professes to be "quite an admirer of the Marx brothers and S. J. Perelman."[7] He drinks beer, wine, and Scotch whether writing or not, and the drawings of Francis Bacon and Picasso are his favorites. Among his literary tastes is a liking for novels—Hemingway, Dostoevski, Joyce, Henry Miller, and especially Kafka and Beckett's novels ("Beckett is the best prose writer living,"[8] he once claimed, though by 1971 his familiarity with Beckett's dramas was sufficient for him to include them in his assessment of Beckett as "a great writer," far beyond anything he himself has achieved—"he's the most remarkable writer

6. Ironically, in July 1975, Vivien Merchant sued Pinter for divorce, naming au-thoress Lady Antonia Frazer as corespondent and scandalizing London society. The suit was later dropped.

7. Quoted from a letter to me dated 17 Dec. 1971.

8. Bensky, p. 20.

in the world").⁹ Hardy and Proust are other novelists he has admired. His taste in poets embraces Donne, Pope, Yeats, Hopkins, Eliot, and Philip Larkin. Among modern playwrights Pinter has expressed admiration for Edward Bond, Joe Orton, Bertolt Brecht, Peter Weiss, Edward Albee, Heathcote Williams, and David Storey, and he has directed plays by Robert Shaw, Gray, John Hopkins, and Joyce. He denies an early acquaintanceship with Brecht and Pirandello and states, "I'd never heard of Ionesco until after I'd written the first few plays," though this seems strange in a veteran repertory actor.

9. Quoted in Mel Gussow, "A Conversation (Pause) with Harold Pinter," p. 128. In *Beckett at Sixty: A Festschrift* (London: Calder and Boyers, 1967) this paragraph from one of Pinter's letters to a friend written in 1954 is included among the tributes: "The farther he goes the more good it does me. I don't want philosophies, tracts, dogmas, creeds, way outs, truths, answers, *nothing from the bargain basement*. He is the most courageous, remorseless writer going and the more he grinds my nose in the shit the more I am grateful to him. He's not fucking me about, he's not leading me up any garden, he's not slipping me any wind, he's not flogging me a remedy or a path or a revelation or a basinful of bread crumbs, he's not selling me anything I don't want to buy, he doesn't give a bollock whether I buy or not, *he hasn't got his hand over his heart*. Well, I'll buy his goods, hook, line, and sinker, because he leaves no stone unturned and no maggot lonely. He brings forth a body of beauty. His work is beautiful" (p. 86).

Chapter II. Basic Concepts

. . . a shared . . . quicksand . . .

The Themes

Harold Pinter's plays are complex collections of interrelated themes. Bernard Dukore, for instance, sees Pinter's theatre as "a picture of contemporary man beaten down by the social forces around him," partially based on "man's failure to communicate with other men."[1] Ruby Cohn claims that "Man vs. the System" with a "central victim-villain conflict" is Pinter's primary theme.[2] Both critics insist that there are religious overtones present. Lois Gordon in *Stratagems to Uncover Nakedness* (1969) has commented on sex and role playing as themes in the plays. Though not thematic studies, Martin Esslin's important volumes *The Theatre of the Absurd* (1961, revised 1969) and *The Peopled Wound: The Work of Harold Pinter* (1970) consider a combination

1. Dukore, "The Theatre of Harold Pinter," p. 54.
2. Cohn, "The World of Harold Pinter," p. 56.

of Freudian and existential aspects in Pinter's writing which create a "poetic image of a basic human situation"; and Walter Kerr's *Harold Pinter* (1967) assumes an existential basis to all of the dramatist's plays, even claiming that they are existentially structured. Pinter himself has admitted that "the question of dominance and subservience . . . is possibly a repeated theme in my plays," in his interview with Lawrence Bensky.[3]

When Pinter began his playwrighting career in 1957, however, one idea was foremost in his mind as a major theme: fear. As a young Jew living through the early days of World War II, he had gone to bed afraid that he might be awakened in the night by a knock at the door and that he and his parents would be taken forcibly from their home by unknown assailants, a picture vividly impressed on his mind by tales of Hitler's Germany. Translated into dramatic terms in *The Room*, his fear becomes a mysterious and undefined something which snuffles about outside the door, trying to get in. Those inside the room realize that there is something on the other side of the door and that they are in danger from its intrusion. The constant threat of invasion produces an atmosphere of menace, menace being any threat of disruption of the status quo, though the threat is more significant than that of mere change: the inhabitants of the room will be exposed to expulsion and further unknown dangers, possibly including physical harm. Twenty years later Pinter's dramas are still concerned with menace, but the emphasis has changed. A plot based on the threat of actual physical harm being visited on the individual by an outside source is replaced by considerations of the posssible sources of menace. The author focuses not merely on the existence of menace and the actions of people trying to avoid confrontations with their personal nemeses, but on the origin of menace and the attempts of characters to remedy the causal situation. Menace is no longer an indeterminate threat derived from a vague source; it grows out of what the writer has called "love and the lack of love,"[4] something which may be equated with "need" (see Chapter IV below).

Love

Pinter has expressly declared that at least two of his plays are "about love." He says this about *The Caretaker*[5] and about *The Homecoming*.[6] Nowhere, though, has he defined the term, and his plays make it clear that he is not speaking of conventional love—unselfish devotion and "affection based on admiration or benevolence." What Pinter calls "love" really amounts to an individual psychological need which must be fulfilled for the emotional well-being of the organism. In psychological jargon this need is categorized as a

3. Bensky, "Harold Pinter: An Interview."
4. Pinter, in Henry Hewes, "Probing Pinter's Play," p. 57.
5. In Marowitz, "Theatre Abroad."
6. In Hewes, "Probing Pinter's Play."

primary appetite (something which is necessary for homeostatic balance—and a drive is that state within an organism which directs behavior toward a goal of creating or maintaining that balance). Pinter's characters require certain things from one another for their own psychological well-being, and the author considers the relationship between individuals stemming from this need to be love.

Traditionally love is a relationship between individuals sustained because of an emotional attachment in which the other is intrinsically important; Pinter's lovers have an emotional dependence on each other which is based on fulfilling their own psychological requirements. The motivation for his characters' action is selfish. It is based on a necessity for emotional fulfillment, and everything that the characters do in the dramas is aimed at satisfying their personal requirements. Indeed, there is a question whether Pinter's characters are even capable of feeling love in the customary sense, since most of the later characters share primary appetites for acceptance, affection, and emotional attachment—elements similar to those in conventional love, but essentially selfish drives. Whereas Pinter's early plays express the existence of menace, then, his later dramas are psychological portrayals of individuals trying to create viable relationships with one another in attempts to fulfill the emotional needs which produce a threat to their welfare.

Loneliness

Pinter has insisted that his writings deal with "the terror of the loneliness of the human situation,"[7] and this statement fits the thematic development indicated above. There is concurrent need for and absence of psychological stability, and this discrepancy is the source of the terror. That is to say, people require emotional relationships, but often such ties do not exist, and the resulting situation is unbearable. Or if ties do exist, there is the fear that they will be broken and the original lack of ties will recur. Pinter's later dramas demonstrate the desperate lengths to which an individual will go to acquire or preserve relationships. Instead of running from something, there is an active seeking for something. There is, thus, a thematic change involved in Pinter's writing as his prime concern becomes a search for psychological well-being through mutual dependence rather than confrontations with an abstract menace. His latest works suggest that the evolution is continuing.

In tracing the thematic evolution from generalized to particularized menace in Pinter's plays, four periods in his writing are distinguishable: the early plays or "comedies of menace," which are more concerned with the idea of fear than the origin of fear; a time of transition during which Pinter consciously begins exploring the cause of menace; the later plays in which attention is

7. Boulton, "Harold Pinter: *The Caretaker* and Other Plays," p. 132.

centered on the lack of emotional fulfillment as a source of menace; and, finally, a fourth period, concerned with the idea of memory, which seems to be developing in *Landscape, Silence, Night, Old Times,* and *No Man's Land.*

Menace, Communication, and Verification

Pinter's first three plays, the "comedies of menace"—*The Room, The Dumb Waiter,* and *The Birthday Party*—introduce his basic ideas about menace, communication, and verification (see Chapter III below for discussions of these terms). In the world pictured in his plays there is an a priori underlying terror of loneliness which creates a feeling of *menace.* In order to help assuage this feeling of menace, characters try to communicate with one another, but the *communication* is inefficient and a circular effect is created as the lack of communication intensifies the menace, which in turn further weakens the ability to communicate. There is also a need for *verification* (see the discussion of *The Dwarfs* in Chapter VI), determining what is true and what is false, the distinction between appearance and reality. Unfortunately, it is sometimes impossible to verify the "truth" of something because of the very nature of the universe. The presence of menace demands additional verification as a safeguard, a means of determining what is a threat, but that same menace hinders even further the attempts to perceive reality. Moreover, verification depends on communication, just as communication cannot exist without a verifiable, arbitrary base of shared knowledge. The lack of verification, therefore, destroys communication and the absence of communication prohibits verification. Which serves to magnify the original feeling of menace, and so on. As Pinter says in "Between the Lines," "we prefer to subscribe to the view that there's a shared, common ground. I think there's a shared common ground all right, but that it's more like quicksand. Because 'reality' is quite a strong, firm word, we tend to think, or to hope, that the state to which it refers is equally firm, settled, and unequivocal. It doesn't seem to be."

The Comedies of Menace. In terms of Pinter's development as a writer it is significant that the threat in *The Room* remains undefined. In the next two plays he evolves a pattern from the base established by *The Room,* though with variation. *The Birthday Party* hints that the menace which threatens and eventually destroys the individual originates in society. The suggestion that society is the destructive force is brought out much more clearly in *The Dumb Waiter,* though the source is still vague, with no specific facets of society singled out as responsible for the threat. While these two plays develop the idea of menace and define Pinter's related notions about communication and verification, they are really extensions of elements introduced in *The Room.* All in all, the first three plays pivot around a menace of general origin.

Plays in Transition. At this point Pinter wrote a series of short revue sketches which revolve around his basic subjects and were useful in developing his techniques, but which are essentially an interlude, a marking of time, although they contain some of his most humorous material. The group of major plays that followed, however, marks a transition, *A Slight Ache* representing the next step in Pinter's thematic development. Most of the fundamental themes are the same as in the earlier works, but for the first time Pinter uses the subject of emotional needs as the hub around which he displays his ideas (communication, verification, and so forth) and menace obviously develops from these needs. Henceforth, need is an increasingly important subject of study, emerging as the main subject in the author's more recent plays.

In *A Slight Ache* the failure to fulfill his wife's psychological demands is the element which causes a husband's downfall. *The Caretaker* explores three characters' attempts to form or confirm attachments, and it is in connection with this play that Pinter first admits using love as a theme. His dramas thereafter deal with the situation which arises when people strive to achieve the emotional satisfaction they need, though three minor plays written during this period look backward as well as forward.

The Later Plays. Fulfillment of psychological needs is firmly entrenched as the primary thematic element in the later dramas. *The Collection* displays the actions of people fighting to preserve their relationships with one another. *The Lover* probes the difficulties a husband and wife have in reconciling sex with their idea of "respectability" in marriage. *The Homecoming* shows to what desperate lengths people will go in order to establish relationships. Two additional short dramas, *Tea Party* and *The Basement*, continue in much the same vein. The latest plays, the "memory" plays *Landscape, Silence, Night, Old Times,* and *No Man's Land,* however, suggest that the dramatist is beginning to move in a somewhat new direction, that he is considering memory and verification as functions of each other. The theme is not new, though the emphasis is.

Starting with *A Slight Ache,* the characters in Pinter's plays are menaced, but not by something outside themselves. Instead, they are trying to fill a need within themselves, their mental well-being is threatened by a psychological deficiency: it is no longer a matter of an individual's relationship with the abstract concept of society, but his relationships with other people as individuals. What this amounts to is simply a narrowing of the author's focus. The early plays deal with menace to expose its existence by provoking a mood of terror. Pinter's notions about the interrelationship of communication and verification are depicted, and the plays portray the menace-creating aspect of these elements, menace being anything which threatens an individual's security. After *A Slight Ache* there is still menace present, but not simply as a psychological threat from things that go bump in the night. Pinter is quoted in Esslin's *The Theatre of the Absurd* as saying that by the time he wrote *The Caretaker* he had advanced beyond this stage in his writing and he no longer depends on "cabaret turns and blackouts and screams in the dark."[8] In part this is because the threat has been reduced to an understandable personal level. When psychological inadequacies become a central concern as a source from which menace derives, Pinter moves from discussing the symptom to discussing the disease.

8. Pinter in an interview with Kenneth Tynan, BBC Home Service, 28 Oct. 1960.

Chapter III. The Comedies of Menace

... the terror and loneliness of the human situation ...

Pinter's characteristic mode of expression is comedic, and his first three plays, *The Room*, *The Birthday Party*, and *The Dumb Waiter*, have generally been called "comedies of menace"[1] because they present a mood of terror in humorous terms. Collectively this group of plays defines the themes and establishes the techniques which will be basic in all of his works; yet they also form a distinct set.[2]

The Room

Pinter's earliest play, *The Room*, was originally performed at Bristol University in May 1957 and then in January 1958 at the Festival of University

1. The term was first used as a subtitle for David Campton's play *The Lunatic View* (1957) and applied to Pinter in an article by Irving Wardle in the Sept. 1958 issue of *Encore*.
2. See Hinchcliffe, *Harold Pinter*, Chap. 2, for instance.

Drama. It was presented professionally for the first time at the Hampstead Theatre Club beginning January 21, 1960. The drama introduces the creative pattern, the subject of menace with the related concepts which are explored, and the techniques that Pinter was to utilize for several years. The author's conception of the play and its subsequent evolution in his mind are typical. In *Time*, 10 November 1961, Pinter discusses the actual event in some detail. Attending a party in London, he had seen two men in a small room. The smaller of the two, a little barefooted man, was "carrying on a lively and rather literate conversation, and at the table next to him sat an enormous lorry driver. He had his cap on and never spoke a word. And all the while, as he talked, the little man was feeding the big man—cutting his bread, buttering it, and so on. Well, this image would never leave me." This image had to be expressed: "I went into a room one day and saw a couple of people in it. This stuck with me for some time afterwards, and I felt that the only way I could give it expression and get it off my mind was dramatically. I started off with this picture of two people and let them carry on from there."[3] In interviews, first with Kenneth Tynan and then with Hallam Tennyson, Pinter further explains: "Two people in a room—I am dealing a great deal of the time with this image of two people in a room. The curtain goes up on stage, and I see it as a very potent question: what is going to happen to these two people in the room? Is someone going to open the door and come in? . . . Obviously they are scared of what is outside the room. Outside the room there is a world bearing upon them which is frightening. I am sure it is frightening to you and me as well."[4]

As Pinter has claimed many times, given a situation, he develops it within its own framework: "I've never started a play from any kind of abstract idea or theory. . . . You arrange *and* you listen, following the clues you leave for yourself, through the characters."[5] Elsewhere he says: "Finding the characters and letting them speak for themselves is the greatest excitement of writing. I would never distort the consistency of a character by a kind of hoarding in which I say, 'by the way, these characters are doing this because of such and such.' I find out what they are doing, allow them to do it, and keep out of it."[6] He further explains: "I don't know what kind of characters my plays will have until they . . . well, until they *are*. Until they indicate to me what they are, I don't conceptualize in any way. Once I've got the clues I follow them—that's my job, really, to follow the clues. . . . Sometimes I'm going along and I find myself writing 'C. comes in' when I didn't know that he was going to come in; he *had* to come in at that point, that's all."[7]

3. Pinter, "Writing for Myself," p. 173.
4. Interview with Kenneth Tynan, BBC General Overseas Service, 7 Aug. 1960, quoted in Esslin, *Theatre of the Absurd*, p. 232.
5. Halton, "Pinter," p. 195.
6. Hewes, "Probing Pinter's Play," p. 58.
7. Bensky, "Harold Pinter," pp. 24–25.

Though an artist's words may provide useful insights, it is often danger-ous to take them at face value when he is talking about his own work, and this is especially true of Pinter, who likes to exaggerate at times. The fore-going details of his creative process seem acceptable, however, since they are logical statements in themselves (that is, they explain an act of literary cre-ativity in a reasonable manner for a writer who has demonstrated a "dramatic instinct"), they are consistent, being repeated basically unchanged over a period of time and in varying circumstances, and finally, they appear valid when applied to the particular plays themselves. In essence Pinter is saying that each play creates a logic of its own which dictates the course of action it is to follow, given the original assumption of two people in a room and the idea of some kind of threat on the other side of the door. On the surface much of Pinter's work seems to conform to the Theatre of the Absurd, but this logi-cal progression places his plays outside the Absurd, as will be seen later.

Besides setting the creative method Pinter pursues from this point on, *The Room* contains the essentials of his early works. We are exposed to a small number of people, in this case two, who are enclosed in a room which serves to keep them secure from the horrors outside. Inside the room the in-habitants have created their own versions of reality which, like the very existence of the room, provide them with a sense of security and well-being. As the drama opens, however, the audience realizes that the participants in the play are not really communicating with one another—in fact, it often ap-pears that they are consciously *avoiding* understanding. Their realistic speech, the uncertain and preoccupied pauses, also convey an awareness of something outside the room which threatens them. As the play progresses, there is a movement from apparent reality toward fantastic unreality, a movement emphasized by the use of realistic dialogue to contrast with the increasingly unrealistic situation. The menace on the other side of the door continues to be suggested until it actually intrudes as a physical presence, Riley, and destroys the security of those within the room. The play, then, essentially deals with three problems: the unexplained menace from without which threatens and finally breaks down the security of an individual; the individual's reactions to the disintegrating conditions; and the lack of communication between peo-ple which demands the maintenance of security and at the same time reflects the impossibility of such a goal.

Pinter continually denies using symbols consciously in examining these problems: "I have never been conscious of allegorical significance in my plays, either while writing or after writing. I have never intended any specific re-ligious reference or been conscious of using anything as a symbol for anything else."[8] He explains his position further when he details his approach to writing in "Writing for Myself": "I start off with people, who come into a particular situation. I certainly don't write from any kind of abstract idea. And I wouldn't

8. Hewes, "Probing Pinter's Play," p. 97.

know a symbol if I saw one." As an author, Pinter claims to be working within a limited scope: "All I try to do is describe some particular thing, a particular occurrence in a particular context. The meaning is there for the particular characters as they cope with the situation. My plays are often interpreted symbolically. Well, you can make symbolic meat out of anything."[9]

It is evident, however, that there are symbolic details present which give his play added meaning. Too many references are repeated too many times and the consistency of associations is too great to be summarily dismissed. The very title of the play, *The Room*, is too significant to be ignored: a great deal of the early Pinter criticism focused on the notion of a room/womb association; and a room is a *physical* place, emphasizing the importance to Rose of her surroundings. Instead of calling the play something like "The Intruder," which would shift the emphasis, Pinter draws our attention to the idea of walls, with things inside as well as things outside certain defined boundaries. He wants us to realize the importance of the room itself. And Rose's comments throughout the play indicate that she is cognizant of the room's functioning as more than merely "a living place" in her version of the universe: "Still, the room keeps warm. It's better than the basement anyway. . . . I don't know how they live down there. It's asking for trouble. . . . This is all right for me. . . . I mean, you know where you are. . . . I'm quite happy where I am. We're quiet, we're all right. . . . It's not far up either, when you come in from outside. And we're not bothered. . . . This is a good room. You've got a chance in a place like this. . . . I never go out at night. . . . We've got our room. . . . I never go out."[10] In view of the events which take place later in the play, Rose's positive assertions are ironic, and part of the irony comes from the fact that *she* considers the room symbolically.

While the plot of *The Room* is simple, the meaning of the characters' words and the significance of their actions are not. The play opens with sixty-year-old Rose serving her fifty-year-old husband tea prior to his going out on business, driving his van, on an icy winter's day. As is typical in Pinter, we know neither the date nor the month (the day is probably a Monday), whether Bert is working for himself or someone else, where he is going, or what he is hauling. Since these are outside-the-room matters, they are unimportant. The characters realistically discuss them as they would in actuality, providing no real information, since they would already be acquainted with the details—and as though the audience were fully aware of all the details too. Rose busies herself about the room, all the while talking inanely about the minutiae of breakfast-making and the weather in a motherly way. The author is incidentally establishing Rose's character as being within the range

9. "Pinterview," *Newsweek*, 23 July 1962.
10. Pinter, *The Room* in *The Birthday Party and The Room* (New York: Grove, 1961), pp. 95, 96, 97, 99, 107, 109, and 119. The pagination of the Grove Press edition of the plays usually corresponds with that of the Methuen publication of the same edition.

of normality—which is important, since he is going to present the disintegration of her character and thus needs to provide a standard against which we can measure her at the play's end so that the contrast will be appropriately shocking. Even from the beginning, though, we can see that fear directly alters her behavior, and the initiation of the destructive process is evident. Rose reminds Bert that he has been sick and that it was "good" that they were not in the basement during his illness, although she would "have pulled [him] through" (p. 97). Of course, as the head of the household, Rose is responsible for the important family decisions. Bert did not really have to worry about whether or not she would have pulled him through for she made the right decision in the first place: "I look after you, don't I Bert? Like when they offered us the basement here I said no straight off. I knew that'd be no good. The ceiling right on top of you. No, you've got a window here . . . you can come home at night, if you have to go out . . . you can come home, you're all right. And I'm here. You stand a chance" (p. 99). Although unfocused, a note of menace has been introduced with Rose's comparison of her room to the dark, dank unknown constituted by the mysterious basement. The development of the threat represented by the basement and the characters' reactions to it will be the theme of the drama.

Like a good parent, Rose is ready to applaud her child for his successes and to brag of them to her neighbors. And like an overanxious mother, when Bert is about to leave the room she is careful to bundle him up against the cold; she brings him his jersey and muffler and helps him into them. Although these might be considered wifely activities, Rose treats her husband (who is her junior by ten years) as a child, and by taking the role of a mother Rose seems to be able to reassure herself that everything is indeed "all right." In this role she has some control over events and can thus create a certain amount of order in the chaos of life, although that order is limited to her one room. Things are all right in the room—it may be cold outside, but it is warm and comfortable inside. As a parent speaking to a child, she is allowed constantly to repeat herself so as to assure her "son" that things are all right. Because this contention is repeated over and over, it must be true, and the repetition helps convince Rose herself that she is speaking the truth.

Menace does creep in, though; in spite of all her attempts to ignore it she is constantly reminded of its existence. After Mr. Kidd, who is probably the landlord, has talked about his sister, for example, Rose states that she does not believe he even had a sister, and later she acknowledges that the Sands' account of having just come up the stairs and just come down the stairs contradicts itself. Menace is created because the contradiction disrupts the verification process.

The audience's first clue that there is something menacing Rose comes with her references to the basement. Her first mention of it seems to be an incidental comment in her opening speech when she remarks that, although it is cold outside, their room "keeps warm"—which is "better than the basement . . . I don't know how they live down there." The audience is soon aware that there may be more involved than simple comparison, though, as Rose continues, saying "It's asking for trouble" (p. 95). Moments later a mystery is introduced as she notes, "I've never seen who it is. Who is it? Who lives down there? I'll have to ask . . . it can't be too cozy." Continuing her discourse on the basement, she observes that the walls were "running." During the course of the play, we are informed that the basement is damp and small, has a low ceiling, has no windows, and smells. A bit later Rose returns to the subject of the walls when she reminds Bert that they would have "finished [him] off" in his recent sickness, if she had not "pulled [him] through," and decides that whoever is living in the basement is "taking a big chance"—"Maybe they're foreigners."

At this point in the play the theme of contradiction or "verification" is also introduced. Even though the introduction of the problem of verification is unobtrusive—Rose states that "There isn't room for two down there," and then submits that "Maybe they've got two now" (p. 97)—it becomes more consequential as the play progresses. The question of the landlord's identity, Riley's name, Rose's name, and whether or not the Sands were ascending or descending the stairs are all fragments of this problem. In a note intended to help the director and accidentally inserted in the program for the performance of *The Room* and *The Dumb Waiter* at the Royal Court Theatre in London in March 1960, Pinter declares: "The desire for verification is understandable but cannot always be satisfied. There are no hard distinctions between what is real and what is unreal, nor between what is true or what is false. The thing is not necessarily either true or false; it can be both true and false. The assumption that to verify what has happened and what is happening presents few problems I take to be inaccurate. A character on the stage who can present no convincing argument or information as to his past experience, his present behavior or his aspirations, nor give a comprehensive analysis of his motives is as legitimate and worthy of attention as one who, alarmingly, can do all these things. The more acute the experience the less articulate its expression."

This concept, which appears throughout Pinter's plays, is one of the most important elements in his theatre. John Russell Taylor, in *Anger and After*, his important study of the English theatre since John Osborne's *Look Back in Anger* (1956), points out that the technique involved in presenting this principle consists of "casting doubt upon everything by matching each apparently clear and unequivocal statement with an equally clear and unequivocal statement of its contrary."[11] He goes on to claim that by extending the implications involved in the sense of terror and uncertainty which lurks beneath the surface

11. Taylor, *Anger and After*, rev. ed., p. 325.

of the ordinary surroundings of Pinter's plays, the world of external realities is subjected to question. Is there any such thing as absolute truth and, if so, can it ever be known? Pinter's answer seems to be that in spite of human desire for unqualified distinctions there is no such thing as knowable absolute truth.

The arrival of Mr. Kidd reinforces the enigmas of identity and verification: everything he says is questionable, demonstrating that these concepts are facets of the menace which underlies all action and dialogue in Pinter. He adds the ingredient of humor, too. He seems to be hard of hearing: he does not answer Rose's call to come in after he knocks, and then when she says that she heard his knock and seconds later asks a question, Mr. Kidd replies "Eh?" and characteristically continues his commentary as though never interrupted. It soon becomes apparent that there is more than a case of misunderstanding, though; it is a complete lack or avoidance of understanding or communication. In a music-hall exchange expressed in realistic speech, characteristic of Pinter's brand of humor, the characters ask and answer unrelated questions, move from topic to topic in a non-logical progression in the manner of an S. J. Perelman–Marx Brothers film script. The result is a mixture of humor and frustration, both of which are derived from the ridiculous and yet pathetic canceling out of thoughts:

MR. KIDD. Best room in the house.
ROSE. It must get a bit damp downstairs.
MR. KIDD. Not as bad as upstairs.
ROSE. What about downstairs?

MR. KIDD. Eh?
ROSE. What about downstairs?
MR. KIDD. What about it?
ROSE. Must get a bit damp.
MR. KIDD. A bit. Not as bad as upstairs though.

. . .

ROSE. What about your sister, Mr. Kidd?
MR. KIDD. What about her?
ROSE. Did she have any babies?
MR. KIDD. Yes, she had a resemblance to my old mum, I think. Taller, of course.
ROSE. When did she die then, your sister?
MR. KIDD. Yes, that's right, it was after she died that I must have stopped counting . . .
ROSE. What did she die of?
MR. KIDD. Who?
ROSE. Your sister.
    Pause.
MR. KIDD. I've made ends meet [pp. 102, 103].

Pinter, speaking of the concepts which underlie his plays in general, has said that he feels it is senseless to write about political or social issues.[12] He contends that people neither can nor will communicate with one another because they are afraid of what they might find out about themselves, and because people are always changing, they cannot predict what they are going to do next, let alone what others are going to do. In *The Dwarfs* this idea is graphically dramatized in one of Len's speeches: "The point is, who are you? Not why or how, not even what. . . . It's no use saying you know who you are just because you tell me you can fit your particular key into a particular slot which will only receive your particular key because that's not foolproof and certainly not conclusive. Just because you're inclined to make these statements of faith has nothing to do with me. . . . Occasionally I believe I perceive a little of what you are but that's pure accident. Pure accident on both our parts, the perceived and the perceiver. It's nothing like an accident, it's deliberate, it's a joint pretense. We depend on these accidents. . . . What you are, or appear to be to me, or appear to be to you, changes so quickly, so horrifyingly, I certainly can't keep up with it and I'm damn sure you can't either."[13] It is for this reason that the concept of verification is the only one which can really be discussed and why, therefore, it is useless to try to write about abstractions such as are involved in political or sociological problems. "I feel," Pinter has said, "that instead of any inability to communicate there is a deliberate evasion of communication. Communication itself between people is so frightening that rather than do that there is continual cross-talk, a continual talking about other things, rather than what is at the root of their relationship."[14]

This talking around subjects instead of about them is one of the basic features of Pinter's realistic dialogue; it clouds any attempt at verification because it prohibits a clear-cut linking of questions and answers. "People fall back on anything they can lay their hands on verbally to keep away from the danger of knowing, and of being known."[15] If the questions and answers are not clearly paired, it is difficult or impossible to determine the truth. Again, a key to Pinter's thinking can be found in an example from *The Dwarfs* when Mark's "I see that butter's going up" is answered by Len's "I'm prepared to believe it, but it doesn't answer my question" (p. 89). Pinter's characters often take advantage of the principle of verification, contradicting themselves defensively to avoid self-expression. The statement about the price of butter may

12. Bensky, "Harold Pinter," pp. 27–28.
13. Pinter, *The Dwarfs*, in *Three Plays* (New York: Grove, 1962), p. 103. See also *The Dwarfs*, in *A Slight Ache and Other Plays* (London: Methuen, 1970), which includes corrections (the names of the actors playing Peter and Mark in the Arts Theatre Production were listed in reverse originally, and the photographer's name was misspelled, according to Methuen, though as demonstrated in Chapter XI there are also significant differences in the texts themselves).
14. Bensky, "Harold Pinter," pp. 24–25.
15. Pinter to Bensky, ibid., p. 27.

be perfectly true—it simply has no bearing on the subject being discussed and thereby avoids placing the speaker in jeopardy for having spoken the truth.

The problem of verification is thus raised again in Mr. Kidd's chat with Rose. Mr. Kidd thinks he recognizes a chair he has never seen before and does not recognize one which has been there all the time. He tells Rose that the upstairs rooms are empty now, only to inform her moments later that the whole house is full. Then comes the amusing and revealing passage concerning the number of floors in the house, followed by Mr. Kidd's reflections on his sister and mother:

ROSE. How many floors you got in this house?
MR. KIDD. Floors. (*He laughs.*) Ah, we had a good few of them in the old days.
ROSE. How many have you got now?
MR. KIDD. Well, to tell you the truth, I don't count them now.
ROSE. Oh.
MR. KIDD. No, not now.
ROSE. It must be a bit of a job.
MR. KIDD. Oh, I used to count them, once. Never got tired of it. I used to keep a tack on everything in this house. I had a lot to keep my eye on, then. I was able for it too. That was when my sister was alive. But I lost track a bit, after she died. She's been dead some time now, my sister. It was a good house then. She was a capable woman. Yes. Fine size of a woman too. . . . I think my mum was a Jewess. Yes, I wouldn't be surprised to learn that she was a Jewess. She didn't have many babies [pp. 102–3].

No matter how long one has lived in a house, one must constantly recount the number of floors, for someone may add or subtract a floor at will, apparently. And counting the floors is not as simple as it sounds. There must be a conscious effort; one must approach the task as a job so serious as to require careful direction supplied by an abler person (his sister). Similarly, befuddled old Mr. Kidd is not even sure of his own mother's background.

Before the Sands are discovered on the landing outside the door, there is a suggestion that outsiders pose a threat when Rose thinks that she sees a stranger from the window. Thus, when she opens the door to empty trash, there is a dramatic shock as they are suddenly seen. With the entrance of the young married couple the threat is much closer to being realized. Ironically the contrast between the shock of their appearance, which focuses the building atmosphere of menace on them, and the normality of their first words lulls us into a sense of security and relief, but the Sands soon provide a disruptive element with their arguing and add to the verification problem when they refuse to accept Mr. Kidd's name as that of the landlord. Mr. Sands' decision that his wife did not see a star is the first of many instances in Pinter's drama in which "reality" is determined by a decision—see Lenny's story about the pox-

ridden girl in *The Homecoming*, for example. And the contradictory statements concerning their course on the stairs further compound the question of
truth and reality. The couple brings with them, moreover, information from
the basement which directly affects Rose's security:

ROSE. You won't find any rooms vacant in this house.
MR. SANDS. Why not?
ROSE. Mr. Kidd told me. He told me.
MR. SANDS. Mr. Kidd?
ROSE. He told me he was full up.
MR. SANDS. The man in the basement said there was one. One room. Number
　　seven he said.
　　　Pause.
ROSE. That's this room [p. 112].

　　The final threat to Rose's security comes in the person of Riley, the blind
Negro. The audience knows that nothing good can emerge from the basement
—Rose has certainly made this clear throughout. Mrs. Sands' account of their
meeting with the mysterious inhabitant is no more reassuring: "I didn't like
the look of it much, I mean the feel, we couldn't make much out, it smelt
damp to me. Anyway, we went through a kind of partition, then there was
another partition, and we couldn't see where we were going, well, it seemed
to me it got darker the more we went, the further we went in. . . . And then
. . . a bit of a fright . . . but we never saw him, I don't know why they never
put a light on" (p. 111). Mr. Kidd's information that the basement dweller
desires a confrontation is further evidence of impending trouble. Not only
is the manner of the man suspect, but his instructions to wait until Mr. Hudd
is gone are ominous: "He's downstairs now. He's been there the whole week-
end. He said that when Mr. Hudd went out I was to tell him. . . . he won't
indulge in any conversation . . . wouldn't even play a game of chess. . . . It's
not good for me. He just lies there, that's all, waiting. . . . But he knows you,
Mrs. Hudd, he knows you. . . . He hasn't given me any rest. Just lying there.
In the black dark. Hour after hour. . . . You don't think he's going to go
away without seeing you, after he's come all this way, do you? You don't
think that, do you?" (pp. 114–15). Even though the man just lies there, his
presence is upsetting.
　　With Riley's entrance comes the destruction of Rose's world. There is
another shock, because it has not been mentioned before, when the man from
the dark basement turns out to be a dark man—a Negro, doubly dark because
he is blind. In spite of being blind, the man "looks about the room," notes that
"this is a large room," and answers Rose's question of what he wants with the
reply, "I want to see you." Rose, anxious to keep control, seizes on each of
these events. When Riley glances about, she demands, "What are you looking
at? You're blind, aren't you?" When he comments on the size of the room, she

interjects, "Never mind about the room." To his statement that he wishes to see her, she retorts "Well you can't see me, can you? You're a blind man. An old, poor blind man. Aren't you? Can't see a dickeybird" (pp. 116–17).

Her reaction to the intrustion of this "poor blind man" is acutely defensive. She strives to dominate. He cannot trick her by looking about the room because she can see that he is blind: "What do you think you've got here, a little girl? I can keep up with you." Rose is trying to prove that she is not a helpless innocent but someone who can take care of herself when she again refuses to be tricked, this time in connection with Riley's name: "What? That's not your name. That's not your name. You've got a grown-up woman in this room, do you hear?" (p. 116). Interestingly, Rose had insisted to Mr. Kidd that it was not possible for her to know whoever it was in the basement, and one of the first things she says when Riley comes in is, "I don't know who you are," yet she immediately insists that he is not telling the truth when he says, "My name is Riley."

More ambiguity is involved as the scene develops. Riley claims to have a "message" for Rose—"Your father wants you to come home." Rose replies, "Home? Go now. Come on. It's late. It's late. . . . Stop it. I can't take it." She does not seem especially surprised that Riley represents her father's interests; it is something she never questions. Her reaction moments later is much the same when Riley addresses her as Sal:

RILEY. Come home, Sal.
    Pause.
ROSE. What did you call me?
RILEY. Come home, Sal.
ROSE. Don't call me that [p. 118].

She does not deny the name Sal, she merely does not wish to be called Sal. Another element of ambiguity comes in unobtrusively when Riley switches to the first person and it is no longer "Your father," but "*I* want you to come home" (italics mine). Rose continues the conversation as though she does not even notice the change.

Now that the threat is out in the open, though not understood by the audience because of the amount of information Pinter withholds,[16] Bert re-enters and momentarily ignores the presence of Rose's caller. Speaking for

16. At the beginning of this chapter it was noted that Pinter, in his own words, allows the characters to develop themselves, that he merely follows the *clues.* Withholding information, then, would seem to contradict his statement, but in fact it underscores his contention that he does not interfere ("I find out what [the characters] are doing . . . and keep out of it," not saying, "these characters are doing this because of such and such."). This is the way we live—we see someone doing something and we try to figure out why they are doing it. We do not expect everyone to constantly fill us in on the antecedents in their dialogue (which *they* are well aware of and upon which they base their conversation) or their motivations, just as we do not explain ourselves to a casual passerby. This is one of Pinter's techniques for developing a superrealistic theatre.

the first time in the play, Mr. Hudd expresses some of his own fears as he tells his wife about his drive: "I got back all right. . . . I had a good bowl down there. . . . I drove her down, hard. They got it dark out. . . . They got it very icy out. . . . But I drove her. . . . There was no cars. One there was. He wouldn't move. I bumped him. . . . I got back all right" (pp. 119–20).

Where Rose's terror was based on the idea of something intruding, possibly from the basement, into the security both represented by and created by her room, her husband's menace lies outside the room in the form of an indefinite "they" who go so far as to control the weather in an effort to destroy him.

All through the speech to his wife Mr. Hudd seems unaware of Riley, but when he turns his attention to the intruder, it is with a vengeance. Because he is not his personal menace, Mr. Hudd easily nullifies him. Screaming "Lice," Bert knocks the Negro to the floor and kicks him until he lies still (there is no evidence that the man is dead, as is assumed by some critics). The Negro's blindness is transferred to Rose, now completely isolated, who stands repeating, "I can't see," as there is a blackout and the curtain comes down.

The plot is simple. There is a room. There is a door in the room, the very existence of which contains menace, for it might be opened at any time and who or what might enter is unknown. The people in the room have isolated themselves from the world and have attempted to create a reality of their own, a mother caring for her child in a safe place, so that they may have an illusion of security. They are, in Pinter's words (during an interview with Kenneth Tynan for the BBC's Home Service series "People Today," broadcast October 28, 1960), "at the extreme edge of their living, where they are living pretty much alone."[17] Given this background, how does Pinter produce a play with more than limited private appeal and meaning? In part the answer lies in the plot itself, since so much is generalized by lack of specifics that the events take on an allegorical cast. It is here that a more detailed examination of the play's imagery and symbolism is needed.

The central image of this drama is the room itself. Everything in Rose's life takes place in the room and all her dialogue is in terms of the room. It is, therefore, through the room that Rose is vulnerable. It is Rose's place in the room which is threatened when menace upsets her: the Sands pose a threat when they reveal that the room is to be let, and Riley tries to get her to leave the room. Through constant allusion to an imagery revolving around the room, a symbol is evolved. The room becomes more than a location where the Hudds live, it is a place where "We don't bother anyone else. . . . And nobody bothers us" (pp. 109, 97).

The basement becomes a symbol as it is juxtaposed with the room. Where

17. A similar statement by José Ortega y Gasset contains the essence of Pinter's characters: "Man always travels along precipices; his truest obligation is to keep his balance."

Rose's abode is a large place of life, light, warmth, comfort, happiness, and the known (a world unto itself); the basement, with its running walls, is dark, damp, low-ceilinged with no windows, narrowly partitioned, smelly, the unknown (like coffins in the grave). While the room/basement duality may suggest a conventional trope for the conscious versus the unconscious, the Freudian ego/superego (room) versus the id (basement), it would be difficult to justify the ending satisfactorily in these terms. Rose as the ego, protected by the conventionally safe superego, comes into conflict with unidentified subconscious desires and urges represented by Riley, who issues from the subconscious level of the mind, approximated by the basement, to haunt her. Pinter, referring to psychiatric conjecture about *The Homecoming*, has called such speculation "rubbish" and insists, "I have never read Freud." This does not invalidate psychological or even Freudian interpretations of his work, since the concepts involved are widespread in society today. Traditionally, emotions prevent clarity of vision, and having been exposed, Rose's awareness of her previously unconscious desires demands that she lose the protection of innocence and be initiated into darkness. Resentment of the intrusion of a disruptive element which momentarily interrupts his orderly and comfortable existence may motivate Bert's attack. He is less susceptible to the superego's deterrent influence because he is less imaginative than his wife, so he simply strikes out at what bothers him in order to protect his ego, a practical form of sublimation through force, in Freudian terminology.

Seizing on the view of Rose as victim and therefore the incarnation of the old priest in the sacrificial/mythological rituals explained in Sir James Frazer's *The Golden Bough*, Katherine Burkman describes this drama as a ritual in which contenders for the priesthood battle (an *agon*) for the Golden Bough, the room itself.[18] Several of Pinter's plays do fit the pattern, though this could be because there are certain basic patterns which have become literary conventions. It seems unrealistic to assume that Pinter consciously tried to build his dramas around these patterns, especially when he first began writing; and it is his early plays (excepting a few pieces such as *The Basement*) which often best conform to the traditional models. The cyclical pattern is clearly an important element in Pinter's dramatic workshop, yet it need not be attributed entirely to following the design of the old king/new king conflict. Burkman's discussion of the ritualized aspects of repeated ordinary conversation is more convincing.

Riley, too, has become a symbol even before he appears on stage. A mysterious man who patiently lies waiting in the basement, offering the Sands information unknown to anyone else (the vacancy) and commanding Mr. Kidd, the dark man serves as a personification of death who comes out of the grave to bring darkness to Rose. Though he will not play chess with Mr. Kidd as death is often pictured doing—perhaps because the old man's time has not

18. Burkman, *The Dramatic World of Harold Pinter*, pp. 70–73.

yet come—it is typical of Pinter to offer a fairly obvious bit of symbolism and then at least partially to negate it by introducing a contradictory piece of evidence. As he is blind, Riley might also suggest personified justice, although his beating by Bert indicates that he is ineffective. This is something which would be expected in conforming to Pinter's theory of verification, however, for if absolute truth is unknowable, justice is meaningless.

There may be some undisclosed guilt in Rose's past or an event in her childhood with which Riley is acquainted. The possibility that the sin was prostitution arises from several allusions made by Rose herself; angrily reacting to Mr. Kidd's suggestion that she might have known the visitor downstairs in another district, she retorts, "Do you think I go around knowing men in one district after another? What do you think I am?" (p. 115). Speaking of Riley, she says: "My luck. I get these creeps come in, smelling up my room. . . . Oh, these customers. They come in here and stink the place out." Continuing, she alludes to the fact that Mr. Kidd "lets a respectable house" and Riley has dragged her name into it (p. 117). It is not extremely important, however, to identify the sin in Rose's past specifically; only to know that there is something, real or imagined, is enough; the meaning of the play is general in terms of communication and verification, since everyone has something in his past and *The Room* is not merely a case history of sin and retribution.

While there may be conflicting interpretations of the symbolic matter in *The Room*, there can be no doubt of the effect achieved through the technical device of imagery. Just as the actual events and the symbolism in the drama cumulatively produce the tone and meaning of the work, so Pinter's images lead to an overall feeling which reflects that meaning. Imagery in relation to the basement and its inhabitant adequately conveys the sense of dark, dank filth and decay infested with vermin which is Pinter's picture of the menace haunting the Hudds. For example, Rose would not know Riley "to spit" on him, and Bert's last word to the fallen Negro is the exclamation, "Lice!"

Likewise, the use of completely ordinary phrasing and word choice in the dialogue serves by contrast to emphasize the increasing unreality of the situation in which it is spoken. Mr. Hudd's description of his drive at the end of the play is a sample of the effectiveness of this technique, in which each instance compounds what has gone before and helps build to a final, unmistakable effect, for the contrast between the ordinary conversation and the extraordinary events creates shock and horror; one is not expected within the context of the other. Humor works in much the same way, for the funny things being said in non-humorous situations accentuate the seriousness of what is happening.

The disintegration of Rose's character under the threat of unknown menace is the structure of the play. We see her beaten down to the point where she can no longer be a mother—from rambling garrulity to a sterile repetition of "Yes" and ultimately to being blinded by exposure to the outside world in the form of Riley. But there are other characters and other lines of action in the play, and it is in them that small weaknesses are apparent.

Riley's part is enigmatic and perhaps inconsistent with the roles played by the other characters. Pinter has commented on this fact: "Well, it's very peculiar, when I got to that point in the play the man from the basement had to be introduced, and he just *was* a blind negro. I don't think there's anything radically wrong with the character in himself, but he behaves too differently from the other characters: if I were writing the play now I'd have him sit down, have a cup of tea."[19] Riley's part is not so ill-conceived as Pinter describes, for he seems perfectly natural in his actions and words. Bert's sudden attack is far more out of place, especially since a major part of the terror in the play is verbally expressed and more terrifying because it is vague and not concrete. There is no motivation apparent for Bert's outburst, but one realizes that he reacted in a similar manner in the incident during which his van "bumped" a car. When faced with a threat, he physically attacks. If it were a simple matter of race distinction, his reaction would have been more immediate.

Although there are suggestions that the basement and Riley specifically represent death, this is not necessary to the meaning of Pinter's drama—the basement may simply equal fear of the unknown, and Riley may be equivalent to any outside menace—since the play is about problems faced by all people. The drama is universal, and the symbols thus need not stand for particular incidents or persons.

The themes and techniques displayed in *The Room* will be developed further in Pinter's other plays as he extends his exploration of this concept.

The Birthday Party

Pinter's second play, the three-act *Birthday Party*, his first play to be presented professionally (at the Arts Theatre, Cambridge, on April 28, 1958) was begun immediately upon the completion of *The Room* in 1957 and many of the thematic and technical elements present in his first play reappear. In the characters there are numerous echoes too, though they are presented in different aspects: Rose's motherliness and play acting show up in Meg; Petey is Bert without violence; there is a song about Reilly; and Goldberg and McCann are Riley broken down into more identifiable terms. *The Dumb Waiter*, also written in 1957, carries on the idea complex of menace present in *The Room* and *The Birthday Party*, the menace becoming more specific as an organization (an allegorical representation of society) becomes the source of threat and Pinter explores many of the same questions in still another per-

19. Bensky, "Harold Pinter," p. 36. In *The Birthday Party* this is what actually happens.

spective. Instead of focusing on an intended victim, such as Rose or Stanley, Pinter considers the fate of the tormentor. Goldberg and McCann from *The Birthday Party* become Ben and Gus in *The Dumb Waiter*, and it is discovered that the terrors faced by the haunted are shared by their pursuers, who eventually suffer an end which is no different from that experienced by those they pursue.[20] Although Ben and Gus have voluntarily accepted a place in the system—unlike Rose, who tried to devise a safe environment of her own, and Stan, who tried to flee—their reward is that they become their own executioners. The conclusion that not even the menacers can escape menace was foreshadowed by Riley's beating in *The Room* and the momentary breakdown or loss of confidence of both Goldberg and McCann in *The Birthday Party*.

In *The Birthday Party* the horror becomes more intense than in *The Room* because it derives from an even less logical background. Whatever set the series of events in motion is less mysterious than the causes hinted at in *The Room*, in spite of being less specific. The undefined cause becomes extremely general in nature as a result of the self-contradictory possibilities suggested by the tormentors. Again, it is evident that the terrors undergone by the participants in *The Birthday Party* are representative rather than the portrayal of a single individual's plight. Perhaps because the horror is intensified, by contrast the characters' dialogue sounds much more realistic and the horror comes through much more strongly. Humor becomes more important for the same reason, and the element of irony is also more prevalent.

Like *The Room*, *The Birthday Party* grew out of an experience Pinter himself had. In a letter sent to a friend during one of his tours as an actor about three years before the drama was written, Pinter describes his rooming house: "'I have filthy insane digs, a great bulging scrag of a woman with breasts rolling at her belly, an obscene household, cats, dogs, filth, teastrainers, mess, oh bollocks, talk, chat rubbish shit scratch dung poison, infantility, deficient order in the upper fretwork.' Now the thing about this is *that* was *The Birthday Party*—I was in those digs, and this woman was Meg in the play; and there was a fellow staying there in Eastbourne, on the coast. The whole thing remained with me, and three years later I wrote the play."[21] Like the conception of *The Room*, the incidents behind *The Birthday Party* had been in Pinter's mind for some time, and the release of writing his first play triggered the quick succession of plays which flowed from the thoughts stored in his mind.

As in *The Room*, carried throughout *The Birthday Party* is the theme of the threat to a person's security by unknown outside powers and the disintegration of his individuality under the onslaught of the attacking force.

---

20. Or, as Burkman would contend, in the ritual sacrifice victim and victor alike become victims. Goldberg and McCann, Ben and Gus, Rose and Stanley share some of these same qualities—and they are victims all.

21. Bensky, "Harold Pinter," pp. 16–17.

There is also the generalizing effect which allows the meaning of the play to extend to all members of the audience. This includes the idea of verification, which contains within it the problems of identity. The techniques which Pinter employs to express and expand these two concepts in *The Birthday Party* are the same as those he used in *The Room*.

From the outset of the play we are reminded of characters, events, themes, and devices found in *The Room*. The opening conversation between the Boles, Meg in the kitchen and Petey in the living room reading the newspaper (the society page!), is typical in its natural banality, with no real exchange of information taking place:

MEG. Is that you, Petey?
　Pause.
　Petey, is that you?
　Pause.
　Petey?
PETEY. What?
MEG. Is that you?
PETEY. Yes, it's me.
MEG. What? . . . Are you back?
PETEY. Yes.
MEG. I've got your cornflakes ready. . . . Here's your cornflakes. . . . Are they
　nice?
PETEY. Very nice.
MEG. I thought they'd be nice.[22]

There are numerous minor elements involved in this talk which by the very weight of their numbers create a significant comment on life (mutual avoidance and lack of understanding lead to banality in serious situations) when combined with similar elements during the course of the play. The idiom is natural and familiar, producing, like that in *The Room*, a background against which future events will be magnified by contrast. Both people are talking, yet neither divulges any meaningful data and each continues talking in a circular fashion as though the other were not answering. Meg becomes characterized by her constant desire to know if something is "nice" and by her motherly concern, which will become extremely strong when directed at Stan, recalling Rose's role playing in *The Room*. Unlike Rose, though, Meg is generally oblivious to what is really happening about her. The lack of communication between husband and wife sets the mood for what is to follow, implying unsettling conditions.

In *The Dumb Waiter* similar things are implied in the same way. As this

22. Pinter, *The Birthday Party*, in *The Birthday Party and The Room* (New York: Grove, 1961), p. 9. See Chapter XI, below, for explanation of how textual alterations in later editions affect interpretations.

underrated little gem of a play opens, even before the first words are spoken, a feeling of uneasiness is established by the motions of the two men, Gus and Ben. Gus has difficulty tying his shoelaces, partly because there is a matchbox in one shoe and a packet of cigarettes in the other. While determining what the problem is, he wanders about the room. Ben, who is trying to read a newspaper, is continually disturbed by Gus's actions. Gus goes into the bathroom and pulls the chain, but nothing happens—the first of several times this pattern is followed. When he comes back into the room, Ben slams his paper down, exclaims "Kaw," and reads an article to Gus about an eighty-seven-year-old man who was run over when he crawled under a lorry because he could not see to cross the road. The appalled manner with which the two men react to an incident of violence unrelated to themselves is humorous, and in light of the subsequent revelation of their business, morbidly ironic. They display little emotion over the murder they are about to commit, but the accidental death of an unknown old man seems so unbelievable that they become upset. The difference is that one event reflects order, predictability, while the other does not. Their nervousness is similar to that shown by McCann in *The Birthday Party* before a job. The work begun, though, they will probably settle down and demonstrate their ability as he did.

Like McCann and Goldberg, Gus and Ben in *The Dumb Waiter* talk about their unconventional jobs in conventional terms. Gus notices that "he's laid on some very nice crockery, this time," and confesses to being "quite taken with the crockery." He goes on to note that he always manages to bring a few biscuits for the tea break and like most employees half-seriously gripes that he hopes "it won't be a long job, this one."[23] As before, there is humor and irony based on the disparity between the words and the context in which they are spoken.

It is not long before the seemingly innocuous opening scene of *The Birthday Party* begins to involve the dimension of terror, too, with Petey's unobtrusive remark to Meg that two men had approached him the night before, inquiring about a room to rent. The next clue which serves to tell us that things are not as they should be is the noise coming from Stan's bedroom when Meg goes to wake him:

MEG. I always take him up his cup of tea. . . .

PETEY. Did he drink it?

MEG. I made him. I stood there till he did. I tried to get him up then. But he wouldn't, the little monkey. I'm going to call him. (*She goes to the door.*) Stan! Stanny! (*She listens.*) Stan! . . . I'm coming up! I'm going to count to three! One! Two! Three! I'm coming to get you! (*She exits and goes upstairs. In a moment, shouts from* STANLEY, *wild laughter from* MEG.

23. Pinter, *The Dumb Waiter*, in *The Caretaker and The Dumb Waiter; Two Plays* (New York: Grove, 1961), p. 87.

PETEY *takes his plate to the hatch. Shouts. Laughter.* PETEY *sits at the table. Silence. She returns.*) He's coming down. (*She is panting and arranges her hair.*) I told him if he didn't hurry up he'd get no breakfast.
PETEY. That did it, eh?
MEG. I'll get his cornflakes [p. 14].

Meg's words and actions are more like those of a combination mother/mistress than landlady, as she calls her boarder a "little monkey" and "Stanny" and counts before going after him, returning with mussed hair. Moreover, when Meg gives Stanley his "birthday" present later, it is not just a drum, it is a *boy's* drum, bringing home Meg's relationship to her boarder quite vividly. Furthermore, Petey hears the entire exchange as one of the members of the game even to the extent of saying "Ta-ta, Stan" as he exits, rather than objecting to his wife's antics with the younger man as might be expected. Although neither exceptionally bright nor brave, Petey does have an aware and sympathetic nature. He is willing to indulge in inane conversations with his wife to keep her happy, and he recognizes that her games with Stanley are just that, games. There is nothing threatening to his marriage in her actions, so he allows her to continue. And he shows a fondness for Stan that is more than simply a landlord's interest in his tenant. Ultimately, it is through Petey that we understand that Goldberg and McCann are not merely businessmen stopping for a night who become unwillingly involved in Stanley's mental breakdown. Petey knows that these men are actually representatives of a force which is seeking Stan and that their intentions are not innocent. As a matter of fact, he goes so far as to try to stop them from taking Stanley away with them at the end of the drama. It is this action which gives us the perspective to see the two menacers as menacers, inasmuch as Petey immediately comprehends Goldberg's threat (that he ought to go with them) and subsequently refrains from attempting to protect their victim, demonstrating that there is truly something to be wary of.

Meg continues her role playing, switching from mother to mistress through most of Act I. She tells Petey that Stan does not deserve any breakfast because he came downstairs late, and then cajoles Stan to eat his cornflakes "like a good boy." When Stan does not agree that the cornflakes are lovely and refreshing, she calls him a "little liar." To Stan's answer to her question about whether the fried bread was nice, she responds like a playful mistress:

MEG. Was it nice?
STANLEY. What?
MEG. The fried bread.
STANLEY. Succulent.
MEG. You shouldn't say that word.
STANLEY. What word?
MEG. That word you said.

STANLEY. What, succulent—?
MEG. Don't say it!
STANLEY. What's the matter with it?
MEG. You shouldn't say that word to a married woman.
STANLEY. Is that a fact? [pp. 17–18].

Meg's misunderstanding of the word succulent is symbolic both as a summary of her character and as a statement about life. It is not that she just does not understand this particular word, she has no true grasp of the meaning of most words and so, although she talks and listens, she says and hears nothing which bears on life as a meaningful experience. Later, for example, when Goldberg offers the compliment that she will "look like a tulip" in her party dress, she responds by asking, "What colour?" Again, by extension, life is meaningless. The absurdity of life is humorous when expressed in terms of an elderly woman being shocked by the use of a harmless word, but the tragedy of such a situation is also pathetically evident. For Pinter, as explained in an interview with Hallam Tennyson on the BBC General Overseas Service broadcast of August 7, 1960, "Everything is funny; the greatest earnestness is funny. Even tragedy is funny. And I think what I try to do in my plays is to get to this recognizable reality of the absurdity of what we do and how we behave and how we speak. The point about tragedy is that it is *no longer funny*. It is funny, and then it becomes no longer funny."

Later, Pinter will also use humor to intensify the horror contained in *The Birthday Party*, just as he used it in *The Room*. First, the good-naturedness with which Goldberg and McCann plan the party enhances the terror of the inquisition which precedes the festivities. Then Lulu's exchange with Goldberg after spending the night with him is amusing. The correlation between the event and the language used in discussing the event is a fine example of the dramatist's contention that "everything is funny"; all that is needed is an objective perspective:

LULU. You used me for a night. A passing fancy.
GOLDBERG. Who used who?
LULU. You made use of me by cunning when my defences were down.
GOLDBERG. Who took them down?
LULU. That's what you did. You quenched your ugly thirst. You took advantage of me when I was overwrought. I wouldn't do those things again, not even for a Sultan!
GOLDBERG. One night doesn't make a harem.
LULU. You taught me things a girl shouldn't know before she's been married at least three times!
GOLDBERG. Now you're a jump ahead. What are you complaining about?
       . . .

LULU. You didn't appreciate me for myself. You took all those liberties only
   to satisfy your appetite.
GOLDBERG. Now you're giving me indigestion.[24]

Pinter's view of the affinity between what is comic and what is tragic provides
an insight into his use of incidents such as Lulu's meeting with Goldberg;
her "earnestness" is undercut by the "recognizable reality of that absurdity"
of her behavior and the words spoken in this context. A similar brand of
humor comes into being when social ritual is unthinkingly applied in *all*
circumstances.

Further discussing with Tennyson the effect of recognizing the absurdities and uncertainties in life, Pinter says, "the fact that it [life] is verging on
the unknown leads us to the next step, which seems to occur in my plays.
There is a kind of horror about and I think this horror and absurdity go together." Having provided a background through colloquial dialogue and
interactions between the characters, Pinter is now ready to amplify his hints
of terror.

The first hint, of course, is Petey's revelation about the presence of strangers. The hints become less vague and more obviously facets of the building
terror when Stan recalls for us that he is a boarder and not a son, even though
he is treated like a member of the family: when Meg decides not to give him
something cooked for breakfast because he rose late, Stan casually considers
going "down to one of those smart hotels on the front" (p. 16), and a bit after
reminds Meg that he is the only lodger they have had since he has been there.
In the first case Meg does not react to his casual comment casually as she
quickly goes into the kitchen to get him some fried bread, indicating that
not only does she take him literally but also that the threat that she might lose
him is of a serious enough nature that it must be thwarted quickly. Stan's
observation on the lack of visitors is dramatic irony since the audience already
knows that visitors are on their way, maybe even outside the door at this very
moment. From this point on actions and imagery coalesce to form the mount-
ing mood which is explicitly realized with the arrival of Goldberg and Mc-
Cann. Stan derides Meg for not making her husband a cup of tea and accuses
her of serving him sour milk instead. He calls her an "old washing bag," tells
her that it is not her place to come into a man's bedroom, says he cannot drink
"this muck," and violently attacks her housekeeping, calling the place a
"pigsty" and cataloguing the various things that need improving, finally re-
coiling from her in disgust. This picture of decay and corruption reinforces
the audience's realization that this is not a normal household.

Now comes the actual introduction of menace, and it is evident from

24. *The Birthday Party*, p. 84. Pinter's deletions in the revised edition destroy some
of the humor of this confrontation.

Stan's actions that he recognizes the existence of that menace. Meg simply mentions that she has got to get ready "for the two gentlemen.—*A pause.* STANLEY *slowly raises his head. He speaks without turning.*" Acting as though he does not understand, he asks her what she is talking about, then claims that he does not believe her and she is "saying it on purpose," as if childishly to upset him. He demands to know more about the men and then solves the problem like Rose, trying to protect himself from menace by denying its existence, by "*decisively*" insisting that "they won't come. . . . Someone's taking the Michael. . . . It's a false alarm" (p. 21). The fact that no one else has lodged in the house for over a year makes the "sudden" interest of the two strangers suspect, and Stan's reaction indicates that not only does he have something to fear, but these men may represent the threat he has been trying to hide from for that past year.

Ignored on the spoken level, the news has a causal effect and things are suddenly no longer as they were. A concern with identity emerges, and Stan asserts himself by asking Meg who she thinks she is talking to, and then proceeding to tell her: "I've played the piano all over the world. All over the country. (*Pause.*) I once gave a concert. . . . (*reflectively*) Yes. It was a good one, too. They were all there that night. Every single one of them. It was a great success. Yes. A concert. At Lower Edmonton . . . (*to himself*) I had a unique touch. Absolutely unique. They came up to me. They came up to me and said they were grateful. Champagne we had that night, the lot. (*Pause.*) My father nearly came down to hear me. Well, I dropped him a card anyway. But I don't think he could make it. No, I—I lost the address, that was it. (*Pause.*) Yes, Lower Edmonton. Then after that, you know what they did? They carved me up. Carved me up. It was all arranged, it was all worked out. My next concert. Somewhere else it was. In winter. I went down there to play. Then, when I got there, the hall was closed, the place was shuttered up. . . . (*Takes off his glasses and wipes them on his pyjama jacket.*) A fast one. They pulled a fast one. I'd like to know who was responsible for that. (*Bitterly.*) All right, Jack, I can take a tip. They want me to crawl down on my bended knees. Well I can take a tip . . . any day of the week" (pp. 23–24).

The pattern of contradiction lends itself to humor as each positive statement is lessened by another positive, albeit not so grand, statement: the world becomes the country, which becomes Lower Edmonton; everyone attended—except his father, who was nearly there because Stan "dropped him a card," only the address was lost. On another level Stan's history is pitiful. The manner in which he relates his tale shows his defeat and he seems quietly amazed that such outlandish things could happen to him, yet he is resigned. The whole speech has the same ring to it that Mr. Kidd's remembrances of his mother and sister had in *The Room.*

This apocryphal tale seems to be just the opposite of the existential idea that "man makes himself," for Stanley is certainly *unmaking* himself as his story progresses. Similarly, he moves from essence to existence. There is a feeling of *angst* present, though, not only in Stan's thoughts and actions but also in those around him. Meg reacts immediately to his suggestion about the van and the wheelbarrow, as though this anxiety were part of her daily life; and there is truly anguish in Goldberg's lost, incomplete utterance of his belief about the world.

The progression of the dialogue in this scene is a fine example of Pinter's dramatic technique in revealing multiple layers of meaning as related to characterization. Stanley is obviously upset by the news that there are strangers nearby, and his story about his piano-playing career is an attempt to shift the conversation to another subject while it simultaneously suggests that people have been "out to get him" for some time. The intermittent pauses during Stan's recital reveal that he is engaged in an emotional struggle within himself which is created by the unpleasant memories that he is recalling and trying to reconcile himself with. Underscoring the feeling of menace (some unknown horror brooding in the background ready to pounce), which derives from the character's awareness that an unidentified threat exists, is the realization that they are talking but not communicating. Like Meg's constant repetition of the tag, "Is it nice?" it is as though they were following a ritual which has lost its meaning. The landlady's announcement about the prospective lodgers triggers Stan's tale, so the disturbing information and his past must be connected in some manner; yet Meg is unable to realize where the source of his uneasiness lies, because they are not thinking on compatible levels (she worries about whether he has "paid a visit").

Meg's unhesitating acceptance of Stan's implication that "they" might really be after her as being well within the realm of possibility is just as terrifying as his reaction. The atmosphere of menace is almost overpowering. And here the author's technical mastery of the stage is demonstrated in an effective *coup de théâtre*; for as Meg's fear reaches its highest pitch under Stanley's urging, there is a sudden Macbethian knock at that door through which something unimaginable might emerge. This must be the two strangers, and the audience fears what will happen to Stan in the resulting confrontation, a confrontation which he obviously dreads. When the door is opened, however, Lulu, the neighbor girl, is discovered; and there is an immediate release of the tension which has been building throughout the scene.

The ensuing conversation between Stan and Lulu serves two purposes. First, it reinforces our awareness of Stanley's sloppy physical appearance. Under the pressure of the still unknown menace he apparently has let his grooming go and is deteriorating physically—a symptom of his mental deterioration, too. The imagery employed suggests that he is truly a "washout" and is right at home in Meg's "pigsty" of a house. Second, Stanley is seen making a half-hearted attempt to get away from the approaching menace as he tries to persuade Lulu to run off with him; but he has nowhere to go and almost fatalistically does not really try very hard to persuade the girl to leave with him. Again, though, the basic importance of Lulu's knock at the door lies in the fact that Pinter is carefully working to create a maximum effect. The audience's fears are alleviated by the girl's appearance, thus ironically making the arrival of Goldberg and McCann moments later seem devoid of sinister implications by diminishing expectations; but then it is quickly made clear through their conversation that there is, indeed, something menacing about the pair.

With the entrance of Goldberg and McCann soon after Stan's sinister insinuations about the van and his admission that someone was unhappy with him, we have to reorient ourselves, for the pair come in with no introductory information and are immersed in a conversation which has no logical connection with anything that has preceded it, yet at the same time reinforces the basic concepts which have been emerging. Immediately the questions of identity and verification are part of the dialogue: Goldberg admits to having a son named Emanuel, Manny for short, whom he calls Timmy. Goldberg's own name will be questioned by McCann later because he calls himself Nat, but his father called him Benny and his mother and wife both call him Simey.[25] Similarly, Goldberg attaches two names to McCann—Dermot and Seamus (pp. 73, 81). He also refers to other things in a confusing manner. When he calls Meg "A good woman. A charming woman" in Act III, he mentions that his "mother was the same" and his "wife was identical" (p. 73). This yoking of the two women in his life may be more than a simple comparison; there may be literal truth in the statement because on previous occasions he had discussed the two in parallel terms. Compare "Up the street, into my gate, inside the door, home. 'Simey,' my old mum used to shout, 'quick, before it gets cold!' And there on the table what would I see? The nicest piece of gefilte fish you could wish to find on a plate" (p. 46), and "back I'd go, back to my bungalow with the flat roof. 'Simey,' my wife used to shout, 'quick, before it gets cold!' And there on the table what would I see? The nicest piece of rollmop and pickled cucumber you could wish to find on a plate" (p. 62). A good representative of middle-class ideals, he married "a girl, just like the girl that married dear old dad"—no incest involved, but the concept of verification is involved, since the two women are referred to in terms confusingly alike. Similarly, when McCann replies "That's true" to Goldberg's assertion that "everywhere you go these days it's like a funeral," Goldberg answers, "True?

25. Ibid., pp. 81, 46, and 62. Emanuel, "God with us," was applied to Christ; Timothy was a Christian convert who was associated with Paul in spreading the Gospel; Nathan was a prophet who rebuked David for sinning; Benjamin was the youngest and favorite son of Jacob (Jacob figures in the patriarchal drama and has been interpreted as an idealized cluster of religiously originated tribal traditions); among the numerous Simons was Judas' father, and Simeon, another son of Jacob, partook in the cruel massacre at Shechem. See Chapter XI regarding textual changes resulting in the removal of these names in the revised edition, 1965.

Of course it's true. It's more than true. It's a fact" (p. 30), a further comment on the distinction between truth and falsity. Another dimension of mystery is added as Goldberg and McCann discuss the job they are to perform, but do not say what the job is, and the fatalistic element is emphasized when McCann is not sure that they have come to the right place, but Goldberg has no doubt—in fact he did not even have to look for the number on the house. A sense of inevitability will evolve from this sort of revelation.

When Meg returns, the two visitors demonstrate an interest in Stanley, quizzing the landlady about him. Several things are working here. Stan's earlier uneasiness at the mention of strangers is recalled, and it is implied that their job has something to do with him. Humor and irony are present even in a tense situation as Goldberg asks Meg if McCann might go into her kitchen for "a little gargle" (p. 33), and when Meg tells Goldberg that Stan has "been down in the dumps lately," Goldberg replies, "We'll bring him out of himself" (p. 36), a statement the true impact of which comes out only in Act III. Also mixed with the humor is Meg's simplicity and inability to comprehend the world about her. She repeats a confused version of Stan's life story: "He once gave a concert . . . (falteringly). In . . . a big hall. His father gave him champagne. But then they locked the place up and he couldn't get out. The caretaker had gone home. So he had to wait until the morning before he could get out. (With confidence.) They were very grateful. (Pause.) And then they all wanted to give him a tip. And so he took the tip" (p. 34). The distortion of Stanley's tale is also important because it allows the realization that Meg, like Rose in The Room, is coincidentally bragging about the exploits of her "son" and creating a universe which has some meaning for her; she becomes more sure of herself as she proceeds, even though she is producing a garbled version of reality (a practical demonstration of the verification theme, for her story is as acceptable as his; in his latest "memory" plays Pinter implies that this is the structure of life, that we create reality, past as well as present, from moment to moment). The verification concept is displayed pragmatically in The Dumb Waiter, too, when Gus notices pictures on the wall:

GUS. Hello, what's this? (Peering at it.) "The First Eleven." Cricketers. You seen this Ben?
BEN. (reading) What?
GUS. There's a photo here of the first eleven.
BEN. What first eleven?
GUS. (studying the photo): It doesn't say.
BEN. What about that tea?
GUS. They all look a bit old to me [p. 89].

The world view revealed by Pinter is full of objects and events which are real, yet divulge no meaning because they are incomplete or are so unconnected with the context in which they are found that no meaningful relationship can be easily discovered. The verification element is also used later to reinforce the feeling of menace. In an argument about a soccer game Ben first claims that he was not present, then contradicts himself by offering a judgment on a disputed play which took place in the game:

GUS. You were there yourself?
BEN. Not me.
GUS. Yes, you were there. Don't you remember the disputed penalty?
BEN. No.
GUS. . . . I didn't think the other bloke touched him myself . . .
BEN. Didn't touch him! What are you talking about? He laid him out flat! [p. 93].

In *The Birthday Party* Stan's terror becomes centered on Goldberg and McCann, but it is some time before the full impact of the menace is realized. When Goldberg suggests that they hold a birthday party for Stan that night, the plot has been provided for in two ways: the action can logically follow a prescribed course, since the audience knows what the general plan is; and at the same time the idea of the birthday party has quite clearly been linked with Goldberg, an ominous overtone thereby being attached to what would normally be a happy celebration. This ominous overtone is emphasized as the connection between the intruding strangers and Stan is made stronger by the indication that there is something inevitable about their meeting. The knowledge that Stan cannot escape and that the birthday party tonight will probably be the focal point of his confrontation brings the atmosphere of menace to another peak. The abrupt ending of Act I, with Stanley beating wildly on the toy drum, is further evidence that he is losing control of himself under the influence of menace. Stan's savage possession similarly ties the action of the play to a ritualistic theme and his beating of the drum is a desperate, semimagical attempt to try to drive away a set of demons.

Once the men actually meet, there is a brief interlude during which Stan and his tormentors spar, allowing the mood of terror to increase, and then all pressures are brought to bear on him. When his attackers finally accuse him of something concrete, they accuse him of everything—the generalizing effect which says, it does not matter what you did, all that matters is that you did *something*. Stan reinforces this idea by never replying in specifics or demanding an account of what he has done. He knows that he has guilt of one sort or another in his past. Whether it is a matter of stuffing himself with dry toast or of contaminating womankind, he has been antisocial.

The progression of Stan's inquisition is a study in psychological warfare in which the subject is assaulted from all sides at once, with varying periods of aggression and restraint. It begins in Act II when Stan walks in on McCann, who is methodically tearing a newspaper into five equal strips (destruction of a medium of communication or part of the ritual of his job which serves both to calm the Irishman and to unnerve Stan). After exchanging simple social amenities, Stan attempts to leave, but McCann blocks him. The first really explicit act of terror contained in the play, this action serves to substantialize the hint of menace, as it is now clear that the evolving mood of the drama is more than purely a mood; it is representative of a definite, though as yet still undefined, horror. Stan quickly begins to explain before anyone can charge him with being guilty of anything. To McCann's question of whether he is in business, Stanley answers: "No, I think I'll give it up. I've got a small private income, you see. . . . Don't like being away from home. I used to live very quietly—playing records, that's about all. Everything delivered to the door. Then I started a little private business, in a small way, and it compelled me to come down here—kept me longer than I expected. . . . I lived so quietly. . . . You know what? To look at me, I bet you wouldn't think I'd led such a quiet life. The lines on my face, eh? It's the drink. Been drinking a bit down here. But what I mean is . . . you know how it is . . . away from your own . . . all wrong, of course. . . . I'll be right when I get back . . . but what I mean is, the way some people look at me you'd think I was a different person. I suppose I have changed, but I'm still the same man I always was. I mean, you wouldn't think, to look at me, really . . . I mean, not really, that I was the sort of bloke to—to cause any trouble, would you?" (p. 43). Nobody could blame Stanley for anything after such a blanket denial, and minor items such as the lines on his face are easily explained away (is it not admirable that a man should miss his "own" so much that he has done a little drinking to help ease himself through?).

Several times during the conversation Stan moves to pick up a strip of the torn paper and McCann warns him, "Mind that," a threat which, like blocking him from leaving, keeps the thought of physical violence present. There is actual physical action when Stan becomes so involved in his attempts to persuade McCann of his innocence that he grips the other man's arm, as though the physical touch will add credibility to his plea. McCann strikes out savagely, hitting Stanley's arm. Stan switches tactics, seeking McCann's friendship by professing a liking and admiration for Ireland and the Irish people, but Goldberg enters before he has a chance to proceed very far, and Stanley's introduction to terror is about to begin in earnest. Stan is nearly ignored as Goldberg, Petey, and McCann talk about the good old days when young men did not take "liberties" and "knew the meaning of respect." It is in the course of this conversation that Goldberg recalls his old mum's calling him "Simey" and the problem of verifying names is initiated.

When Petey (Stanley's last hope, the only thing that might actually stand between him and his tormentors) and McCann leave, Stan moves on a new tack, telling Goldberg that he runs the house, which is presently "booked out," so they will have to find other accommodations. Overlooking Stan's description of the rooming situation, Goldberg again exercises his image-making power and control of words in a portrayal of getting up in the morning: "Some people don't like the idea of getting up in the morning. I've heard them. Getting up in the morning, they say, what is it? Your skin's crabby, you need a shave, your eyes are full of muck, your mouth is like boghouse, the palms of your hands are full of sweat, your nose is clogged up, your feet stink, what are you but a corpse waiting to be washed" (p. 48). Characteristic of Pinter, the strongest, most effective imagery is that which centers around filth, decay, and odor. The notion of filth, decay, and odor which accompanies and reinforces Pinter's theme of menace comes into play in *The Dumb Waiter*, for instance, when Gus objects that he has been sleeping on dirty sheets—"I thought these sheets didn't look too bright. I thought they ponged a bit" (p. 92).

Game playing is reintroduced in *The Birthday Party* when McCann comes back and Goldberg, McCann, and Stan suggest to one another that they take a seat:

GOLDBERG. Sit down.
STANLEY. No.
    GOLDBERG *sighs, and sits at the table right.*
GOLDBERG. McCann.
MC CANN. Nat?
GOLDBERG. Ask him to sit down.
MC CANN. Yes, Nat. (MC CANN *moves to* STANLEY.) Do you mind sitting down?
STANLEY. Yes, I do mind.
MC CANN. Yes, now, but—it's better if you did.
STANLEY. Why don't you sit down?
MC CANN. No, not me—you.
STANLEY. No thanks.
    Pause.
MC CANN. Nat.
GOLDBERG. What?
MC CANN. He won't sit down.
GOLDBERG. Well, ask him.
MC CANN. I've asked him.
GOLDBERG. Ask him again.
MC CANN (*to* STANLEY). Sit down.
STANLEY. Why?
MC CANN. You'd be more comfortable.
STANLEY. So would you.
    Pause.
MC CANN. All right. If you will I will.
STANLEY. You first. [p. 49].

This little interplay is a serious attempt by the characters to assert their superiority over one another. Similar events occurred in *The Room* between Mr. and Mrs. Sands (pp. 106, 110) and earlier in *The Birthday Party* when Goldberg and McCann first appeared. The problem is solved by Goldberg's suggestion that they both sit down. McCann was upset when Goldberg suggested that he sit down earlier because this simple act would establish which of the two parties is dominant and McCann is unsure about the nature of this particular job (as Gus will be in *The Dumb Waiter*) and does not trust his partner. It appears that getting the victim to sit down is part of the ritual pattern followed in the psychological warfare these men subject their victims to. Now they are using their weapons on Stan. Although this seems to be an innocent bit of game playing, Stan's reaction when he tricks McCann into sitting down first indicates that he recognizes the seriousness of the interplay. He has made an effort, unsuccessful of course, to defend himself by forcing McCann to sit down first. But he is playing their game; they are masters of it, and they control their victim almost effortlessly.

The semantic game which occurs in *The Dumb Waiter*, Ben saying "light the kettle" and Gus insisting on "put on the kettle" as proper usage (p. 97), is another version of the sit-down game. It is a means through which the characters try to demonstrate their superiority over each other, to dominate each other. Like the envelope scene, though, the kettle argument serves a dual purpose; superficially the sight of two grown men arguing over the correctness of a phrase is humorous, yet that such an insignificant item can excite such intense interest, well beyond its intrinsic value, indicates that something is amiss, and the underlying current of menace flows closer to the surface again. That there is more involved than whose choice of words is correct is humorously exposed by Ben's denial of ever having heard the phrase before and his subsequent use of the term in a manner suggesting that it is not foreign to him after all.

In *The Birthday Party*, the question of seating settled, the inquisition begins in earnest, with full emotional force. Standing on either side of Stan, the two interrogators rapidly fire *non sequitur* questions at their subject, matching his earlier blanket denial:

GOLDBERG. When did you last wash up a cup?
STANLEY. The Christmas before last.
GOLDBERG. Where?
STANLEY. Lyons Corner House.
GOLDBERG. Which one?
STANLEY. Marble Arch.
GOLDBERG. Where was your wife?
STANLEY. In—
GOLDBERG. Answer.

STANLEY (*turning, crouched*). What wife?
GOLDBERG. What have you done with your wife?
MC CANN. He's killed his wife!
GOLDBERG. Why did you kill your wife?
STANLEY (*sitting, his back to the audience*). What wife?
MC CANN. How did he kill her?
GOLDBERG. How did you kill her?
MC CANN. You throttled her.
GOLDBERG. With arsenic.
MC CANN. There's your man!
GOLDBERG. Where's your old mum?
STANLEY. In the sanatorium.
MC CANN. Yes!
GOLDBERG. Why did you never get married?
MC CANN. She was waiting at the porch.
GOLDBERG. You skedaddled from the wedding.
MC CANN. He left her in the lurch.
GOLDBERG. You left her in the pudding club.
MC CANN. She was waiting at the church.

. . .

GOLDBERG. Do you recognize an external force?
MC CANN. That's the question!
GOLDBERG. Do you recognize an external force, responsible for you, suffering for you?
STANLEY. It's late.
GOLDBERG. Late! Late enough! When did you last pray?
MC CANN. He's sweating!

. . .

GOLDBERG. Where is your lechery leading you?
MC CANN. You'll pay for this.
GOLDBERG. You stuff yourself with dry toast.
MC CANN. You contaminate womankind.
GOLDBERG. Why don't you pay the rent?
MC CANN. Mother defiler!
GOLDBERG. Why do you pick your nose?
MC CANN. I demand justice!
GOLDBERG. What's your trade?
MC CANN. What about Ireland? [pp. 52–55].

The controllers of Stanley's ordeal charge their victim with such a magnificent array of crimes, sins, and *faux pas* that he must have committed some of them; yet Pinter's ambivalent concept of verification contradicting reality is sustained when, for instance, Stan's mistreatment and murder of his wife are denounced only to be followed by a condemnation for never marrying. The two charges are mutually exclusive, of course. And Stan's examiners do not pursue the reference to his piano-playing career—the one allegation which might be credible to the audience.

As a matter of fact, Pinter does include a clue that Stan's problem derives from the period when he lived near Maidenhead and that it might be directly connected with Goldberg somehow. When they first meet, Stanley tells Mc-Cann about his quiet life in Basingstoke (leading a life remarkably like that led by Rose in *The Room*; apparently he has tried her method of escape and found it unsuccessful, which is why he fled to the seacoast) and asks if the Irishman ever had tea at Fuller's or visited Boots Library (p. 42). At the party Goldberg also recalls these two establishments (p. 59). If the two men frequented the same places, it may be that they were more than casually acquainted; perhaps they worked for the same people. And the people they worked for may have belonged to the underworld, which would explain the fact that someone is after Stanley, the tormentors' practiced approach, and Stan's reactions. Such an interpretation (although probably much too narrow) gains credibility from the realization that Stan is literally taken for a ride as the play ends (to see Monty, the gang leader?) and Goldberg's pride in his car which has a boot with just the "right amount" of room—to hold a body, perhaps?

The confrontation scene is the crux of the play. Again, it is not a particular which is important; since there is no way to escape the all-encompassing catalogue, the stress is on the idea of inevitability which ultimately defeats Stanley. The scene ends in violence with Stan physically attacking Goldberg (he kicks him in the stomach) and Stan and McCann circling each other, each ready to bash the other with a chair, Stan repeating "Uuuuuuhhhhh!"

The potential battle is interrupted by a drumbeat, and Meg enters to announce the beginning of the birthday party. The party is ironic. It simultaneously celebrates the death of Stan as an individual (symbolically an artist, though the idea of the artist is more useful as a conventional representation of human sensitivity than as a literal fact—at best Stan was a second-rate performer) and his rebirth as a nonentity conforming to the dictates of society (when the play ends Stan is dressed as though for his own funeral).[26] Thus the party might better be described as a wake celebrating the death of Stan as an individual. The members of the party play out their own interests, oblivious to Stanley's presence. Meg talks about her childhood, McCann reminisces about Ireland, Goldberg and Lulu practice mutual seduction, Stan sits silently.

In the ensuing game of blindman's buff, McCann touches Stan's glasses,

26. In the revised edition Pinter unfortunately reduces the symbolic impact of this scene by having Stan wear clothes of a more businesslike nature.

which he breaks after Stan is blindfolded. Stan is forced back into an active role by the game. No longer able to see (the linking of blindness and guilt, as in *The Room*), he destroys the drum when McCann places it in his way, and then, as if released from social conventions by the mask or by the thought that if he is going to be damned he may as well be condemned for a concrete reason, he turns on the two women, first trying to strangle Meg and then trying to rape Lulu.

Act III is an epilogue in which we see the results of Stanley's ordeal. Meg is still unaware of reality—mentioning Goldberg and McCann's relationship to Stan, she says, "I think they're old friends" (p. 71)—and is only concerned with having been the "belle of the ball." Petey is aware of events, inquiring about Stan's condition, but he is not strong enough to stand up to the tormentors. McCann and Goldberg are less polished as a team now that the mission is accomplished, and Goldberg stands around spouting aphorisms. Lulu has undergone an experience with Goldberg which should have taught her a lesson, but (in the extremely funny exchange already quoted) she gives no indication that her future conduct will be any different. Armed with a suitcase, Goldberg "took advantage" of her, but he is willing to "let bygones be bygones." Bolstered by moral indignation and assuming the stance of a misused woman who has been exposed to exotic and degrading practices, the neighbor complains bitterly about her treatment, though she shows no outward physical signs of having been damaged in any way and Goldberg dismisses her by neatly turning her phrases back on her and refusing to put up with her hysterics. A younger version of Meg, she is used by the forces of society for their own ends, though she is aware enough to understand that she has been used. Like Petey, she also knows that she does not have the power to do more than object ineffectually. Technically, it is Lulu who carefully draws the audience's attention to the fact that Stanley's personal appearance is on a par with the run-down condition of the boarding house when her description of him parallels his attack on Meg's "housekeeping," and she functions as a focus for Stanley's attention as the breakdown becomes complete, perhaps a comment on society's repression of sex. Along with Petey it is Lulu's recognition of Goldberg's nature which gives us the perspective to see him as he really is. With both Petey and Lulu coming to the same conclusions, it is doubtful that Goldberg and McCann are innocent.

No sooner is Lulu out the door than McCann brings poor Stan in. The transformation is shocking. Lulu had met Goldberg and suffered at his hands during the night, but it was only a passing moment and brought no physical change to mirror the mental alteration. With Stan the effect is greater in proportion to the amount of attention he receives—and the contrast between Lulu's appearance and Stan's is indicative of just how much attention was involved. He has been reduced to the level of a cipher—a nonthinking, nonreacting member of a smoothly running mechanistic society in his neat, conservative dress of *"striped trousers, black jacket, and white collar. He carries a bowler hat in one hand and his broken glasses in the other. He is clean-shaven"* (p. 85). He cannot talk. "Still the same old Stan," comments Goldberg (p. 89). These are the results of exposure to menace.

The Birthday Party, like The Room, lends itself to a symbolic interpretation.[27] Keeping in mind the alternative symbolism contained in the metaphor of the birthday party, Stan's change of character, and his funeral attire in Act III, the dramatization may be seen as an allegory of death. There is also ample evidence that Goldberg and McCann may represent the ideals of society, with Stan filling the role of the artist forced back into the mold of conventionality. Stanley as a pianist was not much of a performer, *vide* his concert story, but even as a quasi-artist his piano playing represents a threat to the status quo because it is not a thing that everyone can do equally well and because it requires a different set of goals from those held by the ordinary workingman; he is thus set apart from his fellow man, whether as an artist or merely as a sensitive individual.

The brooding Irishman McCann, a recently unfrocked priest, as a representative of traditional society, focuses on treachery and politics, religion and heresy, while Goldberg is more concerned with sex, property, and social propriety. One of Goldberg's characteristics is the continual repetition of cultural clichés; but like the advice of Polonius, the rules laid down are meaningless because they depend on learning by rote instead of understanding: "Uncle Barney taught me that the word of a gentleman is enough. . . . my name was good. . . . Do your duty and keep your observations. Always bid a good morning to the neighbors. Never, never forget your family, for they are the rock, the constitution and the core. . . . play up, and play the game. Honour thy father and thy mother. . . . Follow the line, McCann, and you can't go wrong. What do you think, I'm a self-made man? No! I sat where I was told to sit. I kept my eye on the ball. School? Don't talk to me about school. Top in all subjects. And for why? Because I'm telling you, I'm telling you, follow my line? Follow my mental? Learn by heart. Never write down a thing. No. And don't go too near the water. And you'll find—that what I say is true. Because I believe that the world . . . (*Vacant.*). . . . Because I believe that the world . . . (*Desperate.*). . . . BECAUSE I BELIEVE THAT THE WORLD . . . (*Lost.*)" (pp. 30, 81, 80). Goldberg has lost his faith in himself and finds nothing to believe about the world. Retreating into the past, though, he finds a renewal of strength, and like Meg creating a meaningful world for herself when she recounts Stanley's

27. Burkman's reading of *The Birthday Party*, for example, pictures the action as an *agon* between Stanley and the "reigning priest-king" Monty who is alluded to by his lieutenants, Goldberg and McCann, on one level, while on a second level Stan serves as both victim and victor in the dual role of the sacrificed/resurrected god. As a scapegoat (*pharmakos*), Stanley is destroyed, "only to be reborn in the image of Monty" (p. 23), whom Burkman sees as shaping the entire action. Other critics have noted Stanley's Christ-like assumption of the guilt of mankind, but Pinter does not develop this parallel.

tale of pianistic accomplishments in Act I, Goldberg grows more certain of himself as he proceeds with his repetition of the advice his father used to give him.

Another characteristic is his faith in panaceas: "The secret is breathing. Take my tip. It's a well-known fact. Breathe in, breathe out, take a chance" (p. 29). Later he will claim success because he never lost a tooth, will have McCann check his throat and then blow in his mouth, and will stretch a chest expander (which he carries with him) until it breaks to prove his vitality.

The crimes attributed to Stan are mostly antisocial—murder, failure to keep a clean house, refusal to marry. The catalogue of cliché awards Goldberg and McCann offer Stanley for his rehabilitation likewise reflects socially desirable goals and prizes. Stan has been cockeyed for years, but now he has friends who will help him see straight again. Having broken his glasses, they will get him a new pair. They suggest that he has had a nervous breakdown, a socially acceptable modern illness, and should have a long convalescence "Somewhere over the rainbow," "Where angels fear to tread" (p. 86). Once Stanley has followed this program he will be set for life, as McCann and Goldberg recite in rhythmical stichomythia:

MC CANN. We'll renew your season ticket.
GOLDBERG. We'll take tuppence off your morning tea.
MC CANN. We'll give you a discount on all inflammable goods.
GOLDBERG. We'll watch over you.
MC CANN. Advise you.
GOLDBERG. Give you proper care and treatment.
MC CANN. Let you use the club car.
GOLDBERG. Keep a table reserved.
MC CANN. Help you acknowledge the fast days.
GOLDBERG. Bake you cakes [p. 87].

Goldberg and McCann may also represent another form of conventionality—organized religion. Their names, the foods mentioned by Goldberg and his Jewish phrasing of "sacred" clichés, their ritualistic approach, the reference to McCann's recent leaving the cloth ("He's only been unfrocked six months," p. 85) have been seen by Ruby Cohn[28] and Bernard Dukore[29] as evidence of this limiting force which is brought to bear on the artist by the Judeo-Christian tradition (Cohn insists on the use of clichés while Dukore concentrates on the significance of the name changes and the circumstances in which they occur). McCann even calls Goldberg "Judas" during the interrogation. The two men also convey a feeling of inevitability, an aspect of most religions. As Goldberg tells Meg when she professes happiness that the two men arrived when they did, "If we hadn't come today, we'd have come

28. Cohn, "The World of Harold Pinter," pp. 55–68.
29. Dukore, "The Theatre of Harold Pinter," pp. 43–54.

tomorrow" (p. 35). Other critics have agreed that Goldberg stands for family, school, and social relationships, and McCann serves the interests of politics and religion.

In view of one of the most characteristic elements in Pinter's stage crafts- manship, his attention to details, it is interesting to note throughout the play, and in particular during the inquisition and party scenes, McCann's accusa- tions and references, which are clear evidence of his preoccupation with politics (especially Irish independence) and religion (primarily Catholi- cism). The probability that Pinter intended for McCann to be seen as a representative, with Goldberg, of the repressive aspects of the Judeo-Christian tradition which is the basis of Western society is enhanced by the extent to which the dramatist expresses the Irishman's allegiances through even less obvious allusions. For example, while Stanley's interrogation in Act II is filled with outright statements of his having betrayed "the organization," it also con- tains McCann's mention of the Black and Tan (p. 51), a special police force composed of army veterans which was created in 1919 to reinforce the Royal Irish Constabulary in its battle with the revolutionary Irish Republican Army. Later McCann sings a song at the birthday party about "the bold Fenian men" (p. 63). The Fenians were a legendary band of warriors who fought to defend Ireland in the second and third centuries. In the nineteenth century the name was revived to identify members of a secret organization of Irish and Irish-American patriots devoted to the overthrow of British rule in Ire- land.

There are also religious concerns demonstrated during the inquisition scene which go beyond the simple accusation that Stan stinks "of sin," when McCann refers to "the Albigensenist heresy" and "the blessed Oliver Plun- kett" (p. 54). The members of the Albigensian heresy belonged to a Cath- aristic sect in southern France between the eleventh and thirteenth centuries, and Oliver Plunkett was the last English Catholic martyr to die (in the seventeenth century).

McCann's dialogue is filled with the mention of place names, too, and these usually serve to combine the political and religious themes as they are located in various parts of Ireland. (Pinter may well have gained acquaintance with them during his eighteen-month acting tour of the Irish provinces before he turned playwright.) The names figure in Irish history either as places in the battle for independence or as sites of religious significance or both. Drogheda, for instance, is the subject of one of the questions with which Mc- Cann confronts Stan in Act II (p. 55). The seemingly inconsequential query takes on meaning when the history of the town is revealed. Located on the southern border of County Louth on the Boyne about 30 miles northwest of Dublin, Drogheda was a stronghold first of the Danes and then the Anglo- Normans and the site of several parliaments. In a rebellion in 1641 the town was besieged but relieved, only to fall to Oliver Cromwell in 1649, when the inhabitants were massacred. After the Battle of the Boyne, Drogheda was garrisoned by King James's troops. In addition a synod was convened in Drogheda in 1157. Very little remains of the ancient fortifications, though the Magdalen tower of a Dominican friary founded in 1224 remains, as does a tower of the Augustinian abbey of St. Mary d'Urso, built in 1206; and six miles west of Drogheda are the ruins of a Cistercian abbey. The Franciscans, Carmelites, and Knights of St. John also established themselves in Drogheda; none of their buildings now remain. Ruins may be found at the other cities mentioned by McCann, too, thus linking them to the political/religious content of the drama.[30]

Though there is an artist-versus-society motif in *The Birthday Party*, as in *The Room*, the meaning need not be so limited. Because neither the original deed which stimulated the menace nor the source from which the menace generates is identified, and because of the generalizing effect created by the inclusiveness of the sins attributed to Stan, once again it is implied that everyone is vulnerable to such terror. The meaning of the drama does not depend on whether we know what Stanley did. All we have to know is that at some time or other in his past he, like all of us, did something—he is guilty. *The Birthday Party* continues the theme of menace initiated in *The Room*, but the menace is less mysterious and more specifically concerned with matters of society in the second play, and in addition, where we fear for Rose in the first drama, Stan makes us aware that we should fear for *ourselves*. We cannot create a secure environment as attempted by Rose, nor can we hide from

30. The Irishman wonders if Meg has ever been to Carrickmacross (Carrikmacross, p. 61), a marketplace 57 miles northwest of Dublin in County Monaghan, where there are remains of an Elizabethan castle which was destroyed in 1641; he discusses Roscrea (p. 63), a small mountain village in south-central Ireland (County Tipperary) which contains the medieval ruins of the Castle of Mormonder (1213), a seventh-century priory, and a Franciscan friary (dating from 1490); and he asks about Tullamore (p. 63), an urban district in the central Irish county of Offaly in which bronze age and early Christian monuments are to be found, including the ruined Sraith Ui Chatharnaigh castle which dates from 1588. Finally, when McCann verbally abuses Lulu in Act III the former priest declares that he has seen her "hanging about the Rock of Cashel, profaning the soil" (p. 85). The Rock of Cashel is a 300-foot-high hill located in the city of Cashel (County Tipperary) which was supposedly blessed by an angel in the fourth century, leading the kings of Munster to establish a stronghold there which was turned over to the church in 1101. Situated on the summit of the hill are the remains of St. Peter's cathedral (burned by the earl of Kildare in 1495), a round tower, Cormac's chapel, and an ancient cross, on the pedestal of which the kings were crowned. Part of the Rock's defenses are still intact and at the base of the hill there is a Cistercian abbey (Hore) which was founded in 1266. Within the town itself there is a Dominican priory (1243) and the city (now the seat of a Protestant bishop) is also the site at which Henry II received homage from the king of Thomond in 1171 and at which Edward Bruce held his Irish parliament in 1315. Cashel was captured for the last time in 1647 by Lord Inchiquin. Beccause of the abundance of references throughout McCann's speeches which are both politically and religiously significant, it is clear that such allusions are not merely coincidental. Almost certainly Pinter does intend McCann to represent these two social elements.

insecurity in an already existing situation as tried by Stan. *The Dumb Waiter*, Pinter's third play, will explore further sources of horror and the possible consequences of exposure to menace.

The Dumb Waiter

That it is an organization which Ben and Gus serve and Gus criticizes in *The Dumb Waiter* is clear. Somebody selects the victim, someone else rents the room and notifies the enforcement squad, and someone else is in charge of cleaning up whatever mess is made. As Ben says, "They got departments for everything" (p. 103). This picture of a job for everyone and everything, with everyone performing his own specialty is close enough to a description of modern society for a correlation to be drawn. Here, then, the play becomes a depiction of the fate of a sensitive man (one who begins to ask questions because his last victim was a girl who came apart so messily that he wonders who clears up the remains), presenting a threat to society because he questions rather than accepts, and who must therefore be destroyed before he destroys.

Gus's recent penchant for asking questions, which is brought to his attention by Ben ("You're always asking me questions. . . . You never used to ask me so many damn questions. What's come over you? . . . Stop wondering. You've got a job to do. Why don't you just do it and shut up?" p. 99), serves as a foreboding, since society requires obedience. Because Ben accepts everything as it is, as Goldberg advised McCann to do in *The Birthday Party*, he has no problems. His secret of success, "just do it and shut up," is reminiscent of Goldberg's words in the earlier play (Act I). Gus's questioning of the system leads him in front of Ben's pistol by the end of the drama. Unlike Stan, he cannot be forced back into an acceptable mold—he pays no attention to Ben's pleas that he remain silent.

Symbolically the dumbwaiter has a twofold significance. Most obviously it is a mystery. It represents the unknown and thus is a potential source of menace, for it begins functioning suddenly, for no apparent reason. It continues to operate in the same manner, making demands on the occupants of the room, but it is as though it were working automatically, since it takes no notice of the responses stimulated by its actions. Allied with the sense of mystery centering on the dumbwaiter is the religious symbolism connected with it.

Religion is an aspect of society which does, of course, contain and depend on mystery. The actions of the machine are godlike too. It preexisted, and it initiates action of its own volition. As a representative of authority, it descends to present demands for food sacrifices. The demands are unreasonable—tea when there is no gas, for example. Although the originator of the demands remains hidden from the eyes of its two subjects, there is a means of direct communication. Ben speaks "with great deference" through the speaking tube. After unquestioningly trying to appease the authority upstairs, Gus fantasizes about what heavenly, albeit somewhat prosaic, conditions must exist up there: "Who knows what he's got upstairs? He's probably got a salad bowl. They must have something up there. . . . They've probably got a salad bowl up there. Cold meat, radishes, cucumbers. Watercress. Roll mops. . . *Pause*. The lot. They've probably got a crate of beer too" (pp. 113–14). The final and most frightening quality of godhood displayed by the controller of the dumbwaiter is his power over life—it is through the speaking tube that Ben receives the order that the next person to come through the outside door is to be the victim.

While on the subject of religious symbolism, it should be pointed out that some critics have detected aspects of Christianity symbolized in the play. The attempt to link the twelve matches in the envelope to Christ's apostles, and the trinity of rings on the stove to the Christian tradition, seems rather far-fetched, however. Pinter has commented: "When I say there are three rings, I mean there are three rings. But all of us are indeed surrounded by the remnants of a Christian civilization. This question of understanding is on so many different levels—after all, you can understand with your big toe."[31] In spite of his denial Pinter as a poet/dramatist is clearly aware of the significance of symbols, but the linking of rings on a stove to the Christian tradition when there is no other evidence in the play that the author is trying to make such a connection seems pointless. Pinter may be using the audience's awareness as part of his technique, though. By ignoring the audience's expectation that the number of matches will be made into a symbol, the playwright is demonstrating that there are things, like the gas stove, which simply exist in the universe, unconnected, and that we need not, indeed perhaps cannot, expect to find a meaning in everything.

Aside from any symbolic significance, Pinter's use of the incident of the envelope of matches being pushed under the door is admirable. Terror of the unknown is evoked from the fact that no logical explanation is offered for the existence of the envelope: there is no writing on it, no message in it—just the twelve matches. The element of the unknown is further compounded when no one is discovered in the passageway who could have pushed the enigmatic object under the door. It is here, too, that the audience is given the first solid indication as to what kind of job Ben and Gus perform when Gus approaches the door, gun in hand. That the men have something to fear is obvious from the presence of the gun, and a door is once more established as a likely source from which the expected menace will emerge. Ironically, though, it is the still unnoticed dumbwaiter which will prove most terrifying.

31. "Pinterview," p. 69.

Pinter also employs humor in this incident, with a twofold result. When Ben notes that whoever left the packet "must have been pretty quick" (p. 96) to have been able to disappear before Gus could get to the door, it is funny because the audience is aware that the actual amount of time which elapsed between the envelope's appearance and Gus's opening of the door is not a matter of mere seconds, and from this discrepancy some insight into the characters' very subjective view of the universe is gained.

The differing reactions of Ben and Gus to the dumbwaiter phenomenon likewise offer a chance to distinguish some of the differences in their natures, which in turn helps elucidate the meaning of the play. Their attitudes toward the dumbwaiter and its demands are identical to their attitudes toward other subjects and events in the drama. Ben accepts without question the absurdity of the situation and tries his best to fill the impossible demands made of him. In Pope's phrase, for Ben whatever is, is right. Gus, on the other hand, neither accepts nor totally acquiesces; he complains and questions the whole set of events: "We send him up all we've got and he's not satisfied. No, honest, it's enough to make the cat laugh. Why did you send him up all that stuff? (*Thoughtfully.*) Why did I send it up?" (p. 113). The distinction between the positions of the two men is forcefully demonstrated frequently, as when Gus looks up the shaft and Ben "*flings him away in alarm*" (p. 105). Significantly the speaking tube works only for Ben.

The presence of the infernal machine has so influenced the thoughts and emotions of the two men that they no longer mesh. Ben reprimands Gus for not polishing his gun: pride in one's work is a middle-class virtue. The speaking tube settles the question of usage argued earlier, in Ben's favor. In catechistic style the pair then goes through a dry run of the procedure they follow in an actual murder—but for the first time Ben forgets the point at which Gus is to take his gun out. Gus persists in asking questions, and Ben becomes more and more nervous as the questions continue, ultimately turning on his partner physically. The men repeat the newspaper routine for a few moments, but like everything else which has been repeated since the first intrusion of the dumbwaiter, the sincerity and enthusiasm of the previous occurrence is missing. Ben does not even read the article, a fact which makes no difference in this new context.

When Gus goes offstage for a glass of water, Ben receives the instructions that the victim is coming. When Gus returns, he enters "*stripped of his jacket, waistcoat,* [and] *tie*" (p. 121), a conventional use of the removal of clothing (the accoutrements of society) to signify the reduction of a man to his most basic and vulnerable state. The situation which exists as the curtain falls is overwhelming in its implications: Gus has been questioning the organization (society) and the organization has ordered him destroyed; it is Ben, though, who finds himself in an incredible predicament—if he follows orders and kills his companion, he is sure to start thinking himself, for it was a traumatic experience which started Gus's mental processes, and will in turn have to be destroyed by the organization; if he does not shoot Gus, they will both be pursued (representatives of the organization must already be upstairs waiting, for whatever was ordering Ormitha Macarounada and the like also sent the fatal message). Ben has been given an impossible choice, one to which there is no correct answer, and one which is faced by most members of society in one form or another at one time or another.

When initiative and imagination are stifled, they are destroyed. And they must be stifled to a great extent for a society to survive, since society is based on order and the willingness of the majority to accept without question menial tasks and the rationale explaining them. A figure such as Gus represents quite a threat to a status quo founded on such principles, since he initiates questioning.

The gradual build-up of terror follows much the same pattern in *The Dumb Waiter* as in *The Room* and *The Birthday Party*, though this time the menace is already in the room, waiting for the victim to enter. At first seemingly inconsequential facts and thoughts mentioned in the course of normal conversation take on completely new meaning, *in toto* and in juxtaposition with one another, until the menace becomes obvious on an intellectual level, echoing the underlying tone which has been evolving throughout. The final point of the play comes when these two elements are joined, each reinforcing the other.

Ambiguity is a keystone in Pinter's drama, and the title of this play is in line with such a technique. Does it refer to the actual machine, Ben's lack of insight, or the silent killer waiting for his prey? Probably all three are involved. Such ambiguity is symptomatic of Pinter's view of the universe. The machine which does not work is another evidence of his view. That the toilet does not flush properly for Gus does not greatly surprise us, for in a universe such as ours the traditional is no longer valid and we only partly expect machines to function properly; there seems to be no logical reason why they should. This point of discontinuity or lack of connection was likewise displayed in the picture of the "first eleven."

As in the two preceding plays, humor and dialogue play dual roles. Humor, besides providing something to laugh at, serves simultaneously as comic relief and a means of heightening the feeling of terror by contrast. Examples have already been cited, but it is important to reiterate that a good deal of Pinter's comedy rests on an ironic base. Dialogue is used to keep the action flowing and to establish a realistic framework, once more allowing an intensification of the atmosphere of menace through contrast with the unrealistic context in which it is uttered. But for Pinter there is much more involved. In "Between the Lines," an article he wrote for the *Sunday Times* (London), he delineates his theory of language and paralanguage: "Language, under these conditions, is a highly ambiguous commerce. So often, below

the words spoken, is the thing known and unspoken. . . . There are two silences. One when no word is spoken. The other when perhaps a torrent of
language is being employed. . . . The speech we hear is an indication of that
we don't hear. It is a necessary avoidance, a violent, shy, anguished or mocking
smokescreen which keeps the other in its place. When true silence falls we
are still left with echo but are nearer nakedness. One way of looking at speech
is to say it is a constant stratagem to cover nakedness. . . . I think that we communicate only too well, in our silence, in what is unsaid, and that what takes
place is continual evasion, desperate rearguard attempts to keep ourselves
to ourselves. Communication is too alarming. To enter into someone else's
life is too frightening. To disclose to others the poverty within us is too fear-
some a possibility. . . . I'm not suggesting that no character in a play can ever
say what he in fact means. Not at all. I have found that there invariably does
come a moment when this happens, where he says something, perhaps, which
he has never said before. And where this happens, what he says is irrevocable
and can never be taken back. . . . There is another factor which I think has
considerable bearing on this matter and that is the immense difficulty, if not
impossibility, of verifying the past. I don't mean merely years ago, but yesterday, this morning. What took place, what was the nature of what took place,
what happened. If one can speak of the difficulty of knowing what in fact
took place yesterday one can I think treat the present in the same way. *What's
happening now?* We won't know until tomorrow or six months time, and we
won't know then, we'll have forgotten or our imagination will have attributed
quite false characteristics to today. A moment is sucked away and distorted,
often even at the same time of its birth. We will all interpret a common experience quite differently, though we prefer to subscribe to the view that
there's a shared, common ground, a known ground. I think there's a shared
common ground all right, but that it's more like quicksand. Because 'reality'
is quite a strong, firm word, we tend to think, or to hope, that the state to which
it refers is equally firm, settled, and unequivocal. It doesn't seem to be, and
in my opinion it's no worse or better for that."[32] The entire conversation of
The Dumb Waiter (or any Pinter play, for that matter) is an example of Pinter's concept of language in practice, which in turn reflects the interrelationship of his themes of menace, communication, and verification. As can be
seen in his comments on language, the three are inseparable components of a
whole and all three must be considered in the discussion of any single one.

While clearly related to *The Room*, *The Dumb Waiter* is more closely
allied to *The Birthday Party*, which openly sets the individual against society
(or the system, or the organization) and demonstrates that the man who
questions must either be made to conform or be destroyed by society for its
own preservation.

In the first three "comedies of menace" Pinter clearly defines and estab-

32. *Sunday Times* (London), 4 March 1962, p. 25.

lishes the interrelationship between the three concepts which are basic in his thought (menace, communication, and verification). He also develops his techniques of expression, including humor based on *non sequiturs* and funny things being said in unfunny circumstances as a means of contrasting with and thereby accentuating the prevailing mood of menace. The idea of an outside threat to a character's security or individual identity is fundamental in his work during this period. Moreover, a distinguishing feature of the menace is its indeterminate source; the threat itself is never truly identified, although in *The Birthday Party* and *The Dumb Waiter* it is evident that society is involved. Pinter's next major play, *A Slight Ache*, is pivotal in his dramatic evolution, showing the beginning of a change in content as he starts a new thematic exploration, though a brief interlude during which he experimented with his techniques in a series of revue sketches followed his initial outpouring of plays in 1957.

Chapter IV. An Interlude—The Revue Sketches

. . . a complete play
which just happened to be four
minutes long . . .

One typical Pinter ingredient which is not as prevalent in *A Slight Ache* and the dramas which follow as it was in the preceding plays is humor, especially that based on *non sequiturs*, inconsistency, and verbal incongruity. This may in part be due to the fact that Pinter wrote a series of comic and semicomic revue sketches during the year 1959.

The sketches themselves were not really planned but came into being more or less on the spur of the moment. While putting together the new musical revue *One to Another*, Disley Jones, having worked on *The Birthday Party* with the author, asked Pinter if he had anything that could be used in the show. Pinter produced "The Black and White" (an early monologue which he changed into a dialogue) and "Trouble in the Works" for the revue, which was performed at the Lyric Opera House, Hammersmith, and at the Apollo Theatre in London in 1959. "Getting Acquainted," "Special Offer," "Last to Go," and "Request Stop" were then written for an even more popular revue,

Pieces of Eight, which was also performed at the Apollo Theatre in London later in 1959. Historically these performances were important to the dramatist's career because, writes Charles Marowitz in the *New York Times* (1 October 1967), "One of these revues was seen by the script head of Rediffusion Television and, as a result, Pinter's first play was unearthed, read and ultimately televised." Other sketches have appeared in collections of his works: "Applicant" was published in *A Slight Ache and Other Plays* (1961), "Interview," "That's All," and "That's Your Trouble" in *The Dwarfs and Eight Revue Sketches* (1965), and "Dialogue for Three" in an issue of *Stand* (Vol. 6, No. 3, 1963). *Pinter People*, a fifty-eight-minute film combining live action (including an interview with Pinter) and animation, and produced, directed, and designed by Gerald Potterton (who worked on the Beatle's *Yellow Submarine*) recreated "Trouble in the Works," "Request Stop," "Applicant," "The Black and White," and "Last to Go" in cartoon form. Voices for the characters in this 1969 film were supplied by Pinter himself, Vivien Merchant, Donald Pleasence, Dandy Nichols, Kathleen Harrison, and Richard Brier.[1]

"The Black and White"

"The Black and White" portrays a moment in the lives of two old women who apparently pass their evenings in milk bars, watching all-night buses go by. Seated at a table eating soup and bread, they discuss transit schedules, reminisce, and glance out the window. The picture is one of a meaningless existence in which nothing important happens, but which continues to go on and on, always following the same mundane pattern. Aside from depicting a simple, lonely existence, this sketch contains two elements common in Pinter's work, a realistic dialogue coupled with a touch of humor:

SECOND. How's your bread? (*Pause.*)
FIRST. Eh?
SECOND. Your bread.
FIRST. All right. How's yours? (*Pause.*)
SECOND. They don't charge for bread if you have soup.

1. THE VOICES:
"Trouble in the Works"   Mr. Fibbs: Harold Pinter
(running time: 3 minutes)   Mr. Wills: Donald Pleasence
"Request Stop"   Woman: Vivien Merchant
(3 minutes, 35 seconds)
"Applicant"   Lamb: Richard Brier
(4 minutes, 15 seconds)   Miss Piffs: Vivien Merchant
"The Black and White"   First Old Woman: Kathleen Harrison
(4 minutes, 35 seconds)   Second Old Woman: Dandy Nichols
"Last to Go"   Barman: Harold Pinter
(4 minutes, 45 seconds)   Newspaper Seller: Donald Pleasence

FIRST. They do if you have tea.
SECOND. If you have tea they do. (*Pause.*)[2]

It is the conversation of two people who have nothing to say—realistic sounding, but imparting no information and ignoring responses.

"Trouble in the Works"

"Trouble in the Works" brings two men together (Fibbs representing management and Wills labor—there is an amusing "appropriateness" in their names), as Pinter has fun with language, using pseudo-mechanical jargon about products in a factory to demonstrate a failure in communications:

FIBBS. . . . we've got the reputation of having the finest machine part turnover in the country. They're the best paid men in the industry. We've got the cheapest canteen in Yorkshire. No two menus are alike. We've got a billiard hall, haven't we . . . we've got a swimming pool. . . . And you tell me they're dissatisfied?
        . . .

WILLS. They don't want to have anything more to do with it.
FIBBS. This is shattering. Shattering. What else? . . .
WILLS. Well, I hate to say it, but they've gone very vicious about the high speed taper shank spiral flute reamers.
FIBBS. The high speed taper shank spiral flute reamers! But that's absolutely ridiculous! What could they possibly have against the high speed taper shank spiral flute reamers?
WILLS. All I can say is they're in a state of very bad agitation about them. And then there's the gunmetal side outlet relief with handwheel.
FIBBS. What!
WILLS. There's the nippled connector and the nippled adaptor and the vertical mechanical comparator.
FIBBS. No!
WILLS. And the one they can't speak about without trembling is the jaw for Jacob's chuck for use on portable drill.
FIBBS. My own Jacob's chuck? Not my very own Jacob's chuck?
WILLS. They've just taken a turn against the whole lot of them, I tell you. Male elbow adaptors, tubing nuts, grub screws . . .
FIBBS. But not, surely not my lovely parallel male stud couplings.
WILLS. They hate and detest your lovely parallel male stud couplings . . . *and* the bronzedraw off cock with handwheel and the bronzedraw off cock without handwheel!

2. "The Black and White," in *The Dwarfs and Eight Revue Sketches* (New York: Dramatists Play Service, 1965), p. 33.

FIBBS. Not the bronzedraw off cock with handwheel?
WILLS. And without handwheel.
FIBBS. Without handwheel?
WILLS. And with handwheel.
FIBBS. Not with handwheel?
WILLS. And without handwheel.
FIBBS. Without handwheel?
WILLS. With handwheel *and* without handwheel.
FIBBS. With handwheel *and* without handwheel?
WILLS. With or without! (*Pause.*)
FIBBS. (*Broken.*) Tell me. What do they want to make in its place?
WILLS. Brandy balls.³

This amusing exchange with its sexual overtones grew out of a job Pinter held in a factory service department for half a day: " 'Trouble in the Works' came right out of that half day in the office, which made the work . . . well worthwhile, because I had to copy down all the names—these extraordinary names of machine part tools, which I had never seen before."⁴ When the sketch was presented as part of the NBC Experiment in Television production of *Pinter People*, Wills' last line was unfortunately changed from "Brandy balls" to "Love," perhaps a concession to the mass audience, its cliché nature weakening the final effect.

"Getting Acquainted" and "Special Offer"

Two of the pieces from *Pieces of Eight*, "Getting Acquainted" and "Special Offer," are considered so slight by Pinter himself that he has not tried to preserve them—indeed, he claims that the script of "Getting Acquainted," "a farcical episode built around a Civil Defense practice,"⁵ has been lost. "Special Offer" is a short selection in which a BBC secretary is disturbed by a sale at a London firm:

SECRETARY. . . . this old crone suddenly came right up to me and sat beside me. . . . I've got just the thing for you, she said, and put a little card into my hand. . . . MEN FOR SALE! . . . It's an international congress, she said, got up for the entertainment and relief of lady members of the civil service. You can hear some of the boys . . . singing little folk tunes. . . . Tea is on the house . . . the boys do a rare dance imported all the way from Buenos Aires, dressed in nothing but a pair of cricket pads. Every single one of them is tried and tested, very best quality, and at very reasonable

3. "Trouble in the Works," ibid., pp. 29–31.
4. Pinter talking, in *Pinter People*, 1969.
5. Taylor, *Anger and After* (1969), p. 333.

rates. If you like one of them . . . you can buy him, but for you not at retail price. . . . What an extraordinary idea! I've never heard of anything so outrageous, have you? Look—here's the card.
(*Pause.*)
Do you think it's a joke . . . or serious?[6]

The sketch is amusingly suggestive in its premise that men should be provided for the "entertainment and relief" of working ladies, just as call girls are supplied for male executives. And the language of merchandising applied to the proposal adds to the fun (and the sense of indecency?) and looks forward to the collective bargaining session at the end of *The Homecoming*.

"Last to Go"

"Last to Go" is a bit of Pinter humor at its best. As might be expected, the humor is based on short, quick exchanges, a sort of skewed stichomythia, in which the prime element is a lack of communication again. Two characters, a barman and an old newspaper seller, talk at rather than to one another, each bouncing words off the wall that is the other, their responses being related though not necessarily relevant to the words of the other as they go through the motions of making conversation. The form is there, it is the meaning which is absent, and it is this which creates the humor. The situation is a fine example of Henri Bergson's definition of comedy as "something mechanical encrusted on the living":

MAN. You was a bit busier earlier.
BARMAN. Ah.
MAN. Round about ten.
BARMAN. Ten, was it?
MAN. About then. (*Pause.*) I passed by here about then.
BARMAN. Oh yes?
MAN. I noticed you were doing a bit of trade. (*Pause.*)
BARMAN. Yes, trade was very brisk here about ten.
MAN. Yes, I noticed. (*Pause.*) I sold my last one about then. Yes. About nine forty-five.
BARMAN. Sold your last then, did you?
MAN. Yes, my last "Evening News" it was. Went about twenty to ten. (*Pause.*)
BARMAN. "Evening News," was it?
MAN. Yes. (*Pause.*) Sometimes it's the "Star" is the last to go.
BARMAN. Ah.
MAN. Or the . . . whatsisname.
BARMAN. "Standard."

6. "Special Offer," printed in Hinchcliffe, *Harold Pinter*, pp. 73–74.

MAN. Yes. (*Pause.*) All I had left tonight was the "Evening News." (*Pause.*)
BARMAN. Then that went, did it?
MAN. Yes. (*Pause.*) Like a shot. (*Pause.*)
BARMAN. You didn't have any left, eh?
MAN. No. Not after I sold that one. (*Pause.*)
BARMAN. It was after that you must have come by here then was it?
MAN. Yes, I come by here after that, see, after I packed up.
BARMAN. You didn't stop here though, did you?
MAN. When?[7]

The men are engaging in a ritual exchange; there is no meaning or any real attempt to communicate anything other than the ritual. They are satisfied with the form itself.

"Request Stop"

The repetition of a ritual is essential in "Request Stop," too, but the lack of communication demonstrated has taken on much more serious overtones. In the sketch five people are queued up at a bus stop when one of the women asks the small man next to her a question about the scheduling. The incident quickly becomes frightening in its implications as she suddenly acts as though he has made an indecent proposal to her and makes wild, unrelated accusations indicative of the senselessness of most prejudices, yet which are seriously considered (see also Davies' reactions in *The Caretaker*): ". . . Nobody asked you to start making insinuations. . . . One of my best friends is a plain clothes detective. (*Pause.*) I know all about it. Standing there as if butter wouldn't melt in your mouth. Meet you in a dark alley it'd be . . . another story. . . . Anyone can tell you're a foreigner. I was born just around the corner. Anyone can tell you're just up from the country for a bit of a lark. I know your sort. . . ."[8] When the aggravated woman turns to another of the women in the line and asks her to be a witness, the lady ignores her request, hails a taxi, and disappears, allowing the first woman to turn her wrath on the noninvolved: "We know what sort she is. . . . I was first in this queue. (*Pause.*) Born just round the corner. Born and bred. These people haven't the faintest idea of how to behave. Peruvians."[9] The terms used are the same as those directed at the original focus of her verbal attack, the small man. A bus goes by and everyone runs after it, leaving the first woman alone. Another man walks up to the bus stop to wait and the whole ritual begins again, even more terrifying in its repetition as the woman *"speaks shyly, hesitantly, with a slight smile"* asking the newcomer a question about the bus route (Le Roi Jones's *Dutchman*, 1964, is a more sinister expression of a similar theme).

7. "Last to Go," in *The Dwarfs and Eight Revue Sketches*, p. 37.
8. "Request Stop," ibid., p. 35.
9. Ibid.

Applicant

In "Applicant" (a sketch based on an episode in the "discarded" play *The Hothouse,* circa November 1958) a physicist, Lamb, enters an office *"eager, cheerful, enthusiastic"* to apply for a vacant post. Once there he is subjected "to a little test to determine his psychological suitability" by a Miss Piffs, *"the essence of efficiency."* The test consists of sitting Lamb in a chair, attaching electrodes to his palms, and placing earphones on his head, then asking a series of unrelated questions: "Would you say you were an excitable person? . . . Are you often puzzled by women? . . . Unable to sleep? . . . Unable to remain seated? . . . Do you suffer from eczema, listlessness, or falling coat? . . . Are you virgo intacta? . . . Have you always been virgo intacta?"[10]

The last several queries are funny by themselves, but even more so considering the job for which Lamb is trying to establish his qualifications. At various times during the quizzing Pinter employs stage effects—*"a piercing high pitched buzz-hum,"* a red lighting of the stage which flashes on and off in time with Miss Piffs' questions, and the substitution of numerous instrument sounds (drums, cymbals, trombone, bass) for words, something he will indulge in much less frequently from here on. The NBC Experiment in Television presentation is in cartoon form and during the inquisition the two characters assume the outward appearance of robots.

Lamb's condition at the end of the interrogation contrasts starkly with his initial appearance, bringing to mind Stanley's experience in *The Birthday Party,* as he collapses to lie still and silent on the floor while Miss Piffs bends over him to close the interview with the conventional "Thank you very much, Mr. Lamb. We'll let you know."[11]

"Interview"

The keynote to "Interview" is incongruity. Conducted in the form of an interview, the tone of the sketch is set by the opening line: "Well, Mr. Jakes, how would you say things are in the pornographic book trade?" Having established a somewhat bizarre framework, Pinter compounds the effect (as in "Special Offer," where prosaic language is used to apply to a nontypical situation) by having Jakes make a perfectly logical and acceptable statement regarding a socially unacceptable subject: "you don't get all that many people sending pornographic books for Xmas presents." It is only fitting that Jakes uses the term "Xmas."

An innocuous question from the interviewer ("What sort of people do you get in your shop?") soon leads into another track as Jakes's answer shifts the focus of the sketch. Jakes begins to talk sinisterly of security police and secret

10. "Applicant," in *A Slight Ache and Other Plays* (London: Methuen, 1970), pp. 134–35.
11. Ibid., p. 136.

dossiers, leaving the interviewer bewildered and at a loss as he loses control of the interview and the direction it is taking (see also "Kullus," and "The Examination"). But Jakes has the answer—he is compiling his own set of dossiers! In the final line of the sketch Jakes reveals who is behind the moral disintegration of the country: it is the clientele which patronizes his shop. And who are those customers? "They're all the same, every single one of them. COMMUNISTS."[12] This insight into the workings of the human mind which can rationalize about almost anything is presented in a typically Pinteresque manner, humorous and horrifying at the same time.

"That's All"

"That's All" is another slice of life on the order of "The Black and White." Once again the dramatist presents two women who are discussing the everyday nature of their lives. Mrs. A and Mrs. B go round in circles like the barman and the newspaper vendor in "Last to Go" as they discuss a mutual friend who used to live in the neighborhood but who has moved away, returning occasionally to visit a nearby butcher's shop. The main topic of the conversation is what day of the week she used to come on, when she comes now, and on and on. The monotony of certain kinds of existence is the point.

"That's Your Trouble"

"That's Your Trouble" takes place in a park. Two men observe a third man, offstage, carrying a sandwich board on his back. An argument ensues between the first two men over whether the third man will develop a headache or a neckache from carrying his burden. They become emotionally involved and almost violent as they debate a question which not only does not concern them but which could be easily answered by simply asking the third man. In the end they revert to the childish level reached when an argument loses any semblance of logic (communication) and the participants resort to name-calling:

B. You just don't know how to listen to what other people tell you, that's your trouble.
A. I know what my trouble is.
B. You don't know what your trouble is, my friend. That's your trouble.[13]

Summary

Speaking of the sketches in general, Taylor claims that they constitute Pinter's "first unmistakable success with a wider public."[14] Possibly the

12. "Interview," in *The Dwarfs and Eight Revue Sketches*, pp. 42 and 44.
13. "That's Your Trouble," ibid., p. 48.
14. Taylor, *Anger and After*, p. 332.

popular acceptance grows out of the fact that the sketches are amusing and simple, being playlets in which two or more characters are placed in a one-idea situation and allowed to react to themselves and to the circumstances. The general idea explored in most of these sketches is pretty straightforward too—the inability or unwillingness to communicate.

Pinter has called his revue sketches plays in miniature and has further stated: "As far as I am concerned there is no real difference between my sketches and my plays. In both I am interested primarily in people: I want to present living people to the audience, worthy of their interest primarily because they *are*, they exist, not because of any moral the author may draw from them."[15] Of "The Black and White," which is exactly as described above and is a representative example of his sketches, he claims, "I had never done anything with the tramp women because they fitted naturally into a complete play which just happened to be four minutes long: it couldn't be expanded or worked into a more general framework, but on the other hand what can you do with a one-act play which lasts only four minutes? The only thing, of course, though I would never have considered it a possibility unprompted, is to fit it into a revue as a sketch."[16]

In these concentrated exercises Pinter seems to have been working to perfect his techniques for dealing with dialogue and to explore various means for humorous expression. Apparently he decided to discard some of the methods used in the comedies of menace (maybe even writing himself out in certain veins of expression). The later plays show more subtle approaches and it is clear that the dramatist benefited from this interlude.

15. Ibid., p. 335.   16. Ibid., pp. 333–34.

Chapter V. A New Direction

... *it's about love* ...

A Slight Ache

A Slight Ache represents another measure of Pinter's growing success and popular acceptance, for it was originally commissioned to be performed on the BBC Third Programme for July 29, 1959. It was later presented at the Arts Theatre in London on January 18, 1961, as a stage play, the first of several plays written for a radio or television medium and subsequently adapted for the stage. More important, the drama shows a departure from one of the main themes of the preceding plays and indicates the new direction Pinter will explore more fully in the plays to follow. Whereas *The Room*, *The Birthday Party*, and *The Dumb Waiter* are based on an actual menace and the action which grows out of that menace, *A Slight Ache* represents a new development as it concentrates on the *derivation* of menace. A quite simple detail marks this play as the beginning of a shift in thematic direction: the play starts out with an unknown lurking just outside the door, but the supposed threat is brought *inside* and examined and it becomes evident that it is nothing to fear; the danger is *internal*, in the minds and actions of the players. Instead of something external posing a threat because it is trying to get at the individual, the peril exists because there is some *need* within the individual which is not fulfilled. Stanley in *The Birthday Party*, for example, retreats to seaside lodgings in an attempt to escape, to cut himself off from an outside world which has rejected him, and he creates a self-contained universe which serves as a sanctuary. With the arrival of Goldberg and McCann, the outside world has intruded. They are factual manifestations of external physical menace and actually attack their prey, reducing him to a babbling, impotent figure by the end of the drama. In *A Slight Ache* the matchseller provides no true threat to either Flora or Edward, except insofar as everything has the potential to destroy Edward's identity. In *The Birthday Party* menace is derived from Goldberg and McCann's actual pursuit of their quarry. In *A Slight Ache*, the unfulfilled emotional needs of the man and woman are the source of menace.

Just as important, in *A Slight Ache* the menace starts to become explicitly definable; it revolves around a central theme of the drive to satisfy primary appetites. Where menace present in the earlier plays is to varying degrees general in nature and the audience never learns specifically what initiated the threat, from *A Slight Ache* on, the origin of menace is more explicit. Pinter narrows his field of study from generalized vulnerability to need as a source of insecurity. A threat to an individual's mental well-being arises from the disparity between the need for and the absence of certain psychological elements. Identification of need as a source of menace simultaneously provides the characters with a change in motivation, for rather than trying to escape something, they seek to fulfill their emotional needs through relationships with other people.

In a familiar opening, though for the first time with a middle-class setting and a middle-class idiom, the two main characters, Flora and Edward, a husband and wife, are discovered sitting at the breakfast table, engaged in an inane conversation. Pinter is already preparing for his primary comments however, for he quickly establishes a communications problem between the man and the woman, creates an atmosphere of contradiction and alienation, and demonstrates the husband's inadequacies. First of all, Flora corrects her husband when he misnames the flowers in their garden. Then Edward has trouble disposing of the wasp; he cannot even issue orders properly, telling his wife to cover the pot and in almost the same breath demanding that she stay still, a contradictory set of commands.

Edward's reaction to Flora's misuse of the word "bite," like the argument in *The Dumb Waiter*, parallels and thereby prepares us for his sudden actions when he first sees the matchseller through the window: "[*He stops suddenly*]

. . . [*thickly*]: 'He's there . . . [*low, murmuring*]: Blast and damn it, he's there.' "¹ The audience becomes increasingly aware of the intimidating image of the matchseller unfolding in Edward's mind as additional bits of information are revealed. Edward notes that the stranger has been posted outside the back gate for two months, denying him, purely through physical presence apparently, the pleasure of using the gate; whereas the wasp had initially been called "vicious" and actually presented no problem, both husband and wife classify the matchseller as "harmless" (p. 16) in spite of their worried reactions to his existence, the suggestion being that since the "vicious" wasp was harmless, the "harmless" tramp may conversely prove troublesome.

It is significant that Flora refers to the intruder in physical terms—as a large animal, a "bullock"—and that Edward soon picks up her remark (pp. 17 and 19). When Flora admits that she cannot say that she finds the bothersome old man a "nuisance" (p. 19), we are given a foreshadowing of what is to come, for she seemingly is attracted to him and she has "nodded" to him on occasion. Her picture of the matchseller may indicate part of the reason that events will occur as they do, since Flora's concern with the stranger's animal-like appearance indicates a preoccupation with physical matters, and Edward is certainly not physically impressive. In addition Edward has earlier admitted to sleeping "Uninterrupted. As always." So he probably has not been fulfilling his husbandly duties. To this point in the play there is little to differentiate it from the comedies of menace.

The ragged matchseller is invited into the house by Flora on Edward's insistence. When he proves harmless (unlike the forbidding pair in *The Birthday Party*, who represent external menace intruding on an individual's sanctuary), it becomes evident that Pinter is introducing something new: the man does not come in as a real physical threat as Goldberg and McCann do—the menace already resides in the couple. The confrontation between Edward and the old man brings disastrous results, though: the matchseller never says a word, and Edward, faced with silence, only exposes his own fears and inadequacies. When the old man enters, Edward begins speaking. At first his conversation seems to be mere rambling, as he talks about the villagers' former squire and his red-haired daughters. The speech seems to be a series of memories, each triggered by association in Edward's mind with what he has just said but having no relevance to the action of the play and being meaningless trivia to the audience. A veiled clue to the identities which lie behind the tale is included when he tells of the squire's youngest daughter, whose name he has difficulty recalling, and refers to her (p. 23) as "the best of the bunch. . . . A flower" (in *Who's Afraid of Virginia Woolf?* a year and a half later, Edward Albee produces similar dialogues). Edward goes on to mention that he writes "theological and philosophical essays" and "observations on certain tropical phenomena," being especially fond of "Africa . . . my happy hunting ground."

1. Pinter, *A Slight Ache*, in *Three Plays* (New York: Grove, 1962), p. 14.

His expertise in African matters is made questionable seconds later, though, when he includes the Gobi in his discussion, in a way suggesting that he does not distinguish between Africa and Asia geographically, a situation which will be recalled when Teddy is quizzed on his specialty in *The Homecoming*. Question-asking usually leads to calamity in Pinter's dramas.

The speech gives some insight into Edward's make-up and is a pivotal point in the play in terms of the relationship between husband and wife. We learn something about Edward and his history of failures and partial successes in life from the knowledge that the essays he is so proud of are probably faulty, since they have not taught him that the Gobi is in Asia. Edward's reminiscences indicate that while he has never been especially successful before, he cannot even live up to his past now. See the monologue, for instance, in which he includes pouring "hot water down the spoon-hole" and adjusting the lens of his telescope among his accomplishments (pp. 35–36)—not too impressive as points of pride. The validity of all of his statements is made questionable by his reference to the hot water when we realize that the wasp incident earlier this very day is probably the foundation for his claim. His assertion that he was "number one sprinter at Howells" is opened to doubt when he alludes to having been "a stripling . . . like [Barnabas]" (p. 39), for it is obvious that Barnabas is not a stripling.

Edward has been a relative failure in creative life, and the play shows that this carries over in his attempts to form relationships with those about him. We learn that things are not as they should be between Edward and his wife when we realize that one of the squire's daughters is Flora and that Edward is trying to conceal this information. He relates how Flora has stuck with him "in season and out of season" (note the floral imagery connecting the description of the squire's youngest daughter who "was the best of the bunch," "a flower," and Flora) and remembers her "flaming red hair" in youth —and stops abruptly (pp. 23–24). Up to this point there has been nothing to explain Edward's and Flora's actions toward each other, but now a little understanding of their motivation has been added. Although Pinter's play is not realistic, the actions which take place in it do proceed from a realistic base of psychological need.

In the sequence following, even more information is imparted. Now that he "can get down to brass tacks," the host informs his silent guest that he was not alarmed by the matchseller's physical appearance. Edward goes on to proclaim that "nothing outside this room has ever alarmed me," and that the matchseller disgusts him (p. 27). Since he is agitated, however, one begins to wonder what there is inside the room which bothers him if nothing outside causes him to worry. Then Edward unwittingly provides a clue: "You're no more disgusting than Fanny, the squire's daughter, after all. In appearance you differ but not in essence" (p. 27). We will be reminded of this admission later when Edward verbally abuses his wife.

When Flora returns, Edward's understated appraisal of the situation produces humor, but there is always the underlying current of menace. Asked how the two men are "getting on," Edward replies, ". . . remarkably well. He's a little . . . reticent. Somewhat withdrawn" (p. 28)—this describing the completely one-sided talk. Flora offers to examine their quarry, who will "admit everything," to which Edward hisses, "What are you plotting?" The sequence which follows brings Pinter's new theme into focus, for it indicates that the wife's unfulfilled desires are uppermost in her thoughts.

Sex immediately comes to Flora's mind as she asks the matchseller if he has ever been a poacher, a question that seems irrelevant until she, like Edward before her, reveals something of her past—in this case a Laurentian "rape" with humorous overtones implying her attitude toward sex: "Of course, life was perilous in those days. It was my first canter unchaperoned" (p. 31). Years later, she goes on to relate, the man was brought before her for poaching, but she acquitted him: "He's grown a red beard, I remember. Yes. A bit of a stinker"—not much of a condemnation of the man, considering what had happened.

Her phrasing indicates that the story is not to be taken seriously, but it is a means for introducing the subject of sex. The fantasy itself is interesting because it suggests that she is seeking a stronger, more domineering man. Having brought sex into the conversation, Flora mops her victim's brow, leans on the arm of his chair and intimately asks if he has a woman. She then rapidly alternates a castigating attack with a seducing attack. She tells him that he smells vile, doubts that he realizes sex is "a very vital experience," commands him to "speak to [her] of love," admires his solid body (perhaps picturing him as the strong, silent type as opposed to her weak husband, and also contradicting Edward's contention that the man is "like jelly"), and ends by deciding to "keep" him and giving him the name Barnabas (an apostle; interpreted, the Son of Consolation, Acts 4.36), which is appropriate, since she turns to him for solace. Flora then asks if he has been waiting for her and reveals for the first time that she is aware of the symbolic content of the situation when she says that she is going to put him to bed—his deathbed. The connection of death with the sex act, as a Freudian symbol representing death, may be implied by this image, but it is more likely that Flora is acknowledging her selfish motivation that compels her to kill his individuality so that she can subordinate his personality to her desires.

When Edward resumes his confrontation with the matchseller, he continues to expose himself, gaining no knowledge of Barnabas in return. The drama nears conclusion as Edward finally completes his self-induced breakdown. His last spoken words are a question which comes with great effort: "What are you?" (p. 39). In view of what follows and his jumbled and inconsistent insertion of the matchseller into his own biography, "Who am *I*?" is really the question. Ironically, his wife's offstage calling to Barnabas answers the question by indicating the role exchange which has already been prepared for by Edward's projections and partial identification with this silent old man (who, among other things, was young "at the same time, perhaps"). Flora's act of replacing Edward with Barnabas brings the curtain down and sums up Pinter's new theme, for she has actively moved to find psychological satisfaction.

The title of the play alludes to the problem Edward has with his eyes, the advancing physical symptom reflecting his advancing mental disintegration. At first he feels only a slight ache in them after his battle with the wasp. With the introduction of the mysterious stranger outside his garden gate, however, the pain increases in proportion to his lack of success in dealing with the outsider, until at the conclusion of the drama the other man has become a mote in his eye that no longer allows him to see clearly, for Barnabas looks younger, "extraordinarily . . . youthful." Pinter has a minor preoccupation with vision: Riley is blind and Rose loses her sight at the end of *The Room*; Stanley's glasses are purposely broken in *The Birthday Party* and he is accused of having been "cock-eyed"; Edward speaks of blinding the wasp, decides that the matchseller cannot see straight, and wonders if he has a glass eye in *A Slight Ache*; Davies is attacked by Mick in a dark room in *The Caretaker*; Disson experiences problems with his sight in *Tea Party*; and so forth. As there is a fracturing of routine and as characters lose control of events about them, there is a corresponding interruption of their sensory mechanisms.[2]

As in Pinter's previous works, the strongest images in *A Slight Ache* are those of filth and decay, in which all the senses are abused, emphasizing the mood of menace by presenting an unpleasant background. One of the first things that Edward mentions about the stranger is that he can smell him, not a surprising statement considering that the man is dressed filthily and has been standing in the rain—even Flora exclaims later that his clothes look and feel as though he had been rolling in the mud. The vegetation imagery might be considered in conjuction with the role exchange at the conclusion of the play as a reflection of the traditional literary pattern which grows out of the fertility ritual in which the old year-king is conquered by the new year-king. The fact that the action takes place on "the longest day of the year" may have some relevance here too. After all, Flora's interest in Barnabas certainly involves some sort of sexual desire.

2. In the light of these occurrences it is interesting to note that the author's childhood friend Henry Woolf (who was responsible for his writing *The Room*) claims, though not entirely convincingly for people with good vision, that Pinter himself has poor eyesight and that this is one of the reasons he writes about perception, literal and figurative. Since he has difficulty focusing on peripheral objects, he is more aware of the shadowy borderlines of reality.

Symbolically it is the figure of the matchseller which is most significant. Some critics have suggested that the matchseller, like the dagger in *Macbeth*, does not really exist, but is, instead, a projection of the couple's anxieties.[3] For evidence, they point to the facts that he never is heard and that *A Slight Ache* was originally a radio play. Questioning his existence is unjustified for two reasons: first, the matchseller is included as a character in the stage directions of the stage version, so he exists by definition; second, and more important, the other two characters act as though he exists. Whether he is real or not is not as important as the fact that they use him as a focal point in their struggle for affection.

Physically the stranger, somewhat like the symbolic figure which visits Rose, is described as a dark old man; he is dirty, and he is pictured in animal images. This last item is important to the overall meaning of the play, for the imagery in Edward's speeches indicates that he sees the man in physical terms, especially in regard to himself and failure: Barnabas symbolically comes to represent the antithesis of Edward, even though he intrinsically presents no threat. Flora's depiction of Barnabas as a bullock sheds some light on her motives. A bullock is an ox or young bull—a large, powerful animal full of vitality (incidentally, while Pinter refers to a bullock in other plays, he never uses the word bull in his dramas). "Bullock" is a term also applied to a castrated bull, so Flora's interest may not be entirely sexual (besides, she is not eager to bring Barnabas into the house and once he is in she mothers him to an extent, but there is no question that sex is involved, because of her insistence on it as a subject. Flora may be using the matchseller as a challenge to her husband, or perhaps there is a clue here to the reasons for Edward's failures: Flora's reaction to sex may not be natural (after all, she seems attracted by a dirty, sick, passive old man) and she looks to the stranger as a strong replacement for her weak husband. In either case, she is game-playing, employing a third party as a challenge, in an effort to find fulfillment, either by forcing her husband into a role acceptable to her or by making him allow her to engage a substitute. Pinter will explore the game-playing theme more fully in subsequent plays such as *The Lover*. That Flora lacks fulfillment in her marriage, though, is clear. The fact that she is willing to turn to an outsider indicates that her husband has been unable to satisfy her psychological demands. She is so desperate in her need that she seizes on Barnabas as a symbol of fulfillment, even though she is clearly deluding herself.

Taken together, the imagery describing the matchseller, the roles assigned him by the two main characters, and the symbolic elements attached to him all combine to produce a character whose prime purpose in the play is to serve as a catalyst which will allow the problems of a husband and wife to be exposed and, after a fashion, to be solved. All in all, then, *A Slight Ache* is basically the story of a woman's psychological needs, the failure of her hus-

3. Hinchcliffe, *Harold Pinter*, p. 70; Esslin, *Theatre of the Absurd*, p. 208.

band to adequately fulfill those needs, and the wife's solution. We still may not know the truth of what happened in the past to start the chain of events in *A Slight Ache*, but the motives become clearer as they become less symbolic and more applicable to the individuals involved. Edward needs to be needed as the master of all situations, as is evidenced in his handling of the rampaging wasp, but he is emotionally and physically unable to fulfill Flora's desires. Flora needs more or a different kind of emotional satisfaction than Edward can provide, so she turns to a substitute who *may* satisfy her need. Clearly the existential question of identity is not important to Flora. She is flexible in creating herself to the point that she is able and willing, like Ruth in *The Homecoming*, to adopt any role that answers her purpose.

At this point in Pinter's development it is not clear whether the failure is meant to represent all failures in life or if the connection has been made between menace and need as a primary source of threat. Until this drama, need has only been incidentally present. While Edward and Flora do not discuss their needs, their actions provide evidence that needs are the source of their motivation. Barnabas is not likely to supply Flora with what she needs, but he is a change from her husband. Since Edward has been a failure, she can be no worse off, and the old man might even afford her some hope. The importance both husband and wife attach to the matchseller is related to their own relationship and reveals that their primary appetites are the basic motivational ingredients in the drama. The next few plays still center on individual needs and the drives they create ambiguously, but it is evident that in *A Slight Ache* a new thematic direction is beginning to develop in Pinter's mind as his focus switches from the *physical* forces which threaten the individual from without to the *psychological* deficiencies which menace from within.

The Caretaker

The Caretaker, first presented at the Arts Theatre in London on April 27, 1960,[4] continues the thematic direction started in *A Slight Ache*, in which the menace is no longer outside the room, creating terror as it snuffles about trying to get in but is a part of the characters within the room and is carried with them. The drama is significant for reasons that go beyond merely being an

---

4. *The Caretaker*, which opened the same week as Ionesco's *Rhinoceros*, was produced on Broadway as a result of a personal artistic stipend awarded by producer Roger Stevens. Gottfried, who interprets the drama in terms of "mutual responsibility," feels that this instance of "patronage" allowed the playwright to take advantage of the wave of internationalism just then reaching the United States and that Pinter's success in the American theatre has come about because he manages to please all elements of the play-going audience through his ability to "combine basic right-wing theatre values (mystery, suspense, comedy) with a left-wing sense of strangeness and unreality." *A Theatre Divided*, pp. 288–89.

extension into a trend or the fact that it is the dramatist's first real public success; it is a vital point in Pinter's development, for it is in connection with this play that the author admits his *awareness* that the theme of need is becoming central in his work. Charles Marowitz reports in an article in the *Village Voice* that Pinter has said about the play, "It's about love."[5] When "love" is equated with "need," a certain pattern falls into place. This is as close as the author has come to supplying a definition of what will become his major thematic element, and it provides an understandable basis for his character's actions. As stated in Chapter II, love in a Pinter play differs from the conventional definition of love. When Pinter talks about love he means a psychological *need* for acceptance or affection or emotional attachment. What he is trying to say in *The Caretaker* becomes clear when one realizes that Davies, Aston, and Mick all need to satisfy a primary appetite for acceptance, affection, or emotional attachment, and the acts of all three are designed to fulfill their needs (the difference between these three men and Stanley, for example, is that they actively move *toward* fulfillment while he was content with trying to avoid confronting his needs by retreating).

The meaning of this play has been discussed by the critics more than all the rest of Pinter's work put together, in Taylor's opinion, though no one has yet come up with a satisfactory explication.[6] The reason is probably that the alternative possibilities are all at least partly true. As usual, the minimal plot action provides only a few clues. Donald Pleasence, who created the role of Davies in the original production and in the film version, has comically reduced the plot to a six word summary: "boy meets tramp, boy loses tramp."[7] With few exceptions during his career, Pinter, like Shakespeare, has not been especially concerned with plot *per se*. There is in a Pinter play a series of events which holds together, but the meaning of the drama lies in the characters. The actual events are not as important as the psychological reactions to them by the individuals involved. So it is with *The Caretaker*. Two brothers, one a former mental patient, and an old tramp become locked in a battle of wills when the recuperating brother rescues the tramp from an unpleasant situation and invites him into his room, which is in a house owned by the younger brother. The drama evolves in a series of confrontations between these three characters as they try to establish their relationships to one another. The result of these confrontations is the expulsion of the old man.

In interpreting the play the items to be considered include the questions of identity and verification clustering around Davies; Aston's attempted reorientation, as well as his suggested Christ-figure qualities and his role in the society-versus-artist confrontation; and the problem of communication and

5. "Theatre Abroad," 1 Sept. 1960.
6. *Harold Pinter* (1969), pp. 15–16.
7. Quoted in Henry Popkin, Introduction to *Modern British Drama* (New York: Grove, 1969), p. 24.

interaction between individuals. This last element is probably the most important in determining the ultimate meaning of the play, for the actions of the three characters make sense when one realizes that each is trying to establish an attachment with one of the others. Simultaneously each is trying to protect that relationship from an outside interference, the third member, which threatens to destroy it by forming a new pairing. Although not as apparent as in *A Slight Ache* and some of the later plays, need is a basic theme of the drama, and it is Pinter's conscious revelation of this that marks *The Caretaker* as an advance in his thematic development.

Mixed throughout the play, serving as unifying elements, are the minor problems which, though not of consequence in this play, plague early Pinter characters constantly—racial tensions, the battle between men and machines. The opening scene uses one of these minor elements as a device to introduce one of the real problems of the play. Davies complains that he could not sit down during his tea break because the seats were full of foreigners. Davies is upset further because everybody in the place is "treating [him] like dirt":[8] there are some things which a man cannot allow if he is to retain his "manhood" and it is important to Davies that he be accepted as an individual.

The first clue to Davies' nature comes when he explains to Aston why he is in trouble: "Comes up to me, parks a bucket of rubbish at me tells me to take it out the back. It's not my job to take out the bucket! They got a boy there for taking out the bucket. . . . My job's cleaning the floor" (p. 9). Although, considering his admitted tasks, Davies' complaint is amusing (it sounds like a parody of a couple of union workers squabbling about "jurisdiction" over an insignificant item), there is an extremely important concept being explored here, one vital to Davies' makeup. Identity, a sense of the integrity of his self-picture, has been threatened. Roles must be kept separate in order for Davies to maintain his conception of his own identity, for if he is forced into a different role, doing someone else's job, he is not being allowed to be true to his self-image. His intense bigotry is another example of this facet of his character, for he needs to see someone as inferior in order to emphasize his own "superiority." Being accepted as an individual is an important part of the old man's motivation, as evidenced in his activities with the two brothers and in the importance with which he regards the identity papers he left in Sidcup fifteen years ago; he claims that recovery of those papers will solve all of his problems, but he is always waiting for the weather to break, or, when it is nice out, is unable to undertake the journey because his shoes are unsuitable. A background of rejection has led him to seeming apathy: if he does not ask, he cannot be refused. Actually, his apathy is superficial, for he is in fact neither simply passive nor neutral. He is involved in performing negative actions actively designed to lead to self-destruction. The

---

8. Pinter, *The Caretaker* (New York: Grove, 1965), p. 8. See Chapter XI for an explanation of how textual alterations in later editions affect interpretations.

old man can do nothing constructive to save himself. Like Edward in *A Slight Ache*, even when he tries to control events about him, he is the destructive agent who keeps things from happening as he hopes they will.

Davies has a long history of seeking attachments, a place where he can "belong," yet finding reasons for rejecting relationships when they are tendered him. As Esslin says, Davies is "a man *seeking* for a place for himself, fighting for that little patch of light and warmth in the vast menacing darkness."[9] His most recent experience is the one from which Aston rescued him. He had been given a job, but could not get along with his co-workers: ". . . who was this git to come up and give me orders? We got the same standing. He's not my boss. He's nothing superior to me. . . . If you hadn't come out and stopped that Scotch git I'd be inside the hospital now. I'd have cracked my head on that pavement if he'd have landed. I'll get him" (pp. 9–10). As the tramp reveals his biography, it is evident that this incident is part of a pattern. He once found a woman who was willing to marry him, so he immediately imposed upon the situation an attitude which allowed him to reject her: "That's why I left my wife. Fortnight after I married her, no, not so much as that, no more than a week, I took the lid off a saucepan, you know what was in it? A pile of her underclothing, unwashed. The pan for vegetables, it was. The vegetable pan. That's when I left her and I haven't seen her since" (p. 9).

On another occasion he turned to a monastic order, a group which orients its actions around charity based on love, but again he was unable to accept their offering and found reason to reject them or cause them to reject him: "Them bastards at the monastery let me down again. . . . I said to this monk, here, I said, look here, mister, he opened the door. . . . mister, I said, I come all the way down here. . . . you haven't got a pair of shoes, have you. . . . I heard you got a stock of shoes here. Piss off, he said to me. Now look here, I said, I'm an old man, you can't talk to me like that. . . . If you don't piss off, he says, I'll kick you all the way to the gate . . . . get out round the corner, and when you've had your meal, piss off out of it. . . . Right, they said to me, you've had your meal, get off out of it. Meal? I said, what do you think I am, a dog? . . . One of them, an Irish hooligan, come at me. I cleared out" (pp. 13–14). The sequence of events as reported by Davies is doubtful. It is much more likely that he offended his potential benefactors (who did, after all, feed him) in some way—the phrasing of his request alone would not endear him to them and it is unlikely that they would use the language he attributes to them.

Apparently Davies feels too inferior to be able to accept the psychological elements that he needs. His expressed fears and prejudices concerning blacks and foreigners are indicative of his feelings of insecurity based on his self-portrait of inferiority: "How many more Blacks you got around here then? . . . I mean you don't share the toilet with them Blacks, do you? . . . Because, you

9. Esslin, "Godot and His Children," p. 142.

know . . . I mean . . . fair's fair" (pp. 14, 18–19). To a bigot, sharing the facilities with inferiors would be degrading. Davies needs to know that there is something which makes him better than others, even if it is merely a matter of ancestry or nationality. For instance, he suggests that people prefer to have an Englishman "to pour their tea" (p. 27). This attitude is likewise mirrored in his reference to the "Scotch git" at the café and the "Irish hooligan" at the monastery: the fact that Davies, like the woman in Pinter's revue piece "Request Stop," is English and they are not is sufficient proof of his superiority. Ironically he may not even be English—his names are Welsh and he ignores Mick's question about his ancestry—but he has assumed the nationality as a means of bettering himself.

Still, the old man has needs and he continues trying to fulfill his requirement for some sort of attachment, demonstrated by his following Aston home. That this is his intent is suggested by a lack of any other reason for tagging along as opposed to simply disappearing, perhaps to Sidcup. Pinter's stage directions make it quite clear that Davies is following his host like a lost dog.[10] Not only does he go to Aston's, he is willing to stay there. Gordon feels that "Davies has offered and welcomed the exchange of mutual feeling only because it promised Aston's favor."[11] Boulton sees the tramp as "a man who is seeking sympathy,"[12] while Esslin contends that "his need for a place in the world is pathetically obvious."[13] The existence of papers in Sidcup would, thus, represent proof of his place—they "prove who I am" (p. 20). Since he never gets them, and since he alternately calls them identity papers, insurance cards, and references according to his need at the moment, they may simply be a symbol of his dream of such a place. Because of his self-defeating drives and corresponding actions, though, he is doomed to failure. Davies, "the unfortunate Everyman, whose forsaken nature demands kindness and charity," according to Gordon, "cannot conceal . . . selfish, greedy, and possessive traits,"[14] and Esslin agrees that "he is unable to subdue his own nature."[15] As a personification of human weaknesses, he is continually led by his *hubris* to his own downfall; just as he cannot find or accept shoes that fit him, he does not fit into society.

The Caretaker shows that, as Davies is granted the acceptance he craves, he once again will manage to achieve rejection. Filled with mistrust, self-deception, and having lived a life of evasion, he cannot believe his benefactor helped him simply because he was in trouble. When it becomes evident that he can be secure in Aston's acceptance, he no longer desires it and turns to

10. In the film, which shows the two men walking on the street on their way to the room, this comparison is clearly indicated by Davies' shuffling back and forth after Aston.
11. Gordon, *Stratagems to Uncover Nakedness*, p. 44.
12. Boulton, "Harold Pinter," p. 138.
13. Esslin, *The Theatre of the Absurd*, p. 244.
14. Gordon, *Stratagems*, p. 42.
15. Esslin, *The Theatre of the Absurd*, p. 244.

Mick as another possible source, repudiating his original patron. This, of course, will lead to his eventual expulsion. That Aston does accept him is proved by the older brother's friendliness (sharing his tobacco and offering a place to stay and a pair of shoes), trust (he is willing to leave the old man alone in the house), and interest in the tramp's plight (he gives him money, offers him a job, and attempts to replace the missing bag). Davies, therefore, might be considered a poor strategist. However, his consistent choice of words and actions which will lead to defeat indicates that he is working toward failure. He always makes the wrong choice, indicating more than pure coincidence.

Act III contains a good example of the old man's self-destructive tendencies as he tries to play the brothers against each other in his effort to form an attachment with either of them, only to turn both men against himself. He argues first with Aston, asserting himself as the better of the two, reminding his host that he has never been "inside one of them places," and referring to Mick as his "friend" and "true pal"! Aston suggests that "it's about time you found somewhere else" as he notes, "I don't think we're hitting it off" (pp. 67, 68). Davies returns with Mick, whom he is telling what happened, obviously sure that the younger brother will back him (Mick had, after all, offered him the caretaker's job earlier too). It soon becomes apparent, though, that Davies has miscalculated. "You get a bit out of your depth sometimes, don't you?" says Mick (p. 71). When Davies refers to Aston as "nutty," Mick starts a diatribe that ends with his sending the old man away: "What did you call my brother? . . . Did you call my brother nutty? My brother. . . . that's a bit of an impertinent thing to say, isn't it? . . . It's all most regrettable but it looks as though I'm compelled to pay you off for your caretaking work. Here's half a dollar" (pp. 73–74).[16] Mick's reasons for dismissing the tramp are adequate: "You're really strange. Ever since you come into this house there's been nothing but trouble. . . . I can take nothing you say at face value. Every word you speak is open to any number of different interpretations. Most of what you say is lies. You're violent, you're erratic, you're completely unpredictable" (p. 73).

In this speech Mick recognizes Davies' nature, which grows out of his contradictory motivations. On the one hand the old man's primary appetite for acceptance leads him to seek relationships with others, while on the other hand his need for identity will not allow him to compromise to the degree necessary to maintain a relationship. If he compromises with his wife about the proper use of a vegetable pan or with Aston about whether or not to close the window, his sense of inferiority is so strong that he feels his identity is in danger. If he does not compromise, the relationship may be destroyed. The

16. The "half a dollar" or half-crown is an interesting figure since it is the same amount that Albert gives the prostitute as a "pay off" in *A Night Out*.

opposition of these two mutually exclusive driving forces leads to his "erratic" behavior.

The younger brother also attacks his rival on emotional, illogical grounds. He accuses the old man of not being something he never claimed to be: "You come here recommending yourself as an interior decorator . . . and what happens? You make a long speech about all the references you've got down at Sidcup. . . . I haven't noticed you go down . . . to obtain them" (p. 74). Davies does indicate that he could "give [Mick] a hand" in decorating the house (p. 63), though this is not the same as calling himself an interior decorator, and he never states what his references recommend him for. Surely his appearance and obvious lack of knowledge are in themselves enough to indicate to Mick that he is not an experienced decorator.

It really does not matter what the nature of the accusation is, though. Mick has wanted to get rid of Davies, and the caretaker has given him an excuse to do so, something which Davies' previous life would lead us to expect. Davies' "blunder" has been in alienating himself from Aston and allying himself with Mick, for in doing so he has placed the direction of his future in the hands of a man who has a motive for wanting him displaced. Even after their estrangement Aston was willing to give his guest "a few bob" to "get down to Sidcup" (p. 68), but Mick never intended to befriend his brother's visitor. Mick's position is clear when he concludes his dreams for refurbishing the flat with the claim that "it wouldn't be a flat it'd be a palace." Davies agrees with him and asks, "Who would live there?" to which Mick replies, "I would. My brother and me." Davies wants to know, "What about me?" Mick "*quietly*" changes the subject, ignoring the question (pp. 60, 61).

Throughout the play Davies demonstrates that he needs to form relationships with others, to find his "place" (his taking up with the brothers), first with Aston, then with Mick when the original relationship disintegrates, yet he is unable to create permanent attachments. The play concludes with this vulnerable, pathetic character desperately trying to reestablish the convivial relationship with Aston which was present at the beginning of the play, plaintively crying, "What am I going to do? . . . Where am I going to go?" (pp. 77–78), but it is clear that his needs will never be satisfied. It is difficult to feel much compassion for him, though, because of his unsympathetic nature—he seems to deserve what he gets.

Aston, on the other hand, arouses our sympathies. Like Davies, he is always about to do something which he never quite gets around to (building a shed out back). He is stuck, as T. S. Eliot puts it, "Between the idea/ And the reality/ Between the motion and the act." The reason for Aston's behavior, however, is different from that which keeps Davies inactive. Aston is the sensitive man, and the shadow has fallen because he did not conform to society. Unlike Davies' nonconformity, though, his was active and therefore a threat, so he was made a nonthreat by society in an act of self-preservation, as per Gus's fate in *The Dumb Waiter*.

There is a suggestion of Christ symbolism in Aston. He is in his early thirties, calls himself a carpenter, is sensitive, helps people, and has a cross to bear in the form of the damaged mentality forced on him by society. It seems more likely, though, that if he is meant to be a symbolic figure, he fits the role of the sensitive person who is crushed by a society which can neither understand nor tolerate the differences in his makeup which set him apart from ordinary men, a role previously suggested by the treatment of Stanley in *The Birthday Party*. In the closing speech of Act II Aston explains, almost to himself really, how he used to think (in nearly Messianic terms), what happened to him, and how he is now. Pinter's style is straightforward here, and the true horror lies in Aston's calm telling of the simple truth. The gap between pain and suffering and articulation of the experience—an experience in which society, including his mother, was trying to help him, but because they did not understand, only succeeded in destroying his essential character —creates a rendering of that experience which is detached and deeply involved and moving at the same time: ". . . he wasn't supposed to do it while I was standing up . . . anyway, he did it. So I did get out. I got out of the place . . . but I couldn't walk very well. . . . The trouble was . . . my thoughts . . . had become very slow . . . I couldn't think at all . . . I couldn't . . . get . . . my thoughts . . . together . . . . uuuhh . . . . I couldn't hear what people were saying. I couldn't look to the right or the left . . . because if I turned my head round . . . I couldn't keep . . . upright. And I had these headaches . . . . I should have died. Anyway, I feel much better now" (p. 57). Through an accident in a mental hospital over ten years ago a sensitive individual's imaginative powers have been destroyed and he is left nearly emotionless. His attitude toward other people is changed too.

Essentially, as reported in his troubled history at the end of Act II, Aston needs contact with other people. He suffered a breakdown when he found out that others did not pay attention to him: ". . . they always used to listen. I thought . . . they understood what I said. I mean I used to talk to them. I talked too much. That was my mistake . . . . they used to listen, whenever I . . . had anything to say . . . but maybe I was wrong. Anyway, someone must have said something . . . . some kind of lie . . . people started being funny" (pp. 54–55). Even his mother failed him: "I knew I was a minor. I knew [the doctor] couldn't do anything to me without getting permission. I knew he had to get permission from my mother. So I wrote to her and told her what they were trying to do. But she signed their form, you see, giving them permission. I know that because he showed me her signature when I brought it up" (pp. 55–56).

Because of his rejection by those about him (the men at the café, the men at work, his mother), Aston has developed feelings of insecurity, and his life has now been reduced to the point where he is watched over by his younger brother at his brother's flat. He no longer actively seeks out others at work or at the café. He has adopted a comparatively passive role in which he generally remains silent and tries to figure out what is wrong with the world. This is reflected in his continuing attempts to repair broken objects such as the toaster. If simple mechanical things can be made to function correctly, then he can obtain a solid base in reality, for he will have something in which he can place his trust. People have let him down before, after all, and he needs some place to start over again. He still needs contact with people, though, and Davies seems to be suitable to begin with, since his position when Aston befriends him, a busboy in a poor establishment being attacked by his fellow workers, certainly indicates that the tramp will pose no threat. Davies does become a menace to Aston's current mode of existence, however, and Aston is forced to throw out the man who would displace him in the security of the flat and in his relationship with his brother. A result of the two brothers' experience with the old man may be that they are brought closer together than before as they unite to overthrow a potential usurper. "ASTON *comes in. He closes the door, moves into the room and faces* MICK. *They look at each other. Both are smiling, faintly*" (p. 75). Now that Aston's faith in his brother is reestablished, he has the strength to begin work on his shed.

In Pinter's screenplay for the movie version of *The Caretaker* (*The Guest*), as Hinchcliffe points out, the significance of the glance between the two brothers is more emphatic (especially the hint of triumph on Mick's part) because of the camera's focusing ability, while in the play there is only a slight implication. Discussing the film in an article by Pinter and Clive Donner, the director, Pinter acknowledges this when he writes, "I think in the film one has been able to hit the relationship of the brothers more clearly than in the play." [17]

Aston, then, is a character whose need for human contact has led him to disillusionment, since his overtures to others have been rejected because of their unusual nature, yet he keeps trying to establish a relationship with someone and in the end the union between him and his brother is stronger for his efforts. Still, Aston's role is basically that of an object over which his brother and his new-found "friend" battle.

Davies sees reality only as it pertains to him in terms of physical things such as shoes. His inadequacies and fears are represented by the ever-present foreigners (the blacks next door) and machinery. The unconnected stove which might gas him, for example, is a perfect symbol of his irrational fears, and at the same time it embodies both Pinter's sense of menace—perhaps especially fitting in view of the fate of millions of Jews in World War II Germany—and the Theatre of the Absurd notion of man's all-inclusive lack of connection with his chaotic universe. Davies is unable to function in a complex

17. Pinter and Donner, "Filming 'The Caretaker'."

society, yet his arrogant actions lead to his expulsion from any sanctuary. Where Davies had his Sidcup, Aston has his shed, as he too is ineffective in the modern world. As Aston tells Davies at the end of Act II, he *used* to see things very clearly. Since he has lost his imaginative ability (as evidenced by his simple dream of building a shed and his straightforward description of the events at the hospital, especially when these are compared to Mick's elaborately described dreams of renovating the house and his fantastic accounts of uncles and friends), Aston has turned to his tools as an answer in an act of replacement. It is through the interaction of these two men that their characters are portrayed, a cause-and-effect pattern in which the actions of one determine the actions of the other. And it is solely because of his relationship with the other two men that we understand Mick at all.

Mick's motivations are harder to decipher than are those of either Davies or Aston, but love for his brother is a primary factor. This is demonstrated by his immediate reaction to Davies as a threat; he attacks the newcomer without hesitation. As Taylor points out, it is evident that Aston "likes [Davies] and likes his company. Mick's jealousy is instantly aroused, and his one thought is to get the old man out."[18] Taylor goes on to say that Mick's methods are devious, but they are all aimed at repelling the intruder Davies because of jealousy. He needs his brother to the extent that he will fight for him. And because Aston can no longer adequately take care of himself, Mick's own affection for his brother demands that he take care of him. Once these facts are recognized, Mick's actions make a great deal of sense, for they are directed toward helping his older brother and at preserving the relationship which exists between them. Except that he is in the building trade and owns a van and this house, we are given very little substantial information about Mick, but he does display the physical violence and brutality of Davies, who is quick to pull a knife and who does not hesitate to attack Aston's vulnerability for much the same reason, if from a different position. Where Davies acts to ally himself with one of the brothers, Mick is trying to preserve the status quo (loosely, this pattern is repeated as the basis for *The Collection*). The two men react to each other with apprehension, for each represents a threat to the security of the other. Most of Mick's actions stem ultimately from affection for his brother and a desire to help and protect him, a reversal of the normal big brother/little brother relationship. He has provided Aston with a place to live and encourages his interests. In the earlier conversation with Davies, Mick indicates that when the flat is redecorated he and his brother will live there together. His ignoring of Davies' question pointedly excludes the old man from this future. Later he explains why his brother is living in the house and what he is doing there: "I'm not worried about this house. I'm not interested. My brother can worry about it. He can do it up, he can decorate it, he can do what he likes with it. . . . I thought I was doing him a favour, letting

18. Taylor, *Anger and After*, p. 337.

him live here" (p. 74). The house itself does not interest him; even his elaborately conceived plans for redecorating seem to be unimportant in themselves (contingent on living with his brother). It is only in terms of providing his brother with something to do that the house becomes important, and Mick thought that he was helping Aston by letting him stay there. His attacks on Davies are partly self-protective, since Davies might replace him in his brother's eyes, yet they are meant to help Aston too, for Davies has nothing to offer Aston. Now that his brother has turned the tramp out, Mick can stop playing with him. As he tells the old man, "Ever since you come into this house there's been nothing but trouble," for "You're nothing else but a wild animal, when you come down to it" (pp. 73–74).

Mick's strategy in expelling the tramp indicates that his protective stance regarding Aston derives from fraternal affection rather than merely from a sense of duty. It is clear that Mick recognizes Davies as an opponent from the very beginning, and it is also clear that he would have little trouble driving the intruder out with physical force. His immediate reaction to the presence of a guest in his brother's room is an attack which completely overpowers its victim. In the interrogation which follows, the younger brother repeatedly speaks Davies' alias with an emphasis that gives the name a curselike quality: "Jen . . . kins." Eric Partridge in A *Dictionary of Slang and Unconventional English* notes that "kins" is a suffix, colloquial in tendency, seen in the "euphemizing of oaths." Mick's pronunciation of the surname, coupled with the comparisons of Davies to people he reminds him of (the "my uncle's brother" and "a bloke I once knew in Shoreditch" tales) and his description of the old man, "You're stinking the place out. You're an old robber . . . . an old skate . . . . an old barbarian" (p. 35), show that he has unhesitatingly categorized his adversary as an enemy, and an unsavory one at that. The younger brother also shows his quick awareness of the situation when he asks (p. 34), "You intending to settle down here?" Yet he does not try to force a withdrawal. Instead, he initiates a plan of attack whereby Aston will himself eventually reject the old man voluntarily and therefore will not turn against his brother for having banished his friend and so that banishment will not in itself make the tramp more appealing.

Mick builds up Davies' confidence in their relationship, offering him the caretaker's job and implying dissatisfaction with his brother, so that Davies will overstep the bounds, "get a bit out of [his] depth" (p. 71), when he says, "I'm a bit worried about my brother. . . . He doesn't like work. . . . It's a terrible thing to have to say about your own brother" (p. 48). Ironically, Davies does not see the evidence which contradicts this assertion, such as Aston's tarring the roof. Davies does overreach himself, threatening his host with a knife and reminding him that "I never been inside a nuthouse" (p. 67), and Mick's plan is successful when Aston literally turns his back on the old man as the final curtain falls.

If Mick were simply being protective, he would have removed the threat instantly and permanently by force and the implication of future violence or even legal recourse, but he undertakes the slower, more devious procedure because his brother's feelings are important to him; he wants to be sure that his actions do not cost him the relationship he has with his brother. The relationship between Mick and Aston is emphasized by the fact that they always refer to each other as "brother," never by name. The motivation, then, is fraternal affection, as opposed to duty.

Finally, as mentioned above, when Mick leaves the stage for the last time, having defeated Davies, the two brothers smile faintly at each other. Clifford Leech sees this smile as a token that things are again as they should be—the family tie has been reunited and there is hope for the future: "They are brothers, and . . . they are together for a moment, in silence . . . as they smile . . . there is understanding and affection."[19] Director Peter Hall has pointed out the importance of specific actions in Pinter's plays.[20] If the author calls for an action, it is not merely a piece of "business," but something which has a direct bearing on the meaning of the drama. The called-for smile, then, is meant to be significant. This last glance between the two brothers helps emphasize the theme of need, for it signifies their dependence upon each other, thereby placing their actions and motives in perspective. They have proved to each other their affection, and Mick's going out indicates a realization that the situation is now secure. He can rely on his brother to expel Davies, and, therefore, his presence is no longer necessary. In this first play dealing with the dynamics of the family unit "the two brothers jointly seem to symbolize . . . family compatibility," according to Ruby Cohn,[21] and "a study of the unexpected strength of family ties against an intruder . . . the workings of the English mind today," in John Arden's words,[22] and Boulton finds that "despite their lack of communication there is a bond of sympathetic understanding between them; they are the unified centre of the play's action."[23] It might be mentioned that the mysterious and conspicuous figure of Buddha which Mick smashes (much as society crushed Aston) is the statue of a sensitive man; yet the statue in the play appears to have no significance other than its mere existence. Like the stove, it has no connection, it is absurd—unless it represents the uselessness of religion and/or the meaninglessness of symbols. It does take on the suggestion of a signal between the two brothers, though, indicating Mick's statement that the Davies affair is closed; and Aston's lack of reaction seems to be a concurrence.

Interestingly, even though it is the reason for the conflicts which arise in

19. Leech, "Two Romantics," p. 29.
20. See Irving Wardle, "A Director's Approach," an interview with Hall, and see Chapter XI, below.
21. Cohn, "The World of Harold Pinter," p. 67.
22. *New Theatre Magazine*, 1, No. 4 (July 1960), 29–30.
23. Boulton, "Harold Pinter," p. 132.

the drama, contrary to the conclusion of *A Night Out*, love is presented as potentially positive, the source which may bind brothers together and offer hope for the future in their reconfirmed allegiance to each other. This is simply the other side of the coin; if the lack of something leads to menace, the presence of that thing should displace menace.

Pinter himself has said a great deal about the meaning of this particular play, though one feels at times that he is like the Davies who replies to Mick's query, "Are you Welsh?" by saying "Well, I been around you know." In answering the criticism by Leonard Russell in the *Sunday Times* that the audience laughed at *The Caretaker* as if it were a farce, Pinter wrote: "Certainly I laughed myself while writing 'The Caretaker' but not all the time, not 'indiscriminately.' An element of the absurd is, I think, one of the features of the play, but at the same time I did not intend it to be merely a laughable farce. If there hadn't been other issues at stake the play would not have been written. . . . As far as I'm concerned, 'The Caretaker' is funny, up to a point. Beyond that point it ceases to be funny, and it was because of that point that I wrote it."[24] This sounds like Pinter's definition of tragedy.[25] What happens at that point is the play, but the author recognizes a certain self-direction imposed by the drama itself: "At the end [of *The Caretaker*] there are two people alone in a room, and one of them must go in such a way as to produce a sense of complete separation and finality. I thought originally that the play must end with the violent death of one at the hands of the other. But then I realized, when I got to the point, that the characters as they had grown could never act in this way."[26] As developed in the drama, it is clear that neither Aston nor Davies is of a homicidal nature. It is evident why one of the people did have to go, though. In the relationship between the two brothers the intrusion of an outsider could weaken their bonds and their power to help each other might be diminished as a consequence. Aston is dependent on Mick to provide a sanctuary where no one will bother him and where he can work things out in peace. Mick is his brother's keeper, his caretaker. Aston may feel some insecurity in his relationship with Mick, however. After all, people he had trusted had failed him before and it is taking him a long time to regain his confidence, even in his brother. One need only remember the friends who had turned him in, and the mother who had signed the consent papers, to understand Aston's reluctance to accept any situation as secure. Nevertheless, he does desire human companionship, so when Davies follows him home, he is willing to take a chance and the circumstances for the play are set. When Aston recognizes what kind of person Davies is (he complains that Davies is "stinking the place out,"[27] as his brother claimed earlier), he realizes that the

24. *Sunday Times*, London, 14 August 1960.
25. See Chapter II.
26. Pinter quoted in Taylor, *Anger and After*, p. 336.
27. Pinter, *The Caretaker*, p. 69.

tramp lacks any redeeming qualities, and may endanger his association with his brother as well. This being the case, it is Davies who "must go" so that the original relationship may remain intact. In an interview with Kenneth Tynan, Pinter is even more explicit about how the drama might have ended and how it does end, incidentally recognizing that his techniques have improved: "The original idea . . . was . . . to end the play with the violent death of the tramp. . . . It suddenly struck me that it was not necessary. And I think that in this play . . . I *have* developed, that I have no need to use cabaret turns and black-outs and screams in the dark to the extent that I enjoyed using them before. I feel that I can deal, without resorting to that kind of thing, with a human situation. . . . I do see this play as merely . . . a particular human situation, concerning three particular people and not, incidentally . . . symbols."[28] The essence of this statement is further evidence of the author's centralizing of the theme of need. The "human situation" is the confrontation of various characters with various psychological drives. There is no reason to kill the tramp if he does not fulfill someone's needs, because he is important only if he functions as a satisfactory agent, and he ceases to be important when this requirement is not met. His loss, therefore, is not traumatic, so he can be ousted easily (he is not of enough consequence to require killing as a threat to existing relationships). When both brothers are cognizant of this, the play ends.

The final meaning of the play has been simply expressed by Pinter elsewhere, too. Terrence Rattigan claims that, "When I saw *The Caretaker* I told Pinter that I knew what it meant. 'It's about the God of the Old Testament, the God of the New, and Humanity, isn't it?' Pinter said blankly, 'No, Terry, it's about a caretaker and two brothers.' "[29] This statement becomes meaningful when joined with Pinter's assertion in Charles Marowitz's "Theatre Abroad" article that the play is "about love."

What this statement means in terms of the action of the play is that all three characters have individual needs for attachment of some kind and that everything they do is aimed either at creating such a relationship or maintaining one which already exists. Davies tries to form alliances with both Aston and Mick, but fails. In the final analysis it must be admitted that Davies remains an enigmatic, chameleon-like figure who tries to fulfill his own needs for companionship by changing to fit the requirements needed to fulfill the needs of others so that they will form an alliance with him (there are traces of Davies in both Stella in *The Collection* and Ruth in *The Homecoming* in this respect). He allows those around him to play out their own fantasies because he is so indefinite, taking on the shape they need. The irony is that his changeability and lack of selectivity ultimately cost him what he most desires. Mick, who displays his astuteness during his games with Davies when he tricks the old man into contradicting himself, is aware of the tramp's change-

28. Broadcast on the BBC Home Service, 28 Oct. 1960.
29. Quoted by Hinchcliffe, *Harold Pinter*, p. [8].

able nature, and this allows him to manipulate the old man. He recognizes Davies as a threat to the union between himself and his brother and strives to displace the tramp so as to keep his own position secure. What each man does is aimed at fulfilling his personal needs.

It is clear that Pinter was aware of what he was doing when he wrote this play and that he consciously intended to comment on psychological needs. His statement about the meaning of the drama reveals this. Furthermore, it is obvious, in the way he plays the three men off against one another, that he was probably consciously taking their motivation into account and this would certainly create the pattern of situations and actions presented in *The Caretaker*. The structure of the drama and the character development detailed above indicate that this is true. Pinter's comment about how the play "must" end is further evidence of his awareness of need as a thematic element. It is the author's admitted awareness that the concept of psychological need is centralized as his prime subject in this play which makes *The Caretaker* so important in Pinter's development.

As can be seen from the excerpts quoted above, *The Caretaker* includes many characteristics typical of Pinter plays. A combination of the problems of verification, the use of language for defensive purposes rather than for communication, and the fact that individuals are constantly undergoing change to the degree that they cannot predict their own actions, let alone those of others, create a world in which identity is difficult to establish and even harder to maintain. The question of identity which began with Rose's "Who are you?" in *The Room* and was continued by Edward's repetition of the same question in *A Slight Ache* is raised by Mick's interrogation of Davies (who introduces himself as Davies to Aston and as Jenkins to Mick). Davies' search for and insistence upon his integrity as an individual remind us of Stanley's "Do you have any idea who I am?" in *The Birthday Party*. There is a major difference between the comedies of menace and *A Slight Ache* and *The Caretaker*, though, for in the latter dramas the characters are defined in terms of their relationships with one another as they try to form some kind of link, an element which Pinter will expand upon as the exploration of need replaces menace used merely as a stage device to create a mood, complete with "blackouts and screams in the night." The movement from simple menace to need as the primary subject which began in *A Slight Ache* reaches the level of centrality in *The Caretaker* and the playwright turns his attention to his new theme in the major plays which follow.

Chapter VI. Three Short Plays

. . . because of the freedom . . .

The time of change represented by *A Slight Ache* and *The Caretaker* was not a smooth transition for Pinter, and three minor plays written during this period reflect his uncertainty and experimentation. The subject of *A Night Out* shows the movement toward psychological realism, but is contrarily expressed through the use of numerous very patent stage devices. *Night School* is a throwback to the comedies of menace. *The Dwarfs* is in many ways an anomaly, a play standing by itself, though it too shows signs of the transition taking place and, indeed, deals with memory/perception ideas which the author returns to in his latest dramas.

Two things might be kept in mind while considering these three plays. First, they were written between the middle of 1959 and the middle of 1960, shortly after Pinter's revue sketch experimentation; and second, like *A Slight Ache* they were originally written for media other than the stage. Taken together, they constitute an important phase in Pinter's development as a writer, for they gave him an opportunity to experiment outside the limits imposed by the stage, and the freedom he gained contributes to the freer movement and more relaxed style of his later work.

In his article "Writing for Myself," Pinter recognizes that there are different approaches involved when writing for radio or television than when writing for the stage, though he claims not to "make any distinction between kinds of writing"—that is to say, he feels that radio or television work is as valid as stage drama. Technically, when writing for the stage he "always keep[s] a continuity of action," whereas "television lends itself to quick cutting from scene to scene, and nowadays I see it more in terms of pictures. When I think of someone knocking at a door, I see the door opening in close-up and a long shot of someone going up the stairs. Of course the words go with the pictures, but on television, ultimately, the words are of less import than they are on the stage."[1]

This is not true about radio, naturally, but the dramatist does find radio and television alike in one respect: "I don't find television confining or restrictive, and it isn't limited to realism, necessarily. Its possibilities go well beyond that," he says after writing A Night Out, and then goes on to declare, "I like writing for sound radio, because of the freedom. When I wrote The Dwarfs a few months ago, I was able to experiment in form—a mobile, flexible structure, more flexible and mobile than in any other medium. And from the point of view of content I was able to go the whole hog and enjoy myself by exploring to a degree which wouldn't be acceptable in any other medium." His conclusion is that this writing "was extremely valuable to me."

A Night Out

Although written at about the same time as The Caretaker, A Night Out is one of the few Pinter plays in which there is no problem in determining the meaning. Really an extended revue sketch, A Night Out was first produced on the BBC Third Programme, May 1, 1960, and by the Independent Television Authority on April 24, 1960 (with a record audience of between fifteen and eighteen million viewers). The first stage presentation was at the Comedy Theatre, London, on October 2, 1961.

As part of the carry-over from the revue sketches, the basic situation is more familiar than in most of the dramatist's earlier pieces, the action remains realistic throughout, and Gordon notes that there is a "more direct rendering of character."[2] Other traces remaining from the sketches include a realistic

1. "Writing for Myself," pp. 172–75.   2. Gordon, Stratagems, p. 50.

dialogue, comedy composed of a more obvious brand of humor, a lightness of tone, and a resultant lack of the total desperation usually associated with Pinter characters. These elements may also have been influenced by the playwright's awareness of his mass audience.

One clear bit of evidence that *A Night Out* was intended to be seen on television is the large amount of movement from scene to scene, recalling the author's comment about "quick cutting." While still relatively simple in setting, the play is more varied than most of Pinter's works in that it consists of nine scenes, which switch back and forth in four different locales. Scene i takes place in the kitchen of a small house in the South of London where Albert Stokes, a twenty-eight-year-old insurance clerk, lives with his mother. As the play opens, Albert is dressing to go out, an immediate departure from the typical Pinter format, significantly acknowledged in the drama's title. In the revue sketches the setting was occasionally outdoors and in the previous plays characters came and went, but this is the first time in a regular drama that Pinter follows his protagonist outside and does not center on the image of a room.

Albert's mother enters, and the basic premise of the drama instantly becomes clear in the ensuing conversation as the mother's possessive, whining nature is seen dominating that of her "boy." The son is preparing to go to a party at his employer's (Mr. King) where a retiring employee (Mr. Ryan) is to be honored. Mrs. Stokes pretends to be ignorant of the affair, though Albert informed her of it a week ago and asked her to press a tie for him to wear to it only this morning. Mrs. Stokes expresses annoyance there will be no usual Friday night card game tonight and then acts the part of a martyred mother:

MRS. STOKES (*turning away*). Your father would turn in his grave if he heard you raise your voice to me. You're all I've got, Albert. I want you to remember that. I haven't got anyone else. I want you—I want you to bear that in mind.
ALBERT (*with a step towards her*). I'm sorry—I raised my voice. (*He moves on to the landing, mumbling*) I've got to go.
MRS. STOKES (*following Albert*). Albert.
ALBERT. What?
MRS. STOKES. I want to ask you a question.
ALBERT. What?
MRS. STOKES. Are you leading a clean life?
ALBERT. A clean life?
MRS. STOKES. You're not leading an unclean life, are you?
ALBERT. What are you talking about?
MRS. STOKES. You're not messing about with girls are you? You're not messing about with girls tonight?

ALBERT. (*moving to left of the table*). Don't be so ridiculous!
MRS. STOKES. Answer me, Albert. I'm your mother.[3]

Mrs. Stokes's conversion from martyred to accusing mother (who sees sex as being something dirty) completes the primary referents of the play, for the series of scenes which follow will demonstrate that Albert is intimidated by both his mother and sex and cannot adequately assert himself against either force.

Scene ii is set in a coffee stall near a railway arch where two of Albert's co-workers, Kedge and Seeley, are waiting for him to go to the party. This scene, much on the order of "The Black and White" or "Last to Go," could quite easily have been extracted from the play and presented as a revue sketch. An old man informs the two partygoers that their friend "sat there looking very compressed with himself," which the barman explains as meaning depressed (p. 7). Seeley tells Kedge that this may be because of the football game played on Saturday last, information which will explain Gidney's actions later at the party. Kedge was sick, and Albert, switched to Kedge's position from his own normal position on the firm's team, did not play well and the team lost, much to the displeasure of team captain Gidney. Typically the two men do not actually understand Albert and assume that their fellow is distressed because of the game too. There is humor in this scene with the old man and also in the discussion between Kedge and Seeley consisting of a group of contradictory statements about various ballplayers in which Seeley, sounding like Goldberg in *The Birthday Party*, influences Kedge's opinion, perhaps even distorting reality by his domination over the other.

Scene iii cuts back to the kitchen where Albert's mother is prattling on, asking where he is going, repeating that he will miss dinner, and so on, as though they had never talked about it before. While fussing over Albert's dress ("You can't go out and disgrace me, Albert," p. 11), making sure that he has a handkerchief in his breast pocket so that he looks like a gentleman, as his father before him always did, Mrs. Stokes manages to let Albert know that she has made shepherd's pie, his favorite dinner. She is trying to manipulate him as Seeley did Kedge in the preceding scene.

Back at the coffee stall in Scene iv, Albert's attitude toward his mother is exposed. Kedge asks Seeley if he has ever met Albert's mother. The subject seems to bother Seeley, and when he is asked "What's she like," the stage directions indicate that he replies "*shortly*" (p. 12). Kedge observes, "He always gets a bit niggly when she's mentioned, doesn't he? A bit touchy." Albert arrives and is kidded by his cohorts about the presence of women office

3. Pinter, *A Night Out* (London: Methuen, 1961), pp. 5–6. A slightly altered version of this play with division of the action into acts but retaining scenes is also available in *A Slight Ache and Other Plays*, London: 1970.

workers at the party and he fails to understand Kedge's implication that Gidney will be upset with him because of the bad game a week ago. Moments later Kedge's statement that Albert gets "niggly" when his mother is referred to is brought out in the following exchange:

KEDGE (*regarding Albert*). How's your mum, Albert?
ALBERT. All right.
KEDGE. That's the idea.

    . . .

ALBERT (*quietly*). What do you mean, how's my mum?

    . . .

KEDGE. I just asked how she was, that's all.
ALBERT. Why shouldn't she be all right?
KEDGE. I didn't say she wasn't.
ALBERT. Well, she is.
KEDGE. Well, that's all right, then, isn't it?
ALBERT. What are you getting at? [p. 15]

Note the repetition of the line "Well, that's all right, then, isn't it?" which Pinter used as a youth when he kept talking, trying to avoid trouble during his walks through the alley of broken milk bottles. Kedge's irrelevant, trivial, self-centered comments about his own mother at the end of the conversation are typical of Pinter, suggesting that something important has been touched upon but quickly passed over by those who are unaware or who wish to stay uninvolved.

Scene v takes place in the lounge of Mr. King's house, where the party is in progress. The normal cocktail-party conversations are taking place: the boss recommends cycling to everyone, then admits that he drives; Seeley compliments Gidney on his shoes; and so forth. Although the atmosphere is friendly, an ominous note is introduced when Gidney tries to talk Joyce into playing up to Albert. There is a brief moment of tension when Gidney insists that he "could go anywhere" with his qualifications and calls on Albert for affirmation only to have Albert claim that he, too, has the qualifications to go anywhere and be anything he might want to be.

Kedge and Betty flirt; as contrast for the amorous pair, Joyce and Eileen flirt with and tease Albert, who cannot cope with the situation. In a related incident Mr. King's toast to Mr. Ryan is interrupted, and the scene becomes a mixture of comedy and terror as Kedge's buffoonery is juxtaposed with Eileen's sudden screams and claims that somebody touched her, "took a liberty" (p. 25). Although the stage directions make it clear that old Mr. Ryan was the guilty party, Gidney uses the event as an excuse to turn on Albert. There is some name-calling and pushing, and then the group splits in two, everyone but Gidney, Seeley, and Albert standing aside as the lights are lowered on the large group so that the other three become the center of attention. Gidney has been provoked by "that bloody awful game" and the scene swiftly moves to its climax:

GIDNEY (*breathlessly*). I know your trouble.
ALBERT. Oh, yes?
GIDNEY. Yes, sticks out a mile.

 . . .

ALBERT. What's my trouble, then?
GIDNEY. (*very deliberately*). You're a mother's boy. That's what you are. That's your trouble. You're a mother's boy [p. 28].

There is a scuffle following this "That's Your Trouble"-like exchange, after which Albert exits. Blackout.

Scene vi is a short scene back in Mrs. Stokes's kitchen. During the entire time only Mrs. Stokes speaks, her talk being that of the kind of mother who would produce a son like Albert: "Albert! Is that you? . . . What are you creeping up the stairs for? Might have been a burglar. What would I have done then? . . . You leave me in the house all alone. . . . Well, I won't even ask any questions. That's all. . . . What have you been doing—mucking about with girls? . . . Mucking about with girls I suppose. Do you know what time it is? . . . Drunk I suppose. I suppose your dinner's ruined. . . . But you've never brought a girl home here in your life. I suppose you're ashamed of your mother . . . . are you drunk? Where did you go, to one of those pubs in the West End? You'll get into serious trouble, my boy, if you frequent those places, I'm warning you. . . . I hope you're satisfied. . . . I never grumble. . . . I'm not asking for gratitude. But . . . I've never told you about the sacrifices we made, you wouldn't care. . . . Telling me lies. . . . Well, if you don't want to lead a clean life . . . if you want to go mucking about with all sorts of bits of girls, if you're content to leave your own mother sitting here till midnight, and I wasn't feeling well . . . . you don't care . . . . the least you can do is to eat the dinner I cooked for you, especially for you, it's shepherd's pie" (pp. 29–31). Some of the phrases foreshadow Max in *The Homecoming*. The scene ends abruptly as Albert jumps up, grabs a clock and raises it above his head. Mrs. Stokes screams as the lights fade and come up on the coffee stall for Scene vii.

Albert enters the coffee stall where he is joined by a girl who smiles seductively and tries to engage him in a conversation. Her motive is rapidly made obvious and she invites him to go with her just around the corner to her room. They leave, Albert never having said a word.

Scene viii finds the couple entering the girl's room. Her attitude has changed and she is now brisk and nervous, asking Albert not to walk so heavily that the whole house will know he is there. She finally asks him to take his shoes off in order to protect her reputation. She shows Albert a photograph of a little girl, who she says is her daughter who is staying at a very select boarding school. Albert breaks a lace on one of his shoes while trying to remove it and swears under his breath. The girl asks him not to say words like that—"I'm sorry, I can't bear that sort of thing. It's just—not in my personality" (p. 33). Considering the nature of her profession and the fact that she is speaking to a customer, this is a humorous response. Similar responses occur throughout the scene, but they become pathetic when it is revealed that she is attempting to live a lie, being unable to reconcile her self-picture with reality, much like Davies in *The Caretaker*. She is full of contradictions, talking of the log fires in Switzerland, being fond of a smoke with a glass of sherry before dinner or a glass of wine after dinner, then moments later belching. She confides that she is well-educated and does not fit into the neighborhood, which is "full of people of no class at all." She also claims to have been a continuity girl in films at one time, matching Albert's lie that he is in the cinema. Removing her skirt and blouse, she says: "I'm no different from other girls. In fact, I'm better. These so-called respectable girls, for instance, I'm sure they're much worse than I am. Well, you're an assistant director—all your continuity girls and secretaries, I . . . bet they're very loose" (p. 36). She does not seem to realize that her claim of having been a continuity girl and her subsequent appraisal of her "better" self as opposed to "loose" continuity girls do not match.

Albert is also living in a sort of dream (as the final scene will make evident) with, among other things, his invented story about being a free-lance assistant director. His actions are peculiar, too. He chuckles at nothing, comments on the clock on the mantlepiece several times, sinisterly reminding us of the close of Scene vi. He coughs violently, sighs and groans, smiles, and picks up the clock.

When Albert drops his cigarette on the floor the girl becomes outraged, and her diatribe strongly resembles that of Mrs. Stokes. Albert grabs her wrist, forcing her to sit down, while verbally attacking her in terms similar to those used by his mother earlier: "Don't muck me about. . . . Who do you think you are? . . . You never stop talking. Just because you're a woman, you think you can get away with it . . . . you're a dead weight round my neck. . . . Always something. . . . I've had—I've had—just about enough. . . . 'What would your father say, Albert?' . . . So you know what I did? . . . You haven't got any breeding. She hadn't either. And what about those girls tonight. Same kind. And that one. I didn't touch her. . . . I've got as many qualifications as the next man. Let's get that quite—straight. And I got the answer to her. . . . I finished the conversation. . . . I finished her. . . . With this clock! . . . . Of course, I loved her, really" (pp. 39–40). The references to Albert's father and grandmother demonstrate that he is not actually talking to the girl. His imagination and desires get the better of him as the girl assumes the role of a scapegoat, taking on his mother's characteristics in Albert's eyes. He breaks the girl's game of respectability when he points out that she does not have a daughter and that the picture is of her as a child (there is a date on the back of the photograph). Having gained dominance ("I'm giving orders here"), Albert does not know what to do with his power and, blinking uncertainly, tells the girl to pick up his shoes and put them on him. In a final exertion of his individuality Albert calls the flat a "dump," warns the girl about how to talk to him, flips her a half-crown, telling her to buy herself "a seat at the circus," and exits (p. 42).

The concluding scene shows Albert returning to his mother's kitchen, smiling and luxuriously at ease. Suddenly, startlingly, Mrs. Stokes's voice is heard offstage, calling Albert. He stiffens and his mother enters. It is all over, as it never began, and Albert's mother is still Albert's mother: "Do you know what the time is? . . . Where have you been? . . . To raise your hand to your own mother. . . . Aren't I a good mother to you? Everything I do is—is for your own good. You should know that. . . . You're good, you're not bad, you're a good boy" (p. 43). So the play ends.

The terror in *A Night Out* is not an unknown something, it is not in any sense mysterious, it is a stereotype established in the opening seconds of the play. The drama is actually a comic revue sketch which has been extended to portray the problems involved in a mother's domination over her son on the order of Sidney Howard's *The Silver Cord*, the lack of communication between the two, and the trouble brought about (especially with the opposite sex) when such a situation exists. Only the menace is gone.

The play is not, however, outside Pinter's pattern of development. Technically the lack of subtlety in using stage devices ties *A Night Out* to *The Room* and the recently finished sketch, "Applicant." Linguistically, it continues the line of realistic dialogue which Taylor finds superb in this play with its "constant leap-frogging and casting-back in sense, its verbal misunderstandings, anticipations which prove to be mistaken, [and] mishearings."[4] In "Writing for Myself" Pinter admits that the play pleases him in this area: "*A Night Out* did, I think, successfully integrate the picture and the words, although that may be because I wrote it first for radio."[5]

Thematically, the play looks back to *The Room* and *The Birthday Party* in the characters of Albert, who can be as silent as Bert Hudd before a woman's tongue or be accused of attacking girls at parties as Stanley attacked Lulu, and Mrs. Stokes, whose smothering motherliness is reminiscent of Rose (and even somewhat reminiscent of Flora's approach to Barnabas in *A Slight Ache*). And the relationship between Albert and his mother can be equated with that of Stanley and Meg. In addition, the drama looks forward to the later plays in Albert's reaction against the two principles of femininity he comes in contact with, for the combination mother–wife–sex-partner woman is a major figure in Pinter's canon, the aspects of which appear in Sally, Sarah, Ruth,

4. Taylor, *Anger and After*, p. 343.   5. "Writing for Myself," p. 175.

almost all of Pinter's women to some extent. There is also the pathetic need for illusion, shared by the lonely girl and the equally lonely Albert. Finally, the internalizing of the conflict on a psychological level is certainly a thread which the dramatist picked up in A *Slight Ache* and pursues in his subsequent work.

Night School

First presented by Associated Rediffusion Television on July 21, 1960, and later performed in an expanded version on the BBC Third Programme, September 25, 1966, *Night School* is considered by many to be Pinter's weakest play. Although it played before a television audience of sixteen million in one night, Pinter himself has considered the drama a failure and for several years refused to let it be produced or published, claiming that he had lost the script (the play was not brought out in printed form available to the general public until 1967 after the playwright rewrote it during the summer of 1966). Most of Pinter's essentials are present—the dialogue, familiar character types, the struggle for territory (a room), and the problems of communication and verification. Unlike most of his writing, however, the most important components of this play are not these ingredients: it is not read for insights into the human dilemma, but for the pervasive revue sketch brand of humor which is its outstanding feature, and it is in part for this reason that many judge the work a failure. Others, such as Hinchliffe, declare that its greatest fault is conforming to a formula in which Pinter almost parodies himself.[6] As a comedy, though, it must be admitted that *Night School* is a success.

Like A *Night Out*, *Night School* is among Pinter's simplest, most straightforward dramas, and the meaning is relatively easy to discern (especially after the several years' exposure to Pinter's ideas and techniques in the comedies of menace which helped prepare his critical audience). The action opens in a living room where two elderly aunts, Annie and Milly Billet (there is a pun here), are welcoming home their nephew Walter Street, who is returning after a nine-month absence. The conversation is that which one would normally expect in such a situation as Annie asks Walter, "How did they treat you this time, eh?"[7] and the pair discuss the chocolates he brought for Milly and a problem with hanging curtains properly.

Aunt Milly comes in and the conversation continues quite matter-of-factly:

ANNIE. Sit down, Milly. Don't stand up.
MILLY. I've been sitting down, I've been lying down. . . .

6. Hinchliffe, *Harold Pinter*, p. 110. Taylor (*Anger and After*, p. 343) quotes a similar conclusion drawn by Pinter himself: "I was slipping into a formula . . . the worst thing I have written."
7. Pinter, *Night School*, in *Tea Party and Other Plays* (London: Methuen, 1967) p. 81.

WALTER. You haven't been so well, eh?
MILLY. Middling. Only middling.
ANNIE. I'm only middling as well.
MILLY. Yes, Annie's only been middling.
WALTER. Well, I'm back now, eh?
MILLY. How did they treat you this time?
WALTER. Very well. Very well.
MILLY. When you going back?
WALTER. I'm not going back.
MILLY. You ought to be ashamed of yourself, Walter spending half your life
  in prison. Where do you think that's going to get you?
WALTER. Half my life? What do you mean? Twice, that's all.
ANNIE. What about Borstal?
WALTER. That doesn't count.
MILLY. I wouldn't mind if you ever had a bit of luck, but what happens? Every
  time you move yourself they take you inside [p. 83].

The sudden revelation that Walter's absence has been an enforced one, spent
in prison, is made even more surprising by the contrast with the casual way in
which the information is delivered.

  Aunt Milly's next speech is very practical and humorous because of its
inappropriateness to the stereotype of old aunts—a combination of the talk
of the two killers in *The Dumb Waiter* and the two elderly aunts in Joseph
Kesselring's *Arsenic and Old Lace*: "Listen, I've told you before, if you're not
clever in that way you should try something else, you should open up a little
business" (p. 83). A similar piece of advice will be given by the landlord, Mr.
Solto, in much the same manner a while later. The characters' rather indifferent acceptance of a life of crime as a part of society is certainly no more
startling than Gay's *The Beggar's Opera* and is just as funny for the same
reasons (Milly does not say that it is morally bad to spend half one's life in
prison, it simply does not lead anywhere, and Walter does not consider
Borstal important, presumably because Borstals are for juveniles).

  A slightly ominous tone is introduced with Milly's question to Annie,
"Well? Have you told him?" and it becomes apparent that the two old ladies
are hiding something from their nephew, but the seriousness of their secret is
masked by the amusing attempts to avoid the question. Milly eventually reveals that they have let Walter's room to Sally Gibbs, a young schoolteacher
who does not know that she has displaced him:

MILLY. She's always studying books. . . .
ANNIE. She goes out to night school three nights a week.
MILLY. She's a young girl.
ANNIE. She's a very clean girl.
MILLY. She's quiet . . . [p. 86].

Again an amusing round of conversation conceals the serious consequences involved in the revelation:

WALTER. She's sleeping in my room!
MILLY. What's the matter with the put-u-up? . . .
WALTER. The put-u-up? She's sleeping in my bed.
ANNIE. She's bought a lovely coverlet, she's put it on.
WALTER. A coverlet? I could go out now, I could pick up a coverlet as good as hers. What are you talking about coverlets for?
MILLY. Walter, don't shout at your aunt, she's deaf.
WALTER. I can't believe it. I come home after nine months in a dungeon.
ANNIE. The money's been a great help.
WALTER. Have I ever left you short of money?
MILLY. Yes!
WALTER. Well . . . not through my own fault. I've always done my best.
MILLY. And where's it got you? [pp. 86–87].

Milly's question is ironically pertinent because his best has only gotten him into jail and his failure to provide adequately has cost him his room—the crux of the play. The bed becomes symbolic of the struggle for the room:

WALTER. You're asking me to sleep on that put-u-up? The only person who ever slept on that put-u-up was Aunty Gracy. That's why she went to America. . . . I can't believe it. But I'll tell you one thing about that bed she's sleeping in.
ANNIE. What's the matter with it?
WALTER. There's nothing the matter with it. It's mine, that's all—I bought it.
ANNIE. So he did, Milly.
MILLY. You? I thought I bought it.
ANNIE. That's right. You did. I remember.
WALTER. You bought it, you went out and chose it, but who gave you the money to buy it?
ANNIE. Yes, he's right. He did [pp. 87–88].

Then comes one of the funniest and most typical utterances in the drama when Walter, fresh from prison, asserts: "I can't live in these conditions for long. I'm used to something better. I'm used to privacy."

The issue, of course, goes back to Pinter's first play, *The Room*. Walter's security is based on the possession of his bedroom, and if he loses the bedroom, his existence is threatened, for he will have nothing in the world to use as a referent by which he can define himself. The dialogue may be funny, then, but the intolerable situation definitely is not.

In the next scene Mr. Solto has arrived and is being served a piece of pie by the aunts. Speaking in an idiom and cadence remarkably like that of Goldberg in *The Birthday Party*, Solto provides his public view of himself in an apocryphal tale: "They wanted three hundred and fifty pounds income tax off me the other day. My word of honour. I said to them, you must be mad! What are you trying to do, bring me to an early death? Buy me a cheap spade I'll get up first thing in the morning before breakfast and dig my own grave. . . . I'm an old-age pensioner. I'm in receipt of three pound a week. . . . I've always been a lone wolf. The first time I was seduced, I said to myself, Solto, watch your step, mind how you go, go so far but no further. If they want to seduce you, let them seduce you, but marry them? Out of the question. . . . The lady who first seduced me, in Australia—she kicked her own husband out and gave me his room. I bumped into him years later making a speech at Marble Arch. It wasn't a bad speech, it so happens" (pp. 93–95).

The use of reversed clichés (seduction with the man assuming the woman's attitude) is the basis of the humor here. There follows another bit of comedy which, like Walter's play on the word "tart" earlier, has been discredited by Hinchcliffe and other critics:

SOLTO. I killed a man with my own hands, a six-foot Lascar from Madagascar.
ANNIE. From Madagascar?
SOLTO. Sure. A Lascar.
MILLY. Alaska?
SOLTO. Madagascar.
　　　Pause.
WALTER. It's happened before [p. 94].

Like the play's opening dialogue, the talk between Solto and Walter eventually gets around to the problem of a man trying to make a living in a profession which does not suit him. As before, the conversation is conducted in a perfectly ingenuous tone, as if the topic were no more incriminating than the aunt's discussion of the merits of hot versus cold milk in the next scene:

SOLTO. Why don't you go to the Prisoners Help Society. They'll give you a loan. I mean you've done two stretches, you must have a few good references. . . .
WALTER. . . . I'm thinking of going straight.
SOLTO. Why? You getting tired of a life of crime?
WALTER. I'm not good enough. I get caught too many times. I'm not clever enough.
SOLTO. . . . If you want to be a forger you've got to have a gift. It's got to come from the heart.
WALTER. I'm not a good forger.
SOLTO. You're a terrible forger. . . . I'm a better forger than you any day. And I don't forge.
WALTER. I haven't got a gift.
SOLTO. A forger's got to love his work. You don't love your work, that's your trouble, Walter [pp. 95–96].

Walter still has hope though—like Davies' trip to Sidcup in *The Caretaker*, Walter's "if" revolves around getting his room back: "I could get settled in, I could think" (p. 97). The scene ends with Walter asking Solto for help in locating and identifying a girl whose photograph he has found (stolen from Sally's room).

After the hot milk/cold milk debate in the following scene, Annie over-hears Walter and Sally talking. In the conversation Walter lies to Sally, telling her that he is a gunman ("It's not a bad life, all things considered. Plenty of time off. . . . No, there's plenty of worse occupations"—again reminiscent of the discussion Ben and Gus have about job conditions) and a grave robber ("I can recommend it, honest, I mean if you want to taste everything life has to offer," pp. 101–2). There is a short interruption when Annie returns to her own room and humorously cannot recall what the pair were talking about, there being nothing out of the ordinary in their conversation. Annie resumes her post at Milly's insistence only to hear Walter claiming to be a "triple bigamist." Annie returns to her bed again and the scene fades into Sally's room, where Walter is beginning to be affected by the schoolteacher's pres-ence, admitting that he has been telling her lies. The scene closes with Walter having Sally model for him. One is reminded of Albert's ordering the young prostitute around in *A Night Out*. And as in *A Night Out*, the shifting scenes derive from the drama's initial presentation on television. The aunts' lack of perception and inability to determine or understand what is happening bring back memories of Meg at the end of *The Birthday Party*—the women seem to be made of the same stuff.

Solto, meanwhile, has been in pursuit of the girl in the photograph and in the scene which follows is in a club talking to the manager, Tully, an acquaint-ance from the old days, who informs him that the girls in the club are quality: "We got some high-class dolls down here, don't worry. They come all the way from finishing school" (p. 107)—probably similar to the one the girl in *A Night Out* sent her "daughter" to.

A sequence of short scenes here in Sally's "night school" follows. First, Sally is introduced to Solto, who, when she tells him that her name is "Katina," remarks on the coincidence that his childhood sweetheart had the same name; there is an effective switch to Annie and Walter, who are commenting on the fact that Sally is a nice girl and has fixed the room up nicely (verification, ap-pearance versus reality—reinforced by the photograph in the play's closing scene); then back to the club where Solto is trying to proposition Sally by telling her about his beach cottage and inviting her to go down for the week-end. He then tells her that he came looking for her specifically because of Walter's photograph. She denies knowing the forger.

The next scene is funny in the S. J. Perelman, Robert Benchley, surreal-istic tradition as Solto attempts to convince Walter that he has been unable to locate the girl:

WALTER. Didn't you locate that club?

SOLTO. What club?

WALTER. In the photo.

SOLTO. No. What I thought, the best thing to do would be to get hold of the photographer, you see. So I paid him a call.

WALTER. What did he say?

SOLTO. He wasn't there. He'd gone to Canada for a conference.

WALTER. What kind of conference?

SOLTO. A dental conference. He's going to be a dentist.

WALTER. Why'd he give up photography?

SOLTO. He had a change of heart. You know how it is. He gave me a cup of coffee, told me his life story.

WALTER. Who did?

SOLTO. His brother. The chiropodist. He's in dead trouble that boy, he can't meet his overheads.

WALTER. Look here, Mr. Solto, if I were you I'd give up the whole thing.

SOLTO. You want my opinion? I think the photo's a fake. There's no such club. There's no girl. They don't exist.

WALTER. That's exactly what I think.

    Pause.

SOLTO. You do?

WALTER. Exactly.

SOLTO. Who knows? You might be right [pp. 113–14].

From the way Walter goes along with Solto he obviously does not believe the man, and when the landlord leaves, Walter goes upstairs to talk to the other lodger.

    The final scene in the play takes place the next morning when Annie finds that Sally has gone, leaving a note thanking the two old ladies and explaining that an urgent matter has called her away suddenly. Milly enters with another photograph she has found in the schoolteacher's room—a photograph showing Sally holding a netball and surrounded by schoolgirls.

    More superficial than Pinter's previous works, *Night School* contains less emotional intensity and the imagery is not as strong, but the humor is proportionately greater as Pinter exploits techniques, such as the use of *non sequiturs* and puns, embodied in his revue sketches, and shock situations from his earlier pieces in which what is said is entirely out of keeping with the surroundings or circumstances in which it is uttered.

    The two major themes of the drama are a reversion to the battle for territory as a method of establishing identity and security and the problem of verification. The prime motivating force behind Walter's actions is the fact that he has been displaced from the room which he feels defines his character. His chance to establish a relationship which will define his character in terms of human interreactions is ironically lost when he chases Sally away by being a threat to expose her. In some ways Walter, like Davies, is midway between Rose and Ruth. Rose is satisfied with her room, while Ruth is involved with human personalities rather than material structures. Both Davies and Walter are given opportunities to make human contacts, but opt for something less, ultimately losing the potential involvement which would supersede their choices and make those choices unnecessary.

Sally is a combination of natures which she keeps hidden merely by not supplying information. Her overuse of perfume is a form of cheapness completely inconsistent with her studies. Her habit of constant bathing is typical guilt symbolism, yet the knowledge that she is associating with Walter, an ex-convict, does not bother her at all. Sally's actions are concerned with keeping the two segments of her life separate and hidden.

Solto, too, is a mixture, but unlike Sally he hides his true character by raising a cover. His role as a pensioner, whining about taxes, contrasts with his beach property, his scrap works, and his knowledge of clubs and shady former acquaintances. In Solto's case motivation seems based purely on immediate desires.

The question of verification is not terribly important in connection with Walter's lies. His life, in spite of his momentary lies about being a gunman, is basically open and straightforward. He does not try too hard to convince anyone that the lies are true. Solto's pose as a pensioner is, though not immediately, a fairly obvious front for his more nefarious activities. Only with Sally does there seem to be a true discrepancy, but the evidence of the two photographs demonstrates that she was probably both a schoolteacher and a night-club hostess. The photographs, incidentally, connect Sally in *Night School* with the prostitute in *A Night Out*, just as her dual personality of Sally/Katina aligns her with other Pinter women such as Sarah in *The Lover*.

The Dwarfs

Pinter's most difficult play to understand, the most absurd in a Theatre of the Absurd sense, is *The Dwarfs*. The author's facetious reply to a question about what his plays are about, "The weasel under the cocktail cabinet,"[8] is certainly well suited to a play that Taylor has labeled his "most difficult play yet and most daunting to popular taste."[9] The drama is Pinter's most personal statement and is more poetic than dramatic, leading to George Wellwarth's derogatory comment about the author's "personal nightmarish symbols": "Pinter keeps everything deliberately vague and allusive, and it is impossible to get anything out of the play at all."[10] Even the playwright recognizes that the drama is obscure and that his decision to produce it was "regretted by

8. Taylor, *Anger and After*, p. 323.   9. Ibid., p. 345.
10. Wellwarth, *The Theater of Protest and Paradox* (1971), p. 235.

everyone—except me" because the play "is apparently the most intractable, impossible piece of work. Apparently ninety-nine out of a hundred feel it's a waste of time, and the audience hated it."[11]

Based on his partially written autobiographical novel, *The Dwarfs* was first performed on the BBC Third Programme, December 2, 1960, and subsequently staged in a revised version at the New Arts Theatre, London, on September 18, 1963, Harold Pinter directing. A good deal of the confusion in the play results from its genesis as a novel Pinter worked on from 1950 to 1957, and in *The Peopled Wound* Esslin devotes much of his discussion of the work to tracing its relationship to the novel and demonstrating that a large portion of the novel, dealing with the "transition from adolescence to maturity," is drawn from life, something also reflected in the incidents related in John Lahr's unpublished interview with Henry Woolf. Again Pinter has recognized the source of the problem: "The trouble about the novel was that it stretched out over too long a period, and it incorporated too many styles, so that it became rather a hotch-potch. But I've employed certain strains in the book which I thought were worth exploring in my radio play."[12] Elsewhere he admits that he did take "a great deal from [the novel], particularly the kind of state of mind that the characters were in."[13] This internalizing of action and focusing on a mental orientation relates the drama to the transition period he was currently going through in his writing. Furthermore, Pinter understands the play's place in his artistic development: "even though it is . . . more dense, it had great value, great interest for me. From my point of view, the general delirium and states of mind and reactions and relationships in the play—although terribly sparse—are clear to me. I know all the things that aren't said, and the way the characters actually look at each other, and what they mean by looking at each other. It's a play about betrayal and distrust. It does seem very confusing and obviously it can't be successful. But it was good for me to do."[14]

Short, *The Dwarfs* is limited in setting—moving back and forth between two houses in a London suburb, probably Hackney—a division of the stage which is a precursor of *The Collection*; in action (there is no plot); and in number of characters (just three men appear; to concentrate on the states of mind, Pinter eliminated the novel's love-interest, a girl named Virginia). The simplicity of these elements is counterbalanced by a dialogue which is typically Pinterian in its idiom, phrasing, and rhythm and generally seems meaningless. The exchanges between Len, Pete, and Mark are obscure at best, until Len begins his babbling about the dwarfs and the rats. There can be no doubt that he, at least, is as mad as Alice's hatter. But maybe not. As the play

11. Quoted in Bensky, "Harold Pinter," p. 23.
12. Pinter, "Writing for Myself," p. 173.
13. Quoted in Bensky, "Harold Pinter," p. 23.
14. Ibid.

progresses, another possibility arises. The usual questions are explored and related to one another, but the perception-of-reality aspect of the verification problem becomes especially pertinent. It may be that Len is not crazy but is seeing the truth behind the illusions of life, that instead of a distortion, he sees another view of reality, a truer perspective.[15]

The freedom afforded by working in the medium of radio that Pinter alluded to earlier has a bearing on this aspect of the drama in that a goodly proportion of *The Dwarfs* is almost an interior monologue spoken by Len. Mark and Pete are described through his eyes (as a seagull and a spider) and may be projections of his consciousness at times. This is more true for the radio production when Len is speaking to and about one of the other characters as though the other were not present—and he might well not be as far as the radio audience is concerned.

Since there is no plot and little action in the play, the cumulative meaning is a plot equivalent. Essentially there is merely a series of vaguely connected dialogues between three men in their thirties as the setting switches back and forth from Mark's house to Len's house, displaying variations on the themes of reality and fantasy. Moreover, although the conclusions implied or even explicitly stated concern society, Len, Pete, and Mark are practically asocial for they exist in a near social vacuum in which things outside the houses and people aside from the three characters are largely ignored or unknown.

The play opens in a *Dumb Waiter*-ish fashion in Mark's house, where Len and Pete, apparently waiting for their absent friend, engage in everyday banalities, quarreling about who forgot to bring some milk and the fact that mechanical objects are in rebellion—"There's something wrong with this recorder."[16] The milk conversation leads to the information that Mark has been gone for two weeks (he is a traveling actor). The search for milk turns to a discussion of Mark's ancestry (part Portuguese), stemming from an examination of the cooking utensils discovered. Mark's profession and ancestry tenuously identify him with Pinter.

The thematic development is soon begun, however, when attention is centered on the recorder: "There's nothing wrong with it. But it must be broken." Len sneezes and complains, "I've got the most shocking blasted cold I've ever had in all my life," only to state in the next line, "Still, it's not much of a nuisance, really." Pete's comment, "Why don't you pull yourself together? You'll be ready for the loony bin next week if you go on like this" is ironic in view of Len's subsequent mad ramblings and his hospitalization by the end of the play.

In a Goldbergian idiom Len explains to Pete how he spends his nights:

15. The expression of this idea is reminiscent of Theodore Sturgeon's 1941 short story, "Yesterday was Monday," though Pinter claims not to know the story.

16. Pinter, *The Dwarfs*, in *Three Plays*, p. [83]. See Chapter XI for an explanation of how textual alterations in other editions affect interpretations.

"As for the night, that goes without saying. As far as I'm concerned the only thing you can do in the night is eat. It keeps me fit, especially if I'm at home. I have to run downstairs to put the kettle on, run upstairs to finish what I'm doing, run downstairs to cut a sandwich or arrange a salad, run upstairs, run back downstairs to see to the sausages, if I'm having sausages, run back upstairs to finish what I'm doing, run back downstairs . . ." (p. 86). Pete asks him when he last slept, to which he answers, "Sleep? Don't make me laugh. All I do is sleep." The evidence that there is something wrong with Len accumulates when he gets upset over minor things, wanting to know where Pete got his shoes and if he has been wearing them all the while, becoming distraught because Pete is holding his hand palm upwards and, to make matters worse, discovering that there is a straight, horizontal line across the middle of the palm: "You couldn't find two men in a million with a hand like that. It sticks out a mile. A mile. That's what you are, that's exactly what you are, you're a homicidal maniac!" (p. 87).

There is a break at this point in the drama as Pete goes to greet Mark, and Len delivers the first of his mad soliloquies, much in the same wandering style as the Benjy section in William Faulkner's *The Sound and the Fury* or an Ionesco character: "There is my table. There is a table. There is my chair. There is my table. That is a bowl of fruit. There is my chair" (p. 87).

This extremely prosaic speech, trying to make concrete surroundings out of a world of chaos, to structure the world (and incidentally signaling a change in scene location), is interrupted by a piece of imaginative imagery with an allusion to Shakespeare. Len visualizes "my hundred watt bulb like a dagger" in a way similar to Macbeth's experience with a dagger, for the room is his still place at the hub of the wheel (several of Len's speeches contain passages reminiscent of T. S. Eliot's *Four Quartets*) and the light is exposing things, leading him out of the "deep grass," the sanctuary of his room. Immediately Len returns to his simple cataloguing.

Once again, though, his imagination breaks through as he compares himself to Christ, speaking of "my kingdom" and whispering, "They make a hole, in my side." Later he is willing to offer himself as a sacrifice in place of Mark, and he is in his thirties. Along the same lines are Mark's age, Latin origin, ring, and commitment to betting on a "treble chance." Pinter denies ever having "been conscious of allegorical significance in my plays. I have never intended any specific religious reference or been conscious of using anything as a symbol." The religious significance of the "hole" "never occurred" to him. "I certainly didn't mean it. However, I would remind you, on this question [of conscious references], that I live in the world like everyone else and am part of history like everyone else." [17]

Mark now makes an appearance and the tense situation is matched by a humorous interchange:

17. Quoted in Hewes, "Probing Pinter's Play," p. 97.

LEN. What's this, a suit? Where's your carnation?
MARK. What do you think of it?
LEN. It's not a schmutta.
MARK. It's got a zip at the hips.
LEN. A zip at the hips? What for?
MARK. Instead of a buckle. It's neat.
LEN. Neat? I should say it's neat.

    . . .

MARK. What do you think of the cloth?
LEN. The cloth? (*He examines it, gasps and whistles through his teeth. At a great pace.*) What a piece of cloth. What a piece of cloth. What a piece of cloth. What a piece of *cloth.*
MARK. You like the cloth?
LEN. WHAT A PIECE OF CLOTH! [p. 88].

Still in a humorous vein, Pinter now exposes the theme of communication:

LEN. There's a time and place for everything.
MARK. You're right there.
LEN. What do you mean by that?
MARK. There's a time and place for everything.
LEN. You're right there [p. 89].

The next two lines, though, are among the most important in all of Pinter's work; not only are they the key to this particular play, but they provide an insight into most of the concepts he investigates in all his drama:

MARK. I see that butter's going up.
LEN. I'm prepared to believe it, but it doesn't answer my question [p. 89].

These two lines express much of the content of the Theatre of the Absurd, and when they are related to Pinter's previous comments about verification (i.e., something may be true and at the same time irrelevant) and when the dialogues and themes presented throughout his plays are compared to the standard this set of statements provides, many seeming enigmas become clear, though possibly unanswerable.

There follows a short discourse in which Mark speaks of wanting "some bread and honey" and Len remarks that he did not want his guest to become "too curious," that he wanted him to "keep a sense of proportion." Because there are further episodes in the play containing similar expressions, it is evident that Pinter is alluding to A. A. Milne's *Winnie the Pooh* and Lewis Carroll's Alice books, two imaginative examinations of the world of reality. This is especially interesting in the light of the speech which Len makes next, for in it he discusses the nature of his universe, a discussion which indicates why he has to verbalize his room in order to make it concrete: "The rooms we live in. . . . They change shape at their own will. I wouldn't grumble if only they would keep to some consistency. . . . I can't tell the limits, the boundaries, which I've been led to believe are natural. . . . I can't rely on them. When, for example, I look through a train window, at night, and see the yellow lights, very clearly, I can see what they are, and I see . . . they're only still because I'm moving. I know that they do move along with me, and when we go round a bend, they bump off. But I know that they are still, just the same. . . . So they must be still, in their own right, insofar as the earth itself is still, which of course it isn't. The point is . . . that I can only appreciate such facts when I'm moving. When I'm still, nothing around me follows a natural course of conduct. I'm not saying I'm any criterion. . . . After all, when I'm on the train I'm not really moving at all. That's obvious. I'm in the corner seat. I'm still. I am perhaps being moved, but I do not move. Neither do the yellow lights. The train moves, granted, but what's a train got to do with it?" (pp. 89–90). Involved in this recitation is a concept of relativity (with a suggestion of Einstein) which demonstrates the impossibility of belief in a physical world, for stability is prohibited. The only constant is change.

It may be the realization of this continual flux and the resultant unreality of reality which drives Len to seek order in the shape of the mysterious dwarfs he talks about. His description of their activities may well be an attempt to impose his will on the universe, to produce order out of chaos: "The dwarfs are back on the job, keeping an eye on proceedings. They clock in very early, scenting the event . . . . they only work in cities. Certainly they're skilled labourers. . . . They wait for a smoke signal and unpack their kit. They're on the spot with no time wasted and circle the danger area. There, they take up positions, which they are able to change at a moment's notice. But they don't stop work until the job in hand is ended . . ." (p. 92). In the revised edition this monologue has been turned into a three-way conversation and the removal of some of the transitions clouds the original application. Pinter continually rewrites his plays as they are brought out in new editions (*The Caretaker* is another example of this tendency), usually smoothing out and simplifying the language—even cutting when he feels the need.

Pete explains in part the reason for Len's disturbed state when he observes that Len is not elastic: "By elastic I mean being prepared for your own deviations. You don't know where you're going to come out next at the moment. You're like a rotten old shirt. . . . The apprehension of experience must obviously be dependent upon discrimination if it's to be considered valuable. That's what you lack. You've got no idea how to preserve a distance between what you smell and what you think about it" (p. 91).

Later, when he drops a toasting fork, Len demonstrates the easy movement from supposed reality to illusion—in essence he sees through the illusion to reality (though we have only his description to go on). Instead of seeing the images of everyday life, Len thinks that he sees the actuality which lies beneath:

Don't touch it! You don't know what will happen if you touch it! . . . You mustn't bend! Wait. (*Pause.*) I'll bend. I'll . . . pick it up. I'm going to touch it. (*Pause. Softly.*) There. You see? Nothing happens when I touch it. . . . Nothing can happen. No one would bother. . . . You see, I can't see the broken glass. I can't see the mirror I have to look through. I see the other side. But I can't see the mirror side. . . . I want to break it. . . . But how can I break it . . . when I can't see it?

 Silence.

What are the dwarfs doing? They stumble in the gutters and produce their pocket watches. One with a face of chalk chucks the dregs of the daytime into a bin and seats himself on the lid. He is beginning to chew though he has not eaten. Now they collect at the back step. They scrub their veins at the running sink. . . .

 . . .

. . . They've gone on a picnic. . . . They've left me to sweep the yard, to pacify the rats. No sooner do they leave . . . . than in come the rats.

 . . .

. . . Everything is from the corner's point of view. I don't hold the whip. I'm a laboring man. . . .

. . . No dwarf is chef. It's a brotherhood. A true community. They even have hymn singing. . . . So I note their progress. So I commend their industry. So I applaud their motive. So I trust their efficiency. So I find them capable [pp. 94, 96, 98, 99].

Whether Pinter intends Len's vision to represent the truth, an allegorical explanation for the working of society, an attempt to create order, or merely the rantings of a madman is impossible to tell, and it may well be that the dwarf segments are composites of several or all of the implied alternatives.

 As in his earlier plays, Pinter embellishes the presentation of his themes with humor and vivid imagery. *Non sequiturs* serve both as a source of humor and an expression of theme in Len's confession to Mark: "I often wonder about you. But I must keep pedaling. I must. There's a time limit. Who have you got hiding here? You're not alone here. What about your Esperanto? Don't forget, anything over two ounces goes up a penny" (p. 93). A theological talk between Len and Mark creates a similar situation:

LEN. Do you believe in God?
MARK. What?
LEN. Do you believe in God?
MARK. Who?
LEN. God.
MARK. God?
LEN. Do you believe in God?
MARK. Do I believe in God?

LEN. Yes.
MARK. Would you say that again? [pp. 102–3].

Pete's recounting of a dream illustrates Pinter's strong image-making power: "There was some sort of panic. When I looked round I saw everyone's faces were peeling, blotched, blistered. People were screaming, booming down the tunnels. There was a fire bell clanging. When I looked at the girl I saw that her face was coming off in slabs too, like plaster. . . . Black scabs and stains. The skin was dropping off like lumps of cat's meat. I could hear it sizzling on the electric rails" (p. 92). That this description comes after Pete's portraiture of Mark as being as barren as a bombed-out site is apropos.

Identity, verification, the question of reality, exposure of reality, and the problems of communication are all involved in Len's last major speech: "The point is, who are you? Not why or how, not even what. I can see what, perhaps, clearly enough. But who are you? It's no use saying you know who you are just because you tell me you can fit your particular key into a particular slot which will only receive your particular key because that's not foolproof and certainly not conclusive. Just because you're inclined to make these statements of faith has nothing to do with me. It's not my business. Occasionally I believe I perceive a little of what you are but that's pure accident. Pure accident on both our parts, the perceived and the perceiver. It's nothing like an accident, it's deliberate, it's a joint pretence. We depend on these accidents, on these contrived accidents, to continue. It's not important then that it's conspiracy or hallucination. What you are, or appear to be to me, or appear to be to you, changes so quickly, so horrifyingly, I certainly can't keep up with it and I'm damn sure you can't either. But who you are I can't even begin to recognize, and sometimes I recognize it so wholly, so forcibly, I can't look, and how can I be certain of what I see? You have no number. Where am I to look, where am I to look, what is there to locate, so as to have some surety, to have some rest from this whole bloody racket? You're the sum of so many reflections" (p. 103). This is Pinter's most explicit dramatic statement of his concept of verification. Involved by extension, too, is his approach to language, for language depends on arbitrarily agreed-upon definitions, and if nothing remains static, nothing can be used as a standard to which other things can be matched or compared. And the speech also demonstrates why the dramatist confines himself to writing about the problems of individuals: if people change so rapidly and constantly, it is impossible to understand oneself, let alone someone else. Therefore, it is senseless to talk about abstracts such as war; there is no basis for communication, and even if there were, such considerations are unimportant until the more immediate problem of reconciling the individual to life is met.

In the closing words of the play Len speaks in a religious tone of cleansing and purification (as in Eliot again, and sounding like Pinter's detailing of the digs he describes as part of the inspiration for *The Birthday Party*), repeating the idea of change, the cycle of existence: "And this change. All about me the change. The yard as I know it is littered with scraps of cat's meat, pig bollocks, tin cans, bird brains, spare parts of all the little animals, a squelching squealing carpet, all the dwarfs' leavings spittled in the muck, worms stuck in the poisoned shit heaps, the alleys a whirlpool of piss, slime, blood and fruit juice. Now all is bare. All is clean. All is scrubbed. There is a lawn. There is a shrub. There is a flower." (p. 108). The difference between the two pictures is nicely brought out by the contrasting richness of the imagery of before and the simple, sterile imagery of after.

Technically the most important element in *The Dwarfs* is characterization, for this constitutes evidence of Pinter's continuing development. Pete and Mark, although they are largely defined by Len's descriptions, try to control Len's world as Goldberg and McCann sought to direct Stanley, Pete with his dream which works on his victim as *The Birthday Party* inquisition did, and Mark's domination resembling that of Mick in *The Caretaker*. Len's curiosity marks him as one of the line of Pinter victims, which began with Gus in *The Dumb Waiter*, who are threatened because they ask questions. Like Aston, Len "suffers" from hallucinations and goes to the hospital from which he emerges with "sharper" (that is, less imaginative) perceptions. Esslin points out that Stanley, Aston, and Len all undergo an identity crisis and are "cured" at the cost of a dimension of perception.[18] It is the shift in verification as related to identity which is of prime significance, though. The movement of the play is interior—into Len's mind. For the first time the audience is invited to enter a character's mind, and it is no longer a question of the audience attempting to verify who and what is being presented, the characters *themselves* want to know who they are.

While *The Dwarfs* may not be a theatrical success, the obvious expression of Pinter's major concepts coupled with the verification shift makes this one of the author's most important dramas and manifestly places the play among those which helped him determine the direction his future writing would take. The playwright's next play, *The Collection*, continues the examination of verification and reality, but in more general and thus less personal terms. The curious mixture of clearly expounded theory interspersed with obscure excursions of the imagination is replaced with a simple exemplification of theory through dramatic action, as demonstrating the subject of psychological need becomes the center of the writer's attention.

18. Esslin, *The Theatre of the Absurd* (1969), p. 249.

Chapter VIII. A Pattern of Need

. . . love and lack of love . . .

In the dramas following *A Slight Ache* psychological necessity becomes more and more important as a fundamental thesis and it is apparent that Pinter has come to look at this subject as the main theme in his writing. While the menace, established as a prime element in his first three plays, continues to be a basic component in both form and content, as in *A Slight Ache*, it ceases to be important simply as something which threatens an individual, but gains significance when attention centers specifically on primary appetites as a source of menace. The dramatist realized the potential of this subject, introduced in *A Slight Ache*, when he wrote *The Caretaker*, and in his subsequent plays the threats which confront various Pinter characters have their basis in different kinds of need; for instance, *A Night Out* explores the effect of too much of the wrong kind of love, and in *Night School* the plot revolves around a man who cannot accept love.

More important, Pinter's next three major plays—*The Collection, The*

Lover (two more dramas originally written for television), and *The Homecoming*—are all *consciously* concerned with different psychological aspects of need, and they include a view of reality which creates humor based on bizarre situations. There is menace in these extensions of the ideas presented in *A Slight Ache* and consciously studied in *The Caretaker*, but it is a threat to emotional well-being which grows out of the fact that the characters involved are placed in circumstances in which their psychological needs are not being met by those around them. Thus, a threat to an individual's *mental* welfare which grows out of these psychological needs is a common feature of these three plays, although the conclusions which can be drawn from the evidence they present are different. For example, Stella in *The Collection* is not an external menace to Harry and Bill, since, like Barnabas in *A Slight Ache*, she represents no intrinsic danger. Whereas Goldberg and McCann of *The Birthday Party* definitely intimidate Stanley, Stella would pose no danger to the two men if their relationship were stable. The dramas explore some of the ways in which individuals attempt to rectify their situations by forming or strengthening attachments with others.

It might be suggested while examining these three major plays, and in particular *The Homecoming*, that the author's background as an actor be taken into consideration, for not only must any artist perforce try to satisfy his own needs in creating a work of art, as the Freudian Esslin concludes, but Pinter's equal understanding of the actor's similarly special emotional needs to express himself, to reveal aggressive feelings, to dominate, to sublimate conflicts, and so forth, may in part account for some of the roles he creates for his characters to play. As he has said, "I'm writing for the stage, for actors to act. But it comes second. The characters are there first. It's a good part for an actor if the character possesses a proper and full life." [1]

The Collection

The Collection was first presented by Associated Rediffusion Television in London on May 11, 1961, and then staged a year later by the Royal Shakespeare Company at the Aldwych Theatre, London, on June 18, 1962. A wonderfully funny play, it is one of Pinter's most dramatically conventional works. *The Collection* includes a group of characters in the upper middle class and, partly as a result of the class level and partly as a theatrical technique, the setting for the drama is among the most elaborate of all Pinter's plays. The stage is divided into three sections: a telephone booth and two living quarters. The division into three separate areas is important to the action and meaning of the play, since Bill and Stella must not be brought together (the phone booth provides a means for linking the two dwellings). The middle-class

1. Gussow, "A Conversation (Pause) with Harold Pinter," p. 126.

aspect affects the language, too, and Wellwarth notes that dialogue used like a boxing match really becomes pertinent for the first time, while Taylor points out that the educated, articulate characters are not *failing* to communicate.

The action of *The Collection* revolves around the theme of verification which Pinter has been exploring since *The Room*. In this case something happened or it did not happen, and four characters, Bill Lloyd, Harry Kane (a phallic image), and James and Stella Horne (the surname carrying a suggestion of cuckoldry), are involved in finding out or concealing the truth. As a means of exploring the theme of need in this play, Pinter has made the event in question one which has significance in the lives of the four people and their attachments to one another. Hinchcliffe contends that "what happened in the play is that two relationships that had rather fallen into habit . . . [are] jolted" because of the alleged events at Leeds. As a result of this jolt, "the two people in each [pairing] have . . . to rethink the basis for their relationships."[2] It is enough, however, merely to see that the relationships are unstable.

When James and Stella are seen for the first time it is obvious that they are not getting along well. James ignores his wife's questions and Stella slams out of the house. Pinter judiciously switches locales to demonstrate the premise explicitly, and a series of events quickly establishes that the relationship between Harry and his younger companion, Bill, is strained, too, starting when Harry comes down to breakfast, complaining that Bill has not fixed a stair rod as promised—or at least he "didn't fix it very well." Harry is also displeased that Bill has left a glass of fruit juice on a tray, rather than placing it in front of his roommate. Besides displaying disgust over such minor incidents, when Bill says that he is going to see a film the older man sarcastically observes, "Wonderful life you lead." Almost casually, Harry informs Bill that "some maniac" telephoned at four o'clock the night before and wants to know who it was. When Bill states that he has no idea who it might have been, Harry demands to know if he met anyone on his trip the week before. Bill denies meeting anyone.[3]

Apparently relationships within the two pairings have not been completely satisfying, and the action in the drama results from the dissatisfaction of two of the characters. Later evidence will support the assumption that the relationships are in fact still in the process of deteriorating. What happens in the play grows out of a need for love as the four people attempt to protect, solidify, or simply redefine the bonds between themselves and their partners.

Physical menace similar to that found in the "comedies of menace" is introduced when James visits Bill. Nevertheless, it is soon evident that this type of menace is of only secondary importance to the people in the drama. Although neither man recognizes the other, James knows that he wants to talk

2. Hinchcliffe, *Harold Pinter*, p. 117.
3. Pinter, *The Collection*, in *Three Plays* (New York: Grove, 1962), pp. 45, 46.

to Bill Lloyd and forces his way into the room. The element of fear, of a threat existing for an unknown reason, is present now and will be for the remainder of the play, but it never becomes the focus of the author's attention. It can be dismissed because Pinter expresses it only in a humorous context in the drama and does not develop it to the extent he did in *The Birthday Party*, where physical menace caused a breakdown. Instead he focuses on the mental aspect: the menace stems from a fear of being deprived of the emotional affinity the characters in *The Collection* require. The comic is stressed in the absurd dialogue which develops when James asks Bill if he has any olives, as soon as he comes through the door, and then takes a grape out of a bowl of fruit and asks where he should put the pips. When Bill answers, "In your wallet," James takes out his wallet and puts the seeds into it. He then asks Bill if he had a "good time in Leeds last week." Bill expresses ignorance of what the intruder is talking about, so James explains:

JAMES [*with fatigue*]. Aaah. You [went] down there for the dress collection. . . .
BILL. Did I?
JAMES. You stayed at the Westbury Hotel. . . . you had your yellow pyjamas with you.

   . . .

BILL. What was I doing there?
JAMES [*casually*]. My wife was in there. That's where you slept with her.
   Silence.
BILL. Well . . . who told you that?
JAMES. She did.

   . . .

BILL. Mmmm? Who is your wife? [p. 53].

    As evidenced at its production in such varied locales as the Century Playhouse in Los Angeles in 1968 and the Ateneo in San Juan in 1972, the audience's reaction to James' relevations and Bill's responses is a mixture of being offended and amused. Bill would normally be condemned by society for his activities, but the accusation has been in an offhand manner. The immediate implication is that James attaches little importance to the event. And Bill's reactions in no way lessen the viewer's difficulty in determining the truth about what actually happened. This, of course, is one of Pinter's main purposes. When asked to verify whether an affair actually did take place, he has replied, "I am not mystified. . . . When an event occurs—some kind of sexual event in *The Collection*, for example—it is made up of many little events. Each person will take away and remember what is most significant to him. The more other people try to verify, the less they know."[4] This play is a practical demonstration of Pinter's philosophy.

    4. Quoted in Gordon, *Stratagems*, p. 52.

To the abrupt and stunning accusation, Bill defensively replies that he "was nowhere near Leeds last week. . . . Nowhere near your wife either. . . . Apart from that, I . . . just don't do such things. Not in my book" (p. 54). Because of the homosexual implications evolved throughout the play, this statement, "Not in my book," is possibly fact and certainly funny in retrospect. While there are no overt proofs of homosexuality in the play, critics like Esslin, Hinchcliffe, and Gordon assume that its existence is so obvious that they discuss it in their studies, yet feel no need to include evidence of its existence. Some actions which support the contention that homosexuality is present in the play include Harry's jealousy of James, which is evident throughout, and Bill's overt attempts to please James, as when he supplies the olives. There is also Bill's admission that relations with women are not in his "book"; such things have no appeal for him. Then there is the humor of Bill's flippant replies to James' serious charge. Finally, James tells his wife that he has gained a new perspective on life because of his meeting with Bill, and by the end of the play he "can see it both ways, three ways, all ways" (p. 66). James insinuates his recognition of Bill's homosexuality when he tells Stella that their mutual friend reminds him of Hawkins, an acquaintance from his school days. Like Hawkins, Bill is an opera buff and has many friends among the performers. Since James reveals that he is a secret opera fan, he may be admitting his own latent homosexuality, though because nothing develops along this line, he is probably just using the suggestion as a threat.

Violence and terror emerge when James makes a sudden move toward his host and Bill falls over backwards as he starts away from the attack. Lying on the floor, with James standing threateningly over him, Bill makes a confession, the second version of what "really" happened in Leeds: "The truth . . . is that it never happened . . . what you said, anyway. I didn't know she was married . . . you were right, actually, about going up in the lift . . . we . . . got out of the lift, and then suddenly she was in my arms. Really wasn't my fault, nothing further from my mind. . . . Anyway, we just kissed a bit. . . . The rest of it just didn't happen. I mean, I wouldn't do that sort of thing . . . it's just meaningless" (pp. 58–59). It is clear at this point that some, if not all, of the characters will be exposed to some sort of menace and that it is related to the theme of need in some way (James' attack is instigated because his love has been placed in jeopardy, and Bill is a victim, accused of having been the source of peril), but the direction the play will follow has yet to be set.

The meaning of *The Collection* begins to become clear when Harry and Bill have a confrontation in which Harry is upset by the fact that someone has been calling on Bill. Harry's fictionalized account of James' first visit tries to get to the truth in a bantering manner that masks a concern which becomes more evident later. At first he jokes about Bill's caller from a "national survey" who had "lemon hair, nigger brown teeth, [a] wooden leg, bottlegreen eyes and a toupee" who "stood on the top step stark naked . . . [with] a

waterbottle under his arm instead of a hat" (pp. 62, 63). The importance of
the event is revealed seconds afterward when Harry abandons his jocular pose
and demands, "Who is this man and what does he want?" The account also
differs markedly from what the audience knows really happened. This may
be a clue to the general plot of the drama. Harry is using his imagination in
an attempt to clarify his association with Bill, just as all the other characters
are attempting to stabilize personal standings in their respective pairings.

In the living room on the other side of the set the other couple also discuss James' visit as they, too, try to verify the conditions of their relationship.
James announces that he has come to a decision; he intends to go see his wife's
lover. Stella claims that there is no need to, that he was of no importance.
James incidentally mentions that he merely wants to see if the fellow has
changed since they last saw each other, to which Stella reacts in an interesting
progression of thoughts: "You've never seen him. *Pause.* You don't know him.
Pause. You don't know where he lives. *Pause.* When did you see him?" (p.
65). The movement from denial of possibility through partial acceptance, to
a final acknowledgment, all without any prompting on her husband's part,
is characteristic of the thinking of Pinter characters, for it develops on a line
of logic which defines itself as it progresses. It has no referents outside itself,
yet is internally consistent in alternating implied premises with those actually
stated. In essence, the omitted premises contradict those stated: when Stella
says that James does not know Bill, her next step is to concede that they are
acquainted but to deny that he knows where Bill lives. The middle step is ignored. In other words, Stella's movement from denial to acceptance is not as
startling as it may at first seem, for she convinces herself through a series of
small steps, each one dependent on the thought which immediately preceded
it—she simply does not voice each step. The movement in many of Pinter's
plays follows a similar line in that the conclusion appears absurd, yet given
the premises present at the beginning of the play, one arrives at the end
through a progression of steps which follow from what went before and prepare for what is to come. No one step is especially illogical, but the cumulative
effect is that of absurdity (*The Homecoming* being a prime example of this
effect in action).

When Harry meets Stella, he asks if she knows Bill Lloyd personally. She
says no, so Harry tells her that Mr. Horne has been bothering Bill of late with
a fantastic story. Stella is apologetic and after explaining that they have been
happily married for two years offers a third version of events at Leeds: "My
husband has suddenly dreamed up such a fantastic story, for no reason at all,"
something she attributes to the fact that "he's just not been very well lately,
actually . . . overwork" (p. 71).

James' second visit with Bill brings things to a head. Bill brings out some
cheese, commenting on his "splendid" cheese knife, but assuring James that
it will not cut him if he handles it properly. The two men talk about the affair

at Leeds and Bill philosophizes on the nature of women. James picks up a fruit knife and challenges Bill to a mock duel—"First one who's touched is a sissy." During the ensuing action Bill is cut. James remarks, "Now you've got a scar on your hand. You didn't have one before, did you?" a reference to their first confrontation in which Bill claimed innocence because there were no scratches on his body. Harry, who had returned earlier in the scene but remained unnoticed in the hall, observing and not interrupting, enters and begins speaking as if nothing out of the ordinary has happened. His reactions to an attack on his roommate are so out of place that they are funny: "What have you done, nipped your hand? Let's have a look. [*To* JAMES] Only a little nip isn't it? It's his own fault for not ducking. I must have told him dozens of times, you know, that if someone throws a knife at you the silliest thing you can do is to catch it." After proposing an ironic toast, "Healthy minds in healthy bodies," Harry mentions that he has recently met Stella and that she provided him with what is in essence a fourth version of the Leeds incident— she "made a little tiny confession. . . . What she confessed was . . . that she'd made the whole thing up." Bill agrees that it was pure fantasy and that he would not know the woman if he saw her. To James' comment that it was strange that he confirmed her whole story, Bill responds, "You amused me. You wanted me to confirm it. It amused me to do so" (pp. 76–77).

As is typical in Pinter, imagery based on filth is related to the underlying meaning of the play when Bill's attitude prompts Harry to expand a statement he made to Mrs. Horne earlier, in the strongest imagery in the drama, concerning his protégé's origin: "Bill's a slum boy, you see, he's got a slum sense of humour. . . . I have nothing against slum minds per se. . . . There's a certain kind of slum mind which is perfectly all right in a slum, but when this kind of slum mind gets out of the slum it sometimes persists . . . it rots everything. That's what Bill is. There's something faintly putrid about him . . . he's a slum slug . . . he crawls all over the walls of nice houses, leaving slime. . . . He confirms stupid sordid little stories just to amuse himself. . . . All he can do is sit and suck his bloody hand and decompose like the filthy putrid slum slug he is" (pp. 77–78). Harry sees James as a rival for Bill's attentions as much as Stella because Bill procured the olives, set up a cheese tray, and admits that he did something merely to please the other man. Jealous of his roommate, Harry resorts to name-calling. If something (Bill's affection) cannot be obtained, then it is a good idea to degrade its value so that the impending loss is less severe. At the same time Harry is possessively warning James about Bill's ingratitude and his base character in order to discourage James' interest.

James expresses great relief at finding out the full truth of the matter and, using the same words Stella used earlier, excuses his wife's actions with the conventional, "My wife's not been very well lately, actually. Overwork" (p. 78). Bill, however, unexpectedly brings everything which has just been verified into question again with a fifth version of the story: "I never touched her

. . . we sat . . . in the lounge, on a sofa . . . for two hours . . . we talked about it . . . we didn't . . . move from the lounge . . . just talked . . . about what we would do . . . if we did get to her room" (p. 79).

James leaves the house as Harry and Bill remain silently seated. The lights in the house fade to half-light. When James returns home, apparently believing Bill's tale, he tells Stella that he knows that nothing happened—they simply sat and talked. When he asks, "That's the truth . . . isn't it?" Stella looks at him with a Mona Lisa smile, *"neither confirming nor denying. Her face is friendly, sympathetic"* (p. 80).

According to Pinter's comments on verification and the nature of reality, an interesting but probably irrelevant question is which version of the events that took place at Leeds is true. As mentioned previously, Pinter feels that any single event is a composite of many small events and each individual's perceptions will be determined by what is most relevant to himself personally. For example, Harry's version of the meeting is a distortion of Stella's tale, created in an effort to preserve his affinity with Bill. And this may be the key to the play. It is conceivable that *The Collection* is a demonstration of the problems involved in verification which the author has been exploring since *The Room*. The point of the play, then, could be seen as an attempt to expose the tenuousness of relationships because of the inability of the participants to verify those things which constitute the basis of their relationship—i.e., security in their emotional attachments.

Bill's last version is probably closest to the truth in that the facts and reactions throughout the drama most consistently support it. If they talked and Stella, because of her dissatisfaction with the conditions of her marriage, exaggerated in her account of the encounter, we could easily arrive at James' version. Given that version, Bill's reaction is natural, for he is scared and trying to hurt his tormentor, so he tries to shift the blame, claiming simultaneously that the incident was Stella's fault and that it was a product of her imagination. When Harry presents his version, we cannot be sure whether Stella told him, a stranger, anything, and if so we have no assurance that she told him the truth—Harry is simply trying to protect his own interests by taking the easy way out. Bill's final "truth" has been attributed to the stinging humiliation of Harry's "slum" speech,[5] but the version he presents certainly need not bear out this contention. There really is no reason at this point for him to say anything further, unless it is the truth. After we have made the full round through the several possible explanations, this seems to be the only alternative left, and Bill, relieved that the uncomfortable episode is about to end, tells the truth in a gesture of release, to clear the air. It also gives him the last laugh in what started out as an innocent joke, for the story the two men are complacently accepting because it best suits *their* needs is challenged. Harry is once more put on the defensive, since all preceding versions are made

5. Hinchcliffe, *Harold Pinter*, p. 116.

questionable by Bill's confession; the implication is that the present answer may become suspect in the future. Bill, therefore, gains the upper hand in a relationship which has not fully pleased him up to now.

Esslin is of the opinion that the stage version which has Stella visible throughout the proceedings makes her "the true tragic heroine of the piece,"[6] as she is left alone to fondle her white Persian kitten while the men actively form relationships on the other side of the set. This does not take into account, though, that Stella's reaction makes sense too, if Bill's final version is true, for it is evident through the course of the drama that her marriage lacks something. As she admitted earlier, James has been very busy, and perhaps he has not been paying her the attention she desires. She, like Bill, has a better chance of gaining the upper hand in her marriage by keeping her husband unsure—he will no longer take her for granted and thus will provide the attention that she requires. At the end of the play her position has been strengthened in comparison to what it was when the drama opened. We are first exposed to Stella in the role of a wife unsure of a husband over whom she has no control. He does not answer her questions and generally ignores her presence. Not even sure that he will be in that night, the ineffectual Stella can only slam out of the house in frustration. The situation is reversed when the final curtain falls, for now it is James who is unsure of his partner, asking her questions to which he receives no answer. He has been placed in the position of trying to save a marriage which just a few hours before he had merely been accepting. He has been put on the defensive. This entire maneuver is an example of what Eric Berne has called the "Let's You and Him Fight" ploy. Berne claims that the psychology involved is "essentially feminine." "As a maneuver it is romantic. The woman maneuvers or challenges two men into fighting, with the implication or promise that she will surrender herself to the winner. After the competition is decided, she fulfills her bargain. This is an honest transaction, and the presumption is that she and her mate live happily ever after."[7] Pinter uses this dramatic formula again in *The Basement* (1967). How happy James and Stella will be is debatable, but the smile as the play ends indicates that Stella is prepared to live "happily ever after" in the relationship as it now exists.

It may be argued that the sequence of events portrayed in *The Collection* serves to weaken rather than strengthen the bonds between the members of the two couples. After all, the tenuousness of such bonds has certainly been proved, and all four characters are now clearly aware of the possibilities of a change in partners. It might even be suggested that sexual identities may be an issue of verification and that Harry's jealousy of James is well founded, for James has become conscious of the fact that there is potential fulfillment outside his marriage. Gordon goes so far as to claim that James may have in-

6. Esslin, *The Peopled Wound*, p. 131.
7. Eric Berne, *Games People Play* (New York: 1964), p. 124.

stigated the whole chain of events by fabricating the initial charge because of a homosexual interest in Bill,[8] but there seems to be no evidence to support this contention in the drama (James was not even sure of Bill's identity when they first met). James may in fact become aware of this alternate possibility —he thanks Stella for having "opened up a whole new world" for him (p. 67)— but there can be no doubt that he rejects it in favor of returning to his wife: there is never an explicit mention or any other overt sign of any sexual relationship between James and Bill; James convincingly turns on Bill; and he goes back to Stella. More important, perhaps, than the simple fact that the husband returns home at the end of the play is his attitude toward his wife. It is obvious that she is important to him, for, as demonstrated by his uncertainty, he is returning because he wants her and he is still afraid that he might lose her.

The stress of the play seems to be on the difficulty of verification which can lead to an awareness of the possibility of change. The realization that the potential for change exists may weaken the relationships because the partners can no longer be sure of each other. It may, conversely, strengthen the relationships, because the partners will strive to protect their ties, having seen how fragile they are. Or it may not alter them appreciably either way, if Pinter is simply exploring another instance of the problems inherent in the desire for verification. It is impossible to tell what the ultimate outcome might be, the seeds of doubt having been planted; but as *The Collection* ends, the two couples have been reunited in efforts to retain their relationships. In terms of the play, the truth of what happened at Leeds is not significant. Verification means that one version may be true, or any combination of versions. On the order of Pirandello's *Right You Are (If You Think You Are)* or the Japanese tale *Rashomon*, what is important is how and why people react to what they consider the truth.

The Collection is the first of Pinter's plays which deals with sex specifically as a subject. Many of his previous works included sex as an incidental ingredient. In *A Slight Ache* there is a suggestion that Edward is unable to satisfy his wife's desires, some of which are at least partially sexual in nature. The homosexuality in *The Collection* is an extension of that suggested in *The Dwarfs*. From Rose in *The Room* on, Pinter implies that women are almost always either whores or adulteresses. With Rose there is a hint of prostitution. In *The Birthday Party* Meg's relations with Stanley are suspect and Lulu is promiscuous. In *A Slight Ache* Flora opts for the matchseller in place of her husband. Albert in *A Night Out* pays a visit to a streetwalker's room after his misadventures with the firm's girls. The schoolteacher Sally leads a double life as Katina in *Night School*. Since this is the way women are presented, it comes as no surprise that Stella may have strayed. While sex was a minor ele-

8. Gordon, *Stratagems*, p. 52.

ment in the preceding dramas, in *The Collection* the author uses the subject metaphorically for expressing his observations.

The title of the play may refer to the dress collections taken to Leeds which serve as the immediate cause that stimulates the plot, to the collection of human relationships, or, as proposed by Hinchcliffe,[9] to the fragility of human relationships, sexual or otherwise, represented by the Chinese vases. With the circular relationships (the eternal triangle, infidelity, and jealous lovers) which are traditionally present in stage comedies as a background, Pinter has continued to comment on his usual topics from a fresh viewpoint with more sustained humor than heretofore. He has enlarged his study of people in which need is emerging as a motive force. Now he begins to look at some of the ways they might attempt to satisfy their psychological demands.

The Lover

The Lover was first presented by Associated Rediffusion Television in London on March 28, 1963, and subsequently staged at the Arts Theatre on September 18 of the same year, Harold Pinter directing the production. Like *The Collection*, it also appears to be an amusing comedy at first glance. It is, on the surface, the battle of the sexes waged by two urbane, witty people, another modern comedy of manners. The tragic situation underlying soon becomes apparent in spite of the frivolous tone which carries through most of the play from the opening scene—a situation incorporating identity and verification problems, the difficulties in communication which grow out of and simultaneously reinforce those problems, and the emotional requirements which are the basic stimulus of the action.

The Lover continues Pinter's examination of people seeking fulfillment. Sexual adjustment is part of the issue in this play, as the author combines in one couple the ideas of fidelity versus infidelity: wife versus mistress (or whore), husband versus lover. Where the characters in *The Collection* are dissatisfied with the conditions of their relationships, however, the characters in *The Lover* are disturbed by the ideas which underlie their relationship, for those ideas (the refinement in marriage and sexual attraction) seem to be mutually exclusive in the minds of both husband and wife. As in *The Collection* before it, a good deal of the humor in *The Lover* depends on bizarre or absurd situations which grow out of a lack of psychological equilibrium.

Again following the line of *The Collection*, an implication of things not being satisfactory in a relationship is set with the first words spoken in *The Lover*: "RICHARD (*amiably*). Is your lover coming today?"[10] Again, the in-

9. Hinchcliffe, *Harold Pinter*, p. 116.
10. Pinter, *The Lover*, in *The Lover, Tea Party, The Basement* (New York: Grove, 1967), p. 5.

ference is that there is something amiss in the marriage. Since neither husband nor wife seems distressed by what would normally be an intolerable situation, the implication is that the normal marriage relationship is distorted. And, as in the earlier play, it will become clear that this situation exists because the couple has failed to fulfill each other's needs in a conventional fashion.

In *The Collection* the existence of unsatisfactory associations creates a menace tentatively connected with need, but the exact form the threat will take is not developed immediately. In *The Lover* an uneasy marriage partnership is advanced, too, but the drama develops along a different course: psychological need is apparent from the outset. The shock of the first scene is intensified when Richard returns, for everything is still inexplicably quite pleasant. The conversation moves to the lover's visit and how Sarah entertained him: "RICHARD. Pleasant afternoon? . . . Your lover came, did he? . . . Did you show him the hollyhocks?" (p. 7). Sarah remains at ease throughout. Richard's attention is drawn to the Venetian blinds, which are crooked, a malfunctioning mechanism serving as a reflection of a physical universe in which objects do not fulfill their customary roles, in much the same way this husband/wife combination has broken down. There follows an inane exchange between the two concerning the weather. The picture of an essentially typical suburban household begins to evolve from these meaningless observations and comments, but Richard initiates the chain of events which will lead to the dissolution of their present relationship. He starts to ask questions:

RICHARD. Does it ever occur to you that while you're spending the afternoon being unfaithful to me I'm sitting at a desk going through balance sheets and graphs?
SARAH. What a funny question.
RICHARD. No, I'm curious.
SARAH. You've never asked me that before.
RICHARD. I've always wanted to know [p. 9].

A beginning of questioning can upset the balance of the established order; once the questions are asked, things may be irrevocably altered, a new direction is set, and nothing can reverse the process of change. Gus in *The Dumb Waiter* made the mistake of questioning, for example, and ended up in front of his companion's gun.

Sarah's answer provides the first key to the meaning of the play: "Well, of course it occurs to me. . . . It makes it all the more piquant." The play on specific words is especially important throughout this drama, and the following exchange demonstrates the stress created by Sarah's separation of respectability and sex which constitutes the fundamental conflict in the work:

SARAH. How could I forget you?
RICHARD. Quite easily, I should think.

SARAH. But I'm in your house.
RICHARD. With another.
SARAH. But it's you I love [p. 10].

Talking around their subject, ignoring each other's questions, but interspersing comments directly related to the subject is a form of communication for this couple, and each understands what the other is expressing or leaving unexpressed. Richard's admission concerning a mistress indicates the game-playing aspect of their talk as he quibbles over words, but again the words are important indicators of what lies below the surface of the game: "But I haven't got a mistress. I'm very well acquainted with a whore, but I haven't got a mistress. There's a world of difference" (p. 11).

Although he never defines a mistress, the depiction of Richard's whore clearly indicates a linking of sex with man's animal nature (as opposed to a spiritual experience), made explicit by his imagery, and contrasts vividly with the qualities used to describe the type of woman who appeals to him, the type that he will marry. A whore is "a functionary who either pleases or displeases," someone who can "express and engender lust." Where a whore is "cunning," a wife is a person of "grace," "elegance," and "wit" whom one can "respect," "admire," and "love," and who provides a marriage with "dignity" and "sensibility" (pp. 12–13). Readily admitting things Sarah has never asked about so bluntly before, Richard is free and open in delineation of his whore, for he advocates "frankness at all costs" as being "essential to a healthy marriage," a funny statement in the context. Implying that sex is apart from normal married life, Richard answers his wife's objections that the whore cannot be as bad as her husband claims by ironically noting, "You can't sensibly inquire whether a whore is witty. It's of no significance whether she is or she isn't. She's . . . a functionary" (p. 12).

The distinction between wife and whore is further explored in Richard's next speech when his use of words contrasts with the harsh "whore" and "functionary" just mentioned: "I wasn't looking for a woman I could respect, as you, whom I could admire and love. . . . All I wanted was . . . someone who could express and engender lust with all lust's cunning" (p. 13). Indicating that there is a separation between respectable "love" and sexual desire, the speech further explains the characters' actions. The requirements for a marriage partner are so different from those which qualify a woman as a sexual object that they cannot exist simultaneously in one person. The defining of the two individuals and their relationship continues:

SARAH. I'm sorry your affair possesses so little dignity.
RICHARD. The dignity is in my marriage.
SARAH. Or sensibility.
RICHARD. The sensibility likewise. I wasn't looking for such attributes. I find them in you [p. 13].

The words the couple use to discuss sex and marriage emphasize the dichotomy which exists in their minds and the amount of emotion with which they view that dichotomy. Grace, elegance, and wit in a woman and respect, admiration, love, dignity, and sensibility in marriage are opposed to lustful pleasure in the minds of both man and wife. The actions of the couple show that Richard and Sarah are two people who love each other and need each other's love, yet find it impossible to reconcile their sexual wants with their emotional requirements, so their relationship is menaced when the two forces come into conflict. At the same time their requirements for an attachment and emotional involvement demand that they preserve that relationship. The result is a series of "games in the play [which] are elaborate and ritualistic . . . they separate the respectable husband-wife relationship from the more passionate lover-mistress relationship."[11]

The wife/whore duality and the resultant game playing of *The Collection* are occurring again in *The Lover*. The basic idea upon which Pinter built *The Lover* is graphically developed by casting Sarah in the role of both wife and whore. Whereas she was obviously a housewife in the opening segments of the play, she is shown in a different setting later. The first indication that role playing and exchanging is involved comes when Richard notices that Sarah is wearing "unfamiliar" high-heeled shoes and asks her about them. She mutters, "Mistake. Sorry," and goes into the hall, where she puts the high-heeled shoes into a cupboard and puts on a low-heeled pair. "Apparel oft proclaims the man," and Sarah's shoes are a distinguishing mark; they serve as a uniform. At a later date she is discovered wearing a *"very tight, low-cut black dress"* (p. 18). The wife/whore idea again is brought home when she suddenly notices that she has on her low-heeled shoes and hurries to the cupboard to change into her high heels. She sits on the chaise longue, where she goes through a number of poses in rehearsal of the position she will assume upon her lover's arrival. The doorbell rings. It is the milkman wanting to know if she would like some cream (possibly a sexual allusion). The effect of this break in the growing suspense is on the order of the knocking at the gate in *Macbeth* or Lulu's entrance in *The Birthday Party* and provides much the same kind of relief from tension while intensifying the audience's reaction to the next event which takes place. The doorbell rings again and Sarah familiarly greets the man standing without—"Hallo, Max"—but it is Richard who enters (p. 19). As he comes into the room, however, there are some immediately noticeable changes from the Richard who left earlier. The clothing, actions, and words throughout the scene in which Richard is present as Max combine to create a figure more masculine, harsher, more vulgar and coarse, more vital and animalistic than Richard as Richard. Sarah's actions have undergone a transformation too. She seductively postures before her lover, who takes bongo drums from the hall cupboard. While he taps on the drums, she

11. Hinchcliffe, *Harold Pinter*, p. 122.

scratches the back of his hand and the game period has begun. (Stanley in *The Birthday Party* also uses a drum to signal an emotional contest and a new tempo.) The free use of new names (Max, Dolores, Mary) and rapidly switching roles are serious and frighteningly significant to the meaning of the drama, but the fast rhythm of changes, culminating with a gradual sinking into an emotional quicksand, produces a hilarious effect.

Max, however, is still an unsettling influence as he continues the attack on their relationship which began with Richard's questions. Max's insistence that he has played his last game is met by Sarah's seductive attempt to get her lover to play another game; it was teatime before, now she wants it to be "whispering time" (a phrase she will repeat later) and for him to love her. She has expressed the underlying conflict earlier: "You don't really think you could have what we have with your wife, do you?" The divorce of sex from marriage is implied. When Max asks how her husband bears it, she replies, "He's happy for me. He appreciates the way I am. He understands" (p. 26). The distinction between Sarah's conceptions is clear by now—a husband supplies understanding and the "respectable" elements of marriage, a lover provides sexual release. Richard's earlier differentiation between a wife and a mistress was essentially the same. As a lover, though, his reaction is amusingly ridiculous. He denies her, claiming, "You're too bony" (p. 28).

When Richard returns as Richard, he has made an irrevocable decision while caught in a mundane traffic jam: her "debauchery," her "life of depravity," and "path of illegitimate lust" have to stop. He forbids her to entertain her lover on the premises ever again: "Perhaps you would give him my compliments, by letter if you like, and ask him to cease his visits (*He consults calendar.*)—the twelfth inst." (p. 34). Sarah is taken aback by Richard's insistence, for they have been married ten years, have engaged in the masquerade almost from the beginning ("I didn't take my lover ten years ago. Not quite. Not on the honeymoon," p. 34) with no previous reluctance on his part. The picture of a young bride who was unable to reconcile her idealized vision of marriage and her sexual desires and a husband who tried to help her is now complete. The background of what preceded the play having been furnished, the reason for the game playing becomes comprehensible.

Richard is no longer satisfied with the game which has trapped them, for they are no longer in control; they are controlled by the game itself. In an attempt to bring them to a face-to-face confrontation with reality he is trying to destroy the game while staying within its context; i.e., he refuses to admit that they have been playing dual roles. As the outraged husband, he tells his wife to "Take [Max] out into the fields. . . . Find a rubbish dump. . . . Buy a canoe and find a stagnant pond" (p. 35). Aside from the images, reversal makes this discourse amusing; it would have been acceptable earlier in the play, before the audience was aware of the facts, but now it is ironically humorous. With "*quiet anguish*" Sarah recognizes what is happening, and sounding like Martha when George takes their son from her in Edward Albee's *Who's Afraid of Virginia Woolf?*, tries to dissuade him by reminding him of the mutual consent involved: "You've no right to question me. . . . It was our arrangement" (p. 37). When Richard's course cannot be altered, Sarah strikes out, trying to hurt him by extending her fantasy and claiming that she lavishly entertains other callers when he is not at home (her not inviting the milkman back may contradict this).

Whether Richard concedes that he cannot change Sarah or whether he himself cannot give up the game is not clear, but he shifts from inquisitor to playmaker when he stops asking how the drum is used during her illicit afternoons and initiates the "Got a light?" procedure. Sarah is startled and rebels at first: the game is being played in the wrong circumstances. Richard continues to develop the "you're trapped" theme, and she soon falls in line with the appropriate responses: "I'm trapped. . . . You've no right to treat a married woman like this. . . . But my husband will understand" (p. 39). When she says, "I've never seen you before after sunset," it is apparent that they are creating a new situation, one which will allow them to continue—and will add a new stimulus to their relationship. The basis for their problem still exists, however, for they have treated the symptom and not the disease; they are concerned with an anodyne to relieve their suffering as opposed to finding a cure for what is causing the pain. That the couple is where they were at the beginning, still unable to reconcile the conflict, is demonstrated by Sarah's need to change her uniform and Richard's need to have her do so as the play ends:

SARAH. Would you like me to change? . . . I'll change for you, darling. Shall I?. . .
RICHARD. Yes. . . . Change your clothes. . . . You lovely whore [p. 40].

The last word in the play is indicative of the problem Pinter is exploring in *The Lover*, because in order to relate to his wife sexually Richard must see her in a nonrespectable framework. It is clear throughout the drama that Richard and Sarah enforce a distinction between marriage and sex. This is brought out in their dress (Richard and Sarah wear clothes which are "sober" and "demure" in contrast to the suede jacket and low-cut dress of Max and Dolores), their speech (the wife versus whore debate), and their general actions toward one another (a sedate couple as opposed to the game players). Wellwarth claims that the couple indulges in "their sadistic fantasies . . . in order to achieve sexual potency,"[12] and indeed the games do serve as a sort of foreplay, but they are more significant than simply that. Sarah "looked first" (p. 13), taking her lover shortly after her honeymoon because he symbolically represented a reconciliation between her distortion of puritan morali-

12. Wellwarth, *Theatre of Protest* (1971), p. 238.

ty, which conceived of sex as something not to be indulged in for enjoyment, and her natural biological urges. A wife is someone to be proud of for her social graces; a woman who provides sexual satisfaction is a whore who "pleases" "between trains." As a matter of verification (in this case personal identity) it is vital that the two aspects of her life—marriage and sex—be kept separate and carefully labeled. Like Sally in *Night School*, she has segregated the two segments. Thus the differences between her roles are stressed by the way in which Richard treats her—according to the role she is playing at the time. Bamber Gascoigne of the *Observer* sees *The Lover* as "an expressionistic drama about a young couple who can't reconcile their respectable idea of marriage with the violent ritual of their sexual passions. So they keep sex in a separate compartment."[13] This idea is epitomized by Sarah's statements to the effect that one who suggests sexual activity has "no right to treat a married woman like this" (p. 39) when she is confronted by Max. Since Sarah's problem will not allow this married couple to accept sex as a part of marriage, it forces them to mask themselves as sexual participants almost as if they were taking part in a pornographic movie and consequently making sex something outside of marriage. Lust is opposed to respectability or refinement, is expressed as near rape or seduction (force as opposed to overt acceptance), and is therefore acceptable as being undesired or even unavoidable and thus a venial sin. Passion and respectability are thereby reconciled and everything is all right, as indicated by Sarah's constant refrain that her husband "understands."

Although Gordon rates *The Lover* as Pinter's "least interesting play" because the dramatist oversimplifies and spells out too explicitly his theme of the "multiple aspects of personality,"[14] most critics agree more with Wellwarth that the drama is "one of the most brilliant plays to appear in the English language since the end of the war" in its presentation of a "series of interlocking semisadistic fantasy scenes"[15] after the fashion of Genet's *The Balcony*. Other interpretations include Kerr's description of the schizophrenic behavior of Richard and Sarah in their country home somewhere near Windsor as an "existential playfulness" which bears out the existence-precedes-essence maxim in demonstrating that "personality is not something given; it is fluid," for Sarah is proof that "no woman is essentially wife or essentially whore, she is potentially either or both at once."[16] The shifting identities seem to be proof of the statement in *The Dwarfs* that people are a "sum of so many reflections," or, as Taylor says in noting that *The Lover* surpasses Osborne's *Under Plain Cover*, the play shows "human nature in its irrevocably fragmented form."[17] Esslin sees the actions of the husband and wife as erotic

13. Recorded in Hinchcliffe, *Harold Pinter*, p. 124.
14. Gordon, *Stratagems*, p. 52.
15. Wellwarth, *Theatre of Protest*, pp. 210–11.
16. Kerr, *Harold Pinter*, pp. 31–32.
17. Taylor, *Anger and After*, p. 350.

wish-fulfillment literally stated,[18] though Hinchcliffe feels that these games, which are "clearly defined by custom"[19] are remarkably significant beyond this point. It must be admitted that during the course of the piece the illusions are used not for escape but for preservation as the instinctive is opposed to the civilized.

The Lover shows what happens after the game has been established to the extent that one of the partners, Richard, realizes that he is losing his identity to the game and that instead of controlling it, it is controlling him. In effect the archetypal male finds himself intruding upon himself on his own territory, established by night versus day. Richard accepts defeat as the play concludes, rather than lose Sarah. Striving to protect their marriage in terms which will not threaten their integrity as individuals, Richard and Sarah create a new game out of the ashes of their old game. Gerald Berkowitz remarks that this is substantially the opposite conclusion of *The Room*, though the results are the same, for he sees that in *The Lover* "identities are ultimately destroyed, not by an outside force, but by the very relationship that was created to give them meaning."[20] The paradox is that the two people involved must play the game if they are to harmonize areas in their own natures, forcing reality to fit their theories, but in so doing they subordinate themselves to the identity of the game. The play is, then, the story of two people who psychologically need both the sexual and the refined or idealized aspects of marriage, but find them unreconcilable, so turn to a sort of psycho-drama which allows them to fulfill their need, a need so great that loss of personal identity is subordinate to it.

The Homecoming

The playwright's third full-length play—the two-act *The Homecoming*—is at the same time his most representative, his best, and his most important drama. It was first presented by the Royal Shakespeare Company at the Aldwych Theatre on June 3, 1965, where it ran for a year and a half, closing only to take the original cast to New York for the American premiere in 1967. There it won the New York Critics Antoinette Perry Award for Best Play of that year, also earning Pinter the Award for Best Playwright.

The final play of consequence in Pinter's second major period of writing, *The Homecoming* is less conventional and funnier than the first two because the characters are more desperate in their needs, closer to the "extreme edge of living," so that their actions are more exaggerated and even further from normal behavior. The characters have not reached the point where they have to protect viable relationships—they are still trying to create them.

Act I of *The Homecoming* opens with Lenny reading the racing section

18. Esslin, *The Theatre of the Absurd*, p. 250.
19. Hinchcliffe, *Harold Pinter*, p. 120.
20. Gerald Berkowitz, "Harold Pinter" (M. A. thesis Columbia Univ., 1965), p. 63.

of the newspaper. His father, Max, comes in and asks him a question, which the son ignores. When the old man persists, Lenny looks up quietly and answers, "Why don't you shut up, you daft prat?" provoking Max into lifting his walking stick and declaring, "Don't you talk to me like that. I'm warning you."[21] This is a pattern which will be repeated many times during the play as two characters spar with each other, calling names, showing no respect, threatening physical violence, but it is all done half-seriously, half-playfully, as though it were the only way the participants know of expressing affection for each other. As Gordon points out, "this is a game or ritual enacted daily to maintain the *status quo*."[22] Again, a condition parallel to that in *The Collection* and *The Lover* exists in the abnormal relationship which is displayed between father and son. The ritual itself may be normal, but in this family it pervades all actions to such an extent and with such intensity that it goes beyond the customary exchanges between father and sons or siblings.

Just as the element of menace in *The Collection* and *The Lover* develops because of the individual's needs, a picture of uneasiness simultaneously created and held in check by love comes from Lenny's treatment of his father in *The Homecoming*. Max reminisces about the past when he was a "tearaway" and could have taken care of his son "twice over." His powers have faded and, although he still rules the family, he maintains his tyrannical position as the old patriarch who rules a Freudian primal unit at least in part by common assent of the governed. The use of the diminutive form of the sons' names indicates the family's attitudes toward one another—the sons are still seen as children and their names are representative of their subordinate position in the family. Lenny's intelligence and Joey's physique are adequate to overthrow their father, but they lack the necessary ambition. The dialogue between father and son is revealing:

MAX. Mind you, [Jessie] wasn't such a bad woman. Even though it made me sick just to look at her rotten stinking face, she wasn't such a bad bitch. I gave her the best bleeding years of my life, anyway.
LENNY. Plug it, will you, you stupid sod, I'm trying to read the paper.
MAX. Listen! I'll chop your spine off, you talk to me like that! . . . Talking to your lousy filthy father like that! [p. 9].

First, Max contradicts himself and reveals his unflattering impression of women, which includes a reversal of a wife's customary complaint about wasting the best years of her life. Lenny displays no respect for his father, and instead of answering the image painted by the old man by standing up for his mother, he wants Max to be quiet because he is being bothered while trying to read the newspaper. Max's choice of words in describing himself keeps the tone of his exchange with Lenny amusing instead of serious. The two

21. Pinter, *The Homecoming* (New York: Grove, 1967), p. [7].
22. Gordon, *Stratagems*, p. 54.

men threaten, but they do not mean to call anyone's bluff; they tolerate each other. After all, Lenny continues to live in the house and his father allows him to remain. The intensity of the language used raises questions about this family unit, though, which by definition should be close. There is a serious game being played and the presence of potential crisis comes from the expression of the unconventional thoughts in an uncommon manner, but as in the preceding two dramas the emerging pattern of action implies that need is the essential element which defines the game, for it is specific needs which ultimately determine the characters' actions.

The meaning of *The Homecoming* is harder to decipher than that of either *The Collection* or *The Lover*. The plot is simple, inspired by a boyhood friend of Pinter's from Hackney who went to Canada to teach and get secretly married before returning home to surprise his family. In *The Homecoming* a philosophy professor returns to his London home after being away for six years, bringing with him a wife that the family has never been informed of. Once in the house the husband and wife confront the father, uncle, and two brothers who still live there, and the actions and reactions between the various members of the group eventually lead to the professor's returning to his job while the wife remains behind, ostensibly to help support her new family by becoming a prostitute.

A simple plot is no insurance that a play will be either realistic or easily understood, however, and John Normington (Sam in the original production) remembers that the first-night audience in Brighton when the play was on its pre-London tour actually shouted, "What nonsense! Oh, what rubbish!" while the actors were saying their lines and then stormed out without applauding.[23] Drama critics, too, have disagreed about what the play means. Gordon's concentration on homosexuality and Irving Wardle's contention[24] that a sense of territory is the main theme both seem to have a mistaken emphasis, just as Taylor's view of the play as a "battle between intellect and instinct"[25] and Esslin's view, that the drama is a "perfect fusion of extreme realism with the quality of an archetypal dream image of wish-fulfillment" revolving around an oedipal desire for sexual conquest of the mother (Jessie/Ruth) and embarrassment of the father (Max/Teddy), take into account only part of the "inexplicable motivations"[26] of the work. The actions are realistic and logical, given the despair of the characters. The principle of Occam's Razor should be applied, and only those potential interpretations which are valid for the work as a whole should be adopted.

23. Quoted in "An Actor's Approach: An Interview with John Normington," in Lahr, *Casebook*, p. 147.
24. See Wardle's "The Territorial Struggle," in Lahr, *Casebook*, pp. 37–44.
25. Taylor, *Anger and After*, p. 354.
26. Esslin, *The Peopled Wound*, pp. 156–57. This is also true of Esslin's needlessly limiting contention that the play deals with the underworld.

It is apparent that the casual acceptance of the abnormal is an integral part of *The Homecoming*, abnormality occasioned by the characters' sense of desperation. When Teddy and Ruth enter his boyhood home, Teddy assures his wife that she will be welcomed by the family because "They're very warm people, really. Very warm. They're my family" (p. 23). Yet his insistence "doth protest too much methinks." The meaning of the drama begins to unfold when Teddy and Lenny suddenly meet after Teddy's six-year absence and start a casual conversation, making no mention of the absence or return for some moments. The characters' actions in the play indicate an almost overpowering need for emotional attachment, yet they seem unable to admit this, as though they were embarrassed at being so weak that they are dependent upon others. Admittedly, on the surface the family's actions toward one another are not indicative of need, but this is part of what Pinter is trying to say in *The Homecoming*.

Because of difficulties in communication and the resultant frustrations, because of the emotional needs of the characters and their resultant vulnerability, affection is not expressed in a normal fashion. There is a series of minor details which, taken *in toto*, implies that the men are emotionally attached: most obviously they live together—first of all, Max could kick the others out, and secondly, Sam, Lenny, and Joey all work, so they probably could support themselves singly; a wall was torn down to provide a larger living room so that they could all get together freely; when they are together their questions show an interest in one another's jobs (pimping, driving) and hobbies (horses, boxing), though some of the discussions are satiric. They go to football matches together; they cook and do housework for the family unit; and there are affectionate games and bantering which are really attempts at communication. Individually there are further evidences that there is feeling between the members of the family. Max took the responsibility of raising his brothers when his father died, and after Jessie's death managed to hold things together fairly well—"I suffered the pain, I've still got the pangs," he complains. He has made sacrifices for his kin. He did enjoy his family too, though, as he says in his reminiscing about his sons as children, "What fun we used to have in the bath" (pp. 46–47). In Act II Lenny speaks of the family as a "unit" in which Teddy is "an integral part" to the extent that when the whole family sits in the backyard, "there's always an empty chair standing in the circle, which is in fact [Teddy's]" (p. 65). The circle emphasizes their unit. Most important, Teddy cares enough for his family that he does come home.

In spite of the avowed familial relationship, the two brothers, like fighters carefully testing each other in the opening round, amusingly discuss something which has been keeping Lenny awake instead of greeting each other with some acknowledgment that there has been a period of separation.

TEDDY. Hullo, Lenny.
LENNY. Hullo, Teddy.
    Pause.
TEDDY. I didn't hear you come down the stairs.
LENNY. I didn't.
    Pause.
    . . .
TEDDY. How are you?
LENNY. Well, just sleeping a bit restlessly, that's all. Tonight, anyway.
TEDDY. Bad dreams?
LENNY. No, I wouldn't say I was dreaming. It's not exactly a dream. It's just that something keeps waking me up. Some kind of tick.
TEDDY. A tick?
LENNY. Yes.
TEDDY. Well, what is it?
LENNY. I don't know.
    Pause.
TEDDY. Have you got a clock in your room? [p. 25].

This is just one of many instances in which characters react to an extraordinary situation as though it were perfectly natural. Lenny's meeting with his brother's wife is another example of characters' regarding an unusual occurrence as though there were nothing out of the ordinary taking place:

LENNY. Good evening.
RUTH. Morning, I think.
LENNY. You're right there.
    Pause.
    My name's Lenny. What's yours?
RUTH. Ruth.
    . . .
LENNY. Cold?
RUTH. No.
LENNY. It's been a wonderful summer, hasn't it? Remarkable.
    Pause.
    Would you like something? Refreshment of some kind? An aperitif, anything like that?
RUTH. No, thanks.
LENNY. I'm glad you said that. We haven't got a drink in the house. . . . You must be connected with my brother in some way [pp. 27–28].

Although Lenny finds a strange woman letting herself into his house and Ruth is confronted by a man she has never seen before, the two people react as though this were an everyday occurrence, nothing out of the ordinary.

The lovemaking scene in the final act, discussed later, is both shocking and hilarious. These scenes are useful in helping the audience determine the meaning of the play, for they expose the characters' desperateness in that they seem willing to agree to anything, no matter how unusual it may appear on the surface, in hopes that it may lead to solving their unhappy situations. They will and do play, whatever the game.

The first overt clue that *The Homecoming* is concerned with the theme of need comes at the end of Act I when Max welcomes his boy in a manner as extreme as his rejection had been: "Teddy, why don't we have a nice cuddle and kiss, eh? Like the old days?" Teddy agrees, and the first half of the play ends with the two men facing each other, Max happily exclaiming, "He still loves his father!" (p. 44), and lines of affection have been tentatively reestablished. Max's initial reaction to the return of his eldest son can be explained as anger at Teddy's having left in the first place. After all, Max had undergone elaborately described self-sacrifices in order to keep his family together, only to have Teddy fail in his duty as a son when he deserted them. It is ironic that Max initially attacks Teddy by calling Ruth a "tart," a "scrubber," and a "stinking pox-ridden slut," for he has admitted to having a gift with animals, being able to "smell" a good filly. His instinctual reaction is revived when he later figures she can help "scrub the place out a bit"—but does not realize that "she'll do the dirty on us" until he smells it again moments before the final curtain falls (pp. 41, 81).

The effects of need are exposed in different ways with the various characters. Sam is tied to his brother's late wife. Notwithstanding the fact that he knows that she was unfaithful, he acknowledges that there is no other woman in the world who could compare favorably with her (one is reminded of the type of woman commonly portrayed by Pinter). Sam, a "wet wick," has little to recommend him, and just as Teddy retreats from a lack of success by denying the value of success, Sam retreats from any intimate contact with women by adhering to an idealized figure of Jessie. Being dead, she cannot test his devotion or ability as a live woman might.

Lenny's Walter Mittyish flights into fancy concerning women display his lack of emotional equilibrium. One of these ladies made "a certain proposal . . . this proposal wasn't entirely out of order and normally I would have subscribed to it. . . . The only trouble was she was falling apart with the pox . . . this lady was very insistent and started taking liberties . . . which by any criterion I couldn't be expected to tolerate, the facts being what they were, so I clumped her one." [pp. 30–31]. The account is so farfetched, including the clichés and the ridiculous practicality (he decided against murder in spite of the propitious circumstances because he did not want to get into a state of "tension"), that it is humorous. Ruth's question, "How did you know she was diseased?" and Lenny's reply, "I decided she was," make the whole story even more amusing, but they also introduce a more serious note, both relating it to Pinter's verification theme and implying Lenny's view of women. It makes no difference what the "truth" of the matter is, whether or not the girl did indeed have the pox; all that is important is how the characters react to a given statement. Ruth reflects the desire for verification, even though the fact is insignificant in terms of the action completed, and Lenny's answer implies that something can be true and false simultaneously: while there is no evidence that his pursuer was diseased, his reactions are the same as if she were. His refusal to take advantage of her offer (and she had been "searching for [him] for days") tenuously links him with character types such as Davies in *The Caretaker* and James in *The Collection*, for although the tale is probably fantasy, it can be seen as symbolic of his subconscious rejection of women. Davies was unable to accept attention, in the guise of either approval or affection, in spite of his seeking these things. James' easy reception of Stella's tale (aside from such actions' being what one would expect from a woman) in part is due to his recognition of both the difficulty of creating a relationship and the fragility of that relationship once formed. Starting with his own mother, and then by virtue of his profession, Lenny has been exposed to a low order of women, and the only woman for whom he has ever felt affection left him—his mother died. Unable to accept women because he would be vulnerable to desertion again, he rejects them violently in a protective reflex, to keep himself free from emotional entanglements even as he seeks them. When he entertains Ruth with another fantasy, a double entendre revolving around asserting himself physically regarding a little old lady, he again exposes himself in a protective torrent of words: " I had a good mind to give her a workover there and then, but as I was feeling jubilant with the snow-clearing I just gave her a short-arm jab to the belly and jumped on a bus outside" (p. 33).

A clue to Lenny's alleged actions is given when Ruth refers to him as "Leonard" at the conclusion of the story and he asks her not to call him that, because "that's the name my mother gave me" (p. 33). Jessie has been dead for an indeterminate number of years (at least six as evidenced by the missing wall), yet her presence is powerfully felt on stage throughout the drama as she is referred to by every member of the family and her memory affects the actions of each individual in some way or other. That Lenny finds it difficult to establish a normal relationship with women is obvious. This may be due to the reasons noted above, or it may stem from his comparison of women to the standard of his mother (like Sam, he can find no one who is her equal, so he does not even want to be called by the name she gave him), or from his mother's influence on him similar to Albert's situation in *A Night Out* (possibly another reason for not wanting to be called Leonard—his dislike for his mother). Even Ruth is a threat to him. Lenny is amused that he is in his pajamas and Ruth is fully clothed when they first meet, since this a reversal of his normal working conditions, and he jokingly calls attention to the fact. When things start to get serious, he can only retreat in confusion:

RUTH. If you take the glass . . . I'll take you.
　　Pause.
LENNY. How about me taking the glass without you taking me?
RUTH. Why don't I just take you?
　　Pause.
LENNY. You're joking.

　　. . .

RUTH. Have a sip. . . . Sit on my lap. . . . Lie on the floor. . . .
LENNY. What are you doing, making me some kind of proposal? [p. 34]

Teddy's actions provide another means of exploring the theme of need. Like Edward in *A Slight Ache*, whose failure to fulfill the needs of his wife is paralleled in the implied lack of success in other areas of his life (as hinted at in his inclusion of the Gobi in a speech about Africa or seen in his disastrous dealing with the matchseller), Teddy's shortcomings are suggested by his *not* exhibiting his ability in philosophical matters. Lenny and Teddy, joined by Ruth, discuss the nature of the universe, the question of what is true versus what is not true, which Pinter is answering in his plays by merging the two. In the figure of the girl with the pox Lenny creates a debatable premise and then acts as though it were confirmed. Again, it is not the validity of the premise that is important, but the actions stemming from it. The professor's brother (a pimp) and wife (a former body model) demonstrate a better understanding of his subject than he does:

LENNY. Eh, Teddy, you haven't told us much about your Doctorship of Philosophy. What do you teach?
TEDDY. Philosophy.
LENNY. Well, I want to ask you something. Do you detect a certain logical incoherence in the central affirmations of Christian theism?
TEDDY. That question doesn't fall within my province.

　　. . .

LENNY. But you're a philosopher. Come on, be frank. What do you make of all this business of being and not-being?
TEDDY. What do you make of it?
LENNY. Well, for instance, take a table. Philosophically speaking. What is it?
TEDDY. A table [pp. 51–52].

Lenny is aware of a philosophical question and the words in which to phrase it in his burlesque of existentialism; Teddy does not respond in the same vein.

Ruth enters the fray, introducing a new perspective: "You've forgotten something. Look at me. I . . . move my leg. That's all it is. But I wear . . . underwear . . . which moves with me . . . it captures your attention. Perhaps you misinterpret. The action is simple. It's a leg . . . moving. My lips move. Why don't you restrict . . . your observations to that? Perhaps the fact that they move is more significant . . . than the words which come through them. You must bear that . . . possibility . . . in mind" (pp. 52–53). Once more it is the philosopher's family rather than the philosopher which poses a question or an answer demanding philosophical conjecture as opposed to Teddy's superficial responses.

Throughout Pinter's works there is a pattern of individuals' failing in other areas of their lives as a reflection of their lack of success in creating viable relationships with their companions (Davies and Edward are prime examples). While Teddy may simply not wish to discuss his interests with laymen, his chosen profession would be the one area in which he should be able to exhibit his proficiency. In the play Teddy proves himself capable of doing little besides stealing cheese-rolls, however, although there are ample instances in which he meets defeat in the drama (his inability to control his wife earlier, for example).

Teddy may be a material success—he is a professor who is paid enough to take his wife to Europe—but Pinter is not interested in material success in any of his plays. As he has said, there is no point in writing about such things when we do not even know about the basics of human communication. The characters in *A Slight Ache, The Collection,* and *The Lover* are apparently in comfortable economic circumstances, yet they all have emotional problems. It is possible that Teddy is actually a success as a philosopher, for he faces all situations with a philosopher's equanimity, while still not being able to solve essential problems such as meeting his wife's psychological requirements or maintaining a lasting relationship with his father and brothers which will fulfill his own emotional needs. Hinchcliffe remarks that it is an "obvious absurdity . . . that Teddy has a Ph.D. in philosophy" for "Teddy seems to be philosophical only in the contemptible sense of the word . . . incredibly academic and narrow."[27] He goes on to point out that it is Lenny who is speculative and Ruth who is creative in the drama, not the brother/husband. Whether or not Teddy failed in his profession, it is certain that he did not succeed in his return home. He enters the house full of hope and leaves without his wife. No emotional ties have been reestablished—indeed, some have been nullified. Teddy's failure in returning spills over into his marriage, and his own family disregards the fact that Ruth is his wife (Lenny and Max appear deaf to Teddy's protestations that he and Ruth are married), beginning with Lenny's trouble in being convinced that that is her "connection" with his older brother at their first meeting:

27. Hinchcliffe, *Harold Pinter*, p. 159.

RUTH. I'm his wife.

. . .

We're on a visit to Europe.
LENNY. What, both of you?
RUTH. Yes.
LENNY. What, you sort of live with him over there, do you?
RUTH. We're married.
LENNY. On a visit to Europe, eh? . . . [p. 29].

As the couple is about to depart for America, Teddy's family demonstrates the overwhelming selfish motivation which is partly responsible for their alienation:

LENNY (*to* RUTH). What about one dance before you go?
TEDDY. We're going.
LENNY. Just one.

. . .

> RUTH *stands. They dance, slowly.* TEDDY *stands, with* RUTH's *coat.* MAX *and* JOEY *come in the front door and into the room.* LENNY *kisses* RUTH. *They stand, kissing.*
JOEY. Christ, she's wide open. Dad, look at that. *Pause.* She's a tart. . . . JOEY *goes to them. He takes* RUTH's *arm. He smiles at* LENNY. *He sits with* RUTH *on the sofa, embraces and kisses her. . . .* LENNY *sits on the arm of the sofa. He caresses* RUTH's *hair as* JOEY *embraces her.* MAX *comes forward, looks at the cases.*
MAX. You going, Teddy? . . . Look, next time you come over, don't forget to let us know beforehand whether you're married or not. I'll always be glad to meet the wife. . . . You thought I'd be annoyed because you married a woman beneath you. You should have known me better. . . . *He peers to see* RUTH's *face under* JOEY, *turns back to* TEDDY. Mind you, she's a lovely girl. . . . And a Mother too. . . . JOEY *and* RUTH *roll off the sofa on to the floor.* JOEY *clasps her.* LENNY *moves to stand above them* [pp. 58–60].

Probably the single most frequently asked question about *The Homecoming* is, how can a man just sit and watch something like this happening without trying to stop it? Esslin advances the proposition that Teddy and his wife were not getting along anyway, as evidenced by the trip to Venice, which the critic contends was a last effort to save the marriage with the return to London intensifying the already existing conflict, so that there would be no reason for Teddy's interposing since he can now return home with a clear conscience.[28] In keeping with the tone of the play, though, it is more likely

28. Esslin, *The Peopled Wound*, p. 160.

that the answer can be found in Teddy's character. Pinter has answered the question by replying, "Look! What would happen if he interfered. He would have had a messy fight on his hands, wouldn't he? And this particular man would avoid that."[29]

The hilarious farce taking place in front of the non-objecting husband produces the evidence and at the same time the expression of Teddy's failure. His reaction to his wife's performance suggests that he has been led to expect failure. If he has failed in his relations with his father and his brothers, there is no reason to expect success in his marriage, so Ruth's actions come as no real surprise. The rest of the family's easy acceptance of the events as entirely natural indicates their attitude toward one another, for they are too interested in how events affect them personally to be able to look at a situation with sympathy for the participants.

The action also provides an opportunity for Ruth's self-assertion. She finds that she can manipulate the proceedings, and encountering no resistance, by the end of the sequence she has taken control. She also takes the lead in asking questions:

RUTH (*to* TEDDY). Have your family read your critical works?
MAX. That's one thing I've never done. I've never read one of his critical works.
TEDDY. You wouldn't understand them. . . . It's nothing to do with the question of intelligence. It's a way of being able to look at the world. It's a question of how far you can operate on things and not in things. I mean it's a question of your capacity to ally the two, to relate the two, to balance the two . . . . to be able to *see*! I'm the one who can see. That's why I write my critical works . . . . have a look at them . . . see how certain people can view . . . things . . . how certain people can maintain . . . intellectual equilibrium. . . . You're just objects. You just . . . move about. . . . I can observe it. I can see what you do. It's the same as I do. But you're lost in it [pp. 61–62].

The irrelevance of the question in the circumstances is overshadowed by Teddy's response, which reveals a lack of communication and an attempt to find refuge or shelter on an intellectual level, though his failure to answer Lenny's philosophical questions adequately has already suggested that he is not merely detached as he claims, but possibly is incapable. He cannot even express his feelings adequately to his brother when they are reunited after six years' separation. Ties of affection seem beyond him, since his connections with his father, brothers, uncle, and wife are superficial (no one is truly pleased at his return, and Ruth is ready to stay behind), so he no longer expresses interest in participating, though his initial reunion with his father

29. Pinter, quoted in Hewes, "Probing Pinter's Play," pp. 57–58.

implied desire for acceptance. The contrast in Teddy's attitude at the beginning of the play and his attitude at its conclusion illustrates his inability to form lasting bonds as well as it reflects his recognition of his failure. He returns home eagerly, yet soon becomes anxious to leave, having established no relationships within his family, having been unmoved by his uncle's collapse, and having lost his wife. Only by removing himself from the sphere of human emotion can he face his condition.

Teddy's weakness is that he can feel emotion, but cannot excite a reciprocal feeling in those about him. That he was happy to get home was shown in his trying to convince Ruth, who does not recognize the desperate motivation behind his return, that his family would welcome them: he pointed out his father's chair to his wife, specifically mentioned greeting his father in the morning, seemed pleased that they would surprise the old man, and assured Ruth that she would like him. After he was greeted by Lenny, Teddy asked about his dad. When father and son finally meet at the end of Act I, Teddy is "ready for the cuddle" his father proposes. His talks with the family prove that he cannot communicate, and events in the play show that he has no control over anybody. Since he can control no one, Teddy views people as pieces of machinery so that he will not have to relate to them on a personal level, a classic example of the defense-by-withdrawing mechanism. Because he sees everyone as a machine, he feels no emotion toward them and can simply observe their movements. This is a case of defense by restructuring the world, or autism (the tendency to see things as we want to see them), the type of activity commonly engaged in by Davies.

The Homecoming is Pinter's best work. He utilizes his tools well: the setting concentrates the action as the six characters are joined together for unavoidable confrontation in the confining, barren set; the humor and irony enhance the terror involved in the underlying conflicts; the images of corruption produce vividness (note Max's description of his wife and Lenny's description of the girl "falling apart with the pox" in Act I, for example); and the realistic language (phrases and patterns) emphasizes the movement from reality to unreality through contrast. Specifically dealing with interpersonal relationships, in *The Homecoming* Pinter uses love and sex more explicitly than in his previous dramas as a motive force and a means of delving into problems between husband and wife, father and sons, brother and brother.

The basic structural device in the play is the framework of a power struggle in which sex turns out to be the deciding agent. In a series of skirmishes throughout the drama the characters meet, compete, and attempt to gain dominance over one another, with Ruth using her sex to emerge victorious. There is a tension set up by the alternating tonalities (humor versus horror, for example) of the continuing confrontation. Through the form of verbal fencing, the weaponry of the power struggle, Pinter exposes the characters and their beliefs, thus providing the meaning of the play. For example, Teddy and Lenny's discussion of the dual nature of reality can in part be considered a battle for position, but it is also important as a means for discovering some of the characters' individual problems. Teddy, the professional philosopher, the representative of organized thought, fails to solve problems in his own field. Lenny practices logical thinking on his own to devise theoretical answers, establishing his superiority over his older brother, thereby making more concrete their personal identities. Ruth begins with Lenny's assumptions, but rejects them by applying the principle of practicality, reducing them to an emotional level—the level on which they actually function anyway.

So it is throughout the play. There is no need for Pinter to deal with either nature or society, since the family contains within its makeup the things which are nature and society. The family unit provides the circumstances in which variations on several themes may be experimented with. A philosopher and a chauffeur do not have the vitality to stand up to the life forces of a butcher, a pimp, and a boxer, who in turn fall before a woman's sexual wiles (Ruth is not interested in sex so much as in the power of sex). Ironically, these "vital" elementals are impressive only in comparison with Teddy and Sam. The provider of food has been tricked by a gang of crooks so the family has to skimp to get by, the procurer is unable to fill his own demands, and the fighter is not a physical threat to anybody. Each level of living comes closer to the primal components of life itself: Teddy and Sam can exist only in an already created civilization; Max, Lenny, and Joey represent elements (food, sex, battle) necessary to forge a society with enough leisure and ease to permit philosophers and chauffeurs (unessential thought, luxury) to exist; and Ruth is the element out of which life is created and is, therefore, the most important and strongest of all forces, for she is closest to the basic drives of life (without which the others are meaningless).

The reason for the power struggle is essentially that which motivates the majority of Pinter characters in one guise or another. Although Pinter tends to exaggerate when explaining his plays to interviewers, many of his exaggerated comments are based on a valid core and often the basic thought is applicable to the play in question. When asked by Henry Hewes what *The Homecoming* is about, Pinter replied, "It's about love and lack of love. The people are harsh and cruel, to be sure. Still, they aren't acting arbitrarily but for very deep-seated reasons."[30] When applied to *The Homecoming*, this statement explains much of why the characters do what they do. The need to love and to be loved, a primary appetite, is at the center of the characters' actions. It is also the cause of all their troubles. Asked whether the family represents evil, Pinter contends, "There's no question that the family does behave very calculatedly and pretty horribly to each other and to the returning son. But

30. Pinter, in Hewes, "Probing Pinter's Play," p. 57.

they do it out of the texture of their lives and for other reasons which are not evil but slightly desperate."[31] This brings to mind the earlier equation of love and need in connection with *The Caretaker*. If the people in the drama are desperate in their needs, then everything they do may be aimed at satisfying themselves. This would explain how they can do some of the things they do to one another. In a family which feels these needs so vitally, there has been a breakdown in the ability to communicate emotions between the individual members, and as a result they have resorted to game playing and rituals in an attempt to get through to one another. Unfortunately, the game playing and rituals only serve to compound the problem and make expression of feelings more difficult because the stylized forms get in the way of the players, somewhat on the line of *The Lover*, intensifying the very problems they are meant to alleviate. According to Pinter, "The game is the least of it. What takes place is a mode of expression, a chosen device. It's the way the characters face each other under the game that interests me."[32] The game, essentially, is the continual battle for emotional security.

Max, Sam, Joey, and Lenny are involved in roundabout approaches, and the things they do are either aimed at achieving goals or grow out of frustration from lack of achievement. Max's past was not a particularly happy one, and he has continually been placed in roles which demand respect but not affection from those he rules, as demonstrated in his humorously exaggerated account of his duties (which include the unbelievable claim about "leading psychiatrists"; for one thing, Sam is not an invalid, unless the meaning is "emotional cripple"): "My mother was bedridden, my brothers were all invalids. I had to earn the money for the leading psychiatrists. I had to read books! I had to study the disease, so that I could cope with an emergency at every stage" (p. 47). From Jessie's death he has been both mother (doing the cooking, for example) and father to his sons, and he admits that there have been no women in his home since his wife died. As a housekeeper he has kept things neat and clean, perhaps from habits learned when he was a butcher. Lenny mentions that his father is "obsessed with order and clarity" (p. 33) and the set seems to bear this out. Apparently his "obsession" is something which sometimes amusingly carries over into his thinking, too, as when Sam boasts about being called "the best chauffeur" and Max wants to know "from what point of view?" (p. 13). This is a funny but pertinent question which takes nothing for granted, makes no assumptions—like Mr. Kidd's wandering floors. He does crave affection, though: he welcomes Teddy back with "a nice cuddle and kiss" after a shocked outburst; at the beginning of Act II his mellow conversation with his family indicates that his family is important to him; he shows concern when he finds out that Joey has been teased by his sister-in-law ("My Joey? She did that to my boy? *Pause*. To my youngest son? Tch, tch, tch, tch. How you feeling, son? Are you all right?" (pp. 68–69)—ironically,

31. Ibid.   32. Pinter, in Halton, "Pinter," p. 239.

about the only affection or tenderness shown in the entire drama is directed at Joey by Max here, and by Lenny during the love-making sequence); he is eager to have Ruth stay to become part of the family and wonders if Teddy's sons might not enjoy having a photograph of their grandfather (like Ruth, though, he unconcernedly dismisses Teddy when his son is no longer useful—something he threatened Sam with previously).

It is difficult to tell whether he acts toward his family as he does because, like Davies and Lenny, he cannot accept affection, or whether he has forgone that emotion in order to keep his family together. As mentioned before, this would account for his original reaction to Teddy's return as an expression of his anger at his son's having betrayed the family by leaving in the first place. And the concept of a family unit is important to the old man: he followed his own father into trade, assuming his father's masculinity by taking the same professional role.

Besides having been deprived of the attention he desires, Max is beginning to show the insecurity of old age and fears that he may be too old for anyone to be interested in him—he continually asks Ruth, "You think I'm too old for you?" (p. 81)—so that his daughter-in-law can provide the needed attention, simultaneously proving that he is not too old. Whatever the reason, he is now ready to have her stay, for it is Max who reflects, "Perhaps it's not a bad idea to have a woman in the house. . . . Maybe we should keep her," in the first place (p. 69).

Sam, in contrast to his brother, is a ne'er-do-well who apparently has never been able to get close to anyone. He did not care enough to follow his father's trade as a butcher and has been unable to produce anything on his own, for which Max taunts him: "What kind of a son were you, you wet wick? You spent half your time doing crossword puzzles! We took you into the butcher's shop, you couldn't even sweep the dust off the floor. . . . I gave birth to three grown men! . . . What have you done?" (pp. 39–40). As a chauffeur, Sam merely serves the commands of others. His ineffectualness may have grown out of his feelings for his sister-in-law: "Never get a bride like you had. . . . Nothing like [Jessie] . . . going about these days. . . . a charming woman . . . . a very nice companion" (p. 16). His comments about Jessie throughout the play indicate that he loved his brother's wife—possibly the only simple and sincere expression of love found in *The Homecoming*. The uncle is tied to his idealized memories of the dead woman, and even though he witnessed her infidelity with her husband's best friend, no one could ever match her in his eyes.

Sam's collapse at the end of the play can be seen as a shattering of his split self in an attempt to protect Jessie even though he has to tarnish her memory in the process. By introducing his shocking information he hopes to keep the family from replacing Jessie with Ruth. At the same time his "death" demonstrates the selfish orientation of all the characters in the drama, for they are undisturbed by his death (his favorite nephew, Teddy, is irritated because he "was going to ask him to drive me to London airport" p. 79). This attitude was ironically suggested shortly before when Max objected to Lenny's "concentrating too much on the economic considerations" and warned that "the human considerations" must not be forgotten. The family shows no feeling of regret over Sam's prostration; they continue to pursue their own separate needs.

Joey is a picture of impotence. He can create nothing—he is "in demolition in the daytime" and is a boxer in "the evenings, after work." As a boxer he is not an overpowering figure. His father describes his son's inept character with wonderful accuracy when he defines Joey's fighting style: "What you've got to do is you've got to learn to defend yourself, and you've got to learn how to attack. That's your only trouble as a boxer. You don't know how to defend yourself, and you don't know how to attack" (p. 17). As a lover, he is a failure too. He has to be led through the story of his latest exploit with a "bird" near "the Scrubs" (Wormwood Scrubs is the West London prison) by Lenny, and although he initiates the action with Ruth, he "had her up there for two hours and he didn't go the whole hog" (p. 66). Joey does not seem overly upset by his lack of success. He just does not want anyone else to get the credit (even Teddy "don't get no gravy!").

Jessie filled many roles in her relations with the members of the household, and it may well be that Joey turns to Ruth as a substitute mother, since Jessie is gone. If so, he would not look to his sister-in-law as a source of sexual satisfaction. This would explain his lack of concern over not getting "all the way" and is suggested by his actions as the play concludes when he *"walks slowly across the room. He kneels at* [Ruth's] *chair. She touches his head, lightly. He puts his head in her lap. . . . She continues to touch* JOEY's *head, lightly"* (pp. 80, 82). He is really only a little child in his appetites.

Lenny has been shown incapable of satisfactorily coping with situations in which women are involved. Teddy, by his own admission, has withdrawn (because of his failures—the only real threat he poses is to cheese-rolls) and inhumanly views his family as "objects." He is the furthest removed from the human sphere and cannot even take part in the game any more.

Ruth, Biblically the faithful wife, has not been satisfied by her husband or children and seeks attention from her husband's family. The realizations fostered by Teddy's "objects" speech in Act II are foreshadowed in his treatment of Ruth at the beginning of the drama. He apparently regards her as a child or an object and probably has for some time. Ruth asks his permission to sit down, for instance, and he tries to send her to bed because she needs "some rest." This manner of treatment certainly cannot be satisfactory for a mature individual, so Ruth is in a position to seek a more fulfilling relationship elsewhere. As a result of her starvation for acceptance as the person she is (hearkening back to Davies), a woman with desires and emotions, and demanding emotional stimulation on that level, Ruth is forced to disregard socially approved sources of these elements.

Pinter points out that "if this had been a happy marriage it wouldn't have happened. But she didn't want to go back to America."[33] There is evidence in the play that Ruth has not been happy in her marriage. The first clue to this fact is Teddy's attitude toward his wife when they are originally introduced, an attitude reflected in his treating her as an object or a young child rather than a mature woman. It should also be remembered that Ruth was a "model for the body" and that by her own admission she "was ... different ... when [she] met Teddy ... first" (p. 50). She mentions having lived in the vicinity and manages to take a walk without getting lost. In addition she is apparently familiar with the kind of people who inhabit this section of London, for she understands Lenny's semi-underworld jargon. Teddy apparently has forced her into a new and alien role, that of a university professor's wife.

Teddy's description of Ruth's role in their life in America is attractive: "She's a great help to me over there. She's a wonderful wife and mother. She's a very popular woman. She's got lots of friends. It's a great life, at the University ... it's a very good life. ... It's a very stimulating environment" (p. 50). Ruth's description of America differs markedly, indicating that her life there has not been so rosy: "It's all rock. And sand. It stretches . . . so far . . . everywhere you look. And there's lots of insects there. *Pause.* And there's lots of insects there" (p. 53). It is clear from the picture she presents that she has been living a lonely, barren life, and the image of this sterility so preoccupies her that when Lenny asks her if she wants her drink (when he had amusingly denied having any liquor in the house before) "on the rocks" (with ice), she replies, "Rocks? What do you know about rocks?" (p. 61). As a matter of fact, it may be that the European jaunt was to help Ruth recover from a breakdown resulting from her new life; besides the evidence that she had trouble in adjusting to life in America, it is mentioned that she has not been well. The first hint of her willingness to abandon that life and align herself with Lenny's side of the family comes when she remembers that if she had "been a nurse in the Italian campaign" she would have visited Venice before Teddy took her there. That Teddy misunderstands his wife is demonstrated when he tries to convince Ruth to return with him with the appeal, "You can help me with my lectures when we get back" (p. 55).

Probably the second most frequently asked question concerns Ruth's behavior. Esslin insistently dismisses it by labeling her a "nymphomaniac,"[34] in spite of the fact that she never makes love with any one man in the play, let alone more than one (Joey does not "go all the way," and there is not even

33. Pinter, in Hewes, "Probing Pinter's Play," p. 58.
34. Esslin, *The Theatre of the Absurd*, p. 251, and "The Homecoming: An Interpretation" in Lahr, *Casebook*, p. 5.

any evidence that she and Teddy make love, since they go to bed at different times). Pinter has explicitly denied the allegation, and such a reading would invalidate the character and the logic of the drama which the playwright has built up through the course of the play. Her present surroundings are much closer to the type of environment she would be at home in than the situation existing in the United States. "The woman is not a nymphomaniac as some critics have claimed. . . . She's in a kind of despair which gives her a kind of freedom. Certain facts like marriage and the family for this woman have clearly ceased to have any meaning."[35] What this means is that since marriage and the family have failed to satisfy Ruth's primary appetites, they are not fulfilling their functions and may be discarded.

Pinter would disagree with critics who call the play absurd or unrealistic, too. The basic premise of a woman who will turn to anyone in an attempt to find affection is not absurd in the author's world picture. Although humorously exaggerated in its tone, Pinter's contention about Ruth's strange form of exercise is legitimate from a psychological viewpoint: "As for rolling on the couch, there are thousands of women in this very country who at this very moment are rolling off couches with their brothers, or cousins, or next-door neighbors. The most respectable women do this. It's a splendid activity. It's a little curious, certainly, when your husband is looking on, but it doesn't mean you're a harlot."[36] The strength of psychological urges such as the drive for acceptance and the urgency that directs behavior toward such a goal as well as the "affiliation system" in which one turns to others because of anxiety in trying to maximize self-actualization are common psychological topics. Flora's choice of the matchseller for solace in *A Slight Ache* is a previous dramatic example of how desperate a person can become. The motivation for the actions takes them out of the realm of the absurd. Women who are driven to this point by their desperation are not harlots in the sense of selling themselves for money or even for sexual pleasure—they are driven by a need to fill deep emotional voids. Ruth's description of America ("It's all rock. And sand. . . .") has already indicated that for the past six years she has been a very lonely woman in what are for her sterile surroundings.

While the conclusion of the play is astonishing if taken out of context, as in the "comedies of menace" the movement from a realistic beginning has been smooth and logical, each step being a bit more absurd than the one before it, yet based on its predecessor. Many people suffer the same fate as Ruth, but few of them handle their problems as well: she has been "used by this family. But eventually she comes back at them with a whip. She says, 'if you want to play this game I can play it as well as you.' She does not become a harlot. At the end of the play she's in possession of a certain kind of

35. Pinter, in Halton, "Pinter," p. 239.
36. Pinter, in Hewes, "Probing Pinter's Play," p. 58.

freedom. She can do what she wants, and it is not at all certain she will go off to Greek Street. But even if she did, she would not be a harlot in her own mind."[37] Existentially it could be said that Ruth is continually in the process of "becoming." What Pinter is claiming is that Ruth has been placed outside traditional boundaries by the failure of conventions such as marriage to meet her requirements, so that anything she does is acceptable to her if it brings her closer to satisfying those requirements. This is demonstrated in her businesslike bargaining over the details of her contract and place of work—almost like Millamant in *The Way of the World*—when they are talking about setting her up as a prostitute: "I would want at least three rooms and a bathroom . . . a dressing-room, a rest-room, and a bedroom. . . . A personal maid. . . . You would have to regard your original outlay simply as a capital investment. . . . You'd supply my wardrobe. . . . I would naturally want to draw up an inventory of everything I would need, which would require your signatures in the presence of witnesses. . . . All aspects of the agreement and conditions of employment would have to be clarified to our mutual satisfaction before we finalized the contract" (pp. 76–78). Because of the circumstances and her motivation, Ruth does not fit the traditional definition of a harlot (no one in the play ever "gets the gravy" after all). The whole play is epitomized in Ruth's farewell to her husband. She feels no real affection, antipathy, or guilt for him—she has done what she had to do— and as he moves to the front door to leave for America without her, she calls to him: "Eddie. TEDDY *turns. Pause.* Don't become a stranger" (p. 80). In the power struggle Ruth is the strongest; new lines of attachment are established, and at the end of the play she sits with her new family arranged about her as in a traditional family portrait.

In summary, the actions of the characters in *The Homecoming* have their center in psychological needs. Sam treasures the memory of a woman he considers a nonpareil, the woman he loves and whose position in the household he fights to maintain because of his love for her. Joey takes his father's advice to "go and find yourself a mother" (p. 16) literally and is happy with a woman with whom one need not "go the whole hog," a woman who will caress his head as if he were a small child. Teddy has found love unattainable, so he rejects it and acts accordingly. Lenny's attitude toward women was distorted by his mother to such an extent that he cannot relate to women in a normal manner. He cannot accept affection when it is offered to him. Max, on the other hand, is bothered by his advancing years and seeks reassurance that he is still worthy of someone's attention in spite of his old age. The affection of an attractive young woman provides his needed reassurance and demonstrates that he retains his masculine appeal. Ruth is anxious to take on a new role in which everything revolves about her, a state epito-

37. Ibid.

mized by the placing of the characters at the final curtain, where she has clearly taken on many of Jessie's "attributes." She fulfills different needs for the various men in her new family in order to fulfill her own needs.

As might be expected in a Pinter play, the title of *The Homecoming* has a dual application which implies the testing of certain prejudices. Obviously it refers to Teddy, who is returning to see his family after a six-year hiatus. The occasion is not a happy one, though, and there is little rejoicing. On a subtler level the title refers to Ruth, although paradoxically she has never been in the house before, has not even met the family previously. In this case it is not the physical structure which is important, it is the human relationships which are created that define a place as home.

The Homecoming is related to the three basic concepts and techniques utilized by Pinter in the "comedies of menace," but the new themes and devices which began to evolve in *A Slight Ache* have created a complete new set in the author's mind, and this play caps his second period in which psychological needs have become the prime subject he wishes to explore. When the dramatist wrote *The Room* in 1957 he was interested in exploring the effect of fear, of physical menace, on an individual. By the time he completed *The Homecoming* in 1965 the subject of his works had become psychological need. Rose has a psychological need, too, of course, but it is a matter of a shift in perspective: in the later plays, Pinter's emphasis is on the cause rather than the effect. The movement from menace to need is paralleled by the change in his use of a room as a metaphor for a place of security, and his very titles provide a clue to the meaning inherent in this shift. *The Room* deals with a physical structure, *The Homecoming* with abstract thoughts.

For Rose, home is a specific room in which she can feel secure because of the four walls that surround her. She is running from something and the room is more important to her than her husband because it affords her protection. This can be seen in Rose's obsession with the image of a room. For Ruth, home is the emotional context in which she feels secure and is most satisfied. She is oblivious to her surroundings—it is people who are important, and her attention centers on the people about her. The actual building is irrelevant. Her homecoming, therefore, is an emotional one based on sympathetic feeling. Teddy returns to a house that was once his home, but ironically, he is rejected in the end. Ruth is welcomed into the family because she fits into their emotional situation and fulfills their needs. Like Ruth in the Bible, she adopts her husband's family—"thy people shall be my people." The shift in what constitutes a home is indicative of the change in Pinter's theme as he moves from the presentation of menace to a comment on psychological need as a source of menace.

In a Pinter play the characters are concerned with taking, and the search for a room as a place of refuge is extended to a search for a home, any place where psychological requirements are fulfilled. As the focus on need becomes more important, there is a simultaneous deemphasis of the requirement for a material sanctuary; whether it is Harry's posh Belgravia flat or Max's dilapidated North London house does not really matter. Pinter's realization that this is so is the essence of the thematic change which takes place in his work between 1957 and 1968.

Chapter VIII. Additional Indicators

. . . I've often wondered
what "mean" means . . .

Two additional television scripts which reflect Pinter's thinking during *The Lover* period are *The Basement* and *Tea Party*. Although neither was actually produced until several years later, the dramatist's initial work on both pieces can be traced back to around 1963.

The Basement

The Basement, originally titled *The Compartment* when written in 1963, was first televised by the BBC on February 20, 1967. The play was intended to be one of the segments in a Grove Press film project, "Project I: Three Original Motion Picture Scripts by Samuel Beckett, Eugene Ionesco,

Harold Pinter," though neither *The Compartment* nor Ionesco's *The Hard-Boiled Egg* were shot; only Beckett's *Film*, with Buster Keaton, has been made into a movie short. As a stage play, *The Basement* was given its world premiere as a companion piece to *Tea Party* on October 10, 1968, at the Eastside Playhouse in New York.

Like *The Collection* before it, *The Basement* is basically a simple play, the whole purpose of which is to examine a simple concept in another perspective. The author's techniques, such as limited setting and characterization for easy focus and concentration of thought, remain the same as in most of his other dramas up to this time. But, since *The Basement* is a television play, it relies, like *Tea Party*, on visual effects to a large degree and is perforce less dependent upon verbal expression for relaying the meaning of the drama to the audience. There is, for example, even less verbal imagery than usual, and it lacks the witty wordplay of the works in the comedy-of-manners-style preceding it.

The plot is spare. Tim Law is reading in his comfortable flat one winter's night when an old roommate, Charles Stott (played by Pinter himself in the BBC television cast), arrives. Stott brings with him a young girl, Jane, with whom, after brief amenities, he climbs into bed and begins making love. The rest of the play is concerned with Stott's taking over of Law's flat and then Law's replacing Stott as Jane's lover.

The exact amount of time involved in the reversal of positions is not clear, although the stage directions call for winter six distinct times and summer on five different occasions, so a number of years may pass. Yet the time itself is unimportant. What is important is that the seasons are constantly changing, mirroring the human changes on stage. Because of the intermixing of winter and summer, flashbacks or moving ahead in time may be taking place, though again a linear chronological progression of time is not as important as the mere fact that time progresses. The play ends with Stott in Law's place and Law at the front door in otherwise exactly the same attitudes as at the beginning of the action: the role changes from *A Slight Ache* and *The Lover* and the fight for a room from *Night School* are incorporated in one play.

The Basement opens on a rainy winter night at Tim Law's basement flat (undisclosed locale). Charles Stott, wearing a raincoat, stands outside the door. Jane is huddled by the wall behind him. Inside in a *"comfortable, relaxed, heavily furnished"* room with a lot of books, a large double bed, and a big fire, Law is lying in an armchair reading a Persian love manual, complete *"with illustrations."* Stott rings the doorbell and is warmly greeted by Law, who invites him in, though Jane, hidden from his view, remains outside.

LAW (*with great pleasure*). Stott!
STOTT (*smiling*). Hullo, Tim.

LAW. Good God. Come in!
　　LAW *laughs.*
　　Come in!
　　　STOTT *enters.*
　　I can't believe it![1]

Once in the apartment Law exclaims that, with the exception of a new rain-coat, Stott has not changed at all. His talk is that which would normally be expected in such circumstances, pleased, but disjointed and rushed: "You didn't walk here, did you? You're soaking. What happened to your car? You could have driven here. Why didn't you give me a ring? But how did you know my address? My God, it's years" (p. 94).

As usual in Pinter, the drama begins quite realistically both in situation and dialogue. It will only be a moment, however, before things begin to move toward unrealism, yet the progress is unified so that it seems natural. It is not until one suddenly wonders how things got to where they are that there is an awareness of movement. Events are started on their way when Stott says that he is looking for a place to live and Law invites him to stay. Stott accepts, ironically protesting, "I don't want to impose upon you." He then mentions that he has a friend waiting outside and is told to bring her in. An insignificant subject momentarily occupies the trio's attention as they try to collect themselves and adapt to the new situation:

STOTT. . . . Here's a towel. (*He gives it to her.*) Here.
LAW. But that's your towel.
JANE. I don't mind, really.
LAW. I have clean ones, dry ones.
JANE (*patting her face*). This is clean.
LAW. But it's not dry.
JANE. It's very soft.
LAW. I have others [p. 95].

The importance attributed to an unimportant article (a towel) and the non-logical sequence of statements is typical.

Stott begins to establish control as he imposes order on the situation. Commenting that the room is "a little bright," he turns off the lamps. Events become somewhat incredible as Jane takes off her clothes and gets into bed. Law's reaction is one of casual acceptance, as always in Pinter's plays, and he merely asks his guests if they would like some hot chocolate. Stott removes his clothes and gets into bed. Law claims that he has been feeling lonely and reminisces about when he and Stott were roommates, then fits right into the

1. Pinter, *The Basement,* in *The Lover, Tea Party, The Basement* (New York: Grove, 1967), p. 92.

action by shading the only light on in the room with his sweater and settling down to read his Persian manual of love while Stott and Jane make love in the bed (punctuated by her gasps and sighs). Theory versus success through action is thus beautifully demonstrated.

The next scene takes place on a beach on a summer day. While Stott stands watching from a clifftop overlooking the beach, Law and Jane talk about him, and it is evident that he is successful in many fields, possibly to Law's envy; "He has a connection with the French aristocracy. He was educated in France. Speaks French fluently, of course. Have you read his French translations? . . . He got a First in Sanskrit at Oxford. . . . I know for a fact he owns three châteaux . . . an immaculate driver. Have you seen his yachts?" (p. 98). This trend of success even extends to sleeping—"What repose he has."

Back at the flat Law lies on the floor covered by a blanket as Jane and Stott again make love on the bed, after which Stott turns toward the wall and Jane turns toward Law and smiles at him. She is becoming the seemingly passive female who in actuality controls much of the action.

A following scene finds Stott continuing his alteration of the environment to fit the intruders when he removes paintings from the wall. Another indication that the couple have made themselves at home is a glimpse of Jane in the kitchen, cooking and humming.

On a winter day Stott and Law sit in the backyard, discussing Jane. Stott remarks, "She comes from a rather splendid family," and, like Diana in *Tea Party*, she is musically inclined. Law attempts a devaluation by wondering if "she's lacking in maturity," though (p. 100).

Summer finds Jane and Law on the beach once more, but this time Jane has turned seductress, caressing Law and asking why he resists. On another summer day Law and Jane return to the flat and it can be seen that the room has changed completely. "*The room is unrecognizable,*" according to the stage directions, the furnishings having been changed to a Scandinavian decor. Even the fireplace is blocked—only the bed is the same.

A sequence of quick cuts, alternating short related winter scenes with summer episodes, illustrates Esslin's appraisal of *The Basement* as a nonrealistic dream structured like the movements of a symphony on the themes of fighting for possession of a girl and a room as Law imagines how Stott, whom he envies, would defeat him and how in turn he would try to reverse the process.[2] First Stott asks to hear some music on the stereo. This is followed by a scene in a bar in which Stott reveals that he is a happy man in that he has an old friend (Law) and a new one (Jane) and they get along well together. Out in a field on a winter evening Law tries to goad Charles into competing with him in a footrace—he has Jane drop a scarf to start them —but when he runs Stott stands still, refusing to take part in the contest, and

2. Esslin, *The Peopled Wound*, pp. 175–76.

as Law turns to see where his friend is, he trips and falls. Back in the room Stott again asks to hear the hi-fi while Tim and Jane sit uncomfortably in the cold. The two men appear in the backyard in the next scene, Law asking Stott if he does not think "it's a bit crowded in that flat" for the three of them. Stott replies negatively, so Law assures him that "the Council would object strenuously to three people living in these conditions," only to have Stott disagree again (pp. 103–4).

A momentarily destructive outburst develops on Law's part, possibly because the seasonal alliances have been switched, when Jane and Stott are together on a summer day. Stott wants Law to play Debussy, and as Law searches for the record, he destroys the collection by flinging them at the wall as he discards them. It becomes a winter night when Law finds the recording, and Stott and Jane, naked, climb back into bed. Law covers the lamp with his sweater. A summer day follows with Stott attempting to touch Jane's breast, but "She moves her body away from him" (p. 105).

Sitting by a reclining Law in a cove by the sea on another summer evening, Jane provides a clue to the meaning of the drama as her ambiguous statements indicate that perhaps this is part of a repeating pattern: "Why don't you tell him to go? We had such a lovely home. We had such a cosy home. It was so warm. Tell him to go. It's your place. Then we could be happy again. Like we used to. Like we used to. In our first blush of love. Then we could be happy again, like we used to. We could be happy again. Like we used to" (p. 105). It is not clear when "before" was. And it may be that, like the couple in *The Lover*, *The Basement* presents a picture of people who cannot accept sex or love on an ordinary basis and have to create an artificial climate to stimulate or to rationalize their sexual relationships.

The continual changes in both external nature (the seasons) and the interior furnishings reflect the inconstancy of attitudes and emotions of individuals previously stated in *The Dwarfs*. Incidentally, the sole passage in the play which contains some of Pinter's normal imagery (it sounds as if it could have been taken from Harry's speech in *The Collection*) is Law's deliberately whispered accusation/warning to Stott that Jane is capable of transferring allegiances: "She betrays you. She has no loyalty. . . . You've been deluded. She's a savage. A viper. She sullies this room. She dirties this room" (p. 106).

A scene recalling the final actions of *The Homecoming*, and thereby implying that these attitude reversals are connected with the individual's particular need at the moment, follows. Stott lies in bed motionless, with Law and Jane regarding his imminent demise in tones similar to those used following Sam's collapse, the cliché giving a nice touch:

LAW. Is he breathing?
JANE. Just.

LAW. His last, do you think? . . . He was fit. As fit as a fiddle. Perhaps we
should have called a doctor. And now he's dying. Are you heartbroken?
JANE. Yes.
LAW. So am I.
　　Pause.
JANE. What shall we do with the body? [p. 106].

The play has reached a climax and turns in a new direction. Osborne's *Look
Back in Anger* is brought to mind in a brief scene picturing Law and Jane
"*snuffling each other like animals*" in a corner (p. 107). There are other similarities, too. The games, the changing partners, and the open sexual displays
(though more explicit in Pinter) are all reminiscent of the Osborne play.

　　The crucial confrontation comes when Stott, who has obviously survived
his illness, and Law face each other from opposite ends of the room while
Jane is in the kitchen preparing instant coffee. This is the battle which will
decide the entire contest, and the surroundings have therefore been reducd
to an elemental level: "*The room is completely bare. Bare walls. Bare floor-
boards. No furniture. One hanging bulb*" (p. 109). The two gladiators, bare-
foot and sweating, crouch motionless, each holding a broken milk bottle—a
weapon of violence emerging from Pinter's youthful experiences. As the men
advance toward each other, quick shots are interspersed of Jane unconcernedly fixing coffee in the kitchen, emphasizing the animalistic quality of
the scene, for she is as unmoved by the combat which is over her as she
would be if she were a doe with two bucks fighting to possess her. The milk
bottles, in a short thrust, smash together and Debussy's "Girl with the Flaxen
Hair" suddenly plays. Stott has repelled his host. The music signifies his triumph because he had requested Debussy earlier.

　　The play ends as it began, with everything (including the stage directions) exactly as it was before except that Stott has replaced Law, so the
names in the dialogue are reversed. Stott is in the room reading when Law
and Jane approach the door:

STOTT (*with great pleasure*). Law!
LAW (*smiling*). Hullo, Charles.
STOTT. Good God. Come in!
　　STOTT *laughs.*
　Come in!
　　LAW *enters.*
　I can't believe it! [p. 78].

Curtain.
　　The Biblical phrase "To every thing there is a season" fairly well sums
up *The Basement*. The scenario is, in Esslin's words, "a free association of

images around Pinter's favourite concept, the room as territory,"[3] though it clearly goes further than just depicting a territorial dispute. Taylor claims that this "relatively slight work . . . extends Pinter's preoccupation with the fragmented nature of experience beyond character to include physical surroundings."[4] Actually, *The Basement*, although pretty much neglected by Burkman, is a beautiful example of the elements from the sacred-tree-of-Diana myth. (This somewhat esoteric interpretation should not be overemphasized; while valid, it is not central to the impact on the audience as part of the dramatic experience. For that matter, "Request Stop" effectively portrays a cyclical ritual which is entirely divorced from pagan mythology.)

Until the inclusion of a beach, backyard, and bar in this play the dramatist's setting had generally been either a house or a flat, the only exceptions being a phone booth (*The Collection*), a night club (*Night School*), and the locales of *A Night Out*, *The Dwarfs*, and the revue sketches, all of which remain stably decorated. The uses of setting (furnishings) and nature are more ambitious in *The Basement*, and a dual effect is achieved as the different settings mirror the personalities of those involved (allowing a contrast between them) and the seasonal revolutions reflect the attitude of constant change (Jane is commonly with Stott in the winter and with Law in the summer, for instance).

In examining his theme of circularity Pinter exploits the idea of role changing and character fluidity present in *A Slight Ache* and *The Dwarfs* to arrive at the same conclusion—change is the only constant. In some ways this is related to Disson's dilemma in *Tea Party*, yet it goes beyond that point to make a comment about society and the universe as well. The crux of the play is in possession and continual challenge. Apparently man can control either a house (material objects) or a woman (human or spiritual objects), but not both simultaneously. Like the march of civilizations (Greece versus Rome versus the barbarian hordes), once a possession has been gained, decay sets in, and the man of action degenerates to passiveness, permitting others more vital to take over. As in the history of past civilizations, the conqueror is the one most closely allied with life (Jane equals sex, much as Ruth does in *The Homecoming*), the one who defeats those softened by civilization (*The Persian Manual of Love* represents experience and knowledge at second hand); and in the battle between the haves and the have-nots, those with nothing to lose are willing to take bigger risks and are tougher because they are accustomed to living with less.

When the play opens, Law is effective and entertaining, but limited. Stott dispossesses him. Law grows stronger as an outcast (he is not bound by the same laws as he was when he was a host and hospitality was prime) and

3. Esslin, *Theatre of the Absurd*, p. 253.
4. Taylor, *Anger and After*, p. 352.

overthrows Stott. Stott's fit is the next turning point. Having been rejected, Stott avenges himself by going back on the offensive and driving out his tormentors. He has lost the female, so in retaliation he takes over the house. The final scene is proof that the triangle and struggle for territory are eternal patterns of life which start over again as soon as they are concluded.

Tea Party

Although chronologically following *The Lover*, *Tea Party* is a play with a surrealistic presentation hearkening back to *The Dwarfs*. In large part the confusing quality of the drama may be derived from its preparation as a television play, which involves juxtaposition of scenes not normally possible on the stage. This quality likewise owes its existence to the transition from subjective to objective which takes place in the work.

Commissioned by the sixteen member nations of the European Broadcasting Union to be televised by them under the designation "The Largest Theater in the World," *Tea Party* was first read as a short story by Pinter on the BBC Third Programme, June 2, 1964, and published in short-story form in the January 1965 issue of *Playboy*. It was then acted on BBC Television on March 25, 1965, simultaneously being broadcast to Austria, Belgium, Denmark, France, England, Germany, Holland, Luxembourg, Norway, Spain, Sweden, and Switzerland (Italy refused to televise the production). The world premiere of its stage presentation was on the same program as *The Basement* on October 9, 1968, at the Eastside Playhouse in New York.

While there are still many Pinteresque elements present, *Tea Party* is a departure from the author's previous dramas. Much on the order of *The Basement* as a result of its television orientation, it is more visual and depends less on language than did its forerunners. The plot is fairly simple. Pinter has called it "the story of a businessman's reaction to his new secretary and the effect she has on him. He hires her on the day before his marriage,"[5] but the jumping around of scenes prevents it from proceeding in a straight line, so that it becomes somewhat obscure and closer to Theatre of the Absurd than the comparatively traditional plays which were its immediate predecessors. The short-story version of *Tea Party* is of little help in adding to an understanding of the play, for it presents generally the same features in abbreviated form and in a different order. In retrospect the organization of the drama establishes that the protagonist, Robert Disson, is a successful man in many varied areas of endeavor (business, lovemaking, table tennis) whose very successes make him vulnerable to failure, the fear of which leads to his mental breakdown.

The play begins with Wendy Dodd arriving at Disson's office for a job

5. Quoted in the *Daily Mirror* (London), 26 March 1965.

interview. From the fixtures arranged around the walls it can be seen that Disson works with bathroom supplies. Consulting the references contained in Wendy's application, Disson notes, "They seem to be excellent. You've had quite a bit of experience." In a few moments Wendy will explain why she had so many jobs, but as her prospective employer informs her that he manufactures "sanitary ware," she crosses her legs, a seemingly innocent gesture which becomes a characteristic through repetition and hints that she may well be more responsible for the course of her fate than she admits. After explaining that she would serve as a personal assistant, "a very private secretary in fact," he asks her the reason for her leaving her last job "quite suddenly," a question she finds "a little embarrassing" because the reason "is rather personal." Pressured by her future boss, she relates that she could not persuade her chief "to call a halt to his attentions," an accusation which ironically astounds Disson—"What? . . . A firm of this repute? It's unbelievable."[6] Disson pursues his questioning, unwittingly revealing something about himself:

DISSON. What sort of attentions?

· · ·

WENDY. He never stopped touching me. . . .
DISSON. Touching you?
WENDY. Yes.
DISSON. Where? (*Quickly.*) That must have been very disturbing for you.

· · ·

DISSON. Did he make you cry?
WENDY. Oh, just a little, occasionally, sir.
DISSON. What a monster [p. 45].

Disson comes to the conclusion that Wendy possesses "an active and inquiring intelligence and a pleasing demeanour," attributes he considers essential for the post, so he hires her. As her first assignment he asks her to check certain arrangements—he is getting married the next day, a second marriage and to a well-bred woman (which might be seen as an attempt at social betterment).

In the next scene at Disson's home Disson is introduced by his fiancée, Diana, to her brother Willy. Disson is distressed because Peter Disley, his oldest friend and scheduled best man, has the flu and will have to miss the wedding. The absence of Disley is crucial—crucial because of his speech-giving function: "the best man's not important; you can always get a best man—all he's got to do is stand there; it's the speech that's important, the speech in honour of the groom" (p. 47). The lack of Disley will be of over-riding import. Willy offers to give a talk in honor of the groom as well as the one he plans to give in honor of the bride.

6. Pinter, *Tea Party,* in *The Lover, Tea Party, The Basement* (New York: Grove, 1967), pp. 44–45.

The wedding reception at an exclusive restaurant is the setting for the following scene. Willy's two speeches are humorous as he first praises his sister and then praises his new brother-in-law by repraising his sister: "I remember the days my sister and I used to swim together. . . . The grace of her crawl . . . . those long summer evenings . . . . hearing my sister play Brahms . . . . at her needlework. . . . I have not known Robert for a long time. . . . But in that short time I have found him to be a man of integrity, honesty, and humility. . . . Now he has married a girl who equals, if not surpasses, his own austere standards of integrity . . . . my sister, who possesses within her that rare and uncommon attribute known as inner beauty not to mention the loveliness of her exterior. Par excellence as a woman with a needle . . . a woman of taste, discernment, sensibility and imagination. An excellent swimmer who, in all probability, has the beating of her husband in the two hundred metres breast stroke" (pp. 48–49). On the basis of the wedding speeches Disson offers Willy a job in his business as second in command, an offer Willy readily accepts. The two panegyrics mark the start of Disson's downfall in that they cause him to begin doubting his suitability for the marriage—something which will spread to all the other areas of his life.

A sumptuous hotel room in Italy provides the background for the next brief scene. Already the seeds of destruction have begun to sprout. In bed on their honeymoon Disson asks his new bride if she has ever been happier, to which she replies, "Never." He seeks reassurance, insisting, as Teddy did in *The Homecoming*, "I make you happy, don't I? Happier than you've ever been . . . with any other man," and Diana reaffirms his contention (p. 50). The incident demonstrates both his success and his insecurity because she is happy, yet he remains unconvinced that he is the best.

Disson again expresses needless fears about his inferiority at breakfast in a later scene. Diana's eyes are shining with pleasure, but he needs to be told that his wife did not marry a former suitor who was weak where he is strong. John and Tom, Disson's sons by his previous marriage, whisper to each other while they eat. When their father asks them what they are saying, John answers, "Nothing," but Disson takes the answer as a personal affront—"Do you think I'm deaf?" (p. 52).

The scene shifts to Willy's office. Disson is showing him where he will work and explaining that they will seldom meet, but will instead communicate through an intercom. This information prepares for a later scene.

Switching to Disson's office, Willy is treated to an ironic speech of self-characterization by his employer: "I'm a thorough man. I like things to be done and done well. I don't like dithering. I don't like indulgence. I don't like self-doubt. I don't like fuzziness. I like clarity. Clear intention. Precise execution. . . . I've no patience for conceit and self-regard. A man's job is to assess his powers coolly and correctly . . . . he can proceed to establish a balanced and reasonable relationship with his fellows . . . . living is a matter of active and willing participation. . . . Now, dependence isn't a word I would use lightly, but I will use it and I don't regard it as a weakness. To understand the meaning of the term dependence is to understand that one's powers are limited and that to live with others is not only sensible but the only way work can be done and dignity achieved. Nothing is more sterile or lamentable than the man content to live with himself. . . . It seems to me essential that we cultivate the ability to operate lucidly upon our problems and therefore be in a position to solve them. That's why your sister loves me. I don't play about at the periphery of matters. . . . Neither do I ask to be loved. I expect to be given only what I've worked for. . . . Everything has a function . . ." (p. 53). The scene closes with Disson's observation that his second in command needs a secretary, and Willy suggests that his own sister would be perfect. Like her husband, who functions emotionally rather than logically in spite of his protestations to the contrary, Diana wants to work not for reasons of efficiency but because of her emotions—she wants to be near Disson, an interesting reason, considering the speech he has just made (which has obviously made no impression on her brother).

Later Diana and the two boys are engaged in a Lewis Carroll type dialogue expressing sentiments in much the same way they are presented in the Alice books ("JOHN. Children seem to mean a great deal to their parents, I've noticed. Though I've often wondered what 'a great deal' means. / TOM. I've often wondered what 'mean' means," p. 55) and echoing their father's beliefs and self-conceit ("JOHN. Well, it really all depends on how good you are at making adjustments. We're very good at making adjustments, aren't we, Tom?" p. 55). Although the insipid conversation Diana and the twins are having is entirely innocent, when Disson comes in he looks quickly from one face to another as though he has surprised a triumvirate of conspirators in the midst of their plotting.

Disson and Wendy are then seen together as he is dictating a letter to her at the office. The scene turns into a seductive display when Disson notices his secretary wriggling, a condition he attributes to the hardness of her chair. Wendy goes through several contortions and postures while her employer watches before she settles on his desk.

Back home in the game room Disson and Willy play table tennis, Disson performing skillfully as his sons applaud his winning points. Then on one of Willy's serves, Disson thinks two balls have been put into play and he misses the shot (in the television production the camera is from Disson's point of view and two balls *are* served). Willy denies it and the twins confirm him.

The next scene is in Peter Disley's surgery, where Disson has gone to get his eyes checked. In the prose version he wears glasses; on stage Pinter has eliminated them. Disley assures his patient that his eyes are perfect; he had even picked out a small brown stain on the doctor's cheek as an "evident" distinguishing mark which no one had ever noticed before. Most of the time his eyesight is excellent, Disson agrees, but recently "it's become unreliable. It's become . . . erratic," another piece of evidence that he is deficient, as with Rose, Stanley, and Edward before him (p. 60). The idea of physical deterioration is repeated when Disson experiences difficulty in tying his tie correctly.

Back at the office again, Disson touches Wendy's chair while waiting for her to come in, then sits in it. When she enters, she claims to be hurt because he did not notice her new dress. He wants to know when she put it on and where. Exposing her narcissism, she says she put it on in the hall because there is a full-length mirror there. This scene presents the beginning of the theme which Esslin contends will develop into the main subject of *Tea Party* as the protagonist's "inferiority complex towards his wife drives him to lust after his secretary."[7]

In Disson's workshop the boys humorously irritate their father as he tries to demonstrate for them "how to concentrate your physical energies, to do something useful":

DISSON. What are you doing?
TOM. I'm holding this piece of wood.
DISSON. Well, stop it. I've finished chipping. Look at the point now.
JOHN. If you put some lead in there you could make a pencil out of it.
DISSON. They think you're very witty at your school, do they?
JOHN. Well, some do and some don't, actually, Dad [p. 64].

Even his sons are questioning his abilities. While showing them how to saw correctly, Disson makes a mistake in marking a section of wood, for which he sends John to his room, and after making another mistake which almost costs Tom a finger, he accuses the boy of being at fault.

At the office once more, Disson complains that his eyes hurt and asks Wendy to tie her chiffon scarf, which will evolve into a fetish, around his head. After she does so she makes a business call for him. While she is talking he touches her body, and though she moves under his touch, she does not withdraw beyond his reach. Willy calls over the intercom wanting to know if he can borrow Wendy's services for a few minutes because Diana felt unwell and went home. When Wendy disappears into the adjoining office, Disson hears "*giggles, hissing, gurgles, squeals.*" He goes to the door, squats, and tries to see through the keyhole. Finding that he cannot see, he puts his ear to the door. As he squats by the door, it opens and Diana stands over him asking, "What game is this?" Disson immediately becomes defensive, alternately trying to excuse his actions by claiming to be looking for a dropped pencil and assuming a threatening stance: "How dare you speak to me like that? I'll knock your teeth out" (p. 67). The scene closes as he inanely and ironically wants to know why everybody is getting excited.

7. Esslin, *The Theatre of the Absurd*, p. 253.

The following scene pictorially shows Disson's increasing preoccupation with Wendy's body as his imagination enlarges her buttocks so enormously that his hands go up to keep them at bay. To release the tension Disson knocks a lighter from the desk and invites his secretary to play soccer with him, urging her to get the "ball" away from him. He grabs Wendy's arm only to have her call "That's a foul!" and although she wants to go on with the game he sinks to the floor.

At home in bed Disson and his wife talk, Diana noting that he has seemed "a little subdued" lately. He passes off her comment by saying that he is reading the *Life of Napoleon* (an interesting historically parallel success story). Diana reminds him that their first wedding anniversary is coming up, and he tells her that he is giving a little tea party in celebration at the office and his mother and father will be in town for it.

Returning to the office, Disson and Wendy are discussing business correspondence when he experiences momentary blindness and the television screen goes black. Wendy tells him his eyes are open and thinks he is playing another game:

DISSON. You mean my eyes are open? . . . Is this you? This I feel?
WENDY. Yes.
DISSON. What, all this I can feel?
WENDY. You're playing one of your games, Mr. Disson. You're being naughty again.
    Vision back.
    DISSON *looks at her.*
You sly old thing [p. 72].

Back to Disley's surgery, where the ophthalmologist implies that this may not be a physical problem—"I only deal with eyes, old chap. . . . Why don't you go to someone else? . . . Nothing worrying you, is there?" (p. 73). Disson reminds the doctor that he is his oldest friend, who was to have been his best man, and pleads for Disley to help him, but Disley refuses to communicate and asks who gave the testimonial in his place.

Things continue to get worse and Disson's accusations grow wilder in the next scene. Sitting at home with his wife and Willy, he asks them to tell him "about the place where you two were born. Where you played at being brother and sister." The paranoia has progressed to the point that Disson not only distrusts his brother-in-law with his secretary, he questions the actions of his wife and her brother. Willy replies that they were not playing brother and sister. Diana orders her husband to stop drinking and he goes into a tirade about how much he used to drink: "I used to down eleven or nine pints a night! . . . Every night of the stinking week! Me and the boys!" His memories start Willy reminiscing about his old family home and Disson amusingly joins him:

WILLY. Yes, Sunderly was beautiful.
DISSON. The lake.
WILLY. The lake.
DISSON. The long windows.
WILLY. From the withdrawing-room.

. . .

DISSON. Negroes at the gate, under the trees.
WILLY. No Negroes. . . .
DISSON. Why in God's name not?
WILLY. Just one of those family quirks, Robert [p. 74].

Diana invites Disson to bed and he is offended that she "can say that, in front of him" (her brother). He quizzes her on why she married him and she leaves the room, after which Willy asks to have a private word with him and Disson warns his brother-in-law to "mind how you tread." Willy suggests that a mental problem might be developing, repeating Disley's earlier concern: "Is there anything on your mind?" Disson answers that there is no problem and asks if Willy would like to be his partner, "to share full responsibility" (p. 75). The difference between Disson's earlier life and Diana's increases the husband's uneasiness.

Ping-pong for a second time provides evidence of Disson's accelerating breakdown. Where Disson was confident, decisive, and expert in his play before, now he is desperate and performs with difficulty. And again he has trouble with his vision. Possessing an effective backhand in the prior games, he was always able to counter Willy. This time, however, Willy forces his forehand and Disson loses his sight for an instant (which is worse than seeing two balls when only one exists, as in the last game).

Disson's parents have arrived in the next scene. The main topic of the conversation they hold with their son serves as a reminder that he has turned out to be an extremely successful businessman, for they are amazed at the expensive furnishings which decorate his house. Subsequently Disson is shown at the scene of his success, his office, in a nonsuccessful situation. Wendy ties the chiffon round his head at his direction, but he complains that it "stinks" and tears it off. She leans forward to fix the scarf, and as she does so, he touches her, but she stops him, saying, "No—you mustn't touch me, if you're not wearing your chiffon" (p. 79).

Disson has not moved in the following scene, in which Disley has taken Wendy's place and is tying a bandage around his patient's head. This time the blindfold is not applied as in a game, as it was earlier in this play and in *The Birthday Party*. Willy drops in to make sure that the covering is on straight and the knots are tight, and then a series of short cuts of all the characters in differing combinations represents the progression of the tea party, activities which the audience can see, but Disson can only hear, though there are camera shots from Disson's point of view in which the figures are seen *"mouthing silently, in conspiratorial postures"* (p. 83). They seem oblivious to his presence. At one point, though the audience is aware that the conversations being carried on are trite and innocent, the events take on a more sinister cast when Willy smilingly places a Ping-pong ball in Disson's hand. Whether or not this is imaginary is hard to tell. It almost certainly is, for if it were not, nearly every character in the play would have to be implicated in a plot against Disson, and there were instances—loss of sight and so forth—that others would have had no control over; disturbingly, the action does take place on the stage. The following sequence may similarly be attributed to Disson's imagination as a fantasized vision of his sexual inadequacy, but the audience does see Diana and Wendy, giggling silently, hoist themselves up on the desk where they lie head to toe while Willy caresses the face, first of one and then of the other. Disson falls to the floor in his chair. Disley and Willy try to lift him up— they cannot loosen him from the chair. Disley removes the bandage and they turn the chair upright, Disson still seated on it. As John and Willy hold the chair, Disley and Tom try to pull Disson off it, but he cannot be moved. "Anyone would think he was chained to it," Willy exclaims (p. 87). Diana moves to her husband and tries to get him to recognize her, but he sits impassively in a catatonic state as the play ends with a close-up of his eyes staring straight ahead.

Tea Party is the picture of a man who is only superficially threatened by outside forces; it is the menace from within which destroys him, just as surely as it destroyed Edward in *A Slight Ache*. Pinter depicts Robert Disson as a man successful in all fields of endeavor: he is a good businessman, friend, husband, father, and son. And it is his very success which defeats him, somewhat like an Aristotelian tragic hero, though perhaps he is more akin to Joe in Arthur Miller's *All My Sons* because he does not have sufficient stature to make his fall meaningful in Aristotelian terms.

Disson suffers a mental breakdown (as implied in *The Birthday Party*, *The Caretaker*, and *A Slight Ache*, an acceptable solution to an intolerable problem; as in *A Slight Ache* the collapse is the more complete because it comes from inside rather than being imposed from without). His success has led him to fear failure. In order to be a success, one must be unafraid to risk failure (the "nothing ventured, nothing gained" aphorism). Disson is made vulnerable by his triumphs. Willy's reference to him as a self-made man, his own remembrances about the old days, and the appearance of his parents make it obvious how far he has risen. The breakdown may also result from the tension between the desire for social status and respectability, represented by Diana, and sensuality, symbolized by Wendy. Disson would then be confronted with the problem Richard faces in *The Lover*, the split being more obvious in its embodiment in two different carriers as opposed to being combined in one.

The pretension after social position, in spite of the Knightsbridge office and the elegant home in St. John's Wood, which are both "designed with taste," leads Disson to recognize that the gap between his background and his goals cannot be bridged by money alone. Feelings of social inadequacy become expressed as sexual inadequacy and the loss of other skills. As with Edward, who possibly married the squire's daughter to improve his position, the deterioration of his physical body precludes the defeat of his psyche, and blindness is punishment for his pretensions (with perhaps oedipal overtones). We are again reminded of Henry Woolf's revelation of the dramatist's lifelong deficiency in eyesight and that problems with sight plague Pinter characters from Rose's final blindness, Stan's need for glasses, and Edward's ache to Disson's extreme case, all of which signify guilt or an inability to see the world as it really is and symbolize a failure to come to grips with reality.

Disson's preoccupation with the reasons his wife married him is indicative of his mental state. It is a symptom of his insecurity and need for reassurance. The very fact that he explains to Willy that he is secure and does not need love negates his contentions, for if true they would not need to be stated. The game of table tennis is another symbol for his unsettled life; the ball bounces back and forth quickly like the changes of scene as he loses confidence and is forced into a service break which reflects his emotional break.

Tea Party has a more pervasive surrealistic quality to it than many of Pinter's earlier plays, and it is fitting that in a tale of mental disintegration Theatre of the Absurd effects are employed to such a great extent (the two Ping-pong balls, the chiffon scarf, the party, the two women lying on the desk). The blindfold applied at Disson's own insistence compounds the ambiguity of the drama because he cannot confirm his fears and suspicions visually, fears which may have at least some basis in reality, as suggested by the periods of blindness and Willy's actions with the two women, fears which have driven him to the point of suspecting everyone as being ranged against him ("playing at brother and sister").

In an extension of the reality/appearance theme (verification) Disson can no longer trust his senses to make sense out of the world which surrounds him. He cannot coordinate the sum of his many reflections, the kind that in *The Basement* became part of the physical environment. Taylor feels that *Tea Party* signals the dramatist's shift from his concern with verification as related to individual personalities, a rejection of the subjective in favor of the objective.[8] The play starts out with Disson's perspective, but unlike *The Dwarfs*, in which the audience shares Len's mind and view of the universe, there is a separation as the audience is dissociated from Disson's point of view and the stream of consciousness disappears. At the beginning of the play the audience is with Disson; at the conclusion it is watching him from the outside.

8. Taylor, *Anger and After*, p. 353, and *Harold Pinter*, p. 21.

The significance of the tea party itself and the relationship of the title to the play sum up the meaning of Disson's excursion into madness. On stage the tea party is the culmination of the protagonist's life and, like the Mad Hatter's tea party, it presents a state in which all contact with reality has been lost and the main character is reduced to a deaf, dumb, and blind vegetable which has become one with the chair on which it sits.

Although *The Basement* and *Tea Party* both seem to be out of place in terms of Pinter's thematic development, it must be remembered that the dates of composition, the early sixties, link them with his earlier works. The subject matter which the dramatist is considering (flux, verification) shows no thematic evolution, but the dramas come from a period during which he was still considering the potentialities of these themes, which means that he was interested in experimenting with the form of his expression rather than with new content. *The Basement* and *Tea Party*, then, are additional indicators of the playwright's thinking around the time he was working on *The Lover*.

In the "memory" plays which follow it can be seen that Taylor's assessment is only partly true, as the coordination of reality clusters becomes increasingly more difficult exactly because no objectivity is possible. Pinter's new emphasis will require an understanding that everyone subjectively structures the world constantly, and that such efforts create new realities.

Chapter IX. Plays of Memory

. . . sometimes the cause of
the shadow cannot be found . . .

Taylor comes to the conclusion that memory debilitates the men in *The Homecoming*.[1] Pinter's next five plays, *Landscape, Silence, Night, Old Times,* and *No Man's Land* are short (with the exception of the somewhat longer *Old Times*, fittingly compressed after the manner of Beckett's *Play, Krapp's Last Tape,* and *Embers*), they are almost completely devoid of any action, and, most important, they are concerned with memory. Whether this aspect of the verification problem is to be considered the author's new focus of interest can only be determined when his next major play comes out, though it is certain that this quintet of latest dramas does not conform to the "objective phase" which Taylor felt was signaled by *Tea Party*.

As a matter of fact, these latest works clearly differ from their predecessors in two important considerations: "There isn't any menace at all,"[2] at least not

1. Taylor, *Harold Pinter*, p. 23.
2. Pinter, in Dean, "Late Night Line Up."

of the kind found in the earlier plays, and they are deeply, almost totally, involved with the past. Pinter's statements that "I'm not at all interested in 'threatening behavior' any more"[3] and that the dramas lack menace are not completely accurate, since the characters do feel threatened; but the threat is even less explicitly stated than in the love/need pieces, and it definitely has lost its active motivational emphasis. With the resultant focus on the past, a new theme is being opened. But Pinter's interest does not lie merely with what has happened or what has not happened (*vide* his statements in "Between the Lines" quoted earlier, in which he comments on the impossibility of verifying both past and present events). "What interests me a great deal is the mistiness of the past," he says in discussing *Old Times*. This mistiness, whether or not Deeley and Anna met in a pub twenty years ago ("the fact is they might have and they might not have"), for example, allows the playwright to make a jump to the conclusion that we do, indeed, create the past continually, and not just through the passing of time. He goes on to comment: "The fact that [Deeley and Anna] discuss something that he says took place—even if it did not take place—actually seems to me to recreate the time and the moments vividly in the present, so that it is actually taking place before your very eyes."[4] As Anna says, "There are some things one remembers even though they may never have happened."[5] There is of necessity sometimes the concurrent phenomenon of uncreating the past, as Winnie in Beckett's *Happy Days* affirms: "And should one day the earth cover my breasts, then I shall never have seen my breasts, no one ever seen my breasts."[6]

To some extent, apparently, the dramatist feels that the present creation of the past (which is as valid and verifiable as what "really" took place) is a function of what he calls "verification," but there is a new element which he is paying attention to now, a sort of omnipresence of experience. Paradoxically, we are what the past has made us, yet we remake the past according to what we are. Meg's recounting of Stan's history, Lenny's wild tales, all become true because they are told, so there is no longer any way to differentiate between what is true and what is not true, nor any need to. This is subjectivity at its purest. And it grows out of a consciousness "of a kind of ever-present quality in life. . . . the past is not past, . . . it never was past. It's present" because "You carry all the states with you until the end. . . . those previous parts are alive and present."[7]

Possibly it is the mistiness of the past which softens our perceptions of everything that has also led Pinter to write about a different kind of love in these newest plays, a more "romantic" love: "as they say, it's a very important element in all our lives, isn't it? And I think it's the most misunderstood, mal-

3. Gussow, "A Conversation (Pause) with Harold Pinter," p. 126.
4. Ibid., p. 43.
5. Pinter, *Old Times* (New York: Grove, 1971), pp. 31–32.
6. Samuel Beckett, *Happy Days* (New York: Grove, 1961), p. 38.
7. Gussow, pp. 132–33.

treated matter, too."[8] This shift in subject would also account for the stylistic change he is undergoing. Though this applies to prior works, too, he claims "What I'm interested in is emotion which is contained, and felt very, very deeply. . . . But, perhaps, it is ultimately inexpressible. Because I think we express our emotions in so many small ways, all over the place—or can't express them in any other way." Trying to express these feelings more lyrically than before has brought him to "dangerous territory"; "You can fall on your ass very easily in attempting to express in, if you like, 'lyrical' terms what is actually happening to people. . . . I did it, in 'Silence,' but I cut it."[9]

Landscape

Landscape represents a reversal in the author's normal creative process for, although it was first presented on a BBC Third Programme radio broadcast on April 25, 1968, it was originally written for the stage. The reason is quite simple. When the play was submitted to the Lord Chamberlain for approval for production by the Royal Shakespeare Company at the Aldwych Theater in 1968, the Lord Chamberlain (in his last year in the capacity of stage censor) refused to let it be acted without the removal of several "offensive" four-letter words. Pinter refused to alter the play and it was then broadcast by the BBC intact, since radio was not subject to the Lord Chamberlain's jurisdiction. The play made its stage debut on July 2, 1969, at the Aldwych on a double bill with *Silence*.

This history is especially interesting in the light of remarks made by Pinter in Lawrence Bensky's interview two years earlier: "I do object to one thing to do with sex: this scheme afoot on the part of many 'liberal-minded' persons to open up obscene language to general commerce. It should be the dark secret language of the underworld. There are very few words—you shouldn't kill them by overuse. I have used such words once or twice in my plays, but I couldn't get them through the Lord Chamberlain. They're great, wonderful words, but must be used very sparingly. The pure publicity of freedom of language fatigues me, because it's a demonstration rather than something said."[10]

The play itself is confusing. Two people, Beth, a woman in her late forties, and Duff, a man in his early fifties, sit and talk at a kitchen table, but the stage directions make it clear that they are not communicating, maybe not even talking to each other: "DUFF *refers normally to* BETH, *but does not appear to hear her voice.* BETH *never looks at* DUFF, *and does not appear to hear his voice. Both characters are relaxed, in no sense rigid.*"[11] In addition,

8. Ibid., p. 126.   9. Ibid., p. 128.
10. Quoted in Bensky, "Harold Pinter: An Interview," p. 34.
11. Pinter, *Landscape*, in *Landscape and Silence* (New York: Grove, 1970), p 7.

while Duff's chair is at the right corner of the table, Beth "sits in an armchair, which stands away from the table, to its left." The setting is a clue to the meaning of the drama—Beth has withdrawn from life into her imagination and Duff is still involved in living and trying to reinvolve her. Taylor has commented that the "surface realism is perfect" in producing a "tone [which] is quiet, meditative, of emotion recollected . . . in a state where all passion is spent" to present a couple who live in "independent worlds, sublimely unaware of each other." [12]

Beth speaks first, remembering being on a beach with her man and being looked at by two women (possibly Mr. Sykes' mother and sister, two women mentioned later). The image of the beach is the predominant one in Beth's talk, but it is an image from the past, expressed in language which reflects her separation from the world by its lack of syntax. In her frozen position she is clearly not an existential heroine. When Duff speaks it is almost as though the couple were engaged in two monologues instead of a conversation. As he talks about the rainstorm and their dog, though, he remains in the present.

The first hint in the dialogue to the meaning of *Landscape* comes in Beth's continued remembrances when she mentions how everyone used to touch her "lightly"—"With one exception." That exception may be the brutal attack Duff describes later. In her first speech she had claimed to be beautiful; now she declares, "I could be the same. I dress differently, but I am beautiful" (p. 12). The difference is that in the opening lines she was caught up in her depiction of the beach scene. Later she will comment "Of course when I'm older I won't be the same as I am" (p. 24), yet she is listed in the *dramatis personae* as "a woman in her late forties," a description which does not tally with the picture she paints of herself as a girl on the sand. She does not see herself as a middle-aged woman; time has stopped for her and she is still the youngster of happier days; time has no meaning since she has divorced herself from it. This is brought out when Duff relates his account of her standing in the hall and striking the gong—the house is empty, but she acts as though no time had passed, as though everyone were there. Having placed herself outside time, she is not aware of its passage, so she might just as well be calling people to lunch in a moment twenty years past and not know it.

There are three possible explications of *Landscape*, all of which would lead to the situation as presented. First, Beth may have loved her former employer, Mr. Sykes, who is probably dead (Duff refers to him only in the past tense—"I was never sorry for him, at any time, for his lonely life"). The play, then, would be about a woman fondly remembering her deceased lover. Second, Beth has been confronted with her husband's confession of infidelity and she may be retreating into her memory of the good times she and Duff once knew, when he was still "true" to her. A third alternative would be a

12. Taylor, *Anger and After*, p. 356, and *Harold Pinter*, p. 23.

combination of the first two: faced with her husband's acknowledged indiscretion, Beth might be imaginatively striking back at him by creating a fantasy of love. The first explanation would be an instance of a woman's debilitation by the force of memory, as opposed to the men in *The Homecoming*. In the second case the inaction would be the function of a defense mechanism. The third exposition would again combine these two elements in a way which would be natural for a woman as sensitive and sensually oriented as Beth is portrayed as being in both her own detailing of hands and waves caressing her and Duff's observations of her flower gathering and the like.

In a letter to Hans Schweikart, the director of the first German production of *Landscape* (Hamburg, January 1970), which was mistakenly printed in the program, Pinter expresses his feeling that "the man on the beach is Duff. I think there are elements of Mr Sykes in her memory of this Duff, which she might be attributing to Duff, but the man remains Duff. I think that Duff detests and is jealous of Mr Sykes, although I do not believe that Mr Sykes and Beth were ever lovers." He goes on to say that he "formed these conclusions after [he] had written the plays [*Landscape* and *Silence*] and after learning about them through rehearsals."[13]

Whichever interpretation is true, it is evident that Beth and Duff have been together for some time, including the period of her interlude on the beach. She discusses her gravity as a younger woman and how she used to arrange flowers. Duff, too, remembers that she was grave when she was young and is aware of her interest in flowers. His awareness indicates that his character might not be as brutal as it sometimes seems, and his use of her regard for flowers suggests his motives and, therefore, his relationship to this estranged woman; as discussed later, there is no need to oppose the tenderness of the man on the beach with the brutality of Duff. Aside from the fact that Beth and Duff were aware of each other in the past, there are indications that the couple are conscious of each other's presence even now. Each seems to be talking past the other, but they do pick up cues from the words spoken. For instance, Duff announces that he is sleeping soundly of late. Beth recalls her walks in the water, after which Duff attributes his sleeping to thinking about wooing fish (which he may be doing with Beth). Beth talks about going to a hotel for a cup of tea. Duff tells her about his experience in a bar the day before and she incorporates a bar into her discourse. And after Beth remembers some children playing as she watched through a window, Duff describes an evening when he stood behind her and looked at her reflection in a window. The fact that Beth occasionally initiates these incidents seems to invalidate Esslin's argument, based on the stage directions, that everything she says is actually part of an *"internal monologue."*[14]

Duff, however, is the information supplier. It is through him that the

13. Quoted in Esslin's *The Peopled Wound*, p. 187 n.
14. Esslin, *The Theatre of the Absurd*, p. 254.

audience learns that the couple are living in Mr. Sykes' house and that they had once been the man's servants. Duff drove the car for the "gloomy bugger," who lived a lonely life, while Beth did the housework, apparently quite well. Another clue is provided here, for although they are in the house alone and no one else seems to have been on the premises for some time, they have confined themselves to the servants' section of the house. If Beth is so in love with her memory of Sykes, it would seem that she would keep the place as neat as she did when he was there (and for which he complimented her) as a sort of shrine or memorial to him; yet Duff calls her attention to the moths in the drapes and has to tell her that "the dust is bad" all over.

The revelation of Duff's infidelity comes as a surprise: from what has been said so far Beth's account of a day at the beach with her man would seem more likely to be a tale of illicit love. Duff's disclosure, though, provides a reason for both characters acting as they do. It also reveals further evidence of the sensitive side of Duff's nature, because he was "gentle" and "kind" to her afterwards and they took a walk together to the pond, where she fed the ducks (mating for life, ducks are considered faithful birds in folklore, whereas sparrows, the birds Duff would have chosen to feed, are accounted lecherous). The drama thus becomes another example of betrayal, and Beth's tender kiss is a kiss of parting, for life has taken a new direction and she chooses to stay behind with her memories.

Duff's discourse about the dinner Mr. Sykes gave for his mother and sister the Friday evening following the confession of faithlessness leads Beth away from the beach and toward the dreamlike state she is now in. Her imagery of the mistiness which surrounded her when she got up the next morning recalls Edmund's seeking to escape into a dream world of fog in O'Neill's *Long Day's Journey Into Night* (Edmund sought death, but Beth is not really alive any more). It also contrasts starkly with Duff's accompanying cellarman's jargon. The contrast is between one who is not in life and one who is, the ephemeral versus the concrete, a floating lethargic delivery as contrasted with rhythmic rapidity. Compare "The sun was shining. Wet, I mean wetness, all over the ground. . . . Still misty, but thinner, thinning. . . . Wetness all over the air. Sunny. Trees like feathers," and "Give the drayman a hand with the barrels. Down the slide through the cellarflaps. Lower them by rope to the racks. Rock them on the belly, put a rim up them, use balance and leverage, hike them up onto the racks" (p. 25).

The only time Beth's language attains the clarity and technical detail that Duff's has is when she relates her approach to drawing (which he never mentions): "I remembered always . . . the basic principles of shadow and light. Objects intercepting the light cast shadows. Shadow is deprivation of light. The shape of the shadow is determined by that of the object. But not always. Not always directly. Sometimes it is only indirectly affected by it. Sometimes the cause of the shadow cannot be found. (*Pause.*) But I always bore in mind the basic principles of drawing. (*Pause.*) So that I never lost track. Or heart" (pp. 27–28). This may well be the key speech in the play, for Beth is involved with shadows—the shadows of remembered people which fall across her path like the shadow in Eliot's "The Hollow Men," which falls between idea and reality, motion and act, conception and creation, emotion and response. Shadows are concrete to her; previously she told how her man had felt her shadow when it fell on him. The deprivation is the result of Duff's actions, as he has taken true love from her.

Ironically, Duff may be falling under the shadow now, too. His anecdote about his adventure the day before contains elements of previous descriptions of the walk to the pond on the day after his confession. Both tales involve a walk to the pond with the dog, feeding birds, children playing, and a couple under the trees. Perhaps he is incorporating into the verbal level a vision of the two of them on that day in the past (he saw the man and woman when it was raining, but when it cleared they had disappeared; both he and Beth are unsure about the presence of other people, as when she was not sure whether there had been another man on the beach).

The final "action" in the drama is a change in tone with Duff's outburst about when Beth rang the gong: "You stood in the hall and banged the gong. (*Pause.*) What the bloody hell are you doing banging that bloody gong?" (p. 28). Duff slips back and forth between "now" and "then," but what is more important is what he claims followed: "I took the chain off and the thimble, the keys, the scissors slid off it and clattered down. I booted the gong down the hall. . . . I would have had you in front of the dog, like a man, in the hall, on the stone, banging the gong. . . . I'll hang it back on its hook, bang you against it swinging, gonging, . . . bring out the bacon, bang your lovely head . . . . slam . . ." (p. 29). Was she trying to call her lover back and thus bringing on her husband's angry, envious rape? This could be that "one exception" to everyone's treating her lightly. Perhaps the episode was her reaction to Duff's confession. Or did anything even take place?

The story may be exaggerated or even fantasy, since there is nothing else like it in the drama. On the other hand, if it did happen, it ties in with several other events mentioned during the play. Duff may be attempting to force Beth to face reality, to come out of her shell. He probably was the man on the beach she spends her time remembering, not Mr. Sykes. Sykes had hired Duff to drive for him and Duff was a good driver, so Sykes probably would not have taken the car out alone. And Beth mentions the skill with which the driver smoothly put the automobile in reverse. Duff loved his wife, then. He still does. This explains the rape—an attempt to shock his wife out of her reverie represented by the closed house that her mind has become (with moths and dust) into the real world which opposes it, as represented by the life outside the house, which even though it contains "Dogshit, duckshit . . . all kinds of shit" is open and bright with sun, flowers, and butterflies. His opening remark, "The dog's gone" fits into this pattern of shock treatment. It must have been an old dog, since it was with them in their youth, and yesterday in the shelter it went to sleep (died?). Now it is gone. The abrupt news may be calculated to startle her into awareness.

Duff's position is summarized by the fact that he "thinks" Beth likes for him to talk to her. Apparently this situation has existed for some time and he has been attempting communication all along. Besides trying to reach his wife through abrupt, open channels Duff uses ploys much as Mick used them with Aston. He tries to get her interested in something like a walk or sunning herself in the garden. He has gone so far as to put some flowers in the garden in an effort to entice her out of her skull. Unfortunately, he has not succeeded in drawing her out of her shell, as is indicated by the poignant closing speech:

He lay above me and looked down at me. He supported my shoulder.
> *Pause.*
So tender his touch on my neck. So softly his kiss on my cheek.
> *Pause.*
My hand on his rib.
> *Pause*
So sweetly the sand over me. Tiny the sand on my skin.
> *Pause.*
So silent the sky in my eyes. Gently the sound of the tide.
> *Pause.*
Oh my true love I said [pp. 29–30].

Silence

It is impossible to follow the plot line directly in Pinter's next play, *Silence*. As Ellen says in the drama, "Yes, I remember. But I'm never sure that what I remember is of to-day or of yesterday or of a long time ago."[15] Pinter has woven the present, remembrances of the past, and two past times together to create what Esslin terms his "most lyrical . . . mysterious and difficult" play.[16]

First staged by the Royal Shakespeare Company at the Aldwych Theatre on July 2, 1969, as a companion piece to *Landscape*, *Silence* is one of Pinter's most poetic theatrical endeavors and the one which took him longest to write ("the structure was so different"). Like the Benjy section in Faulkner's *The Sound and the Fury*, the drama becomes poetic as the playwright presents a montage of images from three different time sets which creates the overall metaphor and meaning of the play. There are refrains as threads of meaning

---

15. Pinter, *Silence*, in *Landscape and Silence*, p. 46.
16. Esslin, *The Peopled Wound*, p. 188. Interestingly, there are occasional echoes from *The Dwarfs*, possibly an even more difficult work.

and repeated lines weave in and out, reappearing in snatches and new contexts to tie everything together; and there are caesura-like silences which measure stanzaic groupings of lines, marking the changes in time setting, with image clusters that sound like combinations of Eliot, Yeats, and Hopkins, as the dramatist pictures three people trapped by their memories.

By the end of the play the premise itself is fairly clear. Rumsey, a man of forty, knew a young girl, Ellen, now in her twenties, when she was just a child. The events which took place during that period form the first time set. The second time set occurred when Ellen was older and they fell in love. Rumsey recognized that she should find someone else nearer her own age and, against her wishes, Bates, a man now in his middle thirties, entered the picture to assume the role of a rejected suitor. The third time set takes place in the present as Rumsey, still on his farm, and Ellen and Bates, who have moved into town to live separately, face life emotionally cut off from all others as they remember their past relationships, which they would not or could not continue. The isolation of the three is demonstrated in the directions for the set:

Three areas.
A chair in each area.[17]

The difficulty in following the plot comes from Pinter's presentation, for this memory play is appropriately cast as three interior monologues. The drama starts with Rumsey, Ellen, and Bates remembering a period of past emotions in present-tense terms. This is followed by a silence, indicating a shift in time. The three characters now "talk" about the present in the present tense, but their descriptions are lethargic as compared to their thoughts of the past. There is a trace of nonsyntactical country dialect in their speech, especially when they remember the time that was, but it is not used with consistency, for Pinter also employs syntax to duplicate the thought processes. In sections dealing with what has happened the rules of syntactical order are not followed, partly because the ideas are not complete and partly to convey the memories as images which make a mental impression faster than thought and which do not have to be logically structured to impose meaning, feeling, or a picture. Bates' opening dialogue is a good example of this type of representation (pp. 34–35): "Caught a bus to the town. Crowds. Lights round the market, rain and stinking. . . . Black roads and girders. She clutching me. . . . Brought her into this place, my cousin runs it. Undressed her, placed my hand." In the next segment Bates considers his present surroundings. Since this is on a more conscious level, not drifting in a daydream, the syntax is better: "I'm at my last gasp with this unendurable racket. I kicked open the door and stood before them. Someone called me Grandad and told me to button it. It's they should button it. Were I young . . ."

17. Pinter, *Silence*, p. [31].

That Bates is designated "Grandad" and longs to be young again when he is barely middle-aged provides the first intimation of the play's theme. Ellen repeats a similar feeling moments later when she recalls her conversations with a quite elderly drinking companion: "She asks me about my early life, when I was young . . . but I have nothing to tell her about the sexual part of my youth. I'm old, I tell her, my youth was somewhere else, anyway I don't remember" (p. 36). Ellen is in her twenties! Perhaps she feels that sexual experiences are better indicators of age than a simple numbering of years. More likely, however, the three characters look at life as something without meaning, for everything is in the past for them. Displaced in time, they are like old people who must be content with memories.

That memory has trapped these three is evident in the activities they now indulge in. Each of the characters wants to remain alone à la Rose in his or her room, where things are "pleasant": Rumsey is at ease "alone"; Ellen was eager to get back from her drinking companion; Bates stays in his room "suffocating," to his landlady's consternation. When they are outside they still do not come into any real human contact: Rumsey sees people who walk toward him but never reach him; Ellen meets with her elderly woman friend briefly, but there is no communication ("she could never know much of me," p. 36); Bates rejects his landlady's worry about keeping to himself, unsmiling, by announcing, "I've had all that. I've got all that" (p. 43). He has had companionship and he still has it in his mind. Bates could be speaking for all three of the characters.

The only movement in the play comes when decisions affecting the future course of one of the relationships are relived in flashbacks. Significantly, in the first of these three actions, Bates moves to Ellen, who refuses to go with him on a walk or to his cousin's place in town. Ellen moves to Rumsey in the second instance, when they reconstruct the evening during which she changed from a child to a young woman capable of responding to sexual love. The third time Ellen moves to Rumsey as he tells her to "find a young man." She replies, "There aren't any. . . . I hate them," and he finishes the conversation by repeating his admonition to "find one" (pp. 44–45).

Ellen's declining of Bates' invitation when he remembers taking her to his cousin's, undressing her, and placing his hand, and her expressed attitude toward men younger than Rumsey (who has an older man's appeal—perhaps even as a father figure) suggests that Bates' tragedy is that he is caught in a past which never existed. The tragedy for Rumsey and Ellen is that they are also living in the past when they could have carried on their relationship.

Night

Night is a very short one-act play which was first presented as part of a program of plays about marriage called *Mixed Doubles* at the Comedy Theatre, April 9, 1969. This approximately seven-minute sketch is little longer than some of the revue sketches, but it is clearly related to *Landscape* and *Silence* not only by its date of composition but by the theme of memory.

In the play a man and a woman in their forties sit drinking coffee at night. They talk about their first meeting, yet the accounts they recall are so dissimilar that they might be discussing completely unrelated events. About the only thing that their stories have in common is the point of departure: both remember that the meeting took place at a party given by a couple named Doughty and that he knew Mrs. Doughty fairly well. They also probably agree that the party occurred during the winter at a house near a river and that they took a walk together, pausing at some time before a window. Apparently they made love that night and now have children. They do not agree on whether they petted on a bridge or against some railings in a field, whether or not he opened her coat to touch her, or if he stood in front of her or in back of her while playing with her breasts. It may be that he is remembering another night with another girl and that she is remembering another night with another man. He does claim to love her, whatever the case may be.

It may be that the pair is playing a game, making up their stories as they go. Several times the responses given by one partner derive from the story being told by the other, as when he recounts how he felt her breasts and she asks "Really?" then offers, "I wondered whether you would, whether you wanted to, whether you would." [18] And when she remembers "you had me and you told me you had fallen in love with me . . . and that you would adore me always," he answers, "Yes I did" (p. 60).

It may also be that their memories have been altered by time according to their needs or a desire to produce the tale which seems most romantic to them; they are, of course, a middle-aged couple tied down to getting up early because they "have things to do" in the morning.

Or they may be remembering totally isolated actions.

Old Times

Reflecting the playwright's admiration for his most frequent director, Pinter's 1971 *œuvre* is dedicated to the Royal Shakespeare's Peter Hall. Prior to its premiere at the Aldwych on June 1, 1971, Hall was quoted as prophesying that *Old Times* would have the audience rolling in the aisles in laughter. As a matter of fact, some of the playgoers reacted as they had to earlier productions by walking out of the theatre before the first act was over, in spite of the fact that the critics have by now generally reversed themselves and the drama was met by predominantly rave reviews. When the

18. Pinter, *Night* in *Landscape and Silence*, p. 59.

drama crossed the Atlantic for its New York run five and a half months later, the reception was much the same.

Typical of the reviewers who praise the play is Clive Barnes, who labels it "the finest play yet of a master dramatist . . . a marvelous play, beautiful, meaningful and lyric. A joyous, wonderful play, that people will talk about as long as we have a theatre."[19] Contradictorily he finds that "Pinter's ideas leap madly like March hares in desperate need of April" because "the intensity of the writing makes too much concentration on it almost dangerous." Because "Pinter's plays are hand grenades thrown into the perilously conscious subconscious," Barnes continues, "he is a playwright who can be experienced only in the cool instant of the theatre." The reviewer then concludes that thematically *Old Times* is concerned with "time-traveling and personal, minute awareness of the instant . . . of emotion remote from circumstances." "Memory is a fallible defense against the past." Where critics dismissed Pinter's early plays because they did not understand them, they now seem to be accepting them for the same reason; the playwright's name is sufficient to insure critical applause.

George Melloan, writing for the *Wall Street Journal*, calls Pinter a creator of "dramatic abstractions. . . . [whose plays are] a tracery of words, movements and pauses that play with subtle psychological themes in their appeal both to consciousness and to the subconscious." On the basis of this description Melloan makes an amazing deduction: "What does it all mean? The answer is that it has no special message. It is merely theatre and very good theatre. . . . But if the play, like most first-rate drama, has no message [!], it works with psychological materials that will have different meanings to different viewers."[20]

In contrast to Barnes and Melloan, T. E. Kalem's harsh criticism sounds more honest: "Harold Pinter has not fallen on his face in *Old Times*, but he has mistaken a dead end for a new road. Even more surprisingly, he has written a play that is a bit of a bore . . . . [In it there are] scattered clues to nowhere except perhaps the murky recesses of the subconscious mind." This "lethargic play" about the past fails, he reasons, because "dramatically the uses of the past are betrayed in *Old Times*. At the end of the play, nothing about the past has been clarified or illuminated."[21] As usual, an accurate evaluation of *Old Times* probably lies somewhere between Barnes' unadulterated approbation and Kalem's stiff rejection, and in part in opposition to the very reason that Melloan sees the work as a success and Kalem faults it—the drama has meaning and the form helps create that meaning.

Although *Old Times* is, in Pinter's opinion, "very closely grained,"[22] the first draft came spontaneously and took only three days to write: "It was one

19. Barnes, "Stage: Caught in the Sway of a Sea-Changed Pinter."
20. Melloan, "Pinter's Abstract Dramatic Art."
21. Kalem, "Is Memory a Cat or a Mouse?" p. 70.
22. Gussow, "A Conversation," p. 131.

of those times when you think you're never going to write again. I was lying on the sofa . . . reading the paper and something flashed in my mind. It wasn't anything to do with the paper. . . . The sofa perhaps. . . . I rushed upstairs to my room. . . . I think [the thought] was the first couple of lines of the play. I don't know if they were actually the *first* lines. . . . Two people talking about someone else. . . . then I really went at it."[23] The play, given the working title "Others With Dancers," was composed so quickly, "like lightning," that the dramatist did not bother to name the characters the first time through, simply designating them A, B, and C. This all seems quite appropriate to the play itself, since there is virtually no plot and the action consists of the characters' creating episodes in their pasts, moving by association, as the drama progresses, much like the very subjective process the playwright suggests he follows in merely putting down the lines as they come, each triggered by the preceding, to produce an ephemeral, intertwining, flowing effect when staged.

In the drama Anna visits her roommate of twenty years ago, Kate, and her husband, Deeley, at their home in the country. During the course of this autumn evening the three reminisce about things past, comparing memories of a time when they all may or may not have known one another. Confusingly the memories run together, diverge, and recombine so that it is difficult to tell who did what, with whom, when. Like the intermingled stories of Duff and Beth in *Landscape* or of the man and wife in *Night*, the collage of tales recounted in *Old Times* is filled with contradictory cross references, with allusions which fit not only the speaker but other characters as well.

Based on the ambiguities present, interpretations might be advanced in which there are a man and only one woman or even one man alone, though drawing on Pinter's previous works for evidence, we may conclude that there are actually three people involved. The author has provided the key to the play when he says, "It happens. It all happens."[24] Happens, not happened: whatever the "truth" of the past may be, the reality that the characters react to is the one which they are spontaneously inventing.

The drama opens with all three characters on stage, but they remain still and silent in the dim light, creating a feeling of moody apprehension and vague unreality. When the lights come up on Deeley and his wife Kate, Anna remains in the dimly lit background, almost as though her presence is in their minds. Because there are intimations throughout the play that one or more of the characters may not actually exist, it may be literally true that Anna is nothing more than a thought, though as will be seen, there is ample reason to believe that the three people are in fact substantive. However, Pinter immediately introduces the idea that there can be no assumptions into the conversation. Kate's ex-roommate is going to call on the couple, and Kate is trying to recall Anna's nature. The wife's statement that her friend used to

23. Ibid., p. 127.   24. Ibid., p. 135.

be "fuller" is met by Deeley's "She may not be now," and the husband's question about the nature of their friendship is countered by "Oh, what does [the word friend] mean? . . . If you have only one of something you can't say it's the best of anything" (pp. 8–9).

Verification and the uncertainty of the past are soon established as a theme, too, as Deeley's "Can't you remember what you felt?" is answered by Kate's "It is a very long time" (p. 8). If we cannot be sure of what is happening now, it is absurd to expect to be able to remember something which happened twenty years ago. Obviously, of course, someone remembers something, or Anna's visit would not occur, yet when Kate suggests "I suppose because she remembers me" (p. 9), there is more involved than a logical explanation. There is a hint that perhaps it is Kate who is the memory. The issue becomes even more confused because Deeley, who assertedly has never met Anna, informs his wife that he will be watching her to see if the ex-roommate is "the same person" (p. 12).

One of the author's favorite devices, contradiction, also comes into play in the first few minutes of *Old Times*. First, Kate states that she has no friends "except her," and then reveals that "she was a thief" (p. 10). Both assertions will be called into question by comments made later in the play. Next she reminds her husband that "I hardly remember her. I've almost totally forgotten her," and replies that she has no idea what Anna drinks, yet moments later shows no curiosity about her old friend's marriage because "You forget. I know her" (pp. 12, 14). Anna, too, is not really concerned about Kate's marriage, because she knows her friend so well that she can predict what it is like. And when the trio has coffee after dinner, Kate does not hesitate to offer Anna hers with milk and sugar while serving Deeley his black.

The conversation about the number of friends the two girls had prepares for another example of contradiction, for Kate insists that Anna was her "only" friend while the roommate had a "normal amount. . . . Hundreds" (p. 15). This assessment seems accurate when Anna later names various men whom they might invite over and Kate contributes no names, yet in Act II it is Kate who expands the list and Anna admits that she does not intend to visit anyone else in England: "I know no one. Except Kate" (p. 64). Of course, it has been twenty years.

During her conversation with Deeley, Kate also refers to the fact that she and Anna were "living together" (p. 15). Although there is nothing startling about this revelation, the phrasing is suggestive, and her husband's reaction— he apparently does not notice it as he continues the dialogue, then pounces on it *"abruptly"* and begins questioning her—is one of the several hints that the roommates might have engaged in lesbianism. Some of Deeley's actions might be attributable to a suspicion that such activities may have taken place, for at times he responds as though he were sexually jealous of Anna. Pinter does not develop the theme of lesbian relations enough for the audience to be able to know with any certainty that they actually exist, though; and most of the evidence can be explained as the young ladies' simple interest in each other's sexual activities, with a definite touch of *ménage à trois* thrown in.

Before Anna joins the conversation, there are two other statements, both by Deeley, which have direct bearing on the meaning of the play. "I knew you had shared [a flat] with someone at one time," he says, "But I didn't know it was her" (p. 17). If the events in the bedroom when a man saw the two girls together actually took place, it is likely that he would have been aware of this relationship, though the description of the encounter is sufficiently ambiguous that it is difficult to tell whether the lighting was such that he may have been unable to recognize the roommate. And there is never any indication that he is aware of her name, though if the women had been living together when Kate became engaged and if they were such close friends, it is surprising that no introductions were ever made.

Deeley brings the conversation to an end when he says "Anyway, none of this matters" (p. 17), a sentiment echoed throughout the work. Why it does not matter is not only confusing but may also be the first clue as to what the play is saying. It might be that it does not matter because it all took place in the past and is, therefore, no longer relevant; or it might not be relevant because it is not real (if either or both Kate and Anna are imaginary); or, since everything is in a continual state of flux, there is no need to try to verify factual information which will momentarily become invalid.

Deeley's observation also serves as a signal for Anna's participation in the conversation. But when she turns from the window and begins speaking, it is *in medias res*; obviously, a time shift has taken place. This may signify that Pinter sees time as being mixed, that "all time is eternally present," in Eliot's words in "Burnt Norton," and indeed this seems to be the case when Anna and Kate seemingly move into the past while Deeley remains in the present at the end of Act I. In many ways *Old Times* is a dramatization of the opening lines of "Burnt Norton":

> Time present and time past
> Are both perhaps present in time future,
> And time future contained in time past.

On the other hand, Anna's intrusion in this manner makes sense if she is purely a mental image, too. If she exists only in Deeley's mind or if she and Kate represent different personalities residing within the same individual, she will always be present somewhere in the background and there will be no anachronism involved in her sudden emergence.

Until Anna participates, *Old Times* could well belong to an earlier period in the playwright's career, in both subject matter and technique. Her active presence soon proves to be the pivotal factor which distinguishes the play as a member of the memory group. Although her first speech is about the past, it is not about the past as Kate and Deeley's talk has been, trying to remember what somebody looked like in a time gone by. For Anna the past was good, full of parks and innocence and excitement and cafés and artistic friends, which she recalls animatedly as though its essence still remained because it happened so recently. Her remembrance is so alive that it hardly seems possible that it all took place long ago, and her question "Does it still exist I wonder?" (p. 18) has a double answer. The life in London that she describes clearly exists in her mind, whether as a vivid memory, as a spontaneous creation, or as a combination memory/creation.

After Anna recaptures this moment from her youth she comments on how "silent" the country is, inaugurating a sequence that has a ring to it like that of the games played in Pinter's earlier dramas. Deeley agrees that it is normally "quite silent," causing Anna to remark, "how sensible and courageous of both of you to stay permanently in such a silence" (p. 19). Deeley observes that his work often takes him away, although when he describes his work later, he is fantasizing: "I had a great crew in Sicily. A marvellous cameraman. Irving Shultz. Best in the business. We took a pretty austere look at the women in black. The little old women in black. I wrote the film and directed it. My name is Orson Welles" (p. 42).[25] The fantasy combines elements from Edward's detailing of his profession in A Slight Ache and Lenny's imaginings about the girl with the pox in The Homecoming, for it implies that Deeley may in truth stay at home permanently; yet the story may be just as real as anything else which the characters say.

The game continues when Anna states that she would never go far, "lest when I returned the house would be gone" (p. 19). Deeley is more impressed by her use of the word "lest" than her fear that the house may disappear. Later Anna will surprise Deeley by saying "gaze," a word which, like "lest," is the kind that you "don't hear . . . very often" (p. 26). Having made this statement, Deeley himself uses the word perfectly naturally in Act II (p. 51), recalling the "light the kettle" incident in The Dumb Waiter. At this point in the play, words become important. Anna accidentally compliments Deeley on his "wonderful casserole" when she means to refer to his wife (p. 20). Kate interrupts the conversation to observe, "I quite like those kind of things, doing it," and Anna and Deeley are both at a loss to understand what she means (p. 21). Is it cooking, her husband wonders? Or because of the phrasing, is the reference sexual in nature, implying possible lesbianism again? (She has been talking about walking on the beach.)

Now that Anna is talking, Deeley's attention focuses on her, and the two almost exclude Kate from their conversation. Anna reveals that she lives on

25. Incidentally, this film is probably imaginary, unless it refers to Journey Into Fear (1942), which Welles only started, the direction (and credit) being taken over by Norman Foster.

a volcanic island, and Deeley, who supposedly has never met her before and who did not know if she married or not, assures her that he knows where she lives because he has been there. But, responds Anna, she is "delighted to be here" (p. 23), which pleases Deeley, too, since it is nice for Kate—which leads the ex-roommate and the husband to discussing Kate as though she were absent, describing her as a dreamer, among other things. Ironically, the references seem confused, for instead of describing his wife's dreaminess, Deeley explains in dreamlike imagery how he sees her: "Sometimes I take her face in my hands and look at it. . . . I look at it, holding it in my hands. Then I kind of let it go, take my hands away, leave it floating" (p. 24). When Anna and Deeley talk in Act II about Kate's bathing, they again employ dreamlike imagery:

DEELEY. . . . Shiny as a balloon.
ANNA. Yes, a kind of floating. . . . She floats from the bath. Like a dream.
   [p. 54].

They might be talking about an idealized woman like Lord Byron's cousin by marriage, Mrs. Robert John Wilmot, who "walks in beauty," but Kate is more on the order of Shakespeare's mistress who "treads the ground," pragmatically interjecting, "My head is quite fixed. I have it on" (p. 24).

    The ease with which Deeley and Anna move from describing Kate into a new diversion, alternately singing lines from popular songs of the thirties and forties, suggests that this humorous pursuit has been engaged in before:

DEELEY. Fun to live with?
ANNA. Delightful.
DEELEY. Lovely to look at, delightful to know.

    A silence follows the outburst of song, and then Deeley abruptly explains how he met his wife. Apparently the old tunes have stirred up his memories and he relates how one summer afternoon he happened to be in the neighborhood where his father bought him his first, and only, tricycle (notice the repeated pattern), when he saw the film *Odd Man Out*. In the lobby an usherette was sensually stroking her breasts while a second usherette stood by watching, perhaps paralleling the relationship between Kate and Anna as described later—one girl is sexually involved while the other watches. Deeley was especially enjoying Robert Newton's performance in the 1947 British suspense movie about an Irish rebel leader hunted by the police after a daring robbery ("I would commit murder for him, even now," he asserts, p. 29) when he noticed Kate. She was, he says, punningly insinuating the concept of verification, "placed more or less . . . at the dead centre of the auditorium. I was off centre and have remained so" (p. 30). However, he managed a "trueblue" pickup after the film by talking to her about Newton. "Robert Newton . . . brought us together and it is only Robert Newton who can tear us apart," he concludes. At a "slightly later stage," when their "naked bodies met" and he "touched her profoundly all over," Deeley wondered what Newton would think about it (p. 31).

Anna extrapolates from Deeley's story, realizing that "there are things I remember which may never have happened but as I recall them so they take place." Deeley is startled by her theory, but Anna goes on to "recall" coming home one night to find Kate sitting on the bed and a man sobbing in the armchair. Neither paid any attention to her, so she went to bed. Then, "The man came over to me, quickly, looked down at me, but I would have absolutely nothing to do with him." Following on the heels of her comment about creating the past through recall, this story is questionable, and it becomes even more suspect when she immediately modifies her account: "no, I'm quite wrong . . . he didn't move quickly . . ." (p. 32).

Anna continues her recollection and Deeley is shocked when she says that she awoke during the night to find the man "lying across [Kate's] lap on her bed." In the morning, though, he was gone—"It was as if he had never been" (p. 33). And considering the play's conclusion, it may be that Anna's tale is really more of a foreshadowing, a prediction, than a memory. The author's fondness for ritualistic repetition, as in The Basement, and the characters' familiarity with and readiness to join in the games may suggest that such a memory is in fact a prediction at the same time.

Kate rises and offers Anna a cigarette, protesting that they are talking about her as if she were dead. Anna denies the charge, asking how she can say that when "I'm looking at you now, seeing you so shyly poised over me, looking down at me." Deeley breaks in sharply exclaiming, "Stop that!" (p. 35), thereby raising a question about the vehemence of his reaction to her superficially innocent image. Perhaps he is remembering Anna's description moments earlier of her roommate's caller bending over her in the middle of the night. Perhaps the image which she is painting seems too close to a picture of a pair of lesbians.

Although the conversation throughout the drama expresses an awareness of the simultaneity of the present and the past so that both may be spoken about in the same speech, any immediate concentration of the dialogue on one or the other time seems to be signaled either by silence or a physical action. Anna turns from the window, Kate pours coffee, Deeley shouts, someone stands or sits, and the focus shifts. Having broken the mood of the present, the husband moves back into the past again, remembering the girl whom he married. Anna has already stated that Kate uses silence as a defense mechanism; now Deeley lists her silence among the things which attracted him to her because it was her "only claim to virtue" (p. 35).

Anna's reminiscences of the times in London continue, and she recalls going to see Odd Man Out with Kate. Was this the occasion when Kate and Deeley first met, and if so, why were not the girls sitting together and where was Anna when Deeley approached his future wife? Of course, Kate may have met her husband previously or returned alone to see the film another time, but Deeley's reaction to this piece of information is interesting. The pronouncement is followed by a silence, then Deeley, following a pattern established in the earlier plays, begins talking about a completely unrelated subject: "Yes, I do quite a bit of travelling in my job" (p. 38). His lack of comment about the film may imply that he recognizes that Anna is restructuring the past out of the materials afforded by the evening's conversations or that there is no need to say anything because the two girls are really one. This latter hypothesis gains plausibility from the exchange which follows, an exchange sounding very much as if it could have been lifted from *The Lover*, Pinter's 1963 drama concerned with a wife who plays a dual role. Anna asks if Deeley is away on his travels "for long periods." Kate is not sure. "I think, sometimes," she answers, then asks her husband, "Are you?" (p. 39). Without waiting for Deeley's reply, Anna says to Kate, "I think I must come and keep you company when he's away." Deeley wonders "Won't your husband miss you?" and Anna assures him, "Of course. But he would understand."

With the movement back into the present, Anna becomes the center of attention momentarily, and Kate and Deeley ask her questions about her life in Sicily. Deeley admits that he knows Sicily slightly, though his references indicate more than a casual acquaintance with the island because his work took him there. Actually, he continues, his work "concerns itself with life . . . in every part of the globe." Always careful about usage, he explains that "I use the word globe because the word world possesses emotional political sociological and psychological pretensions and resonances which I prefer as a matter of choice to do without, or shall I say to steer clear of, or if you like to reject" (pp. 40–41). Yet when Anna declares that she finds England "Rather beguilingly" damp, he can only wonder, "What the hell does she mean by that?" (p. 41).

Where Anna and Deeley had ignored Kate earlier, the two former roommates now talk about Anna's Sicilian villa and exclude the husband, who tries to regain control through his Welles fantasy. Following another silence, though, it is clear that the women are not just ignoring the man; they have retreated into the past, leaving Deeley by himself in the present. While he talks about the casserole they had for dinner, Anna and Kate discuss what they will do, as though they were back in the London of their youth. They talk about cooking, walking in the park (which is obviously in London and not a nearby country estate because it is filled with people screaming, policemen, traffic, noise, and hotels—not the good old days pictured before!), what they should wear, and whom they might invite over. Act I closes with Kate going to take a bath.

The setting for Act II is the bedroom instead of the front room, but physically it is a mirror image of the first-act set, including the furniture grouping:

"The divans and armchair are disposed in precisely the same relation to each other as the furniture in the first act, but in reversed positions" (p. [47]). The natures of the two women are reversed in this act, too, beginning with the fact that Anna and Deeley are present and Kate is still in the bathroom.

Deeley suggestively initiates the conversation with a short discourse on the advantage of beds on castors which allow "any amount of permutation" in their physical placement. He may mean this to refer to the possible sexual relationships between the three characters, because he immediately continues, "Yes, I remember you quite clearly from The Wayfarers" (p. 48). This statement also opens a whole new level of meaning in *Old Times*, and for the first time the meaning of the play starts to become clear. Anna does not "think" that she has been there, but she does not deny the possibility, and soon she will be modifying Deeley's stories as the two create memories of "things . . . [which] may never have happened." The truth is probably that they do happen, but only in the imaginations of the host and his visitor.

Deeley starts by recalling details of the episode—who was there, where she sat, what she wore. His description resembles that which Anna gave of the cafés she and Kate used to frequent. It is amusing in this play with its undertone of lesbianism that Deeley recalls that a fellow named Luke "didn't like it much" when he talked to Anna, for in his early poem "New Year in the Midlands" Pinter writes about going to "the yellow pub" where he found "the thin Luke of a queer."[26] In spite of Luke's disapproval, though, Deeley and Anna went to a party where Deeley "sat opposite and looked up [her] skirt" and listened to men talk about China. "You didn't object, you found my gaze perfectly acceptable," he remembers, and Anna joins the game when she answers, "I was aware of your gaze, was I?" (p. 51). A girlfriend of hers appeared and they left the party, leaving Deeley behind. The extent to which Anna is becoming involved in creating the past is seen as the exchange continues:

DEELEY. I never saw you again. You disappeared from the area. Perhaps you moved out.
ANNA. No. I didn't.
DEELEY. I never saw you in The Wayfarers Tavern again. Where were you?
ANNA. Oh, at concerts, I should think, or the ballet [pp. 52–53].

As the drama nears its conclusion, Anna incorporates Deeley's story into one of her own: "I had borrowed some of her underwear, to go to a party. . . . I [was] punished for my sin, for a man at the party . . . spent the whole evening looking up my skirt" (p. 65).

A silence follows Anna's suggestion that she must have gone to concerts or the ballet, and when the conversation is resumed, it is in the present tense as Deeley describes the way in which Kate bathes almost as if he were quot-

26. Poem reprinted in part in Esslin, *The Peopled Wound*, p. [52].

ing a passage from J's *The Sensuous Woman*: "Enjoys it. Takes a long time over it. . . . Luxuriates in it. . . . Really soaps herself all over, and then washes the soap off, sud by sud. Meticulously. She's both thorough and, I must say it, sensuous. Gives herself a comprehensive going over, and apart from everything else she does emerge as clean as a new pin" (p. 53). Anna expands the description by mentioning Kate's practice of having someone wrap her in a towel when she emerges from the tub (p. 54), which leads to a discussion of how she should be dried and powdered which Deeley concludes in a different tone: "*Pause. (To himself.)* Christ. *He looks at her slowly.* You must be about forty, I should think, by now" (p. 57). Whether he is fed up with their ridiculous conversation or angered at the idea of Anna's intimate knowledge of Kate's bathing habits is not clear. He has turned mean, though, and where he was sure that it was Anna he met at the pub because, "I never forget a face" (p. 49), he begins a protective attack now, declaring, "If I walked into The Wayfarers Tavern now, . . . I wouldn't recognize you" (p. 57).

At this juncture Kate returns, having dried herself, and ignoring Anna and Deeley's second music-hall songfest, like Ruth in *The Homecoming*, she begins to take control. Refreshed by her bath, she launches into her first long speech of the play, asserting her preference for the country: "Everything's softer. . . . There aren't such edges here. And living close to the sea. . . . You can't say where it begins or ends. That appeals to me. I don't care for harsh lines. I deplore that kind of urgency" (p. 59). She might almost be talking about the nondefinable line between the present and the past. A big city, she says, is attractive only when it rains, because the rain produces a blurred effect. Once more we are reminded of the playwright's eyesight.

Anna tries to regain control by using the description of London in the rain as a background for a sensual depiction of a cozy room with a fire and a warm drink, but Kate retains the lead by affirming her decision to stay in. The positions of the women are reversed as Anna pours the coffee this time and offers to do the hem of Kate's black dress (possibly the same black skirt Deeley claimed Anna was wearing when he saw her in The Wayfarer?). Moreover, when the women move back into the past, it is Kate who directs the move, and the past is much more tenuous, with Deeley's interjections being recognized.

Again Anna strives to retrench, exposing Kate to Deeley by reminiscing about her roommate's character: "she was *so* shy. . . . I put it down to her upbringing, a parson's daughter, and indeed there was a good deal of Brontë about her" (p. 64). Deeley is astounded to find out that his wife is a parson's daughter, but Anna has more damaging information to reveal, as she proves by relating the affair of the borrowed underwear: "But from that night she insisted, from time to time, that I borrow her underwear . . . and each time she proposed this she would blush, but propose it she did, nevertheless. And when there was anything to tell her, when I got back, anything of interest to tell her, I told her" (p. 65). Deeley's reaction is, "Sounds a perfect marriage" (p. 66). His jealousy is fully aroused and he demands, "You say she was Brontë in secrecy but not in passion. What was she in passion?" Anna's reply, "I feel that is your province," stimulates an outraged outburst: "You feel it's my province? Well, you're damn right. It is my province. I'm glad someone's showing a bit of taste at last. Of course it's my bloody province. I'm her husband" (p. 66).

The tone of Deeley's banter has chilled, and he wonders if he is "alone in beginning to find all this distasteful." Besides, he finds himself worrying about Anna's nameless husband "rumbling about alone in his enormous villa living hand to mouth on a few hardboiled eggs and unable to speak a damn word of English . . . lurching up and down the terrace, waiting for . . . a lobster and lobster sauce ideology we know fuck all about. . . . why should I waste valuable space listening to two —." Interrupting, Kate "*swiftly*" challenges him: "If you don't like it go" (p. 67). And, sounding like Lenny unable to recover from Ruth's unexpected reversal, Deeley is answerless. "Go? Where can I go?" he complains. Kate has an answer, though—"To China." Since she was not in the room when her husband mentioned the discussion of China at the party, her suggestion is amusing, but his reason for rejecting the proposal is even more humorous: "I haven't got a white dinner jacket. . . . You know what they'd do to me in China if they found me in a white dinner jacket. They'd bloodywell kill me" (p. 68).

Now that Kate has weakened Deeley's position, Anna moves to reestablish her own dominance by impressing on him that she is present "to celebrate a very old and treasured friendship, something that was forged between [herself and his wife] long before you knew of our existence" (p. 68). The battle is out in the open, and Deeley counters by informing Kate, "We've met before, you know. Anna and I." Incorporating details manufactured out of his previous talk with Anna (his buying her drinks because she had no money), the husband wields his exposé as a weapon: "We had a scene together. She freaked out. She didn't have any bread, so I bought her a drink. She looked at me with big eyes, shy, all that bit. She was pretending to be you at the time. Did it pretty well. Wearing your underwear she was too, at the time. Amiably allowed me a gander. Trueblue generosity. Admirable in a woman. We went to a party" (p. 69).[27] The use of a recent cliché, "freaked out," in a story which supposedly took place twenty years ago enhances the notion that Deeley is making it up instead of remembering it. The tale ends ambiguously: "She thought she was you, said little. . . . Maybe she was you. Maybe it was you, having coffee with me, saying little . . ." (p. 69).

27. Note the references to her eyes, her shyness, her underwear, the party, and the word "trueblue."

Kate's reaction is probably not what Deeley expected. Rather than becoming upset at this revelation, she responds as Ruth might, turning the game back on the players (pp. 70–71). "What do you think attracted her to you?" she asks her nonplussed mate. "She found your face very sensitive, vulnerable. . . . She fell in love with you. . . . You were so unlike the others. We knew men who were brutish, crass." Recovering, Deeley does not stop to ponder Kate's portrayal of the café-society artists as brutish (maybe because of Anna's depiction of the men in the park); he picks up her lead and enters this new game: "There really are such men, then? Crass men?"[28] He wonders how he was different, for after all "I was crass, wasn't I, looking up her skirt? . . . If it was her skirt. If it was her."

And again there is a shift. Another battle, centering on the two women, develops as Anna reenters the fray: "Oh, it was my skirt. It was me. I remember your look . . . very well. I remember you well." Anna's reentrance allows Kate to switch her attack by taking the image of standing over her former roommate in Act I and giving it a completely new meaning: "I remember you lying dead. You didn't know I was watching you. I leaned over you. Your face was dirty. You lay dead, your face scrawled with dirt, all kinds of earnest inscriptions, but unblotted, so that they had run, all over your face, down to your throat." Kate is in full command and she continues her final speech, the longest in the play, expressing her attitude toward the other two characters in images of death and dirt. Of Anna she says: "When you woke my eyes were above you, staring down at you. You tried to do my little trick, one of my tricks you had borrowed, my little slow smile, my little slow shy smile, my bend of the head, my half closing of the eyes, that we knew so well, but it didn't work, the grin only split the dirt at the sides of your mouth and stuck. You stuck in your grin. I looked for tears but could see none. Your pupils weren't in your eyes. Your bones were breaking through your face. But all was serene. There was no suffering. It had all happened elsewhere. Last rites I did not feel necessary. Or any celebration. I felt the time and season appropriate and that by dying alone and dirty you had acted with proper decorum. It was time for my bath" (pp. 71–72). Anna's serenity is due to the action's having happened "elsewhere," probably in Kate's mind.

Deeley is no match for his wife either: ". . . one night I said let me do something, a little thing, a little trick. He lay there in your bed. He looked up at me with great expectation. He was gratified. He thought I had profited from his teaching. He thought I was going to be sexually forthcoming, that I was about to take a long promised initiative. I dug about in the windowbox, where you had planted our pretty pansies, scooped, filled the bowl, and

28. Parenthetically, Anna is contradicting her earlier statement. Her memory, in addition to being part of her attack, may come up now because she has been reminded by Deeley or because the story has created something to remember.

plastered his face with dirt. He resisted . . . with force. He would not let me dirty his face, or smudge it, he wouldn't let me. He suggested a wedding instead, and a change of environment" (pp. 72–73).[29]

The play nears its conclusion with an enactment of the bedroom scene described earlier: "DEELEY *starts to sob. . . . He goes to* ANNA's *divan, looks down at her. . . . He goes towards* KATE's *divan. He sits on her divan, lies across her lap* (pp. 73–74). After a long silence Deeley gets up and sits in the armchair and the curtain comes down with "DEELEY *in armchair.* ANNA *lying on divan.* KATE *sitting on divan*"—all action is stopped and the drama ends with *"Lights up full sharply. Very bright"* (p. 75). The framed, static arrangement of characters recalls the final curtain of *The Homecoming.*

With *Old Times*, as with the other memory plays, part of the difficulty in interpreting the work lies in a simultaneous scarcity and abundance of facts. As in most Pinter dramas, there is not enough information provided on the one hand, yet on the other hand there is too much, since the data available tend to be contradictory. The audience is never completely sure about what happened in the past, but the meaning of the drama may depend on that knowledge. It is reasonable to conclude, for example, that the *"very bright"* lighting at the end of the play symbolizes a return to reality, though it could certainly imply enlightenment just as well, and reality and enlightenment need not be the same thing at all.

One of the possibilities suggested by the action taking place on stage is that one or more of the characters is imaginary. In numerous instances throughout the play it seems almost as though Kate and Anna were alter egos, the divided personality of a single individual. Kate's remembered treatment of her roommate and Deeley in her closing speech and the imagery involved could easily be seen as the final breakdown of a mind at war with itself; so Anna may not really exist. Deeley's suggestion that she change her environment could be seen as a recognition of the problem and an attempt at a cure. Furthermore, Kate's last words imply that Anna's existence is questionable: "He asked me once . . . who had slept in that bed before him. I told him no one. No one at all" (p. 73). The idea of a mental breakdown, of course, occurs in several of the dramatist's other works. Going a step further, Deeley actually breaks down on stage and begins sobbing after Kate finishes her tale, so it is possible that both women are figments of his imagination. However, since there is no doubt about the existence of any of Pinter's characters prior to *Old Times*, with the possible exception of the old matchseller in the radio version of *A Slight Ache* (an argument dismissed in Chapter V above), since the same people fill the dual roles in *The Lover*, the dramatist's sole presentation of split personalities, and since *Old Times* is meaningful with both Kate and Anna, there is no reason for refusing to admit their presence. The play can be taken

29. Teddy made a similar suggestion, apparently, before *The Homecoming* began.

at face value then, and all three characters can be accepted as real. Whatever ambiguity there is regarding the existence of the characters is simply a result of the author's method of commenting on the "reality" of the past.

If the characters are real, then the theme of lesbianism can be considered. Again, there are implications already noted throughout the play which point to the possibility that Anna and Kate had a sexual relationship. Perhaps Kate's comment after she recalls Deeley's suggestion of a wedding and change of environment is further evidence of their bond. "Neither mattered," she says (p. 73)—because she still remembers Anna, and the two get together again? As has been pointed out, the evidence is certainly not conclusive, and Peter Hall absolutely denies that the theme is important: "It's not a play about lesbians. Categorically, no. It's a play about sexuality, and the key to the play is the line, 'Normal, what's normal?'" [30] The line Hall repeats is spoken by Deeley in Act I when he and Kate are discussing what a normal number of friends is.

Pinter's director is on the right track, but he does not go far enough. *Old Times* is about sexuality, but it is also a demonstration of the playwright's concept of the function of memory. Kate, Anna, and Deeley are battling to establish viable relationships, as earlier Pinter characters do, and the relationships may well have a sexual basis. In a sort of reversal of the method employed by Ruth in *The Homecoming*, who uses sex to defeat the memory of Jessie, Kate emerges as the most powerful individual in *Old Times* because of her superior ability to wield memory as a weapon to secure a sexual objective. Whether the relationship depicted at the play's conclusion can be called successful is another question, but Kate has disposed of the threat of Anna.

In retrospect the numerous excursions into the past make sense, then, if memory is the weaponry of Pinter's latest play. Since the past is nonverifiable, it can be used to substantiate or negate any claim any character wants to draw upon it for. Thus it is perfectly legitimate for Anna to recall inconsequentials on the order of "F. J. McCormick was good too" in *Odd Man Out* (p. 30), while Kate, who "was interested once in the arts" finds that she "can't remember now which ones they were" (p. 37). As the past is created according to their present needs, the characters practice selectivity. There are similarities between the use of memory in this play and in *Landscape* and *Silence*, but *Old Times* is more an extension of *Night*, in which the audience sees the process of alternate pasts being manufactured with the comments of one character keying the creative responses of the other.

As in *Landscape* and *Silence*, the past has as much bearing on the conflict as the present has, perhaps even more. The characters create the past, then, in attempts to shape the present, to evolve a sequence of previous events which will lead to a desired end now. Time is a fantasy in Pinter's work. It is

30. Quoted in Gussow, "A Conversation," pp. 42–43.

amorphous and nonlinear in nature. There is therefore no reason to label anything "past."

Old Times is almost a parody melodrama or soap opera: the characters seem to be emotionally involved in a conflict over something with little intrinsic value. Indeed, there are several battles for possession and dominance going on at the same time. Pinter lifts his play out of the melodramatic category, however, in the way the fight is conducted. The characters are engaged in a mental struggle, and words are used to create the battleground. In essence, saying something makes it true—at least until it is contradicted.

London becomes an important symbol or metaphor (a place of wonder) which might be a vision of a new world, "an idyllic, half-remembered happiness above time and space," which William Baker and Stephen Ely Tabachnik see as Pinter's concern in his most recent plays.[31] Through the power of words Anna creates a halcyon past which will lead her to a present where Deeley is hers: "Albert Hall, Covent Garden . . . to do the things we loved . . . giggling and chattering . . . the sheer expectation of it all" (pp. 17–18). But need determines perception, and Anna later recalls a more sordid London as she shifts her ground to meet Kate's attack: "The park is dirty at night, all sorts of horrible people . . . hiding behind trees . . . they scream at you . . . the traffic and the noise" (pp. 43–44).

Kate refuses to give Deeley up, though, and she creates (maintains?) a past which excludes Anna in the present. Just as words are so powerful that they can create a past, so words can also kill. While Kate's imagery is more stark and less imaginative than that employed by Harry in *The Collection*, it is still effective. When she "remembers" Anna dead, Anna in effect ceases to function.

The principle that the past is creatable is the substance of *Old Times*, and the work proves that Pinter has definitely moved from the thematic set epitomized by *The Homecoming* and is now working in a new area of interest. *Old Times* is the longest of the memory plays to date, but it does not have quite the intensity and forcefulness associated with the playwright's previous dramas which mark turning points in his thematic evolution. While it draws together most of the elements from the other plays in the memory group, *Old Times* does not signify the end of Pinter's present cycle, as *No Man's Land* will show.

No Man's Land

Directed by Peter Hall, the National Theatre's production of *No Man's Land* opened at the Old Vic in London on April 23, 1975. Immediate critical reaction tended to focus on the acting as opposed to the meaning of the play.

31. Baker and Tabachnik, *Harold Pinter*, p. 135.

Benedict Nightingale, writing of Sir John Gielgud's portrayal of Spooner, for instance, finds that Pinter "has in fact, written a part rather more memorable than the play that contains it." [32] There are reasons for this kind of critical response. For one thing, the acting during the drama's premiere run was superb, with both Gielgud and Sir Ralph Richardson turning in masterly performances which rivaled their work in David Storey's *Home* several years earlier. For another, *No Man's Land* is a good play, but there are problems with it.

To start with, it seems almost as if *No Man's Land* were written before *Old Times*. While the play may be concerned with the same themes as those developed in *Old Times*, it is nowhere as lyrical or poetic in the expression of those themes and actually comes closer to the idiom of the playwright's earlier pieces. Many of the lines, scenes, character relationships, and situations recall Pinter's previous works. It is a mixture which looks backward, then; in Pinter's combined thematic and stylistic evolution, *No Man's Land* would fit between *The Homecoming* and *Landscape* perfectly well.

Combining an exploration of the nature of time and man's relation to time with previous modes of expression creates an unevenness in the drama and a consequent diminishing of the intensity which marks Pinter's major works. Although the play conforms to the category of "idyllic half-remembered happiness above time and space" to which Baker and Tabachnik assign *Old Times*, still, it is not developing quite the same themes, and the sense of progressive continuation is broken by the methods of presentation. Possibly Pinter has less to say about these topics at this time, so he has relied upon a certain amount of filler. Some of the dialogue seems merely to be witty conversation, for example, and some of the images appear to be references to unconnected images in Pinter's mind—just isolated things which he has seen and which have "stuck" with him until he could "write them out," such as the picture of two men sitting at a table, one eating, one talking. Even the many literary allusions—to Eliot, Beckett, Shakespeare, Tennessee Williams, Christopher Marlowe, Emily Dickinson, and the Bible—seem also at first glance to function as substitutes for content, though ultimately the allusions help to build the mood of *No Man's Land* and they are certainly suitable to the characters. As a result, the final feeling the play gives is much closer to that of a "dramatic abstraction," as Melloan phrased it in connection with *Old Times*, than was the preceding play.

No Man's Land is set in a "well but sparely furnished" house in North West London on a summer night (p. [9]). The play opens with a scene that immediately recalls the opening of *The Caretaker* as Hirst, *"precisely dressed"* in a sports jacket and *"well cut trousers,"* has invited Spooner, *"dressed in a very old and shabby suit, dark faded shirt, creased spotted tie,"* into his home for a drink (p. [15]). While Spooner, speaking the stilted social formu-

32. Benedict Nightingale, "Inaction Replay," *New Statesman*, 2 May 1975, p. 601.

lae of the Georgian era, is much more genteel than Davies was, there are many similarities between the two characters.

Spooner promptly begins to babble, revealing both himself and his circumstances in the process. Paying little attention to Hirst's lack of interest, he proceeds to define strength as having expertise in maintaining "a calculated posture" and then proposes that his own intelligence and perception allow him to deflate those who pose (p. 16). In fact, however, he later tries to build up his host's stance as a poet, a stance for which there is no real evidence.

As usual in Pinter's work, no assumptions are permitted to pass unquestioned. When Spooner asserts that he is "such a man" (p. 16), after having described those who "discern the essential flabbiness of the stance," Hirst humorously wants to make sure that he understands with which group Spooner is allying himself. As if to demonstrate that he is a man of discernment, the guest begins to incorporate literary allusions in his speech: Eliot's *Four Quartets* echoes in "now and in England and in Hampstead and for all eternity" (p. 17). Spooner's self-portrayal continues with his statement that he feels "at peace here. Safe from all danger." Like Davies, and Rose before him, Spooner sees this "remarkably pleasant" room as a sanctuary. His explanation for why the room appeals to him is both funny and pathetic: "My only security . . . rests in the confirmation that I elicit from people of all kinds a common and constant level of indifference." Although this is the reverse of the process which affects Kate in *Old Times*, the result is the same; the perception of nebulousness held by others is replaced by the assurance that he is "fixed, concrete." Spooner also defensively declares that he never stays with other people very long because there is little danger of anyone ever showing enough "positive liking" for him to want him to remain. "And that," he avers, "is a happy state of affairs." His amusing assessment of himself is probably accurate: "To show interest in me or, good gracious, anything tending towards a positive liking for me, would cause in me a condition of the acutest alarm. Fortunately, the danger is remote." As might be expected, though, he soon asks to stay, and his stated proposal is based on the concept of friendship: "You need a friend. . . . I offer myself to you as a friend" (p. 33). Ironically the offer of friendship follows Spooner's definition of the "essential quality of manliness" which he alleges his host lacks: "to pick up a pintpot and know it to be a pintpot, and knowing it to be a pintpot, to declare it as a pintpot, and to stay faithful to that pintpot as though you had given birth to it" (pp. 33–34). Indicating that the pintpot represents himself, Spooner parodies *Hamlet*: his candor in speaking "is not method but madness." Whereas Hamlet was incapacitated by indecision because of a distrust of his knowledge, Spooner, like Davies, acts rashly and Hirst refuses to act. Spooner's offer is further tempered by his depiction of himself as a guide through life, or death. His arguing that Hirst has "a long hike" and that "when we talk of a river we talk of a deep and dank architecture" could refer to standard symbols for life, yet his "Let me perhaps be your boatman" has a Charon-like ring to it.

In the opening sequence another literary allusion which provides insight into both a character and the overall meaning of the play comes as a continuation of Spooner's explanation of the derivation of his "true comfort and solace" (p. 17). Although amusingly phrased ("startling candor"), the underlying seriousness of Spooner's sentiment is reenforced by its resemblance to Blanche's admission in *A Streetcar Named Desire* that she has always depended on the kindness of strangers: "you are a stranger to me, and . . . you are clearly kindness itself" (Hirst expresses a similar sentiment in Act II). Not only do we learn something about Spooner, the literary allusion likewise alerts us to the possibility that a somewhat idealized vision of the past may intrude on reality.

The dialogue exchanged between Spooner and Hirst is a further indication that Pinter is dealing with the past. Spooner's language, variously described as Victorian, Edwardian, and Georgian, is a parody of the upper middle class, the stereotyped colonels who form the solid backdrop of Agatha Christie thrillers. Several of the exchanges also sound like the satirical forays engaged in by Harry and Bill in *The Collection*, as when Spooner recalls being described as a "betwixt twig peeper":

SPOONER. . . . . A most clumsy construction, I thought.
HIRST. Infelicitous.
SPOONER. *Pause.* My Christ you're right.
HIRST. What a wit [p. 18].

The concept of language is more important than its use as a vehicle for humor and satire, though. When Spooner says "All we have left is the English language," Pinter is beginning to reveal the theme of *No Man's Land*. These are men who no longer act—they talk. The question of salvaging the language is raised and Hirst decides that "Its salvation must rest in you," an ironic comment, given his guest's surname.[33] The mixed metaphor being exercised becomes intelligible when Spooner starts to talk about the sex act in linguistic terms: "I don't peep on sex. That's gone forever. . . . When my twigs happen to shall I say rest their peep on sexual conjugations, however periphrastic, I see only whites of eyes" (p. 19). Certainly of a periphrastic nature himself, the sixtyish Spooner appears to have reached an age where there is no true creativity or passion left, only garrulity and sterile word games.

By reason of his age, Spooner can be expected to have experience to draw upon for his understanding. Using sexual word play as a means of transition (he has had experience "behind" and "beneath" him—possibly a

33. Other interesting associations with the word spoon are the definitions relating to love making, to acting foolishly, to stroking a ball, and to spoon feeding, any of which might obliquely have a bearing on the meaning of the play.

bisexual inference), he dismisses the past in favor of the present. Because he is a poet (or perhaps he has become a poet because of his point of view), the immediate is all that is real for him. The past has a fictive ring to it: "Experience is a paltry thing. Everyone has it and will tell his tale of it. I leave experience to psychological interpreters. . . . I myself can do any graph of experience you wish" (p. 20). The implication is that the past is unreal and can be created to suit the individual (a concept examined in *Old Times*), and that the sciences, whether social ("psychological interpreters, the wet-dream world") or hard ("graph"), are not trustworthy because they rely on this unreality for their input and can be no more accurate than the data they use. For Spooner, apparently, even living in the moment of the present is perilous, for the present refuses to follow any set of rules: "The present is truly unscrupulous." What becomes most salient, therefore, is who can remain at the still point of the hub in Eliot's turning wheel: "I am interested in where I am eternally present and active." The double reversal which immediately follows seemingly reduces the significance of Spooner's philosophizing to the rank of long-winded, shallow verbiage. Hirst concedes that he is not interested in Spooner's subject matter and Spooner expresses relief at not being taken seriously.

At this point Hirst "*draws the curtains aside, looks out briefly, lets curtains fall*" (p. 20). In Pinter's earlier dramas silences or pauses often signaled an attempt to avoid further communication, to change the subject, or to focus attention on the significance of the preceding or succeeding statement. In *No Man's Land* these breaks in the dialogue are generally accompanied by some sort of physical action; often one of the characters moves to the antique liquor cabinet. It has been claimed that Pinter's plays are similar to cricket matches; everyone stands around in obscure relationships to one another, occasionally making sudden unexplained movements which are marked off by pauses and silences. Pinter's fondness for cricket from his childhood on has been amply documented. During the season he is captain of the Gaities, a club side that plays mainly in and around Surrey, and in the winter he practices in the indoor nets at the Middlesex Cricket Club on Saturday morning.[34] In *No Man's Land* the playwright may be poking fun at the critics by suggesting that the drama is modeled after a cricket match with the physical action separating the game's innings, somewhat on the order of chess play in Beckett's *Endgame*. The names of the four characters would lend support to such an interpretation, for as D. A. Cairns observes, they "are named after prominent English cricketers of the late nineteenth and early

---

34. "Master of Silence," *Observer* (London), 27 April 1975, p. 11, contains a report by the actor Robert East, a member of Pinter's side, on the writer's form: he is a "moderately aggressive batsman and in-fieldsman (physically he is tallish and well-built); better at facing fast bowling than slow . . . and a ruthless tactician." Pinter also collects cricket bats (100 Wisdens).

twentieth centuries. . . . Hirst, Briggs and Foster . . . were all-rounders, and left-arm bowlers. . . . Spooner, who in the play is the outsider and who claims to be a poet, was a batsman, known for his elegant stroke-play."[35]

Spooner's next speech is bracketed by Hirst's movements, to the window, then to the cabinet. In between lies Spooner's affirmation that he is "a free man" (p. 21). Growing out of his dissertation on experience, this statement must relate to the past. Spooner sees himself as being free from the past, yet ironically the inference is that he is limited to the present instant.[36] The establishing of Spooner's location in time helps define his character, but it also sets the first half of the play's central dichotomy, for as will be seen later, conversely, Hirst is limited to the past by his temperament.

Having reached a pivotal point in the drama, Pinter now retreats and begins building anew. In a pattern of action again reminiscent of Davies, Spooner takes the initiative. He goes to the liquor cabinet and assumes the role of host, the ensuing dialogue being a near repetition of that in the opening sequence, although the words and positions of the two men are reversed (*vide* "Kullus" and *The Basement*). His tale of "an erstwhile member of the Hungarian aristocracy" (p. 24) reads like a B-movie plot told in S. J. Perelman-like style and contains the same kind of ridiculous material as related by Pinter's previous storytellers—Davies, Mick, Lenny, *et al.* Furthermore, it contains a model of phrasing which comes to characterize Spooner's speech in Act I, a type of repetition: "I spoke, suddenly, suddenly spoke."

Spooner's tale leads to additional thematic developments. Hirst asks his guest what the Hungarian said, to which Spooner replies, "You expect me to remember what he said?" The tone of the story suggests that the events described took place some time ago, so Spooner's incredulousness at being asked what the conversation was is reasonable, especially since he has indicated the transitory nature of the past in his observation that something which has gone (the half-pint of beer he drank) is gone forever ("never to be savoured again"). Of course, this contention is strongly undercut by the many carefully itemized details which he has already included in the story. The important thing, however, is what was said, not that he cannot remember what happened. The words themselves are valueless, as he explains in a cliché which is literally true insofar as the words spoken are concerned: "What he said . . . is neither here nor there" (p. 25). The conversation does not exist in the present and has disappeared in the past. In spite of his

35. D. A. Cairns, "Batting for Pinter," *Times* (London), 7 June 1975, p. 13g.

36. The use of von Kleist here as an example is an interesting commentary on how Spooner sees himself surrounded by the pincers of time. Ewald von Kleist (1881–1954) was a German general in World War II who penetrated to the Caucasus Mountains and then had to retreat, narrowly escaping encirclement. According to military historians, that long retreat in the depth of winter was one of the most remarkable feats of extrication from a trap in all history. Although constantly menaced in flank and rear, von Kleist's army got back to safety through the bottleneck while the attacking Russians were held at bay. If one feels the pressure of the past, leave the past.

locquaciousness, Spooner recognizes the actual meaninglessness of words. When he continues "And I met you at the same pub tonight," the audience's reaction is that Hirst may in fact be the Hungarian of "all those years ago," but Spooner has devalued words as carriers of meaning, so it is clear that just because they met at the "same" pub it does not necessarily follow that Hirst is the same man (Spooner later acknowledges that Hirst is English). Moreover, while there is actually an inn called Jack Straw's Castle at Hampstead Heath, it was named after the leader of a party of insurgents from Essex in the Peasants' Rising of 1381 and has no historical connection with the real Jack Straw, so Hirst's question, "Do you find it as beguiling a public house now as it was in the days of the highwaymen, when it was frequented by highwaymen? Notably Jack Straw" (p. 23), obviously is not meant to be taken literally. Spooner could not know if it has changed and the connection between Straw and the pub is invalid anyway. Typically Pinteresque resonances have been set up.

Spooner continues to delineate himself ("a staunch friend of the arts, particularly the art of poetry, and a guide to the young" who has a wife and remembers a "bucolic life") and humor is derived from the absurd statements and questions involved in the process:

SPOONER. I have never been loved. From this I derive my strength. Have you? Ever? Been loved? . . . I looked up once into my mother's face. What I saw there was nothing less than pure malevolence. I was fortunate to escape with my life. You will want to know what I had done to provoke such hatred in my own mother.
HIRST. You'd pissed yourself.
SPOONER. Quite right. How old do you think I was at the time?
HIRST. Twenty eight.
SPOONER. Quite right. However, I left home soon after. . . . Her buns are the best.
HIRST *looks at him.*
Her currant buns [pp. 26–27].

The farcical aspect of the play on words is emphasized by the visual action (Hirst's look), but from these elements certain parallels and connections between Spooner and Hirst start to become evident. Hirst's answers regarding what angered Spooner's mother and how old Spooner was might be taken for the truth, based on his prior acquaintance with Spooner, but it is more likely that his ability to blend into the game is of more consequence than his facts, though possibly some sort of affinity between the two men is also represented here. As Spooner points out, they are related through nationality and the kind of life they have led.

Hirst, though, does not allow this line to evolve any further. Picking up the thread of the bucolic life, the host for the first time initiates conversation.

His recounting of the village folkways demonstrates that symbols are not always valid, for the garlands are hung on the church beams in honor of men who die unmarried (and have lived a "blameless life") as well as in honor of the young women of the parish "reputed" to have been virgins when they died. If the symbol is applied indiscriminately to all classes, it loses the validity of its uniqueness. The inference is that the external resemblances between the two men alluded to by Spooner are invalid, too.

Having been rebuffed, Spooner turns insolent. He demands more information about Hirst's "quaint little perversions" (in mock-pedantic phraseology: "life and times . . . . authority . . . socio-economic-political structure . . . environment . . . attained . . . the age of reason"). Switching to cricket terminology, Spooner mounts an attack. He asks about Hirst's wife: "Tell me with what speed she swung in the air, with what velocity she came off the wicket, whether she was responsive to finger spin, whether you could bowl a shooter with her, or an offbreak with a legbreak action" (p. 30). When his host does not respond, Spooner confides that his own wife "had everything" and then humorously plays with the expectations conjured up by his cliché: "Eyes, a mouth, hair, teeth, buttocks, breasts. . . . And legs" (p. 31).

Hirst reenters the conversation long enough to submit that his guest's wife had walked out on her husband, which only leads Spooner to wondering "Is she here now, your wife? . . . Was she ever here? Was she ever there, in your cottage?" In a sequence which echoes *A Slight Ache* he confesses that Hirst has "failed to convince"—when Hirst has not tried to convince him of anything. The movement from this point on is very different from that in *A Slight Ache*, though. Spooner equates the "truly accurate" with the "essentially poetic." This interesting definition of truth as something poetically perceived is followed by a silence and then the statement/question (which is never refuted/answered), "Her eyes, I take it, were hazel?" Hirst's poetic response is "Hazel shit" (p. 32).

Spooner thinks that there is "a touch of the maudlin" in Hirst's reaction and tenders some pseudo-philosophizing on the nature of reality. "Have I ever seen hazel shit? Or hazel eyes, for that matter?" Hirst, who opened the play by downing his vodka in "*one gulp*," has been reduced so far by his continuing consumption of alcohol that he can merely "*ineffectually*" throw his glass at his sophomoric acquaintance. This brief physical action is followed by Hirst's first attempt at communication: "Tonight . . . my friend . . . you find me in the last lap of a race . . . I had long forgotten to run." Spooner refuses to credit the other man's admission with any importance, and instead switches his attention back to language when he notes that Hirst has spoken metaphorically. Focusing on language eventually permits him to reach his goal in an oblique manner. First he defines manliness in terms of giving birth. Then he continues by way of literary allusion, which he combines with metaphor. The candid proclamation that his host lacks "the essential quality of manliness" is excused on Shakespearean grounds. From this recognition of inadequacy ("impotence") he describes Hirst's position in life and proceeds to proffer his friendship and guidance. This proposition, in spite of his earlier revelation regarding his attitude toward friendship, seems to be what has directed his conversation thus far. As mentioned above, though, it is not clear exactly what kind of guidance he has in mind, for the terms he uses—"boatman," "river," "deep and dank"—bring to mind the mythical conveyor of the dead.

The supposedly generous and conscious offer of a helping hand is soon depreciated. The serious nature of the proposal is contrasted with the light Elizabethan-air-like tone of "You've lost your wife of hazel hue, you've lost her and what can you do, she will no more come back to you, with a tillifola tillifola tillifoladi-foladi-foloo" (p. 34). This evokes Hirst's second outburst, after which he falls to the floor and slowly, tortuously crawls out of the room in front of the watching Spooner, whose concept of a helping hand apparently is not meant to be taken literally.

Hirst's outburst delineates the half of the dichotomy which matches Spooner's previous assertion of freedom from the past. Hirst announces that "No man's land . . . does not move . . . or change . . . or grow old . . . remains . . . forever . . . icy . . . silent" (p. 34). Depending on the stress, no man's land may refer to the human universe which is insubstantial, or to something which is changeless, such as the past. In Act II it will become evident that Hirst is concerned with the past.

After Hirst crawls out of the room Spooner observes "I have known this before. The exit through the door, by way of belly and floor." While amusing, this may reflect his familiarity with the debilitating effects of drink. A more relevant interpretation, which is reenforced by the repetition of the first line later in the drama (pp. [59], 60, 68) and other possible allusions ("After tea and toast," p. 44), is drawn from Eliot's "The Lovesong of J. Alfred Prufrock." Prufrock's lovesong is actually a recitation of a life of failure, brought about by a fear of rejection which paralyzes him to the extent that he is unable to initiate any meaningful relationships with women. Given the thematic development within No Man's Land and the fact that Spooner and Hirst both refer to Eliot's poem, it is evident that the concepts of failure and paralysis are central to the meaning of the drama.

With Hirst's exit the play suddenly takes on a comedy-of-menace atmosphere. The front door is heard opening and then slamming shut. Spooner "stiffens" and remains still, so the opening of doors is obviously related to menace again. With Foster's entrance, though, the initial confrontation between Ruth and Lenny in The Homecoming is recalled. Instead of inquiring into the stranger's reason for being in the house alone, Foster's first question is "What are you drinking?" and his first action is to pour himself a glass of beer (p. 35). There follows a passage of typical Pinter dialogue, a smokescreen of rapid speech composed of seemingly random sentences which contain possibly significant information and which finally include the question "Who are you?" buried in the patter, all of which is passed over so quickly that it barely has time to register. Among the incidentals mentioned are the facts that Foster considers himself defenseless because he does not carry a gun, although he is not bothered by this condition since he has lived in the "East"; he calls the house a "lighthouse"; he asks Spooner if he has met the host; he calls the host "my father"; and he refers to Hirst's desire to listen to some lieder, nineteenth-century German art songs. The allusion to a lighthouse acquires meaning near the end of the second act when Hirst looks out the window and observes "The light . . . out there . . . is gloomy . . . hardly daylight at all" (p. 86). Although the stage directions indicate that Act II takes place in the morning, Hirst feels that the daylight "is falling, rapidly." He finds the situation "distasteful" and asks Briggs to close the curtains and light the lamps. There may be a fear of death involved in this sequence, a conclusion strengthened by other events in the drama, but there is also a strong suggestion that Hirst sees himself living isolated from contemporary society in a world in which he is responsible for the light (whether of art or learning) and the light of his house outshines that of the outside world. This may in turn explain Foster's contention that Hirst is his father, for the play on words would emphasize that he is a foster son and that Hirst is in fact his spiritual father. Ironically, Hirst shuts out the sunlight (reality) and depends on artificial light, like alcohol, to shield him from the truth (lamplight is more flattering, softer, and hides his age better than the harsh light of an August sun).

At the conclusion of Foster's monologue, Spooner informs him that he is a friend of Hirst's. Foster does not think that he is "typical," but why he thinks this is not developed because Briggs now comes in—not that it necessarily would have been developed in any case. Briggs' appearance leads to an introduction which both expresses the importance of names (labeling things while contrarily not taking anything for granted) and diminishes Spooner by arbitrarily attaching a false name to him: "His name's Friend. This is Mr. Briggs. Mr. Friend—Mr. Briggs. I'm Mr. Foster. Old English stock. John Foster. Jack. Jack Foster. Old English name. Foster. John Foster. Jack Foster. Foster. This man's name is Briggs" (p. 36).

The concept of making no assumptions is pursued in a style reminiscent of Goldberg and McCann's treatment of Stanley in *The Birthday Party*. Briggs recognizes Spooner as someone who clears tables at the Bull's Head pub in Chalk Farm (another tie to Davies, too). Spooner agrees that he has served in this capacity, helping the landlord, a friend of his, when the landlord is shorthanded, but Briggs wants to know "Who says the landlord's a friend of yours?" (p. 37). Moments later Foster concedes that the landlord is a friend of his as well, which leads him to describing Hirst as a mutual friend and host—as opposed to the father/son relationship mentioned earlier.

After Foster alludes to his experiences in Siam ("They loved him at first sight," Briggs confirms), he asks Spooner if he is Siamese and if he has ever been "out there" (p. 39). "I've been to Amsterdam," Spooner replies, and goes on to recount his last visit. As in his story about the Hungarian, he recalls an event revolving around a man sitting at a table at a café. In this account he describes the man sitting "in shadow" outside a canalside café. Light and shadow images are important in *No Man's Land*, the title of the drama itself carrying a nebulous, shadowy connotation. If the play is about death, as hinted at in connection with Foster's "lighthouse" allusion and Hirst's concern with the interior lighting, a man at a table in the shadows "whistling under his breath, sitting very still, almost rigid," would have symbolic significance.

It is interesting how other references to light and shadow are incorporated in the work, too. When Hirst returns to the room after his nap, he discloses the nature of the world he inhabits. It is a world of the past which remains with him in the present in the form of pictures filed in an album: "My true friends look out at me from my album. I had my world. I have it. Don't think now that it's gone I'll choose to sneer at it, to cast doubt on it, to wonder if it properly existed. No. We're talking of my youth, which can never leave me. No. It existed. It was solid, the people in it were solid, while . . . transformed by light, while being sensitive . . . to all the changing light" (p. 45). Hirst's memories of his "true" friends and his youth are the most concrete things in his universe. Just because they no longer exist except in two-dimensional representations which are merely images "transformed by light" does not mean that they never did exist. As a matter of fact, those memories are a part of him, and stored in his mind they are perhaps more real to him than the original people were (he has to be reminded by Spooner about who some of the people might have been—if they are the same people, which is doubtful).

Like Beth in *Landscape*, Hirst's memories involve some sort of metaphysical combination of light, sensitivity, and change. In *Landscape* Beth claims that "shadow is deprivation of light. The shape of the shadow is determined by that of the object. But not always" (p. 28). She also describes a scene at the beach where she stood over her man as he lay on the sand and "he felt my shadow. He looked up" (p. 10). As the play ends she remembers how "he lay above me and looked down at me" (p. 29). In *No Man's Land* Hirst describes a similar scene: "When I stood my shadow fell upon her. She looked up" (p. 46). Seemingly unconnected with anything else in the play, these lines come after the photo album disclosure and probably refer to a memory involving someone in the pictures. The link between the light-and-shadow impression in relation to memory in *Landscape* and *No Man's Land* creates some fascinating reverberations, especially since Beth's recollections are suspect and undoubtedly subjective in character. By extension, Hirst's supposed poetic background and nature might be more responsible for what he remembers than the events themselves.

The continuing existence of the "blank dead" preserved in the album is brought up again in Act II when Hirst tells Spooner that he "might even see a face in it which might remind you of your own, of what you once were" (p. 79). He says that "if you can face the good ghost," something might be seen "in shadow." Those whose pictures are in the album, "whom you thought long dead," possess "trapped" emotion which is transmitted from the past through the vehicle of the photographs. The shadow undoubtedly represents death here, but there is still a sense of equivocation. "Allow the love of the good ghost," Hirst demands, "It will assuredly never release them, but . . . who knows how they may quicken. . . . they wish to respond to your touch." In Biblical terms he commands "And so I say to you, tender the dead, as you would yourself be tendered, now, in what you would describe as your life." It is ironic that Briggs sees the photographs as "blank. . . . The blank dead," for Hirst's portrayal of the trapped love of the good ghost presents a parallel to the roles of Briggs and Foster and later he reminds them that "we three . . . are the oldest of friends" (p. 85), almost as though the two younger men were holographic likenesses from his past. The ironies elicited by the connection of shadows with the past are compounded with Hirst's admission that he knows Boris, the wine waiter at the Ritz, very well: "he's been there for years, blinding shadows" (p. 47). The implication is that liquor is used to dispose of the past by clouding the memory of it. There is even an example of this phenomenon occuring within the action of the play when Hirst returns from his alcohol-induced nap and does not remember who Spooner is.

Another complicated pattern of interlocking themes is developed out of Spooner's account of the Amsterdam café scene. His water imagery is picked up by Hirst upon his return: "I was dreaming of a waterfall. No, no, of a lake" (p. 43). Although he declares "It's good to go to sleep in the late afternoon," Hirst finds himself bothered: "Something is depressing me. What is it? It was the dream, yes. Waterfalls. No, no, a lake. Water. Drowning. Not me. Someone else" (p. 44). The water and shadow images are brought together after he talks about light and his shadow falling when his comment "There's too much solitary shittery" conjures up an association. He continues "What was it? Shadows. Brightness, through leaves. Gambolling. In the bushes. Young lovers. A fall of water. It was my dream. The lake. Who was drowning in my dream?" (p. 46). In *Landscape* Duff described a couple (who might have been Beth and her lover) he spied during a rain by a pond surrounded by "all kinds of shit" (p. 12).

No Man's Land almost becomes the exploration of a confrontation between a lover and the husband he has cuckolded, as if Mr. Sykes and Duff had been brought together (though such a reading is much too limited purely in terms of what is developed in this play and it would be foolish to base an explication of one play on the action of one of its predecessors). Hirst's mad ramblings are interrupted and he asks, "Am I asleep? There's no water. No-one is drowning." The juxtaposition of this statement with his remembrance of the beautiful woman makes the statement seem an attempt at self-protection inspired by a feeling of past guilt. The connection is reenforced by Hirst's association of the wine waiter, who blinds shadows, with "a fall of water," which is countered by Spooner's "It was I drowning in your dream" (p. 47). The tale of Hirst's seduction of Spooner's wife in Act II becomes more credible as this sequence is seen in retrospect, though whether such a seduction ever took place and whether it involved Spooner's wife or another woman is not as important as an actual occurrence as it is in building the contrast between the two men. Spooner may be telling Hirst that he has forgiven his host for the incident when he says "I am your true friend. That is why your dream . . . was so distressing. You saw me drowning in your dream. But have no fear. I am not drowned" (p. 48), but, again, while Pinter's plays often hint that specific events took place, the truth is seldom divulged because it is the concepts involved which are the author's concern, not the actions.

The final reference to water in *No Man's Land* is another reminiscence triggered by the present. Hearing the sounds of birds which he has never heard before but which he realizes must have been there when he was young, Hirst is mentally transported into the past, where he confirms that "they sounded about us then": "Yes. It is true. I am walking towards a lake. Someone is following me, through the trees. I lose him, easily. I see a body in the water, floating. I am excited. I look closer and I see I was mistaken. There is nothing in the water. I say to myself, I saw a body, drowning. But I am mistaken. There is nothing there" (p. 95). Was the body he saw in the water simply an image, and so a product of his imagination, or the distortion of reality which caused something to look like a body, or a reflection of himself?

Before Hirst returns from his brief sleep in Act I, Foster manages to extract a bit of additional information from Spooner. The guest freely refers to his house in the country, repeating the idea of a bucolic life he had mentioned to Hirst previously, and discusses his wife and two daughters, though he avoids Foster's question about their possible reaction to Briggs. Foster entertains the older man with his tale of an Eastern tramp and his dog who "only had about one eye between them." Like Mick in *The Caretaker*, Foster's intention seems to be to warn an intruder that he recognizes him as someone to be wary of, for what the tramp returns is worthless. Spooner advises him to grant the disappearing coin illusion "no integrity whatsoever" (p. 42).[37]

37. It is amusing that the two men agree that the Oriental tramp is performing a "typical Eastern contrick. . . . Double Dutch" (p. 43), since double Dutch is a slang ex-

Hirst reenters and reduces the tension by humorously asking for a glass of whiskey and then being surprised by Briggs' sensitivity in knowing that he wanted a drink. He also claims that the drink is "the first today," a direct contradiction of what Spooner and the audience know to be true. His predilection for alcohol is openly recognized by Briggs ("You'd crawl to the bottle and stuff it between your teeth") when Hirst holds up his empty glass and asks "Who is the kindest among you?" This question relates his need for whiskey with Spooner's previously expressed dependence on strangers.

Hirst's failure to recognize Spooner leads him to disclose the existence of the photograph album. When he asks to be introduced, Foster reminds him that Spooner is a friend, and Hirst observes "In the past I knew remarkable people" (p. 44). He goes on to say that he has an album with pictures of these people in it. Precisely what is in the album is not clear, for in remembering his friends he tells Spooner that "under [the girls'] dresses their bodies were white. It's all in my album." How the pictures would show what was under their dresses is not explained and he never produces his treasure for anyone to see.

In a series of statements which sound like a combination of Beckett (particularly recalling lines from *Happy Days* and *Endgame*) and Len's mad monologues in *The Dwarfs*, Hirst's mind travels from subject to subject and through different periods of time. Having moments earlier talked about his youth, "which can never leave me," he becomes uncertain as to whether or not it ever existed as he tries to capture the ambiguity of the past: "It's gone. Did it exist? It's gone. It never existed. It remains" (p. 46). Time, too, is confusing. "I am sitting here forever" indicates that he is frozen in the moment, but "I wish you'd damnwell tell me what night it is, this night or the next night or the other one, the night before last. . . . Is it the night before last?" strengthens the feeling of the ambiguity of time as all time is seen to coexist, blending into a sense of timelessness. This sense of timelessness fits Hirst's character as it is developing, for time only seems to pass or to take on meaning when it is related to events and Hirst is stranded in the past, so he has no adequate frame of reference to judge the movement of time. Since the past is at least as real to him as the present is, he moves freely from time to time, producing a jumbled conglomeration of impressions: "What was it? . . . Brightness, through leaves. . . . It was blinding. I remember it. I've forgotten. . . . The sounds stopped. . . . There's a gap in me. I can't fill it. There's a flood running through me. . . . They're blotting me out. . . . I'm suffocating. It's a muff. A muff, perfumed. Someone is doing me to death. . . . She looked up. . . . I remember nothing. I'm sitting in this room." Contrarily, it may be that he is supersensitive to the passage of time and realizes that he cannot stop it, that

pression generally used to signify talking in a foreign tongue (though Marlowe used the term to stand for gibberish, and in the late nineteenth century it was used to indicate linguistic dexterity).

it flows away constantly. The running flood, then, could be time itself, or his memories, or his life, since man has been defined as the sum of his memories. Or it may be that nothing is substantial enough to hold him in the present and he is present in all time.

Following his monologue, Hirst collapses again. This time Spooner is ready to help his fallen host, and when Foster tells him to "bugger off," he resists, pointing out that it is logical for him to help because he and Hirst are similar: "He has grandchildren. As have I. . . . We both have fathered. We are of an age. I know his wants. . . . Respect our age" (p. 47). Age either may refer to the like number of years the two men have lived or may signify that they both belong to a specific period of time in the past—both interpretations work.

Foster and Briggs object to Spooner's helping Hirst and once more become menacers. Surmising that the two older men must have met at the Bull's Head, Foster tries to impress upon Spooner the social distance between the host and his guest: "You're not in some shithouse down by the docks. You're in the home of a man of means, of a man of achievement" (p. 48). He justifies the roles taken by Briggs and himself: "We protect this gentleman against corruption, against men of craft, against men of evil, we could destroy you without a glance, we take care of this gentleman, we do it out of love" (p. 49). When Spooner counters that he and Hirst have things in common ("I'm the same age as your master. I used to picnic in the country too, at the same time as he"), Foster continues his explanation: "This man in this chair, he's a creative man. He's an artist. We make life possible for him. We're in a position of trust. Don't try to drive a wedge into a happy household. You understand me? Don't try to make a nonsense out of family life" (p. 50). Assuming that Foster is making no impression, Briggs turns threatening, "*He moves to* SPOONER *and beckons to him, with his forefinger*," but the tension is broken by Hirst's incongruous intervention, "Where are the sandwiches? Cut the bread." With the atmosphere of menace broken, Foster expands the mood of incongruity through a series of contradictory statements. Noting that "you don't come across [Siamese or Balinese girls] over here," he comments "You see them occasionally" (p. 51). The image of these girls "on the steps of language schools, they're learning English, they're not prepared to have a giggle and a cuddle in their own language," stimulates a reaction which negates all that he has said about his relationship with Hirst: "I could make another life. I don't have to waste my time looking after a pisshound" (p. 52).

Briggs returns and casually takes Hirst away from Spooner, evoking no objection this time. As they leave the room, Hirst says "I know that man." Whether he recognizes Spooner from the past, from earlier in the evening, or as a type is undetermined.

Left alone with Spooner, Foster tells another of his apocryphal tales. He once saw a man in the Australian desert carrying two umbrellas and it seems equally startling to him that the man had two umbrellas and that this took place in the "outback," as though such an activity might be more acceptable somewhere else, say on Regent Street. Foster never asked the man about his strange behavior because, Lenny-like, "I decided he must be some kind of lunatic. I thought he would only confuse me" (p. 53). If an explanation could only confuse him, Foster must have contrived some sort of explanation of his own already—and the introduction of the idea of lunatic reasoning definitely prepares for one of Pinter's most effective curtain lines (and one which he must have enjoyed writing) when Foster asks, "You know what it's like when you're in a room with the light on and then suddenly the light goes out? . . . It's like this" and turns the light out. Because of the importance given to light throughout *No Man's Land*, Foster's action has more significance than simply being an effective way of ending Act I.

The lighting as Act II opens, *"shafts of light enter the room"* through the windows, like the lighting of O'Neill's *The Hairy Ape*, supplies subliminal cage imagery and accentuates the fact that Spooner is a prisoner in the locked room. Finding himself in this situation does not appear to be uncommon in Spooner's experience: "I have known this before" (p. [59]). The tone is kept light, in spite of Briggs' reappearance, by Spooner's response to Briggs' "I've been asked to inquire if you're hungry"—"Food? I never touch it." The underlying menace is sustained, however, for when Briggs leaves the door unlocked, Spooner, who moments before had "known . . . before. . . . A locked door," now says "I have known this before. The door unlocked," which he recognizes as a distinct threat: "The shark in the harbour" (p. 60). It is as if everything were a threat, though the unlocked door may be more terrifying for being the more unpredictable. In the light of the ending of *No Man's Land* it is possible that the shark is an allusion to the woman tourist's misunderstanding of the significance of Santiago's shark in Ernest Hemingway's *The Old Man and the Sea*. It may also be that the thought of a shark in a harbor is especially unsettling, since harbors are expected to be safe.

While Spooner has his champagne-and-scrambled-eggs breakfast, Briggs entertains him with the story of how he met Foster. "I was standing at a street corner," he says, sounding like Mick detailing the route to Sidcup, "A car drew up. It was him. He asked me the way to Bolsover street. I told him Bolsover street was in the middle of an intricate one-way system. It was a one-way system easy enough to get into. The only trouble was that, once in, you couldn't get out. I told him his best bet, if he really wanted to get to Bolsover street, was to take the first left, first right, second right, third on the left, keep his eye open for a hardware shop, go right round the square, keeping to the inside lane, take the second Mews on the right and then stop. He will find himself facing a very tall office block, with a crescent courtyard. He can take advantage of this office block. He can go round the crescent, come out the other way, follow the arrows, go past two sets of traffic lights and take the next left indicated by the first green filter he comes across. He's got the Post Office Tower in his vision the whole time. All he's got to do is to reverse into the underground car park, change gear, go straight on, and he'll find himself in Bolsover street with no trouble at all. I did warn him, though, that he'll still be faced with the problem, having found Bolsover street, of losing it" (p. 62). Interestingly, Briggs frames his anecdote with the repeated phrases "I should tell you he'll deny this account. His story will be different" (pp. 62, 63). Irving Wardle remarks that "formerly we would have had the alternate story from [Foster], without knowing comments."[38] This is probably true, but that does not necessarily mean that the play has been weakened as a consequence of Pinter's knowing "his own rules too well." There is a reversal here, as the audience is told that there are different versions of the truth as opposed to hearing the different versions and drawing that conclusion. Now the alternate is never verbalized, yet the same resonances are set up, for the audience, instead of wondering which account is "true," is left wondering what the other tale would involve. The concept of alternative realities, whether determined by unlike perceptive mechanisms or created out of individual needs, is still effectively demonstrated, though this time there is a conscious awareness expressed by the person concerned.

A second, and somewhat frustrating, reversal in Pinter's style is also apparent in Briggs' speech. The dramatist has plainly stated that he feels that four-letter words are overused and should appear in a play solely when they are meant to produce a very specific effect. Nevertheless, compared to his previous works, there are an inordinate number of instances in *No Man's Land* when one or another of the characters says "Normally I wouldn't give a fuck" (p. 63) or uses any of several other expletives. The reason for this increased use of obscenities is not clear. As in the writing of Henry Miller, the casual use of such words does not serve a characterizing purpose as well as other techniques the dramatist has already developed, and the result is that the words either bore or shock the audience, causing them to miss the important material being conveyed. On the other hand, the words are humorous in places, too, as when they are used in ways we do not usually hear them or when they are combined with high-class, formal language.

The conversation which follows is relatively inconsequential. Spooner claims to be a poet and young. Since his age is fairly evident, his poetic talent is made suspect by the paralleling of his statements. Briggs informs him that the champagne was furnished by "doctor's orders" (p. 64), momentarily hinting that he is in a sanitarium (for the insane, or even possibly for dipsomaniacs). There is a bit of word play when Spooner refers to Lord Lancer, the patron of his poetry magazine. "He's not one of the Bengal Lancers, is he?" Briggs asks, and Spooner replies, "No, no. He's of Norman

38. Irving Wardle, "No Man's Land," *Times* (London), 25 April 1975, p. 13.

descent" (p. 66). Briggs notes that Foster is a poet, which elicits a suggestion from Spooner reminiscent of Richard's advice to his wife regarding her lover in *The Lover* to have the man "send me some examples of his work, double spaced on quarto, with copies in a separate folder by separate post in case of loss or misappropriation, stamped addressed envelope enclosed" (p. 67). The stilted, mock-serious reaction is not suited to the occasion, though technically it is correct in form. It also turns out, if Briggs' information is reliable, that Hirst is a slightly jealous poet, essayist, and critic. Spooner thinks that it must be in connection with these activities that he is familiar with his host's face.

Another break in the action occurs with Briggs' departure and a new movement is heralded by Spooner's refrain, "I have known this before" (p. 68). Pinter reminds us of *The Dumb Waiter* when Spooner cites "The voice unheard. A listener. The command from an upper floor." Hirst's reentrance has been prepared for by Briggs' discussion of him and Spooner's reflection on the "command from an upper floor," but when he strides into the room with the hail, "Charles. How nice of you to drop in," the playwright seems almost to be playing with his audience. In this drama about the commingling of memory, dreams, and actuality, Pinter stimulates the audience's memories constantly, introducing lines which might have been taken from one of his other plays. Hirst's entrance lines recall Law and Stott and the opening and conclusion of *The Basement*, for instance. Much like Goldberg's switching of McCann's name in *The Birthday Party*, Hirst calls Briggs Denson, though later alluding to him as Albert (p. 82). His abrupt assumption of the offensive by remembering his past acquaintance with Spooner and his confession that he seduced Spooner's wife could have come from many of Pinter's prior works.

Hirst, who has become verbal, verbose in contrast to his reticence in Act I, gives plausibility to his remembrances by the amount of detail he recalls. Despite the fact that Hirst did not seem to know Spooner in Act I and now calls him by a first name never given before in the play, Spooner does not deny that his name is Charles, so there is no reason for the audience to reject Hirst's choice of names. Similarly, his contention that the two men knew each other at Oxford and last saw one another at the Pavilion at Lords during the West Indies cricket match in 1939 seems acceptable. The added details (the names of the cricketers, the "fine bottle of port") lend authority to the recollection. Having established an atmosphere of authenticity with this tale, Hirst openly attacks Spooner with his account of the seduction. Spooner had earlier questioned Hirst's relationship with Mrs. Hirst; Hirst strikes back in the same vein. Again, certain items are included to provide believability: the wife's name is mentioned (and later used by Spooner—p. 76); the culinary temptations and flowers are duly catalogued; the course of the seduction is carefully outlined—dates, locations, all are listed. Hirst assumes that Spooner knew nothing of the events, although his guest later refutes this assumption. Moreover, Hirst concludes, "we're too old now for it to matter" (p. 69), which may be true, if the seduction really took place and Spooner knew about it, or Spooner would have entered the house in a different frame of mind. Most likely the story is fiction. Hirst concludes his monologue by observing that he and Spooner were never close, possibly because he was "successful awfully early" (p. 70), as evidenced in his power to persuade with words (Emily's seduction), in contrast to the Prufrockian nature of Spooner, who has never achieved comparable stature.

Nonetheless, Spooner is not a pushover. He soon turns Hirst's tale back on him and uses it as a point of departure in his counterattack. *No Man's Land* has become a battleground. He asks Hirst if he ever sees Stella Winstanley, a name his host does not acknowledge until Spooner reminds him that she is Bunty Winstanley's sister. Hirst says that he never sees her, whereupon Spooner announces that Hirst was "rather taken with her" and that Bunty was annoyed with Hirst because he seduced her (p. 73).

As in other Pinter plays, it is not immediately clear whether the two men are discussing mutual acquaintances or are picking up the threads of each other's fantasies and building details on one another's creations. Spooner elaborates on his own connection with the Winstanleys until Hirst actively enters the exercise. First Hirst says that Bunty "never had the guts to speak to me himself" (p. 74). Then, when his guest uses the name Arabella, he asks if Arabella Hinscott is being referred to and warns Spooner that he "was always extremely fond of Arabella. Her father was my tutor [at Oxford]. I used to stay at their house" (p. 75). This is the same kind of activity engaged in in *Old Times*, though the frame of reference for these imaginings is the Victorian novel as opposed to the contemporary jet set. Spooner alludes to his riding with Arabella and a "form of an affair" he had with her, once more turning the tale on Hirst by seizing upon the theme of seduction and applying it to Hirst's own invention. Pinter's amusing spoof of the Victorian model is underscored by his phrasing: "I'm beginning to believe you're a scoundrel. How dare you. . . . I'll have you blackballed from your club! . . . you betrayed . . . . your insane and corrosive sexual absolutism . . . . your friendship with and corruption of Geoffrey Ramsden at Oxford was the talk of Balliol. . . . I'll have you horsewhipped! . . . [You] behaved unnaturally and scandalously, to the woman who was joined to me in God" (pp. 76–77).

The form and the vocabulary of this particular game have been established. Spooner brings these elements together by referring back to Hirst's adulterous admission, contradicting his host's contention that the seduction was secret when he claims that it was "a fact known at the time throughout the Home Counties" (p. 76). He continues, claiming that he knew of their scandalous behavior because "she told me all" (p. 77), so it could not have been of great moment to her.

Humor is an indication that sufficient points have been scored and a new direction is to be explored when Hirst asks Spooner if he listens to "the drivellings of a farmer's wife" and Spooner says yes, since he was the farmer (tying in with the earlier allusions to his country life). Hirst repudiates Spooner's bucolic background and labels him a "weekend wanker" (masturbator), which causes Spooner to recall, "I wrote my Homage to Wessex in the summerhouse at West Upfield." The change in subject matter may suggest that the original topic was not serious, or that it was too serious, or that the new subject is more serious. Spooner's humorous display of professional pride and snobbery would seem to devalue the present subject: "It is written in terza rima, a form which, if you will forgive my saying so, you have never been able to master." Spooner has diminished Hirst's character by attacking his manhood (he seduced Hirst's Arabella and knew about the supposedly secret incident of adultery) and now denigrates the other man's poetic ability. It is this last which draws a response from his adversary: "This is outrageous! Who are you? What are you doing in my house?" (p. 78). The intensity of Hirst's reaction indicates that something vital has been touched upon. He walks about the room and calls on Denson (Briggs) to bring him a whiskey and soda. This, too, is a pattern which is repeated, with variations, throughout the drama as a precursor of an important statement. "The Charles Wetherby I knew was a gentleman," he declares. In other words, Spooner is not Wetherby, a fact evident by Spooner's introduction of himself as Spooner (though not necessarily to be taken purely on faith because of that, as witness Davies in *The Caretaker* and Len's commentary in *The Dwarfs*). Hirst goes on as though Spooner were Wetherby, however: "I see a figure reduced. . . . Where is the moral ardour that sustained you once?" This thought carries him a step further, "In my day nobody changed," and it is this thought which leads him, condescendingly, to offer to show Spooner his photograph album— where the ghosts of long ago are, indeed, unchangingly preserved.

There is a brief jockeying for position as Hirst and Briggs are involved in a test of dominance. Briggs refuses to give his boss the whiskey bottle and Hirst threatens to dismiss him. The younger man says that he will not leave if dismissed and there is a standoff which is solved by Spooner assuming Briggs' role and supplying Hirst with liquor. Briggs helps himself to a drink, bringing Hirst's charge of impertinence and the observation that Briggs' "*was* always a scallywag" (p. 81, italics mine). The ensuing description of England during the August rains is another echo of Eliot.

With the return of Foster, Hirst's second request of Briggs for a bottle, this time using the name Albert, is met with acquiescence. Hirst notes that he has to write a critical essay, and Spooner offers to help for a second time. Foster and Spooner engage in a verbal skirmish, Foster claiming that he is Hirst's secretary (he had been referred to earlier as a housekeeper—p. 52), Spooner suggesting that as an aspiring poet the young man should travel.

Spooner also offers to assist Hirst with his photograph album. "I could put names to the faces," he maintains, implying that he really is familiar with his host's past. The idea that the album contains the images of the dead is enhanced by his observation that "a proper exhumation could take place" (pp. 83–84), though Foster's interjection, "Those faces are nameless," strengthens the supposition that the pictures are fictional. Hirst's "There are places in my heart . . . where no living soul . . . has . . . or can ever . . . trespass," supports the interpretation that the album is imaginary and represents his past, his youth, his dreams, his ideal of a perfect, unchanging world, all of which no longer exist. When Briggs returns with a bottle, Hirst declines any more liquor, insisting, "No, no. I'll stay . . . where I am." More than simply a decision not to imbibe any more, the phrasing of Hirst's refusal to drink is evidence that he does not wish to retreat to the past again, rejecting "the great malt which wounds." Alcohol has been his means of forgetting the present. It has functioned as a kind of time machine which permits him to travel out of and through the present to a time when whatever he wants to forget does not exist or whatever he desires to remember does exist.

Liquor also has a social operation, Hirst reminds Foster. It aids one in consorting with the society to which they are "attached as if by bonds of steel" (p. 85). The significance of this remark is underscored by Hirst's affirmation of their friendship. Since the men are decades apart in age, there is an undeveloped suggestion that Foster ("*a man in his thirties*") and Briggs ("*a man in his forties*") are memories of friends out of Hirst's past ("*a man in his sixties*").

Following the lamp lighting, Hirst states that he is ready to resolve "certain matters" (p. 86). Spooner says that he will help, but Foster again intrudes with a story of how he was called from Bali to be the secretary, chauffeur, housekeeper, and amanuensis of a "famous writer." He is not willing to be replaced, although he does not directly stake his claim. Foster concludes by asking "How did he know of me?" Spooner answers "He made an imaginative leap. Few can do it. Few do it. He did it. And that's why God loves him" (recalling the folk adage that God loves fools and drunks). The truth, according to Briggs, is that he recommended Foster to Hirst, in language similar to that used in Goldberg's recommendation of McCann in *The Birthday Party*. Foster finds his work "fruitful," especially so because he is "in touch with a very special intelligence" (p. 87) which enriches and enlarges him, but does not make unnatural or illegal demands on him.

Still, Hirst is approving of Spooner: "he's a good man at heart. I knew him at Oxford" (p. 88). After a silence, Spooner paraphrases Christopher Marlowe's "The Passionate Shepherd to His Love" (or John Donne's parody, "The Bait"): "Let me live with you and be your secretary." Hirst replies with a question of his own: "Is there a big fly in here? I hear buzzing." Hirst appears to be drawing a metaphor, comparing Spooner with a fly, and his constant entreaty correspondingly has no more meaning than a fly's buzzing. What is more significant, though, is that Spooner's literary allusion allies him with the forces of life, while Hirst's metaphor reverberates with overtones of death, because it recalls Emily Dickinson's "I heard a fly buzz when I died."

Ironically stressing that "I am I" (p. 89), Spooner attempts to convince Hirst that he is perfectly suited to serving his host. Starting fairly modestly with the assertions that he is good with tradespeople, an imaginative and intelligent conversationalist, not too old to learn, and a good cook (who favors French cuisine, but is equally competent with plainer fare), Spooner offers himself with pride as a warrior "who will accept death's challenge on your behalf."

This prolonged overture is met by a silence. Petrified in attitude, statue-like, "HIRST *is still, sitting.* / FOSTER *and* BRIGGS *are still, standing*" (p. 90). One last rambling attempt, an appeal to Hirst as an author to appear before the young and the elderly (with the serious "social implications" balancing the free drinks and Indian food), is greeted by a matching silence. After the second silence, Hirst says "Let us change the subject. / *Pause* / For the last time. / *Pause* / What have I said?" (p. 91). Foster answers, obviously, "you're changing the subject for the last time." Hirst is uncertain—"But what does that mean?" Foster insists that it "means that you'll never change the subject again. . . . Never. . . . It means that the subject is changed once and for all and for the last time forever." The significance of the change is the death-in-life paralysis which emerges from his description of the subject: "If the subject is winter, for instance, it'll be winter forever. . . . The subject is now winter. So it'll therefore be winter forever. . . . The previous subject is closed. . . . nothing else will happen forever. You'll simply be sitting here forever" (pp. 92–94). Hirst is comforted that he will not be alone ("We'll be with you. Briggs and me."), but he recognizes that "it's night" (p. 94). "And will always be night," "Because the subject—" "Can never be changed," Foster and Briggs maintain. Hirst feels a last flicker of life when he hears "sounds of birds," yet he slips back into remembrances of when he was young. The sounds take him to the lake where there is no body floating. There is a silence, then Spooner tenders his final opinion: "You are in no man's land. Which never moves, which never changes, which never grows older, but which remains forever, icy and silent" (p. 95). Another silence follows, and Hirst allows, "I'll drink to that." With this last proof that Hirst supports himself in the present by drink, the lights slowly fade.

No Man's Land is a difficult drama to work with, in part because it is not easy to determine whether Hirst or Spooner is meant to be the major character. In some ways it is Hirst's play. Spooner is used to reveal the nature of Hirst's situation (unlike Davies, who is trying to intrude—and Spooner is not as degenerate as Davies). Yet while we are told that Hirst is a poet, there is no evidence, only hearsay, and Spooner has more claim to being a poet-critic. He shows a familiarity with poetry and he has a definite ability to parody. It would be more accurate to say that he presents an alternative to Hirst's situation.

Hirst is limited by his intimations of mortality. He relies on his view of the past to endure in the present. In working with the concept of time *No Man's Land* is not quite as effective as *Old Times*, however. It is more realistic, and, therefore, does not produce as strong a sense of creating the past as *Old Times* did, where Anna is present but not present when the play opens. The fact that Hirst does not seem sure about things is not enough to convince the audience that he does not simply have a faulty memory; after all, when he arose from that short nap he did not recollect having met Spooner before. If Spooner is meant to represent an alternative to Hirst's method of facing the present, he represents failure, for notwithstanding his efforts, like Duff in *Landscape*, he has not been able to pull Hirst into a viable present and Hirst remains pretty much unmoved at the end of the drama. The literary allusions of paralysis, *Hamlet, Endgame*, "The Lovesong of J. Alfred Prufrock," probably foretell such a conclusion.

No Man's Land is marvellously wrought, with its intricate structure and sustained humor, and is an effective mode of expression for Pinter's concerns. It proves that he is an accomplished craftsman, but it would seem that the culminating play in the dramatist's exploration of the relationship between time and the human mind is still in the future.

Chapter X. Miscellaneous Writings and Films

. . . the dislocated

word . . .

In addition to the plays and revue sketches Pinter has also published a small body of miscellaneous writings and done work in the cinema. Among his miscellaneous writings are poems; a memoir; his short story, "The Examination"; four articles which discuss his theories and techniques; a discarded play, *The Hothouse*; a monologue; and twelve filmscripts.

Poetry

When Pinter turned to playwrighting at the age of twenty-seven he had already published five poems in *Poetry London*: "New Year in the Midlands" and "Chandeliers and Shadows" (with a motto from John Webster's *The Duchess of Malfi*) in the August 1950 edition; "New Year in the Midlands," reprinted because of a typographical error in the original publication,[1] togeth-

1. The concluding stanzas of "New Year in the Midlands" and "Chandeliers and

er with "Rural Idyll," and "European Revels" in the issue for November 1950; and "One a Story, Two a Death," which appeared in the Summer 1951 issue. With the exception of the last two poems, these works appeared in a collected edition of the author's poetry simply called *Poems* in 1968. Included also were "Kullus" (1949), "Jig" (1952), "Stranger" (1953), "The Task" (1954), "The Error of Alarm" (1956), and "Afternoon" (1957). Pinter's most recent individually published poetic endeavors are "Afternoon," which was published in *Twentieth Century* (February 1961), a 1970 poem, "All of That," printed in the *Times Literary Supplement* (December 11) and reprinted in *Vogue* the following year, and the short "poem" which appeared in the December 5, 1971, edition of the *New York Times Magazine*.

Several of Pinter's poems deal with sexual relationships. In "Stranger" the dead narrator berates his widow's new lover for coming between the woman and her memories of the deceased. "You did cajole," he accuses the intruder, "you interposed/in her curious dream." A slight kinship with the situation in *Landscape* might be glimpsed here, but the speaker concludes that life goes on normally and he has "no case" against his replacer (*Poems*, p. 11).

"The Error of Alarm" and "Afternoon" are companion pieces, the former expressing a woman's perspective on the female role as regards male sexual desires, and the latter reversing the point of view, with man portrayed as completely at the mercy of woman's sexual wishes. The woman's predicament is stated in the opening stanza of "The Error of Alarm." Sexual drives ("A pulse in the dark/I could not arrest") will not allow her to avoid men. Unhappily, she recognizes that men perceive her as being nothing more than a sexual object: either she is possessed in the sexual act or she finds herself discarded, as men do not share her need for emotional intercourse. Her reactions to this situation are recorded, and the poem concludes with her capitulation to male demands for purely physical sex. The contrary is expressed in "Afternoon." In this poem it is the male who is the victim of the self-concerned female. As a result of the female's efforts to gain sexual satisfaction, the male is castrated.

"Jig" presents a bitter statement on the sexual conflict in an image of the sexes locked in a sort of St. Vitus' dance:

> Women and men together,
> All in a seaquick temper,
> Tick the cabin clock.

(p. 7)

In the emotionally barren world of male/female sexual relationships, both sexes destroy their partners as a consequence of fulfilling their own needs.

Shadows" were interchanged. The reprint and other poems were attributed to "Harold Pinta."

In some ways, of course, this attitude toward need looks forward to the themes found in Pinter's later plays.

Esslin points out that the dramatist's poetry shows many of the elements to be found in his plays. For example, "New Year in the Midlands" displays "the dreamlike quality of the world in all its sordid reality" through a "Dylan Thomas-like idiom": [2]

> . . . we went to the yellow pub, cramped in an alley bin,
> A shoot from the market,
> And found the thin Luke of a queer. . . .[3]

A line from "Chandeliers and Shadows," "To plunder and verminate man's pastures," recalls Goldberg's accusation that Stanley "verminate[s] the sheet," and Esslin contends that the people referred to in the lines "Her men lovers plasterlads, who / Felled rich women" in the poem "European Revels" are forerunners of Pinter's later destructive females and the violent men of *The Dumb Waiter* and *The Birthday Party*.

The images of "One a Story, Two a Death" are precursors of *The Dwarfs* in their private meaning:

> Brought in a bowl of flaming crocuses
> In an ebon mirrorless age,
> Let fall to her face
> Till her cheeks lit in tongues.[4]

The poem also talks about a "giant negro," who Esslin sees foreshadowing Riley as a death symbol in *The Room*.[5] He further demonstrates that "I Shall Tear Off My Terrible Cap" presents a character which both Len in *The Dwarfs* and Aston in *The Caretaker* resemble in expression, experience, and type, as seen in the following excerpt:

> Only the deaf can hear and the blind understand
> The miles I gabble.
> Through these my dances of dunce and devil,
> It's only the dumb can speak through the rubble.
> Time shall drop his spit in my cup,
> With this vicious cut he shall close my trap
> And gob me up in a drunkard's lap.[6]

Another poem which parallels Aston's situation, "The Anaesthetist's Pin," links an operation and a speech problem:

2. Esslin, *The Peopled Wound*, p. 52.
3. Quoted in *The Peopled Wound*, p. 52.
4. Ibid., pp. 53–54.
5. Ibid.
6. Ibid., p. 55.

> At that incision sound
> The lout is at the throat
> And the dislocated word
> Becomes articulate.[7]

The piece, "A View of the Party," dated 1958, is a poetic treatment of the characters from *The Birthday Party*, though it should be emphasized that the title calls the poem *a* view. In this view Goldberg is not merely an agent of menace in pursuit of Stanley, he assumes the aspect of the menace itself, possibly as the concept of menace. The importance of the room theme is brought out, too, and the conclusion focuses on McCann's breaking of Stanley's glasses, as *The Room* ended with Rose's blindness.

Finally, Pinter's latest pieces of poetry to be published are "All of That" and an interesting little seven-line work which took thirteen drafts, "poem," a quick look at three people: two lovers kissing and an observer. The lovers' kiss is affected by the presence of the observer, even though they see him only with eyes blinded by their own self-involvement. This causal effect may relate "poem" to the author's latest dramas, in which reality is continually being created. There may be a shift in perspectives involved as the "I" becomes "we," or it may simply be that all three people are momentarily united by the light which falls upon them as they create reality at this moment.

Mac

Mac, published in a limited edition in 1968, is a memoir of Pinter's eighteen-month tour with Anew McMaster's repertory company in Ireland, beginning in September 1951. Pinter affectionately recalls the period as "a golden age for me."[8]

"The Examination"

Except for the prose version of *Tea Party*, Pinter's only published short story is "The Examination," which appeared in the Summer 1959 issue of *Prospect* and was later read by the author on a BBC Third Programme broadcast, September 7, 1962. Written at about the same time as *A Slight Ache*, the story has definite thematic connections with this play, with the prose poem "Kullus," and with the later screenplay *The Basement*, as well as aspects which reappear from *The Room* (the territorial struggle) to *Landscape* and *Silence* (the distinctive use of silences to represent activity).

7. Ibid.   8. Pinter, *Mac*, p. 16.

Taylor stresses that the tale can be seen as a gloss to *A Slight Ache* in that it presents the same process that involves Edward and the matchseller from within. He feels that it completes Pinter's first cycle of interest in integrity and identity and represents a shift to the definition of character through social interaction and communication which occupies the dramatist henceforth.[9] Pinter sees "The Examination" as the point from which he developed his themes of violence, dominance, and subservience, though he admits that the themes had been present in his work before: "I wrote a short story . . . called 'The Examination,' and my ideas of violence carried on from there. That short story dealt very explicitly with two people in one room having a battle of unspecified nature, in which the question was one of who was dominant at what point and how they were going to be dominant and what tools they would use to achieve dominance and how they would try to undermine the other person's dominance. A threat is constantly there: it's got to do with this question of being in the uppermost position, or attempting to be . . . . it's a very common, everyday thing."[10]

Through first-person narration an unidentified examiner tells of his relationship with Kullus (as in the poem of the same name). As in Kafka's *The Trial*, the subject of the examination is never disclosed. During the examination, which begins with the examiner in control, marking "proposed times on the blackboard" with a piece of chalk, a fatal mistake is made: "I allowed him intervals."[11] Kullus takes advantage of these intervals to remain silent, but silence does not mean a cessation of activity, "For if Kullus fell silent, he did not cease to participate." Actually, the examiner notes later, the silences are a means of communication, since the intensity can be deepened as a form of activity. The dramatist has applied this technique in his own writing.

The idea of verification is introduced when the examiner remarks that he was obliged to verify any changes in his subject's manner. This leads to the first indication of what is happening in the story, because through his observations "gradually it appeared that these intervals proceeded according to [Kullus's] terms" (p. 88). Kullus is assuming the dominant position. His preoccupation with the windows in the room brings about the examiner's realization that "we were no longer in Kullus's room," for his subject stops maintaining a "particular arrangement of window and curtain," determined by the time of day. The roles are ritually reversed, as in *A Slight Ache* and, more nearly parallel, *The Basement*.

Now Kullus enters the room unattended and the examiner mistakenly assumes a dominant attitude because "I was naturally dominant, by virtue of

9. Taylor, *Harold Pinter*, p. 13.
10. Quoted in Bensky, "Harold Pinter: An Interview," pp. 30–31.
11. Pinter, "The Examination," in *The Collection and The Lover* (London: Methuen, 1970), p. [87].

my owning the room." He arrives at this conclusion through a progression established on the premise that his "visitor" would recognize the "especial properties of my abode" and thus "through recognition to acknowledgement and through acknowledgement to appreciation, and through appreciation to subservience. . . . Had not Kullus been obliged to attend this examination? And was not his attendance an admission of that obligation? And was not his admission an acknowledgement of my position? And my position therefore a position of dominance?" (p. 90). Ultimately, though, Kullus regains the room, too, as the final line states—"we were now in Kullus's room" (p. 92).

Articles

Five articles that Pinter has written are useful in providing insights into his way of thinking when he approaches an artistic problem; they give a picture of the writer's mind at work, summarize some of the concepts which underlie his writing, and explain his techniques. In order of publication these articles are "Writing for Myself," "Filming 'The Caretaker,' " "Writing for the Theatre," "Between the Lines," and "Beckett."

"Writing for Myself"

"Writing for Myself" is Pinter's side of a conversation with Richard Findlater which appeared in the *Twentieth Century* for February 1961.[12] In it he comments on his dramatic background and then discusses the difficulty of writing for the stage, as opposed to other literary forms, though he recognizes the freedom allowed in radio and television writing and the fact that there have been developments in the theatre which have helped him—"*The Caretaker* wouldn't have been put on . . . before 1957."

Essentially he concludes that he does not write to please an audience, but because there is something within himself which has to be written out. As a result he does not see himself fulfilling "any particular social function. . . . I don't carry any banners. Ultimately I distrust any definitive labels."[13]

"Between the Lines"

"Between the Lines," originally an address delivered by Pinter to the Seventh National Student Drama Festival in Bristol, was printed in the London *Sunday Times* on March 4, 1962. The role of the "playwright as prophet" is disposed of and the majority of the article is related to language and para-language—the problem of verification as related to words, and the "two sorts

12. Pinter is reportedly not happy with this interview.
13. Pinter, "Writing for Myself," p. 175.

of silence" which are used to avoid communication. The article supplies a clear definition of Pinter's conception of language and how he applies his ideas to his work.

"Filming 'The Caretaker' "

Written in collaboration with Clive Donner, the director of the movie version of *The Caretaker*, "Filming 'The Caretaker' " was published in the Summer 1963 issue of *Transatlantic Review* and is the transcription of another interview, this time by Kenneth Cavander. The article deals with the difference between staging and filming the play, naturally, and it relates the advantages the film medium provides. Pinter states that the filming allowed the play to be "opened out" in several ways, one of them concerning close-ups and focusing techniques which made the cinematic version more intimate and at the same time gave him a chance to establish relationships between the characters more clearly. He also was pleased with the reality aspect of film, for "in the film, as opposed to the play, we see a real house."

"Writing for the Theatre"

In "Writing for the Theatre," *Evergreen Review*, 1964, Pinter discusses the impossibility of distinguishing between what is real and what is not real, the difficulty, if not impossibility, of verifying the past, the ambiguity of words, and the use of silence for communication. The playwright's conscious understanding and expression of these concepts which structure his work is useful for arriving at consistent interpretations of his dramas.

"Beckett"

"Beckett" is a short tribute included in *Beckett at Sixty*, a festschrift published by Calder and Boyars (London) in 1967. In a letter Pinter explains why he finds Beckett "the finest writer writing" (see Chapter I, n. 8, above, for his reasons).

The Hothouse

In 1966 Pinter told Lawrence Bensky, "I have occasionally out of irritation thought about writing a play with a satirical point. I once did, actually, a play that no one knows about. A full-length play written after *The Caretaker*. Wrote the whole damn thing in three drafts. It was called *The Hothouse* and was about an institution in which patients were kept: all that was presented was the hierarchy, the people who ran the institution; one never knew what happened to the patients or what they were there for or who they were.

It was heavily satirical and it was quite useless. I never began to like any of the characters, they really didn't live at all. So I discarded the play at once. The characters were so purely cardboard. I was intentionally—for the only time, I think—trying to make a point, an explicit point, that these were nasty people and I disapproved of them. And therefore they didn't begin to live. Whereas in other plays of mine every single character, even a bastard like Goldberg in *The Birthday Party*, I care for."[14]

Esslin, who has been given access to the script, reports that this unpublished and unperformed drama bears a handwritten note on the title page which reads, "Final Draft. Discarded play."[15] Although undated, the work is apparently the source of a synopsis for a radio play that Pinter submitted to the BBC on November 12, 1958, which would correspond with the author's declaration that it had been written at about the same time as *The Caretaker*. From Esslin's relation of the plot, there are distinct parallels between the two pieces.

The action takes place in a government-run psychological-research station in the country which is referred to as a "rest home" by a staff filled with caricatures named Roote (an ex-Army officer), Hogg, Lush, Beck, Budd, Tuck, Dodds, Tate, Peck, Gibbs, Lamb, Cutts, Tibb, and Lobb. The idiom, according to Esslin, is "of grotesque farce which points in the direction of Ionesco."[16]

In this setting Miss Cutts, the only woman present, has an affair with Roote and his aide, Gibbs; Lamb is subjected to torturous experiments by Gibbs and Cutts (one of which was extracted as the revue sketch "Applicant"; several other lines from the play reappear in "Dialogue for Three"); a patient dies and his mother is told that he has been transferred elsewhere; another patient gives birth to an illegitimate child; Gibbs reports to "a bureaucrat in Whitehall" that the entire staff has been bloodily disposed of; and Lamb remains forgotten in the soundproofed experimental room, still attached to the electronic equipment.

Links between *The Hothouse* and *The Caretaker* include using Lamb to show the experience Aston underwent, the grotesquely abrupt and unconcerned sexually oriented questions asked by Miss Cutts which might relate to Aston's fear of women, and the superintendent's using the name Jenkins as an example in a discussion about helping the inmates regain their names.

Apparently Pinter decided to abandon *The Hothouse* when he realized that he was exploiting "Pinteresque" elements—was, in fact, copying or even parodying himself. Esslin agrees that Pinter's rejection of the drama was wise, for it allows the playwright to avoid problems which might arise if he did not start from a naturalistic basis in developing his poetic images.

14. Quoted in Bensky, pp. 28–29.   16. Ibid.
15. Esslin, *The Peopled Wound*, p. 103.

Monologue

Between 1971, when he wrote *Old Times*, and 1974, when he wrote *No Man's Land*, Pinter's only piece of original dramatic writing was *Monologue*. A twenty-minute monologue which he created for British television, the play was televised in 1973.

Films

While Pinter's artistic achievements have primarily been connected with his work in the theatre, he has also quietly been building, since his first scripted film, *The Servant*, appeared in 1962, a reputation as a master screenwriter. In the fifteen years since then, he has had numerous cinematic successes, in terms of both popular acceptance and critical acclaim, and he has won several prestigious awards for his work. Besides being entered in major festivals, his films have consistently been listed among the year's ten best, and he received the Berlin Film Festival Silver Bear and an Edinburgh Festival Certificate of Merit for *The Caretaker* in 1963, the British Screenwriters Guild Award and the New York Film Critics Award for *The Servant* in 1964, the British Film Academy Award for *The Pumpkin Eater* in 1965, the Cannes Film Festival Special Jury Prize for *Accident* in 1967, and the Cannes Film Festival Golden Palm for *The Go-Between* in 1971. Indeed, critics claim that Pinter's distinctive style and unmistakable writing ability have been responsible for the best work done by several of his directors.

The extent of Pinter's filmic accomplishments is implied by Andrew Sarris's conclusions in his examination of *The American Cinema*: "The Servant and Accident have done more for [Joseph] Losey's general reputation than all his other [20] pictures put together,"[17] and "Michael Anderson's career [thirteen previous films] is so undistinguished until *The Quiller Memorandum* that two conclusions are unavoidable, one that Harold Pinter was the true auteur of *The Quiller Memorandum*, and two that Pinter found in Anderson an ideal metteur en scène for his (Pinter's) very visual conceits."[18] That Pinter has made such a mark in a field in which the director is the recognized superstar (and the final property is subject to his every whim) is a tribute to his talent as a writer.

Between 1961 and 1973 Pinter wrote an average of almost one screenplay per year, all of them adaptations. Although attaining varying degrees of popular success, the films have all been critically acclaimed and have helped

17. Andrew Sarris, *The American Cinema: Directors and Directions 1929–1968* (New York: Dutton, 1968), p. 96.
18. Ibid., p. 252.

the dramatist achieve a financial security which allows him to be somewhat particular about the production of his plays as well as the choice of stories he wishes to turn into movies.

Of his ten filmscripts, three have been adaptations of his own dramas and seven have been adaptations of novels for the screen (some based on books given him by Director Losey). Taylor concludes that *The Pumpkin Eater* and *The Quiller Memorandum* are "essays in writing technique" and that *The Servant* and *Accident* assume "the character of Pinter creations."[19] Esslin concurs, finding that while in general the artist's approach to the cinema has been in the role of a "conscientious and highly professional craftsman," nevertheless "much of his characteristic quality remains and enriches the films, most notably the ones which have been directed by Joseph Losey [at that time *The Servant* and *Accident*], a film-maker whose sensibility is beautifully attuned to Pinter's terse, elliptic style, his silences and pauses."[20]

The combination of playwriting and screenwriting talent in one author allows a unique opportunity, incidentally, to demonstrate the differences which exist between the dramatic and cinematic versions of his works, and by extension provides some insights into the essential differences between the media of prose writing, drama, and film.

The Servant

Robin (Sir Robert) Maugham's 1948 novel *The Servant* is the original for Pinter's first movie script. Pinter wrote a screen version of *The Servant*, intending it for Michael Anderson, but rewrote it almost completely when Losey decided to do the film.[21] Starring Dirk Bogarde as the servant Hugo Barrett, the movie, Britain's entry at the Venice Film Festival and later at the first New York Film Festival, opened in London in November of 1962.

In his interview with Bensky the scenarist reveals the novel's source of appeal to him when discussing the repeated theme of dominance and subservience in his plays and its particular application to "The Examination" as a question of "who was dominant at what point. . . ." "That's something of

19. Taylor, *Harold Pinter*, p. 20. Perhaps it was only a matter of time before Pinter made his mark in screenwriting, for he showed an early interest in film. As a member of the Hackney Downs School Literary and Debating Society he spoke twice on the subject of cinema. He gave a speech on "Realism and Post-Realism in the French Cinema" (reported in the *Hackney Downs School Magazine*, No. 163, Autumn 1947, p. 13) and then suggested the motion, "In view of its progress in the last decade, the Film is more promising in its future as an art form than the Theatre" (reported ibid., No. 164, Spring 1948, p. 12).

20. Esslin, *The Theatre of the Absurd*, p. 255.

21. Maugham had already written a stage version at this time, but the screenplay is based solely on the novel. Incidentally Losey—an American director forced abroad to find work—finds it ironic that he was voted the best *foreign* director of the year for *Accident* by the Independent Distributors of the United States.

what attracted me to do the screenplay of *The Servant* . . . [the] battle for positions."[22] The early confrontation between Tony and Barrett in which Tony invites his prospective servant to sit down is the first indication of this theme, for by forcing the other man to take a seat, Tony temporarily enjoys a one-up position. This seating game appears in several early Pinter dramas (notably *The Room* and *The Birthday Party*) as a means of demonstrating dominance.

The novel is narrated by one Richard Merton, who tells the story of his relationship with Tony, a friend recently demobilized after five years service in the Orient. Tony moves into an apartment with Barrett and his niece Vera, who is to work as a maid. Tony's girl friend, Sally Grant, starts to worry about Barrett's influence on Tony, and the theme of the movie is set. Like Tony's ex-Nanny, Barrett "insulates" him "from a cold drab world"[23] to the extent that he eventually rejects Sally, Merton, his other friends, and his work even though he has discovered that Vera was Barrett's mistress, brought along to seduce her employer.

As a film, Pinter has improved the product. The narrator is discarded and a secondary conflict grows out of the fiancée's relationship with the manservant, though the fundamental meaning of the movie centers on the theme of domination as related to the male characters. The novel itself is short, only fifty-six pages, and Barrett appears infrequently and often only at second hand as he is mentioned in someone's gossip. He is seldom seen in person. As a matter of fact, the servant is not even introduced until nearly one-sixth of the way into the book, and when he is presented, it is clear from Tony's remark, "I've given up trying to control him," that the servant dominates his master easily from the beginning.[24] There is no sense of conflict between the two men and no tracing of the breakdown of Tony's character. This comes about because of Maugham's conception of Barrett's nature; like Keats's Lamia, Barrett, who is described as a snake, is fundamentally evil. Tony is "lazy, and he likes to be comfortable," according to the narrator, so Barrett's method is simple: "He's found out Tony's weakness, and he's playing on it."[25] The basic difference between the novelist's approach and Pinter's is that in the first instance a tale is told, simply and briefly recounting something which has happened, while the scenarist *demonstrates* the events taking place, leading his audience to a psychological understanding of not only what has happened but also why it has happened. Maugham's work is less imaginative.

In the novel Sally is a minor character, but in the movie, with her name changed to Susan Stewart (acted by Wendy Craig) and incorporating Merton's role and point of view, she becomes a principal force trying to undermine Barrett's unhealthy influence. She fails, however, and by the conclusion there

22. Quoted in Bensky, pp. 30–31.
23. Robin Maugham, *The Servant* (London: Heinemann, 1964), p. 31.
24. Ibid., p. 16.   25. Ibid., p. 20.

has been a role switch between Tony (James Fox) and his servant à la Pinter's dramatic works *A Slight Ache*, "The Examination," and *The Basement*. The latent homosexuality of the book is toned down, too, making it more ambiguous and thereby increasing the stress on the theme of domination.[26] In the novel this is accomplished by having the narrator return to Tony's flat in a final attempt to woo him away from Barrett, only to find that the servant has introduced another girl into the household to entertain his master and himself; in the movie it is Susan who makes the last attempt, arriving at Tony's in the midst of an orgy. She tries to arouse Tony into realizing the situation by kissing Barrett, but Tony is incapable of breaking his servant's hold on him and the kiss serves more tellingly to demonstrate the reversal of roles which has taken place.

There are additional minor differences between Maugham's original and Pinter's adaptation, including the move of the apartment from the basement to the upper story, the inclusion of the ball game on the stairs and the army comradeship talk between Tony and his manservant, the fact that Tony rather than Merton discovers Barrett and Vera together in the film, and Vera's rejoining the two men in the film rather than turning to prostitution. Basically, though, the changes Pinter makes grow out of his attitude toward the material contained within Maugham's story. The novel has a marked sense of a morality play, with the characters obviously representing several of the deadly sins. Everything is clear-cut and almost preordained because Barrett is equated with evil—he destroys from within "by serving [his victim's] particular weakness."[27] Thus, Vera represents lust, her father stands for avarice, and Tony symbolizes the love for comfort and ease, a combination of sloth and gluttony. When Pinter turns these elements into a psychological study, the tale becomes interesting and moving.

Discussing the alterations he effected, Pinter says, "I followed it [the novel] up. I think I did change it in a number of ways. I cut out the particular, a narrator in fact, which I didn't think was very valuable to a film, but I think I did change it quite a lot in one way or another, but I kept to the main core at the same time the end is not quite the same ending that it was in the book. I must have *carte blanche* you know, to explore it."[28]

The changes and additions give Pinter some flexibility to pursue his characteristic interests. The Pinter brand of humor and dialogue both appear in the film (including, incidentally, a scene in a French restaurant which features Pinter, Patrick Magee, and Alun Owen, colleagues from the McMaster tour days, in bit parts). The confused, meaningless, yet funny social small talk that the author captures so well in demonstrating the lack of communication

26. See pp. 20, 21, and 31, for instance, for evidence of the homosexuality found in the novel.
27. Maugham, p. 60.
28. Quoted from a BBC *New Comment* transcript in Hinchliffe, p. 128.

between people is evident in Tony's meeting with Susan's parents, Lord and Lady Mountset:

LADY MOUNTSET. That's where the Ponchos are, of course, on the plains.
SUSAN. Ponchos?
LORD MOUNTSET. South American cowboys.
SUSAN. Are they called Ponchos?
LORD MOUNTSET. They were in my day.
SUSAN. Aren't they those things they wear? You know, with the slit in the middle for the head to go through?
LORD MOUNTSET. What do you mean?
SUSAN. Well, you know . . . hanging down in front and behind . . . the cowboy.
LADY MOUNTSET. They're called cloaks, dear.[29]

In addition, as pointed out by Taylor in a review of *The Servant*, "Tony's house is a sophisticated upper-class extension of the recurrent symbol in Pinter's early plays, the room-womb which offers a measure of security in an insecure world, an area of light in the surrounding darkness. But here the security is a trap sprung on the occupant by his own promptings and by the servant who embodies them and knows too well how to exploit them."[30] The film, then, fits into Pinter's artistic development perfectly, coming between *A Slight Ache* and *The Lover*, for in his writing for the theatre at this time, the playwright was beginning to shift his attention from examining the disintegration of individuals in the presence of outside, physical menace to exploring the interior, psychological source of that menace. Considering that *The Servant* was the author's first attempt at screenwriting, the result is especially impressive.

The Caretaker (The Guest)

Pinter's first trial at transferring one of his own plays to the cinematic medium was a success, too, though there was some difficulty in securing backing for it. The production cost of £30,000, with no guarantee of distribution, was privately financed by a group of backers (Caretaker Films, Ltd.) which included Richard Burton, Leslie Caron, Noël Coward, Peter Hall, Peter Sellers, Elizabeth Taylor, and the continuity girl. The film version of *The Caretaker*, retitled *The Guest* for its American run in 1964,[31] was first publicly screened at the Berlin Film Festival on June 27, 1963, where it was awarded a Silver Bear for "Clive Donner's balanced direction of Harold Pinter's re-

29. Pinter, *The Servant*, in *Five Screenplays* (London: Methuen, 1971), p. 25.
30. Taylor, in *Sight and Sound*, Winter 1963/64, pp. 38–39. See also Penelope Gilliatt's review in the *Observer*, 17 Nov. 1963, for a similar observation.
31. Possibly so as not to be confused with Hal Bartlett's *The Caretakers*, released in 1963.

markable script and the ensemble performances of three fine actors." It was also shown at the Edinburgh Film Festival, where it received a Certificate of Merit—the only British film so honored. Directed by Clive Donner, photographed by Nicholas Roeg, and starring the New York cast of Donald Pleasence, who beautifully brings Davies to life, Robert Shaw as Aston, and Alan Bates as Mick, the film is an excellent cinematic translation of the play.

Stanley Kauffmann's review of the movie emphasizes the effect of exchanging a stage for the screen: "It is a fascinating, funny, eerie film, a work of murky evocations boiling out of grubby naturalistic minutiae [the film was shot in five weeks on location at 31 Downs Road, a derelict house in Hackney, not far from Pinter's childhood home, and at 36 Dover Street, London]. That is, of course, the Pinter method, but in this film we are seeing that method used at its best so far. . . . One feels that, at last, the work has been fully revealed . . . the smallest subtleties of expression can buttress his naturalistic mode, where magnified presence can lend greater implications to silences and hints and physical objects, where the skillful placement and shifting of the audiences by camera movement and angle can underscore his intent to draw us into confined areas, literally and figuratively."[32]

Penelope Gilliatt comments[33] on Davies' defensive use of language in the movie, stating that the old man is "haunted by suspicions of malevolence, but he has no one to ask about them; so when he is talked to he often says 'What?' not because he hasn't heard, but as a hopeless way of gaining time and puzzling out how much ground he has just lost."

These notes are reinforced by Pinter and his director in "Filming 'The Caretaker.'" Pinter sees the situation as cinematic: "It seemed to me, that when you have two people standing on the stairs and one asks the other if he would like to be caretaker in this house, and the other bloke, you know, who is work-shy, doesn't want in fact to say no, he doesn't want the job, but at the same time he wants to edge it round . . . Now it seems to me there's an enormous amount of internal conflict within one of the characters and external conflict between them—and it's exciting cinema" (p. 19).

The author is also in agreement about the work's being "fully revealed": "You can say the play has been 'opened out' . . . that things . . . crystallized when I came to think about it as a film. Until then I didn't know that I wanted to do them [films] because I'd accepted the limitations of the stage. For instance, there's a scene in the garden of the house, which is very silent; two silent figures with a third looking on. I think in the film one has been able to hit the relationship of the brothers more clearly than in the play."

Pinter is also of the opinion that the mechanics of film making, such things as close-ups and focusing techniques, are responsible for a cinematic version that is more intimate, and at the same time they allow him to establish

32. Stanley Kauffmann, "The Guest," in *World on Film*, p. 213.
33. In the *Observer*, 14 March 1964.

the relationships between the characters more clearly, as stated above. For instance, in the theatrical version the stage directions suggest that Davies is following his host like a lost dog when they first enter the room at the beginning of the play. In the film, which shows the two men walking on the street on their way to the room, this comparison is obviously indicated by Davies' shuffling back and forth after Aston. Moreover, in the screenplay, as mentioned before, the significance of the final glance between the two brothers is more emphatic (especially the hint of triumph on Mick's part) because of the camera's focusing ability, while in the drama there is only a slight implication. On the screen the expressions are carefully framed; on the stage there is nothing to direct the audience's attention specifically to the men's faces, so the quick look which passes between them might be missed by the viewers. Since this glance epitomizes the brothers' relationship, it is easy to see why Pinter feels that in the movie the essence of the work is captured "more clearly than in the play."

The opening out is enhanced by the naturalistic capabilities of a cinematic medium, too: "What I'm very pleased about myself is that in the film, as opposed to the play, we see a real house and real snow outside, dirty snow and the streets. We don't see them very often but they're there. . . . and these characters move in the context of a real world—as I believe they do. In the play, when people were confronted with just a set . . . they often assumed it was all taking place in limbo, in a vacuum, and the world outside hardly existed, or had existed at some point but was only half remembered. Now one thing which I think is triumphantly expressed in the film is Clive's concentration on the characters when they are outside the room" (p. 23). In other words that "there is a world outside"[34] is important to the meaning of the work, and this world is better indicated in the film than in the stage version. Ultimately, as mentioned before, it must be remembered that Pinter thinks of his characters as being "real." While Davies may represent the existential Chaplinesque/Beckett tramp on the road of life, he is also a *real* tramp who probably does literally "stink the place out" and who becomes characterized by variations on the tramp's "Thank you, mister," every time he is given something, be it money, cigarettes, or clothing. Aston's acquaintance with the names of tools and their functions and Mick's knowledgeable recital of bus numbers (after the manner of "The Black and White") and his tracing the highway route to Sidcup (added in the film) link them to the real world.

The opening out also reflects the dissimilarities in the two media with which Pinter is working. Because some of the action now takes place outside the room, dialogue must be added, cut, or rearranged in order to accommodate the differences in setting. Partially, too, the dialogue alterations (e.g., the removal of some lines from Aston's hospital monologue) are necessary

34. Quoted from a BBC *New Comment* transcript in Hinchcliffe, p. 99.

because of the kind of flow of action demanded by film. As a matter of fact, the author seems more willing to substitute pure action for words in some cases, as when Aston wordlessly places the ladder under the bed or when he shakes the blanket making Davies sneeze without any preceding comment that it might be dusty. In addition, the scenarist uses the camera's focusing ability for comic effect, as when Davies, close-up in the foreground, notes that there is a "good bit of stuff" in the room, and the piled junk seen behind him almost seems to be closing in, or when the tramp asks, "Is this in use at all?" while he and Aston unload the buried bed.

While the inclusion in the film of outside scenes sacrifices some of the emotional intensity of the stage version evoked by a sense of confinement, Pinter has been able to concentrate on other devices to achieve a like effect on film. The opening shot, for instance, of Mick parked in his van with the house in the background and the following sequence, in which he enters the building, climbs the stairs, and goes into the room tracked by the camera, allow the audience to feel the menace of his waiting figure and also to realize the size of the house and the existence of other rooms, so that Aston's shutting himself off is more starkly recognized. This brings us closer to understanding the play. There are other instances which reinforce the meaning gleaned from this episode: Mick's sudden attack on Davies is more startling as he appears in the frame without warning; the younger brother picks up the old man in his van to take him down to Sidcup, then only drives around a circle and lets his passenger out, showing Mick's unwillingness to be *obviously* responsible for his rival's removal and simultaneously drawing attention to the ritualistic circularity of action and conversation which fills the drama—this scene also functions (as the curtain does on stage) to break the tension generated by Aston's hospital speech at the end of Act II. And finally, shots of Mick's sometimes furtive activities, moving from one room to another and watching through partly open doors when Aston comes home, plus the older brother's realization that this is being done, help make the relationship between the brothers clearer (the fishpond scene implies that they may be working together). All in all, while the transference to film has weakened some aspects of the theatrical version of *The Caretaker*, it has strengthened others, so that Pinter has managed to retain the essence of his play on the screen.

The Pumpkin Eater

The Pumpkin Eater is one of Pinter's less successful ventures artistically, though the film, directed by Jack Clayton, brought an Academy Award to Anne Bancroft in the role of Mrs. Jake Armitage and a British Film Academy Award for best screenplay of 1964 to Pinter.

Based on Penelope Mortimer's novel (1962), the film tells of the conflict between a husband (played by Peter Finch), who wants to escape from the mundane world of work and family into the arms of other women, and his wife, who would be content forever having more children. She becomes pregnant and then has to undergo a hysterectomy, leading to the insertion of a typically Pinteresque symbol (not included in the novel), the sailless windmill in which she lives after the operation. Neither the structure nor its inhabitant can any longer fulfill a primary function.

Another element which Pinter introduces is his characteristic approach to language. A bit of after-party conversation exemplifies the screenwriter's contribution to dialogue, especially representative in its use of repetition:

CONWAY (*his voice coming out of the silence*). I call myself a tradesman, because it's the only thing left to respect, in my honest opinion. In my honest opinion, an honest tradesman is the only thing left to respect in this world. That's my honest opinion.

JAKE. You'd say that in all honesty, would you?

CONWAY. In all honesty, Jake. In complete honesty, boy. Ask Beth. Ask Beth if I mean what I say. (*Pause.*) Ask her![35]

Elsewhere, the use of *non sequiturs* is evident, representing the lack of connection in modern life, as when Jo is confronted by a strange woman while at the hairdresser's: "WOMAN. To tell you the honest truth, my life is an empty place, to tell you the dog's honest truth. Your eyes are more beautiful than in that picture. I bet you didn't always have things so good, that's why you appreciate, don't you? I never dreamed I'd meet you like this and I mean you're so kind, you're so full of sympathy for me. My husband doesn't come near me any more, no, nowhere near me. Don't you think I'm attractive any more? I think I'm still attractive" (pp. 91–92). Finally, the idea that nothing may be taken for granted is expressed in a talk between Jake and his father when the elder Mr. Armitage asks, "Do you like children?" "Of course I like them," his son answers, "Of course I do." Mr. Armitage can only query, "Have you actually known any?" (p. 67).

Two things about the novel which may have interested Pinter are the nervous breakdown the wife is suffering and the fact that the story is told entirely from her point of view, negating any chance for verifying the true motivations lying behind the actions portrayed. The film is more objective in its treatment, and critics agree that there is a clash between the dialogue and the visual presentation which makes it seem too "stagey."[36]

35. Pinter, *The Pumpkin Eater*, in *Five Screenplays*, p. 100.
36. See Ian Wright in the *Guardian*, 17 July 1964, and David Robinson in the *Financial Times*, same date, though Halliwell feels that there are sufficient "brilliantly-handled sequences" to give the film a "feel of life" (*Filmgoer's Companion*, p. 792).

The Quiller Memorandum

Another novel is the source of Pinter's next scenario, *The Quiller Memorandum*. Taken from Adam Hall's *The Berlin Memorandum*, *The Quiller Memorandum* opened in November 1966 with an international cast including Sir Alec Guinness, Max von Sydow, the late George Sanders, Senta Berger, and George Segal (as Quiller). The film version of the 1965 spy-thriller concerning a Western agent who infiltrates a Nazi underground organization was directed by Michael Anderson (for whom *The Servant* was originally intended) and filmed by Ivan Foxwell.

In an act of self-policing, at government request, the United States film industry reportedly agreed to cut all allusions to the villains as members of a neo-Nazi terror organization, though this was not done. When Quiller receives his assignment, for instance, his contact identifies the enemy as "quite a tough bunch. Nazi from top to toe. In the classic tradition";[37] and later the agent poses as a journalist researching an article "about the present day Nazi question in Germany" (p. 154). Obviously, being set in postwar Berlin and dealing with surreptitious military and fascist indoctrination of German youth, the film gains added meaning by drawing on history, and the characters' motivation is better understood when it is seen that the underground group is trying to revive a tradition which had given meaning and structure to their lives. It is ridiculous to try to ignore the historical facts of Nazism, World War II, and the rest. The agreement is simply another instance of the industry's current exercise in catering to oversensitive ethnic groups; the attempt to please everyone perforce demands a complete disregarding of reality. In the cut shown nationwide on American television in 1971 these references were retained.

There are some minor Pinter touches in characterization (verification problems) and dialogue. The opening conversation, for example, is pure Pinter:

GIBBS. What exactly is he doing now?
RUSHINGTON. He's on leave, actually. On vacation.
GIBBS. Ah.
    They eat.
Well, perhaps someone might get in touch with him.
RUSHINGTON. Oh yes, certainly. No difficulty about that.
GIBBS. Ask him if he'd mind popping over to Berlin.
RUSHINGTON. Mmmm. I think so.
GIBBS. Good.
    They eat.
Shame about K.L.J.

37. Pinter, *The Quiller Memorandum*, in *Five Screenplays*, p. 142.

RUSHINGTON. Mmmm.
GIBBS. How was he killed?
RUSHINGTON. Shot.
GIBBS. What gun?
RUSHINGTON. Long shot in spine, actually. Nine point three. Same as Metzler.
GIBBS. Oh, really?
> *They eat.*

How's your lunch?
RUSHINGTON. Rather good.
GIBBS. What is it?
RUSHINGTON. Pheasant.
GIBBS. Ah. Yes, that should be rather good. Is it?
RUSHINGTON. It is rather, yes [p. 140].

The film is only of average interest, though, even as an adventure piece.

Accident

The second Losey film for which Pinter wrote the screenplay, *Accident* probes the relationships between an Oxford University don named Stephen (Dirk Bogarde again), his wife Rosaline (Pinter's actress wife Vivien Merchant), their friend Charley (Stanley Baker), and two of Stephen's students, the aristocrat William (Michael York) and the Austrian princess Anna (Jacqueline Sassard). *Accident*, first shown in February 1967, was England's official entry in the Cannes Film Festival (where it won the special jury prize) and was honored as one of the ten best films of the year by the National Board of Review.

The adaptation, from the book written in 1965 by Nicholas Mosley (who, incidentally, appears as Hedges in the film along with Pinter, who acts the part of Bell), opens with a shot of the don's house. There is the sound of an approaching car and then a crash. But the camera pushes in on the house instead of panning to reveal the accident. Stephen emerges to investigate and finds William dead and a drunken, licenseless Anna in the driver's seat. He carries her into the house before the police arrive and conclude that William was alone. There is a flashback.

The flashback details the events leading to the accident: the don has been attracted to his sloe-eyed student, but is torn by his responsibility as a teacher because of William; he loves his pregnant wife and children, but desires one last fling (and involves his lonely ex-girlfriend, Francesca, played by Delphine Seyrig, who has played Pinter roles on the French stage); Charley, a fellow don, seduces Anna; the unaware, youthful, athletic William is caught in the middle, too young for his fiancée Anna, yet arousing middle-aged envy in Stephen and Charley. With the girl now dependent upon him because of his damaging knowledge that she was driving, Stephen can take advantage of her. The movie ends as it began, with another automobile accident in front of the house (*"Identical shot as at the beginning of the film"*),[38] though this time it is in broad daylight and obviously caused when the family dog runs across the road in front of the oncoming car. In essence the two accidents are the same, but the camera's concentration on Stephen instead of the crash in the first instance provides the meaning of the film, for the wreck is one thing—what the don makes of it is something else. After the second collision he does not bother to investigate.

Reporting on *Accident* for the *Saturday Review*, Hollis Alpert remarks on the atmospheric qualities of Pinter's script, which "is of the evocative kind that concentrates on images rather than dialogue."[39] Judith Crist comes to the opposite conclusion: "Mr. Pinter proves his genius for capturing the essence of our society in the small-talk veneer of our lives, in probing to the heart of the matter with needle-pricks that barely blemish the skin, in turning the commonplace into a portentous suggestion of all the human agony that feeds on its own secrecy."[40] Andrew Sarris disagrees with both Alpert and Crist, calling the movie a "slice of stilled life" in which the "dialogue is almost turgid in its terseness."[41]

Brendan Gill relates the scenario to Pinter's stage work: "Mr. Pinter is fantastically clever at presenting family scenes that, under a smooth surface, are . . . charged with the ability to ravage and destroy. . . . [he] appears to believe that evil is an entity and that man is capable of being invaded and possessed by it. . . . Pinter conveys this progressive, irreversible disaster with words." Gill also makes the point that in *Accident* as in *The Servant*, "a house played a role so important that it became, in effect, one of the leading characters."[42] And Pauline Kael, who likes the film in spite of its faults, feels that the "sensual" dialogue ties the movie to the author's dramatic masterpiece, *The Homecoming*, which it resembles in many ways: "each has its philosophy professor; each has its enigmatic female—the respectable whore to whom all the important male characters are attracted. Each is a satire of home, and in both movie and play Pinter's peculiar talent for dislocating family life and social and sexual relations to a kind of banal horror has some recognizable truth in it and his cadences are funny and reverberating."[43] In

38. Pinter, *Accident*, in *Five Screenplays*, p. 284.
39. Hollis Alpert, "Where It's Happening," *Saturday Review*, 4 April 1967; rpt. in Boyum and Scott, *Film as Film*, p. 27.
40. Judith Crist, "The Agony Beneath the Skin Revealed with Surgical Skill," *New York World Journal Tribune*, 18 April 1967; rpt. in Boyum and Scott, p. 29.
41. Sarris, in the *Village Voice*, 18 May 1967; rpt. in Boyum and Scott, p. 31.
42. Brendan Gill, "Inside the Redoubt," *New Yorker*, 15 April 1967; rpt. in Boyum and Scott, pp. 36–37.
43. Pauline Kael, "The Comedy of Depravity: *Accident*," in *Kiss Kiss Bang Bang*, pp. 131–32.

addition, the author's stage dialogue is characterized by his use of silences and pauses to punctuate and express underlying tensions at moments of psychological stress. This is the case, too, in *Accident*—for example, when Charley and Stephen recognize the emotional conflict which is evolving:

CHARLEY. They're staying.
  Silence.
  Which room . . . is everyone in?
  Pause.
STEPHEN. How the hell should I know?
  Pause.
CHARLEY. Splendid day [p. 252].

Pinter, again discussing the cinematic medium with Taylor, is more interested in the verification of characters and Losey's techniques for exposing this concept: "I do so hate the becauses of drama. Who are we to say that this happens because that happened, that one thing is the consequence of another? How do we know? What reason have we to suppose that life is so neat and tidy? The most we know for sure is that the things which have happened have happened in a certain order . . . . it is this mystery which fascinates me: what happens between the words . . . . when no words are spoken. . . . In this film everything happens, nothing is explained. It has been pared down and down, all unnecessary words and actions are eliminated. If it is interesting to see a man cross a room, then we see him do it; if not, then we leave out the insignificant stages of the action. I think you'll be surprised at the directness, the simplicity with which Losey is directing this film: no elaborations, no odd angles, no darting about [the camera work was by Gerry Fisher]. Just a level, intense look at people, at things. As though if you look at them hard enough they will give up their secrets. Not that they will, for however much you see and guess at there is always something more. . . ."[44]

Interestingly, the scenarist's fascination with the presentation not only of language but also of the meanings present between words echoes master director Ingmar Bergman's thoughts on the subject, that a "dialogue is like a musical score. . . . Its interpretation demands a technical knack . . . how it should be delivered, its rhythm and tempo, what is to take place between the lines."[45]

44. Quoted by Taylor, in "Accident," *Sight and Sound*, Autumn 1966. In a 1967 London interview with Rex Reed (rpt. in Reed's *Conversations in the Raw*, New York: Signet, 1970, pp. 116–20), Director Losey makes much the same point when he praises the terseness of Pinter's script: "It's 100 pages long and only about 60 pages of that is talk, so there's room for the visual things" (p. 118).
45. Ingmar Bergman, "Introduction: Bergman Discusses Film-Making" in *Four Screenplays of Ingmar Bergman*, trans. Lars Malmstrom and David Kushner (New York: Simon and Schuster/Clarion, 1960), p. 16.

The Birthday Party

The second of Pinter's stage dramas to be converted to film was *The Birthday Party*, which opened in New York in December 1968. An excellent and faithful transfer of the play, the movie clearly traces the disintegration of a sensitive man's character as he (Stanley) is exposed to the presence of menace. The film was directed by William Friedkin and starred Robert Shaw (whose *Man in the Glass Booth* Pinter had directed the preceding year) as Stanley in his second Pinter film, Dandy Nichols perfectly cast as Meg, Sidney Tafler as Goldberg, and Pinter's old friend Patrick Magee, also reappearing in a Pinter film, this time in the role of McCann.

The Go-Between

In 1969 Pinter completed the adaptation of L. P. Hartley's novel from 1953, *The Go-Between*. The third collaboration with director Losey, this film brought scenarist Pinter additional honors as it was accorded a best picture award at the 1971 Cannes Film Festival, winning a Golden Palm. Whereas Pinter's early plays were often rejected by public and critics alike, ironically, it now seems that the author's name is sufficient to insure acceptance.

In *The Go-Between* the narrator (Michael Redgrave as the older man, Dominic Guard as the young Leo) relates how he found his old diary and the memories it evokes: in the summer of 1900 he stayed with a school chum in Norfolk where he was the go-between for a pair of lovers (beautiful Julie Christie in the role of Marian, Alan Bates in the role of Ted), carrying their messages back and forth; he discovers them making love, and the man commits suicide. In the epilogue he returns to Norfolk and meets the girl, now an old woman.

The Go-Between is not an entirely faithful cinematic treatment of Hartley's novel, but as in Pinter's adaptation of *The Servant*, it was not meant to be. The major theme has been changed, subordinated really, and *The Go-Between* is not as successful as the earlier film because Hartley's original is better in the first place and because Pinter's choice of subject matter is less compelling in the second place.

Losey sees the film as a "study of people trapped by their class and by society in an improbable situation."[46] According to Esslin, the adaptation is even more "laconic and elliptic than *Accident*," and "Pinter has telescoped the action into that last visit and brilliantly parallels the narrator's arrival, inspection of the place as it now is and meeting with the old lady, with the

---

46. Quoted by Cynthia Grenier in "Americans Sweep Prizes at Cannes Festival," *New York Times*, 28 May 1971, p. 20.

244 · butter's going up

flashbacks of the ancient events, so that the whole culminates in the complete fusion of past and present in the mind of the spectator, who has been gradually drawn into a complex pattern of past and present images and relationships."[47]

Unfortunately, Esslin's evaluation is slightly overenthusiastic. There are bits of Pinterese and Pinteresque humor (the villagers bothered by an insect while sitting on a wagon and watching the cricket match), yet in adapting the novel to the screen Pinter has changed the focus and thereby weakened the end product. As Arthur Schlesinger Jr. points out in a review of the film for *Vogue* (15 September 1971), "The boy in *The Go-Between* not only undergoes an initiation into maturity but is permanently traumatized" by his experience. If the viewer is aware that this is the essence of the story before seeing the film, it is possible to follow the plot line to such a conclusion. However, to an audience unfamiliar with the novel, the movie is mystifying and unconvincing—the meaning is hinted at, but it remains undeveloped. The boy's awareness of the initiation is minimal, so the hinted-at trauma seems unjustified.

Again, unfortunately, the attraction of the piece lies in its beautiful, leisurely evocation of a special time in British history. It is a masterly depiction of stately Edwardian elegance, almost devoid of action rather than filled with the multi-meaning of a Pinter stage play—so much so that the magnificent house and surrounding countryside where the action takes place almost assume the importance of principal characters. Melton Hall, a derelict seventeenth-century manor, was beautifully transformed into a gracious and captivating representation of the turn-of-the-century Brandham Hall by art director Carmen Dillon, who had previously worked with Losey on *Accident*. Shot entirely on location in the county of Norfolk by Gerry Fisher, who had also photographed *Accident*, the film gains much of its atmosphere from the countryside, especially that around the nearby villages of Melton Constable, Hanworth, and Heydon, and the flavor of 1900 captured during Leo's shopping trip in town, shot in the ancient cathedral city of Norwich.

Finally, though, something embedded in the film links it to the playwright's latest dramas, which deal with the subjects of memory, the past, the relationship between the two, and their reality as they create the present or are created in retrospect by the present—in the manner again of T. S. Eliot's "Time present and time past / Are both perhaps present in time future, / And time future contained in time past" or Mary's "The past is the present. . . . It's the future too" in O'Neill's *Long Day's Journey Into Night*. The opening line of both the novel and the film is, "The past is a foreign country: they do things differently there."[48] The promise of this exquisite line is never fulfilled, however, and *The Go-Between* is one of the writer's less successful efforts.

47. Esslin, *The Peopled Wound*, p. 205.
48. L. P. Hartley, *The Go-Between* (New York: Avon, 1971), p. 11.

The Homecoming

Pinter wrote the screenplay for *The Homecoming* in 1970, the third of his dramas to be adapted for the screen. Released in 1973 as part of the highly touted American Film Theatre program, *The Homecoming* was directed by Peter Hall, who had directed the stage version in 1965, and included four of the original cast: Paul Rogers as Max, Ian Holm as Lenny, Terrence Rigby as Joey, and Vivien Merchant as Ruth. The newcomers were Michael Jayston, who replaced Michael Bryant in the role of Teddy, and Cyril Cusack playing Sam, a part originally created by John Normington. Cinematographer David Watkins was responsible for the excellent photography.

Critics, such as Paul D. Zimmerman of *Newsweek*, have agreed that the film version of *The Homecoming* is "more relevant and penetrating than when it first reached Broadway," being both funnier and more frightening because of the "harder, more savage tone" given by Hall's direction.[49] The acting is again superb, with Rogers dominating the outstanding cast, and Merchant and Holm providing fitting support. Zimmerman concludes that the American Film Theatre production nourishes "both the theatre and film," in part because Hall shies "away from . . . cinematic razzle-dazzle." "Closeup," says Zimmerman, "compensates for the loss of intimacy of a live performance," and the "absence of 'exteriors' contributes to the dramatic tension inherent in [this work] about people trapped together."

Jay Cocks, writing for *Time*, also comments on the film's tension.[50] Calling Pinter's film scripts "probably the best scenario writing now being done in English," he credits the immense artistic success of this film to two factors. First, the strength of the original. "No one writes this well originally for films," Cocks contends, not even Pinter himself. The second factor which Cocks cites is the appropriateness of the performances to the material: "Each inflection, every pause and gesture, seems to have been measured by caliper, but this precision never becomes deadening. Instead it draws everything taut, gives an almost musical tension." Pinter seems pleased with the transference to film, too, saying that the movie is "very good."

Butley

In 1973 Pinter directed his first film, an adaptation of Simon Gray's *Butley*, which he had already directed in its theatrical premiere in London in 1970. A part of the American Film Theatre program like the film version of *The Homecoming*, *Butley* was released in 1974. Starring the fine performer Alan Bates, whose tour-de-force stage portrayals of Ben Butley in both Lon-

49. "Theatre in the Camera," *Newsweek*, 3 Dec. 1973, pp. 61–62. Of course it may also be that the audience is better prepared now and more likely to understand what Pinter is saying.
50. "Fire and Ice," *Time*, 17 Dec. 1973, p. 70.

don and New York won best actor awards, the cast also includes Richard O'Callaghan and Michael Byrne from the original London production, along with Jessica Tandy, Susan Engel, Georgina Hale, and Simon Rouse.

The story is a day in the life of an English lecturer at a college of London University. Throughout the piece Butley wittily baits his wife, from whom he is estranged, his homosexual roommate and the roommate's new lover and other members of the staff, avoids students, and occasionally turns to a bottle for reinforcement. The game has become meaningless for him, though, and at the conclusion he cannot muster enough desire to initiate another relationship with a new student (to replace his ex-roommate, also a former student), even though he knows the pattern so well by now that it has become a ritual. In the end he remains isolated from a world of social relationships from which he has deliberately separated himself.

The screenplay is essentially the drama itself with the simple addition of a few non-dialogue scenes outside Butley's office, in his flat, and in a pub. Since the stage version was limited to one set—Butley's office at the university —this would be another example of what Pinter terms the opening out of a play by translating it into the cinematic medium, for again, "these characters [have been shown to] move in the context of the real world."

There are several reasons for Pinter's having chosen *Butley* as his first film to direct. Thematically it is related to his own writing. In an interview on the Shepperton Studios set of *Butley* Pinter talked with Lee Langley about one of his major concerns. "Threat is part of it," he said, "but it's much more than that. It's to do with the sinews of human nature. The complacency of so many people is really quite remarkable. It is . . . pathetic."[51] Pinter's description of Simon Gray's tragi-comedy is close to his descriptions of his own plays, notably *The Caretaker* and *The Homecoming*, for he sees that "it is on the face of it a comedy, but ultimately there's no laughter."

Moreover, Pinter clearly has enjoyed directing on the stage—though he prefers to direct someone else's material because he thinks that the actors are inhibited by his presence when they work on one of his plays. While he states that he is afraid that the actors do not believe that he is objective (he insists that he is, of course), Donald Pleasence proclaims Pinter to be "the most truly honest and indeed best director" with whom he has worked in the theatre.[52] Pinter's acting career created an understanding of an actor's needs and inner processes which makes him an extremely effective director.

Finally, Pinter has found film exciting from his first exposure to cinematic techniques. It is reported that when he first went into a cutting room to see a film edited, he exclaimed, "You can delete dialogue, alter rhythm—a line becomes a pause with a twiddle of knobs, this is marvellous!"

51. "Genius—A Change in Direction," *Daily Telegraph Magazine* (London), 23 Nov. 1973, pp. 30–36.
52. In a letter to me, 9 Nov. 1973.

Given Pinter's interest in directing and his excitement about film, it is not surprising that he has combined the two successfully. In spite of his claim that "I'm still a beginner. Everyone remains a beginner in films for a hell of a long time," Bates found that there was "no sense of an outsider struggling with a new medium" in Pinter's directing. Bates also agrees with Pleasence about Pinter's ability as a director: "Harold is known for a sense of economy, precision and subtlety, all of which are very filmic things. At any rate he seems a totally natural director." Happily, Pinter has emerged from his first experience with film directing enthusiastically. "I'd like to direct more films," he says. "It has been the hardest work I've ever known, but deeply enjoyable."

Remembrance of Things Past

In his interview with Gussow in 1971 Pinter mentioned that he was "going to enter into a film which is going to be the most difficult task I've ever had in my life—and one which is almost impossible."[53] In a letter written at about the same time as the interview, the author answered a question regarding his current projects by stating that he was "not working on any play," but "I'm trying to write a screenplay of 'A la recherche du temps perdu' at the moment!!" and in several subsequent letters he refers to the complexity of his task.[54] The job of translating Marcel Proust's novel to the screen took five months, and the problems presented by the work were immense. In fact, Pinter has replied jokingly to the question of what specific problems he faced in converting the novel to film by saying that the book is 4722 pages long and each page presented a specific problem.

Filming the screenplay did not promise to be easy, either. Losey, the director of several earlier Pinter films, calls *Remembrance* the "best screenplay I've ever seen or known of," but notes that he has a twenty-one-week shooting schedule for the film.[55] With luck to be released in 1977, the finished product will run between three and four hours. Although many lesser characters have been cut (the painter Elstir, the novelist Bergotte, and the musician Vinteuil, for example), Losey reports that there are still forty-nine "important speaking roles" left, and the movie will be filmed on sixty-seven different locations. The shooting has been delayed.

Considering Pinter's preoccupations in his most recent plays and films, it is easy to see why *A la recherche du temps perdu* would appeal to him. In the novel the protagonist finds that he can evoke "the very quality of past experience by simply yielding to the undertow of free association," according to Walter James Miller and Bonnie E. Nelson.[56] This leads to the hero's living

53. Gussow, "A Conversation (Pause) with Harold Pinter," p. 132.
54. Letters to me, 17 Dec. 1971 and 28 March 1972.
55. Eder, "Losey to Film Remembrance," p. 24.
56. In *Samuel Beckett's Waiting for Godot and Other Works* (New York: Monarch, 1971), p. 30.

"subjectively on three levels of 'sensation': recollection, immediacy, antici-
pation." As a result, "The present becomes for him mainly a stage for past
and future."

Losey regards the novel as "a work that concerns itself profoundly with
bisexuality" and indicates that the film will too. The transformation from
homosexuality to heterosexuality is shown, therefore, although the film stays
away from discussions of whether or not Albertine was Albert. The essence of
the book, and the element which probably attracted Pinter most, however,
can be found in *Le temps retrouvé*, the final novel of Proust's lengthy series.
Bits of it are scattered throughout the film and are used to pull everything
together at the end. The final lines of the screenplay, recalling the opening
of *The Go-Between*, can be seen as the key to the film:

Vermeer "View of Delft."
Camera moves in to the yellow wall in the painting.
Yellow screen.
Marcel's voice:
"It was time to begin."[57]

The Last Tycoon

Shooting was begun on *The Last Tycoon* in 1975. Originally to be directed by Mike Nichols, the film was turned over to Elia Kazan by producer
Sam Spiegel when Nichols was delayed in editing his picture, *The Fortune*.

Based on F. Scott Fitzgerald's unfinished novel (1941), *The Last Tycoon*
is the story of a Hollywood producer, Monroe Stahr, as told by Cecilia Brady,
the daughter of his business rival. The themes being developed by the novelist
when he died include the conflict between art and economics, business ethics,
the vulgar debasement of the American dream, the concept of appearance
versus reality as exemplified in the make-believe world of the movies, and
the power struggle between Stahr and Pat Brady. The last two in particular
would appeal to Pinter.

Considering that the much heralded *The Great Gatsby* failed when it
was released in 1974, and that critics attributed its failure partly to the fact
that its British director did not understand the American character (or audience), it is surprising that another Fitzgerald source would be used so soon,
and then given to a British screenwriter to adapt. The choice of Pinter as
scenarist is a tribute to his growing reputation as a major filmwriter.

Langrishe, Go Down

Pinter adapted Aidan Higgins' novel *Langrishe, Go Down* for the screen
in 1971 and revealed to Gussow that he might be interested in directing the

57. Eder, p. 24.

film. According to the dramatist, the story is about "three middle-aged spin-sters living in a house in Ireland in the nineteen-thirties. At the lodge gate there's a cottage and a German philosophy student in his 30's working on a thesis."[58] Although there are no plans to make the film at the moment, Pinter's attention is clearly being focused on the cinema at present.

Summary

In the final analysis it must be said that to this point in his writing career Pinter's screenplays (or perhaps more accurately, his adaptations of other people's works), except for *The Servant*, *The Caretaker*, *The Birthday Party*, and *The Homecoming*, have not been his most successful artistic efforts. The movies certainly are not bad; they just have not always lived up to what might be expected of such a talented author (or the promotional claims, for that matter). While they are full of mood and occasionally contain sparkling bits of Pinteresque dialogue, often they are slow-moving.

Pauline Kael finds that Pinter's weaknesses as a scenarist are "organiza-tion, purpose, [and] dramatic clarity"[59]—the basics of good writing. She also faults him for an "inability to achieve a dramatic climax," an obvious result of his other failings. Probably overstating her point she goes so far as to say that "in movies Pinter doesn't avoid exposition—he's just no good at it."[60] What on stage is cumulative meaning turns into two hours of pictures—a tranquillizing process, since the true poetry is lost—yet the presentation of mood is one of his cinematic strong points.

In the immediacy of the playhouse the audience (or as the French say, the participants) is much more involved with what is taking place on stage than the corresponding moviegoer/screen relationship allows, partly because a film is primarily composed of grouped *visual* images—a montage. Conse-quently, film depends more on action and movement (even if it is only a cut to a different shooting angle) and the intense, psychological, emotional *shared experience* of the play becomes watered down because it takes too much time to express through a building series of cryptic exchanges. With the magnifying and focusing power of the camera, dialogue which is perfectly acceptable spoken across the footlights becomes stilted and drawn out. As a result, a film drags if it tries to transfer plot and conversation to celluloid using stage techniques and conceptual parameters. And Pinter is too intense and subtle to move *directly* into the medium of film with the same artistic success that marks his drama, making his achievements, especially in translat-ing his own plays to the screen, all the more praiseworthy. With *The Home-coming* and *Butley*, however, Pinter has emerged as a major force in the mod-

58. Gussow, p. 132.　　　　　　60. Ibid., p. 133.
59. Kael, p. 130.

ern cinema, as well as in contemporary drama. Indeed, as he continues to concentrate on his filmwriting, it is safe to assume that a writer of Pinter's enormous talent and energy will improve and produce screenplays of even greater quality than those he has already written.

Chapter XI. Technique

. . . always paring away . . .

Pinter's dramatic techniques are, for the most part, quite simple, and much of his success as a dramatist is based on this simplicity. The very setting of the comedies of menace (the single room reflecting the characters' natures and problems) and *The Collection* and *Silence* (with their divided stages), the physical movements of his characters, the realistic dialogue, and the *coups de théâtre* (such as the sudden, unexpected intrusion of Mrs. Stokes' offstage voice at the end of *A Night Out*) are mechanical evidences of the playwright's proficiency in handling his material.

More important, Pinter has joined form and content, possibly more than any other English dramatist, joined them to the extent that Esslin places him in the Theatre of the Absurd because of this aspect of the author's work, while Kerr supports his claim that Pinter is the quintessential existential playwright by the same reasoning. Technique and style, form and content are insepa-rable in his writing. In this respect he may be considered an especially modern playwright, taking what he needs from wherever he finds it and adopting only that which is best suited to his own writing, regardless of how it is classified. Thus he can combine elements from absurdists such as Beckett, Ionesco, and N. F. Simpson with the stark realism of John Osborn, John Arden, and Arnold Wesker, without limiting his writing to any one "school." He seemingly employs Beckett's absurdist approach, say, to language, but he does so in correlation with concepts which place him outside the Theatre of the Absurd (the emotional drives of his characters, that is to say, the expressions of their *motivations*, for example, explain their apparently absurd actions, actions which remain unexplained in *Waiting for Godot*, though the appeal may be visceral understanding in both cases). Likewise he can create realism on the stage without applying it to the social concerns of dramatists such as those belonging to the Kitchen Sink School.

In the early plays Pinter uses blackouts and what he calls cabaret turns to mystify his audience and to underscore his main points, building a mood of menace by exposing the twin lacks of verification and communication. He is emphatic about not being mysterious purely for the sake of being mysterious, though. "I honestly do not willfully keep a secret. I simply only write the play the way I can write. There's no other way I can approach it truthfully," he asserts.[1] "But [meaning] can only come through the work itself. If it's going to move [the audience], it's going to move them. It's entirely their own responsibility."[2] As he progresses in the later dramas, however, he allows his main points to determine his mode of expression more and more, so that meaning and expression are clearly coupled. When a character such as Aston asks, "Where were you born then?" and the answer is "What do you mean?" there are obvious problems in verification and a breakdown of communication which are exemplified by the very words in which they are presented. In his latest works on memory this linking of meaning and expression necessarily leads to a more poetic mode—after the manner of French *avant-gardistes* such as Michel de Ghelderode and Jacques Audiberti—when he comes to grips with a more ephemeral subject that must be evoked metaphorically—the past, which does and does not exist, but which can be created (and which can control actions as surely as if it existed).

As an artist Pinter is cognizant of his development, especially since *A Slight Ache*. His comment on *The Caretaker*, quoted above, shows his initial awareness that his craftsmanship was improving, and in speaking about *Night School* he has demonstrated an understanding of the danger of stylistic stagnation: "Later I realised that . . . there were characteristics that implied I was slipping into a formula. It so happened this was the worst thing I've written. The words and ideas had become automatic, redundant. That was the red light for me and I don't feel I shall fall into that pit again."[3]

1. Gussow, "A Conversation (Pause) with Harold Pinter," p. 135.
2. Ibid., p. 134.
3. "Harold Pinter Replies," *New Theatre Magazine*, 11, No. 2 (Jan. 1961).

The structure, the dramatic portrayal of the concept of verification, the use of humor, and the "Pinteresque" use of language ("Pinterese") create a distinctive style. Often several of these elements are employed in conjuction, either as the means of carrying the meaning or as an actual statement of meaning. For example, humor is utilized to provoke laughter, to provide relief, or to accentuate a contrast. Language is similarly used for specific reasons, but one of the uses of language is as a source of humor, so that both elements can fulfill Pinter's purpose of exposing problems in communication at the same time, as in the example of Aston's question. They function simultaneously as the statement and the means of relating the statement.

Structure

Contrary to what some rather superficial criticism of Pinter's work suggests, a logical structure in which action proceeds with an Aristotelian consistency and is reinforced by a unity of character is important to the dramatist. As he has said, "I am very concerned with the shape and consistency of mood of my plays. I cannot write anything that appears to me to be loose and unfinished. I like a feeling of order in what I write."[4] The internal, inherent structure which is created provides an underlying form that imposes itself upon the author, according to Pinter: "I don't know what kind of characters my plays will have until they . . . well, until they *are* [as in the case of Riley, who "just *was* a blind negro"]. . . . Sometimes I'm going along and I find myself writing 'C. comes in' when I didn't know that he was going to come in; he *had* to come in at that point, that's all."[5]

As mentioned before, the end result of the actions in a Pinter drama may appear to be absurd, but a careful tracing of the movement of the play will prove a steady line of cause and effect, as each event is determined by the nature of the characters participating and the situation which immediately preceded it. And whatever transpires prepares for future events.

Some of the structural criticism of Pinter's work can be traced back to his theory of verification. It is difficult at times for orderly minds to follow the twisting contradictions which his characters' actions seemingly represent. An extension of the concept of verification is also found in the author's attitude toward stage verisimilitude. If, as he remarked to Marshall Pugh, "Sometimes I don't know who I'm looking at in the mirror,"[6] how can he expect his inventions to be able to account for themselves? Or why should we know any more about a character than we know about the passengers in a bus which passes us on the street? In a BBC European Service interview with John Sher-

4. Ibid.
5. Bensky, "Harold Pinter: An Interview," pp. 24–25.
6. In an interview in the *Daily Mirror* (London), 7 March 1964.

wood on March 3, 1960, he offered his opinion: "The explicit form . . . in twentieth-century drama is . . . cheating. The playwright assumes that we have a great deal of information about all his characters, who explain themselves to the audience." What this amounts to, he explained, is "conforming to the author's own ideology. [The characters] don't create themselves as they go along, they are being fixed on the stage for one purpose, to speak for the author, who has a point of view to put over." Contrarily, in one of his own plays Pinter demands that when the curtain goes up, "you are faced with a situation, a particular situation, two people sitting in a room, which hasn't happened before, and is just happening at this moment, and we know no more about them than I know about you, sitting at this table." After all, "the world is full of surprises. A door can open at any moment and someone will come in. We'd love to know who it is, we'd love to know exactly what he has on his mind and why he comes in, but how often do we know what someone has on his mind or who this somebody is, and what goes to make him and make him what he is, and what his relationship is to others?" Besides, that would spoil the fun. Unhappily there are members of the audience who are unable to follow the action of the play without this expected information.

Verification

It has already been pointed out that Pinter's technique for dramatically expressing his concept of verification is extremely simple. He merely juxtaposes mutually contradictory statements of fact. Thus, the Sands can with equanimity claim to have been climbing the stairs one moment and the next moment declare that they were descending. Mark and Len face each other across an abyss widened by their prior knowledge of each other which they each depend upon to determine how the other will react in given circumstances; they are constantly changing, and previous actions may have no bearing on the current situation, since neither one is the person who reacted before. Ironically, there is still a logical underlying structure; it is just that neither knows the chain of events which has transpired and therefore cannot take it into account.

Humor

Pinter's humor contains many of the normal elements of stage humor and is mostly verbal in nature, containing little slapstick. There are puns, misunderstandings, *non sequiturs*, jokes, non-communications, a Yiddish phrasing, witty word play, and reversal, all included for the common reasons of characterization, contrast, relief, plain humorous effects, and so forth. A nice example of reversal is seen in Sam's description of MacGregor for Max: "He was a lousy stinking rotten loudmouth. A bastard uncouth sodding runt. Mind you, he was a good friend of yours,"[7] and repartee is well represented in Lulu's complaint that Goldberg took "all those liberties" only to satisfy his "appetite," which he counters with the assertion that now she is giving him "indigestion."

The most important aspect of humor in Pinter's work is that which grows out of the meaning of a play or the concepts which underlie it. To repeat, in answering the criticism leveled at him by Leonard Russell that the audience's reaction to *The Caretaker* was one of laughter, Pinter replied in the *Sunday Times* (14 August 1960): "Certainly I laughed myself while writing 'The Caretaker' but not all the time, not 'indiscriminately.' An element of the absurd is, I think, one of the features of the play, but at the same time I did not intend it to be merely a laughable farce. If there hadn't been other issues at stake the play would not have been written." It was in this letter that he went on to comment that "everything is funny" and that "the point about tragedy is that it is *no longer funny.*"

This situation produces a kind of humor which basically derives from funny things said in unfunny situations. For instance, there is Harry's gloriously understated reaction to seeing James throw a knife at Bill in *The Collection*: "It's his own fault for not ducking. I must have told him dozens of times, you know, that if someone throws a knife at you the silliest thing you can do is to catch it."[8] Of course, the audience knows that Bill was not trying to catch a knife and nobody could be expected to believe that Harry had advised his roommate "dozens of times" about this sort of experience. The immediate intent is to create a sense of relief that no one was hurt and to create a contrast with the serious confrontation which has been taking place. The "strained expectation," as Kant would put it, is dissolved and the result is laughter. Harry's words are designed to have another effect, too, though. He is jealous of the possible attraction James may be to Bill and wants to make Bill appear foolish in case James is likewise attracted. This is brought out in the "slum boy" speech which soon follows.

Lack of communication and the inability to verify anything sometimes lead to this kind of humor, though more often it hearkens back to the psychological basis of the drama: the characters have reached a stage of desperation where they are perfectly willing to accept anything as normal, any action by another character, no matter how absurd that action might seem, on the chance that it will lead to a relationship which will satisfy their emotional needs. *The Homecoming* is filled with examples of this type.

Humor depends upon a certain amount of detachment, and the psychological problems of the individuals promote detachment, which contributes to funny things being said in unfunny situations, for no one is able to become

7. Pinter, *The Homecoming*, p. 18.   8. Pinter, *The Collection*, p. 76.

sympathetically involved with anyone else. Thus Teddy sits impassively, making the spectacle of his wife and brother rolling around on the floor in an embrace hilarious. If he is not upset, why should the audience become emotionally concerned with the action? And without emotional involvement, the absurdity of what is happening can be appreciated. It becomes a matter of extreme objectivity. Similarly, Max reacts to the information that Ruth has denied Joey not with horror at the event or concern for the imposed-upon woman, but with wonderment that his son could have been treated in such a cavalier manner. He is too concerned with his own selfish desires to identify with another person.

Related to the humor which grows out of the disparity between happenings and characters' reactions to what happens, incidentally, is the approach to acting a play by Pinter. To a large extent the stage directions for *Landscape* which set Duff and Beth together but separated, each blissfully proceeding along the lines of his own existence, can be applied to much of the writer's work. There is violence, explicitly physical violence, present in most of the plays, but the general tone should be subdued—if anything, for example, the character of Teddy should be underplayed. The characters should reflect the idea of accepting everything as being within the realm of the normal so that when this attitude is violated, the effect conveys a greater revelation of motivation than a constant display of histrionics (which would dull into insensitivity) can. As Peter Hall remarks about *The Homecoming*, "To shout in that house is a weakness."[9]

Language

Pinter's use of language and non-language is probably his most important contribution to the contemporary stage. It is certainly the most distinctive device in his collection of dramatic tools. Lahr concludes that the dramatist's "sense of language deploys an actor's intuition for compelling sound, and a poet's precision, discovering a resonance of meaning in the orchestration of silence, pitch, and syntax."[10] As early as November 12, 1960, H. A. L. Craig wrote in the *New Statesman*, "Poetry in the Theatre," that Pinter's work carried a "pervasion of poetry," and Irving Wardle's *Encore* article (also 1960), "There's Music in That Room," attributed the formal quality of music to *The Caretaker*. If poetry is defined as language which conveys something more than the denotative meanings of its words, no one can argue that Pinter's drama is not poetic. Carrying out the musical analogy, Taylor notes that Pinter's "plays are usually built on lines easier to explain in musical

9. Interview with Lahr in *A Casebook on Harold Pinter's The Homecoming*, p. 22.
10. Lahr, "Pinter's Language," in *A Casebook on Harold Pinter's The Homecoming*, p. 123.

terms. They are . . . rhapsodic rather than symphonic, being held together by a series of internal tensions, one of the most frequent being the tension between two opposing tonalities (notably the comic versus the horrific . . .) or two contrasted tempi. . . ." He further elaborates that they are " 'orchestrated' with overtones and reminiscences, with unexpected resonances from what has gone before, so that the result is a tightly knit and intricate texture of which the 'naturalistic' words being spoken at any given moment are only the top line, supported by elusive and intricate harmonies, or appearing sometimes in counterpoint with another theme from earlier in the play."[11]

Economy is the key to Pinter's style. As he told John Kershaw in a 1964 ITV interview, "One of my main concerns is to get things down and down and down. . . . Always paring away. . . . People don't realize that the English language is extremely exciting; it means so much, so many different things at the same time." This economy is related to the playwright's attitude toward words, as he explained in "Between the Lines": "I have mixed feelings about words myself. Moving among them, sorting them out, watching them appear on the page, from this I derive a considerable pleasure. But at the same time I have another strong feeling about words which amounts to nothing less than nausea. Such a weight of words confronts us, day in day out, words spoken in a context such as this, words written by me and others, the bulk of it a stale dead terminology; ideas endlessly repeated and permutated, become platitudinous, trite, meaningless. Given this nausea, it's very easy to be overcome by it and step back into paralysis. But if it is possible to confront this nausea, to follow it to its hilt and move through it, then it is possible to say that something has occurred, that something has even been achieved." Speaking to Bensky about the writing in *The Birthday Party* and *The Caretaker*, Pinter declared, "I want to iron it down, eliminate things. Too many words irritate me sometimes, but I can't help them, they just seem to come out—out of the fellow's mouth. I don't really examine my works too much, but I'm aware that quite often in what I write, some fellow at some point says an awful lot."[12] This irritation has caused him to reexamine some of his works, and his revisions of plays in reprintings show that he does indeed always pare away. For example, John Normington has revealed that the first draft of *The Homecoming* was extraordinarily "much more elaborate" than the acting version and that "some of the speeches were five times as long"[13] to begin with.

The question of textual changes in the plays is an interesting one, and an examination of the alterations provides some insight into Pinter's technique, as well as supplying additional evidence of his thematic evolution. There seem to be three reasons for rearranging the text: first, because something

11. Taylor, *Anger and After*, pp. 357–58.
12. Bensky, p. 26.
13. Lahr interview with Normington, in the galley proof of *A Casebook on Harold Pinter's The Homecoming*, but not included in the published version.

does not work well on the stage; second, as an effort to "tighten" the language; and third, as an attempt to remove some of the confusingly mysterious elements from a piece.

Old Times, like *The Homecoming*, is an instance in which something was changed with the stage presentation in mind: for the London performance Pinter recalls having made a "short pause" out of a "long silence," though he reverted to the original text for the New York production, and the addition of a line of dialogue required a bit of rewriting, as will be discussed below.[14] Pinter's background as an actor serves him well in helping him decide what will be effective on the stage, though he does consider the advice of at least four other people. After a play is finished, his wife, actress Vivien Merchant, reads it, he sends a copy to Beckett (this practice began with *The Homecoming*—Beckett has the "greatest admiration" for Pinter's work), and then he discusses it with the director, often Peter Hall, and the set designer, often John Bury,[15] during rehearsals. He recounts the procedure as it was applied to *Silence*: "I sent the play . . . to Samuel Beckett. . . . He wrote . . . 'Suggest you examine or reconsider . . . fourth speech, page five.' . . . Or whatever it was. . . . I thought it was perfectly all right. Then, after about two weeks' rehearsal, Peter Hall came to me—I hadn't been around for a few days—and said, 'There's one speech in this play that I do not think is working at all.' Off I went and heard it properly again and realized that, of course, Beckett was totally right."[16]

Three other dramas which have undergone textual alteration are *The Caretaker*, *The Dwarfs*, and *The Birthday Party*. Discussion of these alterations chronologically is difficult, since it is almost impossible to trace the printing history of the editions or to determine the exact dates when specific changes were made. Methuen, Pinter's British publisher, for instance, answered a question about dating the textual differences between various editions of *The Dwarfs* by saying that there are no differences; and Grove Press, the American publisher, in answer to the same query replied that they simply reprint the Methuen texts and are, therefore, unaware of any changes. Nevertheless, there are differences.

An examination of *The Caretaker* provides a representative sample of the problems encountered in tracing changes. Originally published in 1960, the play was revised in 1962 and in 1965; yet there are differences between various editions which are supposed to be based on the same text. For example, thirteen lines appear on page 12 in Grove's 1965 revised version which are

14. Gussow, p. 131.
15. In an undated letter to me in December 1971, John Bury refers to this team approach, acknowledging that the apparent simplicity of the results is entirely deceptive and Peter Hall, Pinter, and he work for weeks through many possibilities before they arrive at their solutions.
16. Gussow, p. 128.

not present in either the 1960 Grove edition or the 1962 revised Methuen edition. Yet in later Grove editions, based on the 1965 revised version, these same lines are missing.[17]

All in all, there are forty-six differences between Pinter's original version of *The Caretaker* and the 1965 revision.[18] In Act I these include three typographical errors, six cases in which lines have been omitted in the later text, and four instances of substitution (one word or passage for another). Act II alterations involve six omissions, two substitutions, and three cases in which words or passages have been added. The figures for Act III are fourteen omissions, and four examples each of substitution and addition. For the most part, these alterations are for stylistic reasons and have little or no bearing on the meaning of the drama. There are important exceptions, though, which actually affect the interpretation of the work.

In *The Caretaker* the first example of Pinter's use of revisions to help his audience understand the play, as well as to improve the style, comes in Act I after Aston and Davies discuss who was dreaming. In the original, Aston then asks Davies, "What did you say your name was?" and Davies replies. The revised version moves this exchange to follow the two men's dialogue about women on the next page, and reduces Aston's question, "No, your other name, your real name, what's that?" to "No, your other one?"[19] The playwright thus cuts out several excess words, yet the sequence retains the effect of switching subjects, while at the same time making the thoughts easier to follow by inserting the original question and answer close enough to the second question and answer that the relationship is clearly seen. Later in Act I, Pinter again improves his play when he removes nine lines concerning other jobs Davies might look for and inserts "They want an Englishman to pour their tea," to weave "that's what they want" smoothly back into the dialogue (p. 29; p. 27). This shifts the emphasis of the passage. It is already clear that Davies is not looking for a job and that he improvises as he talks, with no intention of following through, so the original lines are not needed, and the concentration on the "foreigners" theme better exemplifies the tramp's fears and motivations.

At one point in Act I the dramatist removes five lines of stage directions and two exclamations by Davies as the old man examines the contents of the room (p. 30; p. 28) and two lines of action in Act II are similarly replaced by a pause (p. 45). This is an interesting reversal of the pattern Pinter follows in revising other plays later. The reduction of action resulting from these cuts

17. Basically repetitive, they may simply be a mistake corrected later.
18. The figures cannot be considered absolute because many alterations fit more than one category.
19. Pinter, *The Caretaker*, pp. 26 and 27 in the original; p. 25 in the revision. Unless otherwise stated, pages noted first refer to the original edition; pages listed second refer to the revised text.

makes the play more static, which may weaken it, though presumably the cuts were made after Pinter decided from seeing the drama staged that action was unnecessary here.

The only revision of importance in Act II is the omitting of approximately twenty-one lines, about one-sixth of the total, from Aston's hospital speech. A side-by-side examination of sections of the monologue shows how effective Pinter's revisions can be:[20]

Original (pp. 57–60)	*Revision* (pp. 54–57)
Standing there, or in the breaks, I used to . . . talk about things. But it all seemed all right. I mean, some of these men, from the café, we used to knock about together sometimes. I used to tag along on some of their evenings. It was all right. And they used to listen, whenever. . . .	Standing there, or in the breaks, I used to . . . talk about things. And these men, they used to listen, whenever. . . .
. . .	. . .
And I had these headaches. Then I went along to people, but they wanted to take me in, but I wasn't going to go in . . . anywhere. So I couldn't do any work, because I . . . I couldn't write any more, you see. I couldn't write my name. I used to sit in my room. That was when I lived with my mother. And my brother. He was younger than me. And I laid everything out, in order, in my room, all the things I knew were mine, but I didn't die. I never had those hallucinations any more. And I never spoke to anyone any more. The funny thing is, I can't remember much . . . about what I said, what I thought . . . I mean before I went into that place. The thing is, I should have been dead. I should have died. And then, anyway, after a time, I got a bit better, and I started to do things with my hands, and then about two	And I had these headaches. I used to sit in my room. That was when I lived with my mother. And my brother. He was younger than me. And I laid everything out, in order, in my room, all the things I knew were mine, but I didn't die. The thing is, I should have been dead. I should have died. Anyway, I feel much better now. But I don't talk to people now. I steer clear of places like that café. I never go into them now. I don't talk to anyone . . . like that. I've often thought of going back and trying to find the man who did that to me. But I want to do something first. I want to build that shed out in the garden.

20. In this example alone, 330 words have been reduced to 152.

years ago I came here, because my
brother had got this house, and so I
decided to have a go at decorating
it, so I came into this room, and I
started to collect wood, for my shed,
and all these bits and pieces, that I
thought might come in handy for the
flat, or around the house, sometime.
I feel much better now. But I don't
talk to people now. I don't talk to
anyone . . . like that. I've often thought
of going back and trying to find the
man who did that to me. But I want
to do something first. I want to build
that shed out in the garden.

Aside from one substitution and two additions to tie things together around
the omissions, basically Pinter has cut the expansions, the unessential information and explanations, and some repetitions in order to compress the
speech, and to make the transitions more logical and smoother. The overall
effect of this simplification is to make Aston's remembrance starker and, as a
result, more affecting because of the contrast between his understated words
and the emotions which underlie them.

Act III contains a whole series of minor changes which, taken together,
produce a clearer and starker understanding of the relationships between
the two brothers and the intruder at the end of the drama. First, Mick's speech
after breaking the Buddha in the initial version is to be delivered "*To himself,
slowly, broodingly,*" whereas it is spoken "*Passionately*" in the revision—
which better reflects Mick's character and motivation (p. 78; p. 74). Next,
when Aston returns, it is indicated in the original that Mick starts to speak.
In the stronger revision he haltingly says, "Look . . . uh . . . ," and then leaves
(p. 75; appropriate minor alterations are made to incorporate the dialogue).
Dramatically, it is more effective to have Mick stutter than to try to indicate
that he is attempting to speak by wordless actions.

Three and a half obvious and repetitive lines regarding Davies' return
for his pipe are removed in the revision, and the stage direction "*He moves to
ASTON*" is added (p. 75), a nice touch to show Davies' change in position, for
his movement is a subtle act of entreaty. In this last confrontation between
Aston and his guest, nine lines following the dialogue about the plug which
Aston is repairing are discarded. Since most of the omitted lines are Aston's
responses, Davies is, in effect, left talking to himself, underscoring his isolation
and the fact that Aston has completely cut him off. The old man's pleading is
broken with pauses (and four more lines are deleted) to better express his

despair. Also, in the revision Aston does not cross to the window until this point—his not moving before was an additional signal that he was ignoring what the other man was saying. Now he moves because he is paying attention to his unwelcome visitor, but only long enough to dismiss him. The additional alterations in *The Caretaker* are insignificant.[21]

21. Additional textual changes include these, in Act I: on p. 9 of the 1960 edition one comma, obviously misplaced in the original, has been removed and another has been added. On p. 12 beginning with Davies' "This is your house then, is it?" thirteen lines have been removed. Essentially this is not a change, since the exchange between Davies and Aston is repeated almost verbatim on the next page. Although the result is some loss of the sense of wandering attention which the repetition conveyed, the meaning of the passage is retained and the dialogue tightened. On p. 15 a comma has been omitted, affecting the delivery, but not the meaning. On p. 19 a "tin glass" becomes a "thin glass," which may be either an alteration or a correction of a mistake; the passage seems to make sense either way, though "thin" is in the movie version too, and this matches the repetition of "thick" better. On pp. 20 and 21, fourteen lines between ". . . about near of fifteen year ago" and "DAVIES *suddenly becomes aware of the bucket*," dealing with how he would know where to go to find the man with his papers once he got to Sidcup and repeating that the weather is stopping him, are deleted. The idea that he knows the town like the back of his hand is left in, in the later revision, pp. 53 and 51. Six lines about fixing the trouble with the toaster plug are omitted from pp. 21 and 22, following Aston's "I'm mending this plug." "DAVIES *goes towards his bed and stops at the gas stove*" (p. 22) is replaced by "DAVIES *looks at him and then at the gas stove*" (p. 22; p. 21) in the revision, the new stage directions cutting the movement, which probably was not necessary owing to the crowded set. Forty-one lines of "Trouble in the Works" type dialogue about tools, which is not needed, are removed from pp. 25 and 26 before Aston's remembrance of the woman in the cafe who admired his body. In the stage directions on p. 29 three lines after Davies "takes a pair of shoes from under the bed" are omitted (he tries them on, walks), cutting the action and reducing the length of the play. And on p. 29, as a result of the prior action having been omitted, Davies no longer has to take the shoes off, so in the next set of stage directions this action is cut.

In Act II: on p. 45 (p. 43), following "it'd be a matter of a broom . . . isn't it?" six plus lines about a broom are omitted and "Yes," is inserted to join Aston's "and of course." Three lines about Davies using the Electrolux are omitted from p. 45. On p. 48, two lines of action are replaced by "*Pause.*" Instead of sitting on "*the head of DAVIES' bed*" on p. 49, Mick sits on "*junk down right*"—reducing his open challenge of Davies, and "DAVIES *joins* MICK *in junk*" (p. 47) is added. On p. 56, fourteen lines repeating Aston's suggestion that Davies reverse his position on the bed and seven lines about the roof which precede Aston's decision to walk down to Goldhawk Road (p. 53) are omitted; two lines of stage directions regarding a fade-down of the lights are added (p. 54). On p. 59 "week" is changed to "weeks," again perhaps a correction, or possibly just a matter of taste, since either term works in the context.

Act III: on p. [61] five lines about the bucket are omitted, and a period has become a question mark—clearly an error in the newer text. On pp. 62–63, four lines concerning being a caretaker are omitted. On p. 63, two repeated words are omitted. On p. 67 (p. 64), add MICK: "Listen to some Tchaikovsky" after he invites Davies to his place; this increases the humor, which was strong in Act I but decreased in the second half of Act II and in Act III; also a comma is omitted. On p. 68, omit "tin" from "tin lid." P. 71 (p. 67) shows an improvement when five repetitious lines from Davies' speech about his friendship with Mick are eliminated, though unfortunately this includes one nice line, "If only the weather'd break I'd be able to lay my hands on more references than you've seen in a week." Five lines about suitability (p. 71; p. 68) and six lines about staying (p. 72), repetitious in both cases, are removed. On p. 73 (p. 70) action is added as the stage directions "MICK *is sitting in the chair.*/DAVIES *moves about the room*" are replaced by "*Voices on the stairs.* MICK *and* DAVIES *enter.*" On p. 74, four lines are omitted and one word altered to cut repeti-

Like *The Caretaker*, *The Dwarfs* has undergone at least two revisions since the first edition, published in 1961. I have been unable to ascertain the exact date of the third version, which shows the greatest amount of change, though an edition published in 1968 was "*Reprinted . . . with corrections.*" The middle version, published by Dramatists Play Service in 1965, is an acting edition and contains only some of the revisions found in the 1968 version.

There are three basic types of alterations Pinter makes in revising *The Dwarfs*: (i) the addition of movement and the corresponding stage directions (usually inserted in place of the silences used to indicate scene shifts on the radio), which is the result of transferring the play from radio to a stage medium; (ii) a cutting of dialogue; and (iii) a breaking up and rearranging of dialogue, basically Len's soliloquies, often to include action and/or lines by Pete and Mark (this has the effect of shifting the focus away from Len's point of view so that he appears even madder in comparison with the more normal world which now seems to surround him). The Dramatists Play Service edition serves as a bridge between the original and latest texts, for it includes most changes of the first two kinds and yet retains the structure and Len's long monologues as they are presented in the first edition.

The most important single difference between Pinter's original version of *The Dwarfs* and subsequent editions first appears in the 1965 acting edition. There the vital exchange between Mark and Len concerning the price of butter is deleted (without textual notation), and a passage regarding the acting profession, an extension of the Earl's Court reference, is inserted in its place (p. 10). This substitution looks forward to *The Homecoming*, as Len suggests that actors and actresses might prefer not to be watched (though that is their profession!), so he offers a study of mathematics as an alternative to attending their performances, somewhat foreshadowing Teddy's responses in the later drama. Pinter's purpose in making the revision is not clear. He may have felt that the original was too explicit a statement of his theme, or conversely, he may have felt that the public's difficulty in understanding this admittedly obscure play demanded the reduction of mysterious, "absurd" elements. Significantly, a guidepost to the fundamental meaning of *The Dwarfs*, the shifting room discussion, remains intact in all of the editions.

The shifting from Len's point of view can be seen in several sequences. His "The dwarfs are back on the job" soliloquy is altered and the length cut in half, for example; and a chess game between Mark and Pete and their occasional comments (and Len's obvious awareness of their presence) are used to break up the long speech (p. 92; p. 94). The effect is a lessening of ambiguity and a consequent stressing of Len's madness which comes about because of the new perspective gained by contrasting him with the other two

tion. On p. 80 Aston's rising and going to the window is cut, as is one repetitious line of Davies'. And finally, one repetitious line and a pause are removed from Davies' last speech, making it a bit more effective in its stark appeal.

men. Similarly, Len's "They've gone on a picnic" speech is again broken by comments from Mark and Pete, drawing attention to Len's abnormal state of mind by the shift to an external point of view (p. 96; p. 99). The whole meaning of the play changes here, as 94 lines are reduced to 46, with complicated alterations: the "It's to do with beetles and twigs" section, for instance, is placed immediately after an altered version of "I've skivvied" (which becomes "I'm not a skivvy" in the revision; the acting version retains most of the lines of the original). Other changes include "What's up your nose now?" becoming "I'm supposed to be a friend of yours"; five lines beginning "You're too big for me" are cut; eleven lines about Len's being able to take care of himself are removed (p. 98); and Len's comments on the dwarfs and his relationship with them are altered. Pinter seems to be making it clearer by these changes that Len cannot take care of himself and that he is dependent on his friends, by moving farther and farther away from a subjective viewpoint. The drama may be more effective on the stage (i.e., simpler, more easily understood by the audience, who can categorize it as having to do with a man's madness rather than an expression of the playwright's view of the inaccessibility of reality) as a result of the toning down of mystery and ambiguity, but it loses some of its meaning in the process. The numerous other alterations are less important.[22]

22. Additional textual changes include these. On p. 86 "Euston," is altered to read, "Paddington? It's a big railway station" (p. 87). Pete's "Ssshh! That's him" and the following stage directions become four lines of dialogue between Pete and Mark on p. 87 (p. 88). On p. 89 (pp. 90–91), "*Slight pause*" is reduced to "*Pause*," though after "everything" dots are added. Then the "butter's going up" exchange is deleted and the conversation about acting is substituted—"It's a mortuary without a corpse"—the acting version retains the form of the original in part. On p. 90 (p. 92), stage directions replace "*Silence*" and "*Pause*." On p. 91, Pete's apprehension of experience speech omits two lines between "weeds" and "Sometimes," exchanges "We're old pals" for "You can forgive a lot," and omits Len's groaning (p. 93). Between "Here's your mirror" and "Pete asked me to lend him a shilling" on p. 93 is added Len's business with an apple and one line of dialogue—"This is a funny looking apple" (p. 95). On p. 94, an addition, as Len sees the toasting fork (p. 96), then, pp. 94–95, stage directions are added after Len's "mirror" speech, while thirty-one lines of the soliloquy about "What are the dwarfs doing?" are omitted. This includes possible equating of Len and the dwarfs with the words, "*We* watch" (italics mine). The soliloquy is left in, in the acting version. Pete's efficiency speech in the original, pp. 95–96, includes the example of the sun and moon as an "efficient idea" and Len's "The sun and moon? Efficient?" interruption. This is omitted in the revision and Len's insect-squashing comment which follows Pete's speech is moved up in its place with ten lines about Pete's "gamble" and the time to act being added (p. 97), along with stage directions in place of the "*Pause*." On p. 99 Len's vision of Pete moving a boulder is deleted (p. 100). On p. 100, another substitution of stage action for "*Silence*" (p. 100). Again on p. 100, "Old Testament Rabbis" becomes "cheese," and "You want to listen to your friends, mate. Who else have you got?" (p. 101) is added at the end of Pete's "You want to watch your step" admonition (p. 101). Again, Len's relationship with people outside his mind is emphasized, diminishing the effect of his personal perceptions. The conversation between Mark and Len on p. 102 regarding homes is altered somewhat, the stress falling on Len's differentiation between a house and a home (see Ruth in *The Homecoming*, of course, for a fuller expression of this concept), and the improved realization that he does *not* belong. Like Davies in *The Caretaker*, he has no "place" of his own, though

In a letter to me dated 17 December 1971 Pinter answered my questions about some of the changes he made in *The Birthday Party*, saying, "I make alterations in the text, occasionally, in order indeed to tighten and to cut out material which is not working for its keep." And there certainly are differences between the 1959 and 1965 versions of *The Birthday Party*. Altogether there are at least thirteen deletions, five additions, six substitutions, and two occasions of passages being interchanged in Act I alone. In Act II the count is two deletions, four additions, one substitution, and one interchange, and Act III contains alterations amounting to seventeen deletions, two additions, and five substitutions. While many of these changes are inconsequential, several have the effect of altering much of the meaning of the play.

There are four *major* changes in the text of *The Birthday Party*, two in the first act and two in the third. The first comes when Lulu's Macbethian knock at the door at the peak of Stan's reaction (p. 24) is weakened where "LULU's *voice*: Ooh—ooh!" is inserted, reducing the suspense which has been building to this moment. The next comes when Meg returns to find that Goldberg and McCann have arrived. In the revision McCann's gargle is cut; yet there is no indication of what he does and he rejoins the conversation like one who has been out of the room, since Goldberg asks him about things he would have heard if he had remained. The dramatist explains, "I cut McCann's gargling in my own production of The Birthday Party at the Aldwych in 1964. I found it tedious. McCann now gazes out of the window, indifferent to the conversation taking place."[23] This "minor" omission of an action affects the drama significantly on several levels. Pinter undoubtedly removed it to reduce the mystery of why the Irishman would desire a gargle and to tighten both what happens on the stage and the dialogue, but this really defeats the essence of what he has been building to this point. The mystery is lessened, yet the direction of the play has been to create a pervasive mood of mystery

---

there is a vast difference in the kind of belonging these two characters desire. Davies' need is for something physical, Len's need is for something mental, spiritual, psychological. Len's isolation is involved in his added statement to Mark, "You don't understand. You'll never understand" (p. 103). On p. 103, two sets of stage directions concerning the biscuits are added to accommodate the audience's being able to see the action in the stage version. Five sets of stage directions are also added for the same reason after Len concludes his "Who are you" speech (p. 105) and four additional sets of stage directions are included to describe the action (p. 106) when Pete and Mark visit Len in the hospital (sitting, and so on—there is an error in the acting version when both sit on the "left" instead of one on the left and the other on the right). On p. 106, dialogue is added about Len giving Pete and Mark a call when he gets out of the hospital. This seems to function merely as a signal that the scene has ended and as a means of transition from one locale to another on stage (p. 107). Two more sets of stage directions are added and Mark's "You don't give a tinker's shit for any of us" is replaced by "You've been leading me up the garden," which is moved up from his next speech. On p. 108, in the final change, four lines ("Either they've gone dumb or I've gone deaf. Or they've gone deaf and I've gone dumb. Or we're neither dumb nor deaf. In that case it's a conspiracy pure and simple.") are cut. The economy of the language here fits the concluding mood better in the revised version.

23. Pinter to Gale, 17 Dec. 1971.

and menace, and having McCann remain impassively standing, "indifferent" to the events taking place, distorts his role as an active force of menace. Also missing in the newer version is the idea that this gargle is part of the pre-job ritual. And a very nice unity was achieved in the play by the balance of McCann's gargle before Stanley's ordeal and Goldberg's blow in the throat afterward. Other alterations which occur in the first act that affect the meaning of the play include a reduction of the repetition in Meg and Petey's morning talk (pp. 11, 12), a shift in Lulu's attitude toward Stan, which is made less aggressive (pp. 26–28), and a removal of the name changes connected with Goldberg's son.

In Act II nothing particularly important is changed as a result of the multitudinous textual alterations, though Lulu's aggressiveness is reduced even further during the party scene so that she takes on more of the aspect of a victim.

Act III contains two changes of consequence. The extremely comic exchange between Lulu and Goldberg the morning after is destroyed (p. 84), and the symbolic significance of Stanley's clothing at the end of the play is lost when he comes downstairs *"dressed in a dark well cut suit and white collar"* [24] instead of *"dressed in striped trousers, black jacket, and white collar. . . . [with] a bowler hat."* [25] Now he might be a plain businessman, and the ambivalent implication that he may also be outfitted for his own funeral disappears. Also cut from Act III is Goldberg's reference to the car boot (p. 73; this is probably an improvement because it increases the mystery by removing the suggestion that the action in the drama is nothing more than an underworld affair), McCann's narration about Lulu's "nightmares," which leads to Goldberg's revelation that he visited her in the night (p. 77), and the sequence following Goldberg's ironic affirmation about "Not a day's illness" in which he emits a *"high-pitched wheeze-whine,"* then has McCann test him (pp. 81, 82), and ends with the breaking of the chest expander (p. 83). The other alterations in the play are relatively unimportant.[26]

24. Pinter, *The Birthday Party*, p. 81, in the 1965 rev. edition.
25. Ibid., p. 85 in the original edition; Pinter neglects to mention the bowler hat in the rewrite but accidentally retains it in the stage directions, p. 85.
26. Additional textual changes include these. Act I: on pp. 11–12, cut from Meg's "Is it nice out?" to Petey's "I've finished my cornflakes." On p. 12, the mention of bacon is cut. On p. 14, Meg's "I tried to get him up then. But he wouldn't, the little monkey" is removed. On p. 18, after Meg's "You deserve the strap," add "STANLEY. Don't do that!" On p. 19, cut from Meg's "My father wouldn't let you insult me" through "You did" and add "MEG. That's good strong tea, that's all." On p. 21, after Stanley's "But who are they?" cut "I mean, why. . . . ?" On p. 25 after Meg collects her shopping bag, remove, "*Another knock at the door,*" and insert "(*through the letter box*)" after first "VOICE." "It's come" is reduced to two dots, and finally Stan's aggressiveness or appeal is reduced when his "Sit down a minute" is removed at the bottom of the page. On p. 26 there is an improvement, first as Stan's "What are you talking about?" becomes "Stuffy?" and then as twenty-two lines from "Don't you believe me" through "You think I'm a liar then?" are rearranged more effectively and reduced to a mere six lines which flow more evenly with no break in subject groups,

Paradoxically, the earlier version of *The Birthday Party* is generally more effective in ideas, mood, and presentation, the later in the tightening up of language and the removal of mystery, though this goes somewhat contrary to the direction of the play established at the outset. Perhaps the discrepancy can be explained by relating it to the author's thematic development: when he goes back to change passages, he is no longer concerned with the same problems/concepts and therefore weakens the play in trying to polish it

---

though the words themselves are not as interesting. On p. 27, cut Lulu's "Why don't you ever go out?" and the following five lines, and the exchange from Lulu's "Are you going to wash?" through her "Oh," which precedes "Do you have to wear those glasses?" on p. 28—another reduction of the feeling of menace and the ritualistic, meaningless (i.e., non-communicative, non-involved) element of language. In the stage directions at Goldberg and McCann's entrance Stanley's exit changes from "*sidles*" to "*idles*," hopefully a typographical error, since it changes his character and reaction simultaneously. On p. 31, Goldberg's "I'm glad" is removed and "GOLDBERG. As a matter of fact I was talking about you only the other day. I gave you a very good name./ MC CANN. That was kind of you, Nat./ GOLDBERG. And then this job came up out of the blue. Naturally" is tightened to read "GOLDBERG. You know what I said when this job came up. I mean naturally." On p. 33, after the excision of McCann's exit for a gargle, Goldberg sits and, instead of saying "So you," he says "Well, so what do you say? You." Then the "Last week . . . . Or next week. . . . Next week" exchange with Meg is replaced by his "It would, eh?," and "Why?" is inserted before his question about how many are there at the moment. On p. 35, Goldberg's "Well, well, well" becomes "Ah!" and the distortion caused by eliminating McCann's gargle continues on pp. 35–36, as references to it are cut and there is a rearranging of Meg's "I'll invite Lulu this afternoon" speech, placing it before her "Oh, this is going to cheer Stanley up."

Act II: on p. 51, Goldberg's "What's happened to your memory, Webber?" is removed. On p. 55, there is an addition, "STANLEY. Uuuuuhhhhh!" after McCann's "He's sweating." On p. 56, Goldberg's "You drink that one" is replaced by "You've got the Irish." On p. 58, Lulu is given two additional lines, saying "Hallo" after Goldberg introduces himself (and splitting his lines here) and "Come on!" following Meg's "Come on!" On p. 64, "LULU. Come on." is added before Stan and McCann rise. On pp. 66–67, Lulu's role as victim is intensified by removing "LULU (*to* GOLDBERG). Kiss me. (*They kiss*)," and altering "LULU. Someone's touching me!/ GOLDBERG. Who's this?/ MEG. It's me!" to read "GOLDBERG. Who's this?/ LULU. Someone's touching me!" and dropping Meg's response. As in *A Night Out*, the toucher and his intent become more obvious and the touched more imposed upon.

Act III: on pp. 69–70, once more Pinter tightens the dialogue by removing parts of the conversation between Meg and Petey, from Petey's "Good" through his "How are you then, this morning?" and from his "Why don't you have a walk" through Meg's "Did I sleep like a log?" On p. 75, the upstairs door slamming in the stage directions and Petey's "Oh, it's you" are cut, as is Goldberg's "What is what?" On p. 76, Petey no longer sits at the table. On p. 77, in order to accommodate the distortion made when the "nightmare" exchange disappears, "PETEY *rises*" is turned into "*Pause*." On p. 78, McCann and Goldberg's reversal of "What's what?" and "Yes, what is what. . . ." is again cut, as it had been on p. 75. On p. 79, "go and get him" is added to McCann's question, "So do we wait or do we." On p. 80, "No" is removed from Goldberg's speech between "Never write down a thing" and "And don't go too near the water." On p. 82, since Goldberg no longer laughs after the extracted examination, the stage directions are changed from "(*stopping*)" to "GOLDBERG *sits*," and instead of "*shakes his head, and bounds from the chair*," he "*smiles*," and his "Right" becomes an exclamation. On p. 83, similarly, since the chest expander section has been deleted, stage directions must take this into account; and Lulu's entrance is moved and McCann no longer "*exits with the expander*."

technically.[27] Regardless of the outcome, examining Pinter's textual alterations provides a good opportunity to see how the creative mind of this particular artist works.

In his several articles and numerous interviews Pinter has repeatedly
explained that language and paralanguage (the non-use of language in the
form of pauses and silences) can be utilized for both communication and
non-communication, either intentionally or unconsciously. His ability to reproduce human speech with "tape-recorder fidelity" has led to his dialogue
being called realistic or even suprarealistic (see F. J. Bernhard's "Beyond
Realism: The Plays of Harold Pinter" in the September 1965 issue of *Modern
Drama*, for instance). In this context the term suprarealistic means that although the author does not reproduce common speech exactly, he has captured its essence so perfectly that it seems more real than actual street-corner
exchanges.

The reason that Pinter's dialogues sound so real is that, just as he does
not force his characters to provide information which they would not normally
divulge in conversation because it is already shared knowledge, so he does
not force them to follow the pattern of traditional stage commentary, which
is too stylized, too logical in structure as well as content. Moreover, as Pinter
has also pointed out, expression under emotional stress does not tend to be
especially logical and may in fact become unintelligible. An Iago finds it
easier to express himself clearly and effectively than does a bewildered Cassio.
As a dramatist, Pinter has recognized this and incorporated it into his writing;
it is his actor's instinct which serves him as the basic arbiter in determining
whether or not a new work is realistic. Once the piece is written, he makes it
a habit to "read the play aloud to myself, so I know if it's playable. I walk the
characters through. I move them about. I play all the parts."[28]

Director Peter Hall's contention that the plays are "highly wrought"
products in terms of dialogue carries over into the stage business. In a Pinter
play there should be no action on stage except that which is called for in the
stage directions, for every move has a specific purpose. If a character smokes
a cigarette, he should be smoking because the action bears directly on the
meaning of that particular scene and not because he does not happen to have
a line of dialogue at the moment. An example of the importance Pinter places
on stage movement came about with the production of *Old Times* where
"there are problems with coffee cups. You'd be surprised the problems you
can run into with coffee cups. . . . I wrote one new line in rehearsal. It was the
one addition before London. The line is: "Yes, I remember." . . . It came in
the middle of the brandy and the coffee and affected the whole structure. In

27. Ironically, the movie version is more faithful to the earlier edition, retaining
such items as the gargle, though there are some cuts, as when the inquisition is shortened.
28. Gussow, p. 136. In the same interview (p. 126) he rejects the contention made
by Nigel Dennis in the *New York Review of Books*, however, that his plays are "simply
acting exercises."

this play, the lifting of a coffee cup at the wrong moment can damage the next five minutes. As for the *sipping* of coffee, that can ruin the act."[29]

From the beginning critics have stressed that Pinter appeals to his audience in part because his characters speak in the same way that the audience does. The playwright also uses realistic language to contrast with and underscore the events taking place on the stage. Typically in Pinter there is a current of realistic speech running through the drama. Typically there is also a current of absurdity. The progression of his plays appears to be a movement from reality (reading a newspaper) to absurdity (the protagonist, reduced to an inarticulate shambles, literally being taken for a ride). The underlying flow of realistic language persistently contrasts with the "unrealistic" context in which it is uttered, emphasizing the absurdity of the events so that they seem even more absurd than they might otherwise appear. The fact that the characters speak as though engaged in everyday conversation in the midst of these non-normal events heightens the dramatic effect of their outrageous aspects.

Language functions otherwise, too, of course. For Rose it is a way to structure the universe which surrounds her. The slow, careful character of Aston, the quick, imaginative character of Mick, and the bitter, suspicious nature of Davies are clearly marked by their language. For Max, Lenny, Teddy, and Ruth words are weapons of attack or fortifications to provide defense. And in the memory plays, words provide the nebulous metaphor for the past.

The techniques Pinter employs to create his realistic dialogue are many and varied: the use of a common vocabulary, malapropisms, *non sequiturs*, clichés, jargon, tautology, repetition, illogic, imagery, the rhythms and patterns of everyday conversation, and pauses and silences.

A *non sequitur* is an inference which does not follow from the preceding premise, and in a play where the characters are avoiding communication and are completely involved with their personal worries they use *non sequiturs* to talk around rather than at or to one another. They may be talking about the same things, but they skirt around actually admitting their subject. Besides mirroring normal speech patterns, *non sequiturs* can be humorous and/ or convey information about their speakers. When Mr. Kidd moves from his discussion with Rose about his sister to a statement that he has "made ends meet," all three operations are in effect.

Pinter seasons his work with clichés, as though to give it a homey flavor, and they are usually related to the home or family or doing a good job—nice middle-class pronouncements such as those mouthed by Goldberg. Occasionally, however, the very familiarity of the cliché gives it a whole new meaning because of its context. This is the case when McCann tells Stanley that he "can't see straight"—after having deliberately broken Stan's glasses—and the

29. Ibid., p. 131.

exquisite use of cliché which marks Teddy's departure for America at the end of *The Homecoming* ("Don't become a stranger.") certainly merits repeating in this regard.

Jargon similarly serves several purposes in Pinter's writing. The use of technical words is sometimes an attempt to cover an inability to communicate, as with Aston's rhapsody about types of saws, which recalls the classic example of the dramatist's enthusiastic use of technical jargon in the delightful revue sketch "Trouble in the Works." In trying to find the right words to express a meaning, a character often hits upon a set of words which allow him to get sidetracked and therefore postpone his need to continue the attempt to communicate, at least for a while. Jargon works as a defense mechanism in much the same way. It is interesting that Pinter draws on many fields for his passages of jargon, from sailing to phychology, yet theatrical terminology and imagery are surprisingly sparse in his playwriting.

Repetition is one of Pinter's most versatile linguistic devices. A typical pattern can be seen in that conversation between Meg and Petey which opens *The Birthday Party*:

MEG. Is that you, Petey?
    Pause.
    Petey, is that you?
    Pause.
    Petey?
PETEY. What?
MEG. Is that you?
PETEY. Yes, it's me.
MEG. What? . . . Are you back?
PETEY. Yes.
MEG. I've got your cornflakes ready. . . . Here's your cornflakes. . . . Are they nice?
PETEY. Very nice.
MEG. I thought they'd be nice.[30]

Esslin discusses eight different ways that Pinter uses repetition: as a means of conveying dramatic information; with characters who are struggling to find a specific word; because of an enjoyment with the sound of a word once it has been found; as a form of hysteria; to indicate the process of absorbing a fact; as a refrain either to show preoccupation with an idea or as an assertion; to indicate a lack of emotion, which allows a train of associations to evolve; and when a character is lying.[31]

The dialogue quoted above between Meg and Petey is an example of how information may be imparted through repetition, for it displays an in-

30. Pinter, *The Birthday Party*, p. [9].
31. See Esslin, *The Peopled Wound*, Chap. 4.

effectual Meg striving to make conversation, yet shows that there is no worthwhile communication being accomplished.

Lenny's disgust with his father's cooking demonstrates how a character, struggling to find a word which suits his meaning perfectly, uses it over and over once it occurs to him. Having found the word he has been searching for, he becomes enamored with its sound and recites it almost ritualistically and in different combinations. Since Max's cooking is so bad, Lenny asks him why he does not buy a "dog," for he is a "dog cook," he thinks that he is "cooking for a lot of dogs." James' delight with the characterizing nature of Bill's use of "scrumptious" is similar.

As an individual becomes progressively more emotionally upset, specific words echo through his speech more and more frequently. There is a kind of hysteria in Davies' continual repetition of the word "Blacks" when he enters Aston's room and begins to realize that the invitation to stay is being made without any malicious intent. The repetition also indicates the process of his absorbing the fact that he is safe from "foreigners." It is a long process, but by constantly returning to his subject, Davies manages to grasp the concept.

In a very musical or poetic way words continually reappear throughout a Pinter drama until they become a sort of refrain which builds to a cumulative effect having a direct bearing on the meaning of the play. Several such words are frequently repeated in *The Homecoming*. Although "family" and words relating to "home" appear naturally enough in the dialogue, they are what the artist is concerned with in this play, and their overall effect is to serve as indicators which subtly keep the audience's attention fixed on the subject of family and home, though the attention may be at a subconscious level. The continual use of these words also indicates a preoccupation with the abstract concepts referred to by the characters, who incessantly manage to work the words into their conversations.

Finally, speeches which have no emotional impact for the speaker sometimes reveal that lack of emotion through repetition, as in a like manner a character who is lying tends to repeat himself, either trying to get the facts straight in his own mind as he creates them or trying to convince his listener purely by the weight of his repetitions (if someone says something often enough, it must be true). The repetitions in Joey's account of his adventure with the birds in the Scrubs fits both of these categories.

Imagery is another poetic device which Pinter relies upon on occasion, but he deploys it with a great deal of strategy. The dramatist's images are certainly vivid and convey clear mental pictures as he appeals to the senses, but oddly enough, most of the images deal with corruption. It is hard to imagine a description which would have more emotional impact based on sensory involvement than Max's complaint that he is "lumbered" with "One cast-iron bunch of crap after another. One flow of stinking pus after another."[32]

32. Pinter, *The Homecoming*, p. 19.

That rhythm is an important linguistic element is obvious. It can be created in numerous ways, including the jargon and repetition already mentioned. Pinter contends that it can function in a drama as it does in poetry to create characterization and to focus attention on meaning, too: "I'm very conscious of rhythm. It's got to happen 'snap, snap'—just like that or it's wrong. I'm also interested in pitch. . . . I remember when we did *The Collection* Off-Broadway, there was an American actor who was in big trouble with his part. I told him instead of trying to find reasons for his characterization, 'Why don't you read the part and pay attention to the stress of the words?' He did it and he was fine. The point is, the stresses tell you where the meaning is. Saying it up or down can change the whole meaning. It has to be just right."[33] Verifying this, Peter Hall, John Normington, and Paul Rogers have all mentioned that catching the correct rhythm was one of the most important items they had to learn for the original presentation of *The Homecoming*.

In his review of the film *Accident* for the Autumn 1966 edition of *Sight and Sound* Taylor quotes Pinter as saying, "Life is much more mysterious than plays make it out to be. And it is this mystery which fascinates me; what happens between the words, what happens when no words are spoken at all." This is a rephrasing of an idea which the playwright has expressed many times, and it refers to his most distinctive element, especially in the later plays— the use of pauses and silences. This use is something he shares with Beckett, though Pinter's development and refining of the device is unparalleled and adds another rhythmical element.

Frank Marcus recalls, in the *New York Times* of 13 July 1969, that Pinter once told him a story about the time he "had agreed to write a play of one hour's duration for television, had delivered his script and attended the first reading. It went well. Then the producer asked his assistant for the time score. The girl looked at the stop watch. 'Exactly 28 minutes 34 seconds,' she said. Awkward silence. Then the author cleared his throat: 'You see, there are quite a lot of pauses. . . .'" Recognizing the relevance of Pinter's breaks in conversation, Peter Hall held a "dot and pause" rehearsal for the original *The Homecoming* cast, about which the playwright has said, "I do pay great attention to those points. . . . Although it sounds bloody pretentious [the rehearsal] was apparently very valuable."[34] Hall himself has commented on this amusing event: "It drove the actors absolutely mad. I said, 'You don't remember the phrases.' . . . So I said, 'We will now sit down and have a word rehearsal, sitting where we are, and each of you will tell me where your dots are and where your pauses are and where your silences are.' And we went right through it. It only happened once. It was just to try and make the actors understand that we were dealing with something which was highly formed

33. Lahr, "Pinter's Language," in *A Casebook on Harold Pinter's The Homecoming*.
34. Bensky, p. 24.

and highly wrought. And our first responsibility was to know what it was. . . .
I think people who hear that I held a dot and pause rehearsal perhaps mis-
understand its purpose. It wasn't done to imprison the actor, but to add to his
knowledge of the text."[35]

Pinter, as might be expected, has been able to keep his sense of humor
about the importance of pauses and silences as an aspect of language. In
"Between the Lines" he discusses the reason why *The Caretaker* (which ran
a year in London) found a greater critical acceptance when it was first performed than did *The Birthday Party* (which ran a week): "In 'The Birthday
Party' I employed a certain amount of dashes in the text, between phrases. In
'The Caretaker' I cut out the dashes and used dots instead. So that instead
of, say: 'Look, dash, who, dash, I, dash, dash, dash': the text would read: 'Look,
dot, dot, dot, who, dot, dot, dot, I, dot, dot, dot, dot.' So it's possible to deduce
from this that dots are more popular than dashes and that's why 'The Caretaker' had a longer run than 'The Birthday Party.' The fact that in neither case
could you actually hear the dots and dashes in performance is beside the point.
You can't fool the critics for long. They can tell a dot from a dash a mile off,
even when they can hear neither." At the same time these breaks in the dialogue have an important visceral function in the dramas in the author's opinion: "From my point of view, these are not in any sense a formal kind of
arrangement. The pause is a pause because of what has just happened in the
minds and guts of the characters. They spring out of the text. They're not
formal conveniences or stresses but part of the body of the action. I'm simply
suggesting that if [the actors] play it properly they will find that a pause—or
whatever the hell it is—is inevitable. And a silence equally means that something has happened to create the impossibility of anyone speaking for a certain
amount of time—until they can recover from whatever happened before the
silence."[36]

Pauses in the dialogue serve many purposes in Pinter, from actual lapses
in the conversation to indications of extreme emotional involvement. However
they are used, they tend to emphasize the subject matter. Ruth's description
of her home in America as all rock and sand is not long in actual word count,
but the time it takes her to relate it is drawn out by the pauses between her
statements, pauses which make America sound even more barren than her
description of it would indicate. The pauses imply the obvious emotional
effect the sterility of her surroundings has imposed upon her. Since she is so
profoundly affected that she can hardly utter her words, the sterility must be
overpowering.

Recent criticism has come to the conclusion that there is a distinct difference intended when Pinter indicates a pause, as opposed to a silence. Pauses
demonstrate a continuing thought process and contribute to developing ten-

35. In Lahr's interview.   36. Gussow, p. 132.

sion by exposing the intensity of the thought which has not yet broken into a verbally communicable pattern. Silences, on the other hand, signal the conclusion of one line of thinking and the beginning of a new subject of conversation. This difference is apparent when Lenny finishes telling Ruth about the girl with the pox, and his sister-in-law wonders how he knew that the girl was diseased:

> How did I know?
> *Pause.*
> I decided she was.
> *Silence.*
> You and my brother are newly-weds, are you?[37]

The importance of Lenny's answer is conveyed through the use of a pause. And it is an important answer, related to the underlying theme of appearance versus reality, of the idea of verification. The pause tells the audience that Lenny is contemplating his answer, and it is not, therefore, likely to be what normally might be expected—if it has to be considered, it must be of some consequence.

The silence which follows Lenny's pronouncement is another signal for the audience, this time indicating that discussion of the topic of diseased girls is closed and a new topic is to be offered (though it is not really a new topic; this is part of Lenny's pattern of repetition as he tries to assimilate the idea that he is talking to his brother's wife, an idea he has touched on and then dropped several times in the conversation). The break is clear-cut and the audience is thus prepared to go on to something new. In Pinter's latest plays, *Landscape*, *Silence*, and *Night*, the silences almost serve as divisions between chapters, though this is less apparent in *Old Times* and *No Man's Land*.

Stylistically, a comparative reading of Pinter's earliest and latest works reveals that, while there can be no doubt that they were written by the same man, they are very different. As he has gained confidence in his own writing, the dramatist seems more willing to portray the world as he sees it (a blurring of lines) rather than the way others see it (sharp edges) and expect him to see it. Certainly this is true in his imagery. The early descriptions of corruption have given way to a foggy, dreamlike state in *Landscape*, *Silence*, *Night*, and *Old Times*. His style has become less harsh, more impressionistic and lyrical. There is a definite progression, for instance, in the imaginative quality displayed in his characters' fantasies. From Stan to Lenny to the trio in *Old Times* there is a movement toward subtlety and poetic expression. The result is more vital, as the plays contain an emotional flow instead of attempts to delineate. The success of Pinter's method reflects Sir Philip Sidney's contention that poetry ought to move its audience, not try to persuade it. The newer pieces are as emotionally effective as Pinter's earliest writing, though in a

37. Pinter, *The Homecoming*, p. 31

completely different way and effecting quite a different response. This is why Peter Hall could look forward to *Old Times* as a play which would have the audience rolling in the aisles with laughter and Ronald Bryden could review the drama in the *New Statesman* as Pinter's latest "comedy," yet the ritualistic aspects leading to Anna's exorcism could also bring tears to playgoers' eyes at the final curtain.

A Summing Up

. . . I couldn't any longer stay in the room . . .

Harold Pinter has not always been kindly received by either drama critics or audiences. Brustein and Kerr, for example, still have their reservations about him—or maybe they are just disappointed that he does not write as they wish he would. Brustein thinks that the dramatist needs to avoid *coups le théâtre*;[1] Kerr would like for *The Homecoming* to be reduced to a forty-minute one-act.[2] *The Birthday Party* ran only a week and was soundly decried. Pinter tells the story in "Between the Lines" of what happened when he followed the Continental custom of taking a bow with the actors in Düsseldorf after the first night performance of *The Caretaker*: "I was at once booed violently by what must have been the finest collection of booers in the world. I thought they were using megaphones, but it was pure mouth. The cast, though, were as dogged as the audience and we took thirty-four curtain calls, all to boos.

1. Robert Brustein, *The Third Theatre* (New York: Clarion, 1970), pp. 119–22.
2. Kerr, *Harold Pinter*, p. 41.

By the thirty-fourth there were only two people left in the house, still booing."
The Homecoming was harshly received, too, as John Normington recalls in a
passage cited above,[3] when it played to a first-night audience in Brighton
prior to its London run; and people walked out of the recent London performance of *Old Times* before the end of the first act.

Opposed to these reactions, of course, is a preponderance of extremely
favorable opinion, such as that cited in the Introduction and exemplified by
the many awards Pinter has received for his television, stage, and screen
writing. The reason that Pinter can be called *the* outstanding English dramatist of the twentieth century is simple; he started out from a strong base and
has continued to improve. He is exciting, interesting, and fun. His plays are
meaningful. He is imaginative, innovative, and influential. Although traces of
Shakespeare, Albee, Beckett, Pirandello, Ionesco, Chekhov, Joyce, Cary,
Kafka, Céline, Dostoevski, Henry Miller, and Hemingway have been found
in Pinter's writing, he has produced a product which is uniquely his own.

Technically he has shown a steady evolution from the tendency to rely
on stage devices in the "comedies of menace" to the point of becoming the
theatre's most creative realizer of the potentials of language. Thematically he
has clearly continued to develop, too. He has not been content to rewrite
the same play over and over. He examines a problem through a set of plays and
then moves on to another problem. With the "comedies of menace" the playwright was concerned with exposing the existence of menace and its effect
on the individual; from the examination of a physically threatening external
menace he moved to the study of the origin of menace and the desperate attempts of characters to fulfill their psychological needs, an internalization
of the menace of his first dramas; and the portrayal of characters desperately
struggling for emotional satisfaction has led him to his most recent topic,
memory, which is another step in his delving into the workings of the human
mind. This is, perhaps, an even more fundamental concern than those which
preceded it; although the topic is still another variation on the theme of verification, the emphasis now developing focuses our attention on how the individual is responsible for continually creating the reality he exists in.

Criticism, naturally, has reflected the author's continuing changes. The
early critical treatments of Pinter's work, from the late fifties through the early
sixties, concentrated on the room-womb imagery, the atmosphere of the plays,
and the plight of victims being plagued by mysterious outside forces; in the
mid-sixties sociological and linguistic studies were the main focus; the topic
of scholarly attention in the late sixties was the psychological aspect of Pinter's
writing; and more recently, discussions have centered on the subject of memory and his poetic expression.

There is another pattern which can be discovered in the dramatist's
canon: typically Pinter will write a major play, followed by several lesser

3. Cf., above, Chap. VII, n. 23, and the corresponding passage in the text.

endeavors over the next few years as he experiments and gathers himself for another major effort. After each of these major efforts he seems to realize that he has exhausted whatever subject line he has been tracing and that he must move in a new direction (and *Old Times* certainly indicates that the pattern is holding true). There can be no doubt that a progression does exist. First came the three dramas concerning menace *per se*, then the transitional *A Slight Ache* and *The Caretaker*, recognizing that menace is an internal problem, followed by the love/need dramas and the search for the origin of man's desperation; and now the dramatist has moved into the area of memory.

Following *The Homecoming*, Pinter told Kathleen Halton about the drama he was working on at that time: it was about a "woman of fifty . . . who is talking. That's all I bloody well know. I don't know who she is. Certainly it's not a room."[4] Clearly he was talking about Beth in *Landscape*, a play which signaled a shift in thematic concentration as well as setting. As he said to Michael Dean in an interview prior to the opening of *Landscape* and *Silence*, "My last two plays are really rather different. They had to be from my point of view. I felt that after *The Homecoming*, which was the last full-length play I wrote, I couldn't any longer stay in the room with this bunch of people who opened doors and came in and went out. . . ."[5] Although his success has stopped him from creating as frequently as he did during the first eight or ten years of his writing career, if the pattern continues we can expect another major play on his newest theme or the beginning of a new line of development in the near future.

Harold Pinter is still young, in his forties, and he has been writing for a relatively short time, yet he is by general consensus without question the major force in the contemporary English-speaking theatre. As long as he continues his pattern of development, he can only gain in stature.

4. Halton, "Pinter," pp. 194–95.
5. Interview with Michael Dean of BBC TV; rpt. as "Late Night Line-up," *Listener*, 6 March 1969.

Appendix A. Chronology of Pinter's Writings

1946–1947 Juvenilia.

1949 "Kullus" is begun.

1950 "New Year in the Midlands" and "Chandeliers and Shadows" are published. "New Year in the Midlands" is reprinted with "Rural Idyll" and "European Revels" over the name "Harold Pinta." Work is begun on a novel, *The Dwarfs* (unfinished).

1951 "One a Story, Two a Death," by "Harold Pinta" is published.

1957 *The Room, The Birthday Party,* and *The Dumb Waiter* are written.

1958 *Something in Common* (unperformed) and *A Slight Ache* are written.

1959 *A Night Out* is completed. "The Examination" is published. "Getting Acquainted," "Request Stop," "Special Offer," "Last to Go," "The Black and White," and "Trouble in the Works," are performed.

1960 *The Caretaker, Night School,* and *The Dwarfs* (stage play) are performed. *The Hothouse* is finished (unperformed).

1961 *The Collection* is performed. "Writing for Myself" is published.

1962 *The Servant* is filmed. The screenplay is written of *The Caretaker* (*The Guest*).

1963 *The Lover* is presented. "Dialogue for Three" is published. The script is written for *The Pumpkin Eater,* and the script for *The Compartment.* A short story version is made of *Tea Party.* "Filming 'The Caretaker'" is published.

1964 "Applicant," "Interview," "That's All," and "That's Your Trouble" are produced. "Writing for the Theatre" is published. *The Pumpkin Eater* is shown.

1965 *The Homecoming* is presented. "Between the Lines" is published.

1966 The script is written for *The Quiller Memorandum,* and the script for *Accident.*

1967 *The Basement* (originally *The Compartment*) is presented.

1968 *Landscape* is presented. A film version is made of *The Birthday Party. Mac* is published.

1969 *Silence* and *Night* are presented. The script of *The Go-Between* is completed.

1970 The film script of *The Homecoming* is completed. "All of That" is published.

1971 *Old Times* is presented. A movie adaptation of *Langrishe, Go Down* is written. "poem" is published.

1972 The film adaptation of *Remembrance of Things Past* (*A la recherche du temps perdu*) is written. *Monologue* is written.

1973 The film version of *Butley* is made.

1975 The film version of *The Last Tycoon* is made.

Appendix B. Chronology of First Performances of Pinter's Plays

1957 *The Room* is first staged at Bristol University by the Drama Department.

1958 *The Birthday Party* is staged at the Arts Theatre, Cambridge, April 28.

1959 *The world premiere of *The Dumb Waiter* takes place at Frankfurt-am-Main, the Frankfurt Municipal Theatre, on February 28, in German.

*"The Black and White" and *"Trouble in the Works" are performed in *One to Another* at the Lyric Opera House, Hammersmith, July 15.

A *Slight Ache* is first broadcast on the British Broadcasting Corporation's Third Programme, July 29.

*"Getting Acquainted," "Last to Go," "Request Stop," and "Special Offer" are presented in *Pieces of Eight* at the Apollo Theatre, London, September 3.

1960 *The Room* and *The Dumb Waiter* are presented as a double bill at the Hampstead Theatre Club, January 21.

A Night Out is broadcast on the BBC Third Programme, March 1.

The Caretaker is staged at the Arts Theatre, London, April 27.

Night School is televised by Associated Rediffusion Television, July 21.

The Birthday Party becomes the first professional performance of Pinter in America, Actors Workshop, San Francisco, July 27.

The Dwarfs is broadcast on the BBC Third Programme, December 2.

1961 *A Slight Ache* is staged as part of a triple bill, *Three*, at the Arts Theatre Club, London, January 18.

The Collection is televised by Associated Rediffusion Television, May 11.

A Night Out is staged at the Gate Theatre, Dublin, September 17.

1962 *The Collection* is staged at the Aldwych Theatre, London, June 18.

"The Examination" is read by Pinter on the BBC Third Programme, September 7.

The Servant is shown in London in November.

1963 *The Lover* is televised by Associated Rediffusion Television on March 28.

The Caretaker (film) is shown at the Berlin Film Festival on June 27.

*Denotes first stage presentation.

The Lover and *The Dwarfs* are staged at the Arts Theatre Club, London, September 18.

1964 "Applicant," "Dialogue for Three," "Interview," "That's All," and "That's Your Trouble" are broadcast on the BBC Third Programme between February and March.

"Tea Party" is read by Pinter on the BBC Third Programme, June 2.

The *Pumpkin Eater* is shown.

1965 *The Homecoming* begins a pre-London tour in March, staged at the Aldwych Theatre, London, on June 3.

Tea Party is televised by BBC-1 in England and throughout Europe on March 25.

1966 *The Quiller Memorandum* is shown in November.

1967 *The Basement* is televised on BBC-TV on February 28. *Accident* is shown in February.

1968 *Landscape* is broadcast on the BBC Third Programme, April 28.

Tea Party and *The Basement* are staged at the East Side Playhouse, New York, October 19.

The Birthday Party (film) is shown in New York on December 9.

1969 *Night* is staged in a collection of one-act plays, *Mixed Doubles*, at the Comedy Theatre, London, April 9.

Landscape and *Silence* are staged at the Aldwych Theatre, London, July 2.

1971 *The Go-Between* (film) is shown at the Cannes Film Festival.

Old Times is first staged at the Aldwych Theatre, London, June 1, 1971.

1973 *The Homecoming* (film) is shown. *Monologue* is televised.

1974 *Butley* (film) is shown.

1975 *No Man's Land* is staged at the Old Vic, London, April 23.

Appendix C. Casts and Directors of First Performances of Pinter's Plays

A Night Out

Radio Cast

ALBERT STOKES	Barry Foster
MRS. STOKES	Mary O'Farrell
SEELEY	Harold Pinter
KEDGE	John Rye
BARMAN AT THE COFFEE STALL	Walter Hall
OLD MAN	Norman Wynne
MR. KING	David Bird
MR. RYAN	Norman Wynne
GIDNEY	Nicholas Selby
JOYCE	Jane Jordan Rogers
EILEEN	Auriol Smith
BETTY	Margaret Hotine
HORNE	Hugh Dickson
BARROW	David Spenser
THE GIRL	Vivien Merchant

Produced by Donald McWhinnie

Television Cast

ALBERT STOKES	Tom Bell
MRS. STOKES	Madge Ryan
SEELEY	Harold Pinter
KEDGE	Philip Locke
BARMAN AT THE COFFEE STALL	Edmond Bennett
OLD MAN	Gordon Phillott
MR. KING	Arthur Lowe
MR. RYAN	Edward Malin
GIDNEY	Stanley Meadows
JOYCE	Jose Read
EILEEN	Maria Lennard
BETTY	Mary Duddy

HORNE	Stanley Segal
BARROW	Walter Hall
THE GIRL	Vivien Merchant

Produced by Philip Saville

A Slight Ache

Radio Cast

EDWARD	Maurice Denham
FLORA	Vivien Merchant

Produced by Donald McWhinnie

Stage Cast

EDWARD	Emlyn Williams
FLORA	Alison Leggat
MATCHSELLER	Richard Briers

Produced by Donald McWhinnie

Landscape

Radio Cast

BETH	Peggy Ashcroft
DUFF	Eric Porter

Directed by Guy Vaesen

Stage Cast

BETH	Peggy Ashcroft
DUFF	David Waller

Directed by Peter Hall

Night

Stage Cast

MAN	Nigel Stock
WOMAN	Vivien Merchant

Directed by Alexander Doré

Night School

Television Cast

ANNIE	Iris Vandeleur
WALTER	Milo O'Shea
MILLY	Jane Eccles
SALLY	Vivien Merchant
SOLTO	Martin Miller
TULLY	Bernard Spear

Directed by Joan Kemp-Welch

Radio Cast

ANNIE	Mary O'Farrell
WALTER	John Hollis
MILLY	Sylvia Coleridge
SALLY	Prunella Scales
SOLTO	Sydney Tafler
TULLY	Preston Lockwood
BARBARA	Barbara Mitchell
MAVIS	Carol Marsh

Directed by Guy Vaesen

No Man's Land

Stage Cast

HIRST	Ralph Richardson
SPOONER	John Gielgud
FOSTER	Michael Feast
BRIGGS	Terence Rigby

Directed by Peter Hall

Silence

Stage Cast

ELLEN	Frances Cuka
RUMSEY	Anthony Bate
BATES	Norman Rodway

Directed by Peter Hall

Tea Party

Television Cast

DISSON	Leo McKern
WENDY	Vivien Merchant
DIANA	Jennifer Wright
WILLY	Charles Gray
DISLEY	John Le Mesurier
LOIS	Margaret Denyer
FATHER	Frederick Piper
MOTHER	Hilda Barry
TOM	Peter Bartlett
JOHN	Robert Bartlett

Directed by Charles Jarrott

The Basement

Television Cast

STOTT	Harold Pinter

| JANE | Kika Markham |
| LAW | Derek Godfrey |

Directed by Charles Jarrott

The Birthday Party

Stage Cast

PETEY	Willoughby Gray
MEG	Beatrix Lehmann
STANLEY	Richard Pearson
LULU	Wendy Hutchinson
GOLDBERG	John Slater
MC CANN	John Stratton

Directed by Peter Wood

Film Cast

MEG	Dandy Nichols
STANLEY	Robert Shaw
GOLDBERG	Sidney Tafler
MC CANN	Patrick McGee

Directed by William Friedkin

The Caretaker

Stage Cast

MICK	Alan Bates
ASTON	Peter Woodthorpe
DAVIES	Donald Pleasence

Directed by Donald McWhinnie

Film Cast

MICK	Alan Bates
ASTON	Robert Shaw
DAVIES	Donald Pleasence

Directed by Clive Donner

The Collection

Television Cast

HARRY	Griffith Jones
JAMES	Anthony Bate
STELLA	Vivien Merchant
BILL	John Ronane

Directed by Joan Kemp-Welch

Stage Cast

| HARRY | Michael Hordern |

JAMES	Kenneth Haigh
STELLA	Barbara Murray
BILL	John Ronane

Directed by Peter Hall and Harold Pinter

The Dumb Waiter

Stage Cast

| BEN | Nicholas Selby |
| GUS | George Tovey |

Directed by James Roose-Evans

The Dwarfs

Radio Cast

LEN	Richard Pasco
PETE	Jon Rollason
MARK	Alex Scott

Produced by Barbara Bray

Stage Cast

LEN	John Hurt
PETE	Philip Bond
MARK	Michael Forrest

Directed by Harold Pinter
Assisted by Guy Vaesen

The Homecoming

Stage Cast

MAX	Paul Rogers
LENNY	Ian Holm
SAM	John Normington
JOEY	Terence Rigby
TEDDY	Michael Bryant
RUTH	Vivien Merchant

Directed by Peter Hall

Film Cast

MAX	Paul Rogers
LENNY	Ian Holm
SAM	Cyril Cusack
JOEY	Terence Rigby
TEDDY	Michael Jayston
RUTH	Vivien Merchant

Directed by Peter Hall

The Lover

Television Cast

RICHARD	Alan Badel
SARAH	Vivien Merchant
JOHN	Michael Forrest

Directed by Joan Kemp-Welch

Stage Cast

RICHARD	Scott Forbes
SARAH	Vivien Merchant
JOHN	Michael Forrest

Directed by Harold Pinter
Assisted by Guy Vaesen

The Room

Stage Cast

BERT HUDD	Howard Lang
ROSE	Vivien Merchant
MR. KIDD	Henry Woolf
MR. SANDS	John Rees
MRS. SANDS	Auriol Smith
RILEY	Thomas Baptiste

Directed by Harold Pinter

Old Times

Stage Cast

DEELEY	Colin Blakely
KATE	Dorothy Tutin
ANNA	Vivien Merchant

Directed by Peter Hall

Appendix D. Productions Directed by Pinter

The Birthday Party, Oxford and Cambridge, 1958.

The Room, Hampstead Theatre Club, London, 21 January 1960.

The Collection, Aldwych Theatre, London, 18 June 1962, co-directed with Peter Hall.

The Lover, Arts Theatre Club, London, 18 September 1963, assisted by Guy Vaesen.

The Dwarfs, Arts Theatre Club, London, 18 September 1963, assisted by Guy Vaesen.

The Birthday Party, Aldwych Theatre, London, 18 June 1964.

The Man in the Glass Booth (by Robert Shaw), London, 27 July 1967.

The Innocents (by William Archibald, based on Henry James' *The Turn of the Screw*), Morosco Theater, New York, October 1969.

Butley (by Simon Gray), London, August 1970.

Exiles (by James Joyce), London, November 1970.

Butley (film), 1974.

Next of Kin (by John Hopkins), London, 31 May 1974.

Otherwise Engaged (by Simon Gray), London, July 1975; New York, February 1977.

Appendix E. A Partial List of Roles Acted by Pinter

Macbeth, in *Macbeth* at Hackney Downs Grammar School, 1947—first acting role.

Romeo, in *Romeo and Juliet* at Hackney Downs Grammar School, 1948.

In "Focus on Football Pools," BBC Home Service, 19 September 1950—first professional role.

In "Focus on Libraries," BBC Home Service, 31 October 1950.

Abergavenny, in *Henry VIII*, BBC Third Programme, 14 January 1951.

In Shakespearian repertory in Ireland with Anew McMaster's touring company, 1951–1952: Horatio in *Hamlet*, Cassio in *Othello*, Bassanio in *The Merchant of Venice*.

In Donald Wolfit's classical season at the King's Theatre in Hammersmith, 1953, in *As You Like It* and as a king's knight in *King Lear*.

Repertory acting in provincial English theatres, 1954–1957, under the stage name of David Baron.

Seeley, in *A Night Out*, BBC Third Programme, 1 March 1960.

Seeley, in *A Night Out*, ABC-TV, 24 April 1960.

Goldberg, in *The Birthday Party*, Cheltenham, 1960.

Mick, in *The Caretaker*, Duchess Theatre, London, 21 February 1961.

A society man, in *The Servant* (film), 1962.

Reading of "The Examination," on the BBC Third Programme, 7 September 1962.

Reading of the prose version of "Tea Party" on the BBC Third Programme, 2 June 1964.

García, in Jean-Paul Sartre's *No Exit*, BBC Television, 15 November 1965.

Stott, in *The Basement*, BBC Television, 28 February 1967.

Bell, a television producer, in *Accident* (film), 1967.

Lenny, in *The Homecoming*.

Pinter appeared in the "NBC Experiment in Television: *Pinter People*" and was the voice for characters in the cartoon versions of his revue sketches: Mr. Fibbs in "Trouble in the Works" and the Barman in "Last to Go," 1969.

Appendix F. Awards to Pinter

The Evening Standard award for *The Caretaker*, 1960.
Page 1 Award of the Newspaper Guild of New York for *The Caretaker*, 1960.
Berlin Film Festival Silver Bear for *The Caretaker* (film), 1963.
Edinburgh Festival Certificate of Merit for *The Caretaker* (film), 1963.
Prix Italia (Naples) for Television Drama for *The Lover*, 1963.
Guild of British Television Producers and Directors award for *The Lover*, 1963.
British Screenwriters Guild Award for *The Servant*, 1964.
New York Film Critics Best Writing Award for *The Servant*, 1964.
New York Times listing of *The Servant*, one of the ten best films of the year, 1964.
British Film Academy Award for *The Pumpkin Eater*, 1965.
Commander of the Order of the British Empire (C.B.E.) on the Queen's Birthday Honours List, 1966.
Cannes Jury Prize for *Accident*, 1967.
National Board of Review Award, one of the ten best films of the year, for *Accident*, 1967.
Antoinette Perry ("Tony") Award for the best play on Broadway for *The Homecoming*, 1967.
New York Drama Critics Circle Award for the best play on Broadway, for *The Homecoming*, 1967.
Whitbread Anglo-American Award for the best British play on Broadway, for *The Homecoming*, 1967.
Honorary Fellow, Modern Language Association of America, 1970.
Hamburg University Shakespeare Prize, 1970.
Honorary degree conferred by Reading University, 1970.
Honorary degree conferred by the University of Birmingham, 1971.
Golden Palm (Best Picture) Cannes Film Festival award for *The Go-Between*, 1971.

Annotated Bibliography

Adelman, Irving, and Rita Dworkin. "Harold Pinter." In *Modern Drama.* Metuchen, N.J.: Scarecrow Press, 1967. Pp. 241–42.

Allen, Robert Hedley. "The Language of Three Contemporary British Dramatists: John Osborne, Harold Pinter and John Arden." Diss., Univ. of Pennsylvania, 1975.

Allgaier, Dieter. "Die Dramen Harold Pinters: eine Untersuchung von Form und Inhalt." Diss., Frankfurt, 1967. In German.

——. "Harold Pinters 'The Caretaker' als Lese- und Diskussionsstoff in der gymnasialen Oberstufe." *Neueren Sprachen,* 19 (1970), 556–66.

Alpert, Hollis. "Where It's Happening." *Saturday Review,* 24 April 1967; rpt. in Boyum and Scott, *Film as Film,* pp. 26–28. A review of the film *Accident.* Pinter's script concentrates on images rather than dialogue.

Alvarez, A. "The Arts and Entertainment. Wanted—a Language." *New Statesman,* 30 Jan. 1960, pp. 149–50. Review. The violence and horror of *The Room* and *The Dumb Waiter* grow out of Pinter's obsessions with time and the indifference of society.

——. "Death in the Morning." *New Statesman,* 58 (12 Dec. 1959), 836. An examination of *The Birthday Party* as "a classic paranoic set-up," with a discussion of Pinter's symbolism.

——. "Olivier Among the Rhinos." *New Statesman,* 59 (7 May 1960), 666.

Amend, Victor E. "Harold Pinter: Some Credits and Debits." *Modern Drama,* 10 (Sept. 1967), 165–74.

Amette, Jacques-Pierre. "Osborne, Pinter, Saunders and Cie." *Nouvelle Revue Française,* 18 (janv.), 95–99.

Angus, William. "Modern Theatre Reflects the Times." *Queens Quarterly,* 70 (Summer 1963), 155–63. Condemns the modern theatre for not holding the mirror up to nature in its portrayal of a sick society.

Aragones, Juan Emilo. "Dos hermeticas piezas breves de H. Pinter." *La Estafeta Literaria,* No. 31 (Feb. 1967). In Spanish.

Arden, John. "The Caretaker." *New Theater Magazine,* No. 4 (July 1960), pp. 29–30.

Armstrong, William A., ed. *Experimental Drama.* London: Bell, 1963. A collection of lectures given at the University of London, including those by Esslin and Welland.

————. "Tradition and Innovation in the London Theatre, 1960–1961." *Modern Drama*, 4, No. 2 (Sept. 1961), 184–95.

Aronson, Steven M. L. "Pinter's 'Family' and Blood Knowledge." In Lahr, *A Casebook on Harold Pinter's The Homecoming*, pp. 67–86. The formal structure of *The Homecoming* is related to the sense of the family as a unit.

Ashmore, Jerome. "Interdisciplinary Roots of the Theatre of the Absurd." *Modern Drama*, 14, No. 1 (May 1971), 72–83. Pinter's three principal concerns are man's relationship to man, menace, and uncertainty.

Ashworth, Arthur. "New Theatre: Ionesco, Beckett, Pinter." *Southerly*, 22, No. 3 (1962), 145–52. A discussion of Pinter as a Kafkaesque compromise between the Theatre of the Absurd and realistic theatre in that his characters and situations are realistic but become "twisted askew" during the course of their confrontations.

Azarmi, Ahmad A. "The Theatre of the Absurd: A Study of Communication." Dissertation, U. S. International University, 1970.

Baker, William, and Stephen E. Tabachnick. *Harold Pinter*. Writers and Critics series. Edinburgh: Oliver and Boyd, 1973; rpt., New York: Barnes and Noble, 1973. In addition to examining Pinter's works through *Old Times* (emphasis on conflict—masculine vs. feminine, etc.) this study contains a chapter discussing Pinter's background, the modern British Jew from Hackney.

Banks-Smith, Nancy. "Television Is Not Only for Looking At." *Sun* (London), 21 Feb. 1967, p. 12. Review of the television version of *The Basement*.

Barnes, Clive. "Harold Pinter's Debt to James Joyce." *New York Times*, 25 July 1969, D, p. 8.

————. "A Mystery That Asks All the Questions." *Daily Express* (London), 9 March 1960, p. 17. Review of *The Dumb Waiter* and *The Room*.

————. "Stage: Caught in the Sway of a Sea-Changed Pinter." *New York Times*, 18 Oct. 1971, C, p. 8. An extremely laudatory review of *Old Times* as a memory play, mentioning similarities to James Joyce and Proust.

————. "Stage: Pinter's Small Talk of Reality." *New York Times*, 3 Aug. 1971, p. 43. A review of the Lincoln Center production of *Landscape* and *Silence* which sees Pinter's greatness as an "ability to see the world as it exists." However, the critic feels that these poetic plays, perhaps the author's best, suffer from a poor production—an opinion Pinter disputes (see Pinter, "Distressing").

————. "Theater: The Civilized Violence of Harold Pinter." *New York Times*, 16 Oct. 1968, p. 40. Review of *The Tea Party* and *The Basement*.

————. "The Theatre: Pinter's Birthday Party." *New York Times*, 4 Oct. 1967, p. 40. A favorable article calling *The Birthday Party* the newest good thing on Broadway. It mentions that the influence is obviously from Samuel Beckett and comments on the dialogue.

Bensky, Lawrence M. "Harold Pinter: An Interview." *Paris Review,* 10, No. 20 (Fall 1966), 12–37; rpt. in *Writers at Work: The Paris Review Interviews,* 3d series. New York: Viking, 1967. Pp. 347–68; rpt. in *The Playwrights Speak,* ed. Walter Wager. New York, 1967; rpt. in Arthur Ganz, *Pinter,* pp. 19–33. A highly informative and interesting interview in which Pinter talks about his background, his writing career, the influences on his writing, his concepts and techniques, and the writing process. The reprint in the *Writers at Work* series includes a manuscript page from *The Homecoming.*

———. "Pinter: Violence is Natural." *New York Times,* 1 Jan. 1967, p. 7. An interview about dramatic techniques.

Ben-Zvi, Linda. "The Devaluation of Language in Avant-Garde Drama." *Dissertation Abstracts International,* 33 (1973), 1158–59A (Oklahoma).

Berkowitz, Gerald M. "The Question of Identity in the Plays of Harold Pinter." Thesis, Columbia University, 1965. Limited because of the date of its composition.

Bernhard, F. J. "Beyond Realism: The Plays of Harold Pinter." *Modern Drama,* 8, No. 2 (Sept. 1965), 185–91. The poetic quality of Pinter's language and the techniques which make it suprarealistic are examined.

———. "English Theater 1963: In the Wake of the New Wave." *Books Abroad,* 38: 143–44. *The Caretaker* is seen as one of the landmarks in a revolution in the English theatre because it manages to break the conventions of form, yet does not descend to the inane. The article also considers *The Dwarfs* and *The Lover.*

Black, Peter. "TV." *Daily Mail* (London), 26 March 1965, p. 3. Review of the television production of *Tea Party.*

Black, Susan M. Play Reviews Section, *Theatre Arts,* 45 (Dec. 1961), 12. A critical review of *The Caretaker.*

Blau, Herbert. *The Impossible Theatre: A Manifesto.* New York: Macmillan, 1964. Pp. 254–56.

———. "Politics and the Theatre." *Wascana Review,* 2, No. 2 (1967), 5–25.

Bosworth, Patricia. "Why Doesn't He Write More?" *New York Times,* 27 October 1968, D, p. 3.

Boulton, James T. "Harold Pinter: *The Caretaker* and Other Plays." *Modern Drama,* 6, No. 2 (Sept. 1963), 131–40. An examination of themes (especially the terror of man's loneliness) and poetic methods of Pinter's work up to and including *The Caretaker,* with a comparison to Kafka.

Bovie, Palmer. "Seduction: The Amphitryon Theme from Plautus to Pinter." *Minnesota Review,* 7, Nos. 3–4 (1967), 304–13.

Bowen, John. "Accepting the Illusion." *Twentieth Century,* 169 (Feb. 1961), 153–65.

Boyum, Joy Gould, and Adrienne Scott. *Film as Film: Critical Responses to*

Film Art. Boston: Allyn and Bacon, 1971. Critical responses to film art, including six reviews of *Accident*.

Bray, J. J. "The Ham Funeral." *Meanjin*, 21 (March 1962), 32–34. Traces the influence of the Australian Patrick White in Pinter's work.

Brien, Alan. "Chelsea Beaujolais." *Spectator*, 6 May 1960, p. 661. *The Caretaker* presents a realistic picture of man in Hitchcockian terms.

———. "Communications." *Spectator*, 30 May 1958, p. 687. Again compares Pinter to Hitchcock, but this time sees *The Birthday Party* as a failure because of its overuse of reversed clichés and lack of humor (!).

———. "Pinter's First Play." *Sunday Telegraph* (London), 21 June 1964, p. 10. Review of *The Birthday Party* revival.

———. "The Guilty Seam." *Spectator*, 29 Jan. 1960, p. 138. Somewhere between Brecht and Chayefsky, Pinter's dramas of ritualism and manipulation remain "obstinately a-plicit (as opposed to 'explicit')."

Brigg, Peter A. "The Understanding and Uses of Time in the Plays of John Boynton Priestly, Samuel Beckett, and Harold Pinter." *Dissertation Abstracts International*, 32 (1972), 6964A (Toronto).

Brine, Adrian. "Something Blue." *Spectator*, 10 June 1960, p. 836. *The Caretaker* with its assertions about the nature of communication (lack of communication stifles, but actually communicating can lead to something worse) is a change from the earlier plays.

———. "In Search of a Hero." *Spectator*, 26 Feb. 1965, p. 386. Because of the functional non-functioning of dialogue in Pinter's plays, a new type of actor is needed to fulfill the demands of the roles.

———. "MacDavies Is No Clochard." *Drama*, 56 (Summer 1961), 35–37. Davies in *The Caretaker* is portrayed as a peculiarly English character, thus allowing only an inadequate transfer of the drama to other countries.

Brooks, Mary E. "The British Theatre of Metaphysical Despair." *Literature and Ideology*, 12: 49–58. Discusses *The Birthday Party* and Beckett.

Brown, John Russell. "Dialogue in Pinter and Others." *Critical Quarterly*, 7, No. 3 (Autumn 1965), 225–43. Pinter's dialogue, influenced by Beckett and Chekhov, lies behind his success. A study of the texture of that dialogue.

———. "Mr. Pinter's Shakespeare." *Critical Quarterly*, 5, No. 3 (Autumn 1963), 251–65; rpt. in *Essays in the Modern Drama*, ed. Morris Freedman. Boston, 1964. With Beckett, Ionesco, and Shakespeare, Pinter shares the slow exposure of character and motivation through seemingly meaningless repetitions, silences, insistences, and denials which imply the underlying context of the character's actions. See also Bert O. States (below).

———, ed. *Modern British Dramatists: A Collection of Critical Essays*. London, 1968; rpt. in Twentieth Century Views series. Englewood Cliffs,

New Jersey: Prentice Hall/Spectrum, 1968. A discussion of Pinter's work is included as part of this brief survey.

————. *Theatre Language*. New York: Taplinger, 1972. Includes: "Harold Pinter: Action and Control; The Homecoming and Other Plays," pp. 93–117; "Harold Pinter: Gestures, Spectacle and Performance; The Caretaker, The Dwarfs and Other Plays," pp. 55–92; and "Harold Pinter: The Birthday Party and Other Plays," pp. 15–54.

———— and Bernard Harris, eds. *Contemporary Theatre*. Stratford-on-Avon Studies, No. 4, London, 1962. Nine essays, including Leech's comparison of Pinter and Wesker.

Browne, E. Martin. "A Look Round the English Theatre, 1961." *Drama Survey*, 1, pp. 227–31.

B[rulez], R[aymond]. "Nieuwe Dramatick?" *Nieuw Vlaams Tijdschrift*, 18 (1965), 835–36.

Brustein, Robert. "The English Stage." *New Statesman*, 6 Aug. 1965, pp. 193–94; rpt. in J. R. Brown, *Modern British Dramatists*, pp. 164–70. A brief survey. Pinter "excludes statement from his work altogether."

————. "The English Stage." *Tulane Drama Review*, 10 (Spring 1966), 127–33.

————. "A Naturalism of the Grotesque." *New Republic*, 23 Oct. 1961, pp. 29–30; rpt. in *Seasons of Discontent: Dramatic Opinions, 1959–1965*. New York: Simon and Schuster, 1965. *The Caretaker* is about the "spiritual vacancy of modern life" and lack of communication.

————. *The Theater of Revolt: An Approach to the Modern Drama*. Boston: Atlantic/Little, Brown, 1962; rpt. London, 1965. A study of rebellion in the theatre in existential terms; Pinter's debt to Pirandello is cited.

————. *The Third Theatre*. New York: Knopf, 1969; rpt. New York: Simon and Schuster (Clarion), 1970. In his section on "Thoughts from Abroad" Brustein says he does not like *The Homecoming*, which he clearly did not understand.

Bryden, Ronald. "Atavism." *New Statesman*, 27 Sept. 1963, p. 420. Review of *The Dwarfs* and *The Lover*.

————. "A Stink of Pinter." *New Statesman*, 11 June 1965, p. 928. About Pinter's imagery.

————. "Pared to Privacy, Melting Into Silence." *Observer* (London), 6 July 1969, p. 22. Beckett's influence can be seen in *Landscape* and *Silence*.

————. "Pinter." *Observer* (London), 19 Feb. 1967.

————. "Pinter's New Pacemaker." *Observer* (London), 6 June 1971, p. 27. Review of *Old Times*.

————. "Three Men in a Room." *New Statesman*, 26 June 1964, p. 1004. The underlying theme of domination runs through Pinter's work. The plays present a self-contained world in which nothing important is said but everything reflects a battle for control over others.

Burkman, Katharine H. *The Dramatic World of Harold Pinter: Its Basis in Ritual*. Columbus: Ohio State University Press, 1971. Two kinds of ritual —everyday meaningless and meaningful sacrificial—are counterpointed. Draws upon Frazier's *The Golden Bough*. Interesting and valid to a point, but lacks unity.

———. "Pinter's *A Slight Ache* as Ritual." *Modern Drama*, 11 (Dec. 1968), 326–35.

Busch, Lloyd. "The Plot-Within-the-Plot: Harold Pinter's *The Caretaker*." Paper given at an S.A.A. Convention, 8 Dec. 1967, Los Angeles, Calif.

Cairns, D. A. "Batting for Pinter." *Times* (London), 7 June 1975, p. 13g. Correspondence regarding the names of the characters in *No Man's Land* —former cricket players.

Callen, A. "Comedy and Passion in the Plays of Harold Pinter." *Forum for Modern Language Studies*, 3, No. 3, 199–305.

Canaday, Nicholas, Jr. "Harold Pinter's 'Tea Party': Seeing and Not Seeing." *Studies in Short Fiction*, 6: 580–85.

Capone, Giovanna. *Drammi per voci: Dylan Thomas, Samuel Beckett, Harold Pinter*. Bologna, 1967. In Italian.

Carat, J. "Harold Pinter et W. Gombrowicz." *Preuves*, No. 177 (Nov. 1965), 75–77. In French.

Case, L. L. "A Parody on Harold Pinter's Style of Drama." *New York Times*, 16 May 1965, sec. 2, p. 6.

Chapman, John. " 'The Birthday Party,' a Whatsit by Pinter." *New York Daily News*, 4 Oct. 1967, p. 86. Review of the New York production of *The Birthday Party*.

———. "Donald Pleasence Superb Actor and 'Caretaker' Splendid Play." *New York Daily News*, 5 Oct. 1961, p. 73. Review of *The Caretaker*.

Chiari, Joseph. *Landmarks of Contemporary Drama*. London, 1965. Expresses a high opinion of Pinter's ability to create jigsaw puzzle plays as excellent as *The Caretaker*.

Clurman, Harold. *The Naked Image: Observations on the Modern Theatre*. New York: Macmillan, 1966. Pp. 105–14. Includes discussion of *The Caretaker, The Collection, The Dumb Waiter, The Lover, The Room*, and *A Slight Ache*.

———. "Theatre." *Nation*, 28 Dec. 1964, pp. 522–24. Review of *A Slight Ache* and *The Room*.

———. "Theatre." *Nation*, 23 October 1967, pp. 412–14. Review of the New York production of *The Birthday Party*.

———. "Theatre." *Nation*, 21 Oct. 1961, p. 276. A favorable review of *The Caretaker*.

Cocks, Jay. "Fire and Ice." *Time*, 17 Dec. 1973, no. 25, p. 70. An extremely flattering review of the film version of *The Homecoming*, especially of

Pinter's writing: "probably the best scenario writing now being done in English."

——. "Two by Losey." *Time*, 9 Aug. 1971, p. 63. A favorable review of *The Go-Between*.

Cohen, Mark. "The Plays of Harold Pinter." *Jewish Quarterly*, 8 (Summer 1961), 21–22. Mentions Pinter's cliché-filled, repetitious dialogue and themes of domination, menace, security, and the malignant organization.

Cohen, Marshall. "Theater 67." *Partisan Review*, 34, No. 3 (Summer 1967), 436–44.

Cohn, Ruby. "The Absurdly Absurd: Avatars of Godot." *Comparative Literature Studies*, 2 (1965), 233–40. As examples of the Absurd, both *Waiting for Godot* and *The Dumb Waiter* exemplify the Absurd doctrine of man's awareness of his place in the universe through the absurdity of the play's form.

——. *Currents in Contemporary Drama.* Bloomington: Indiana Univ. Press, 1969. Includes an evaluation of Pinter. See pp. 15–17, 78–81, 177–81.

——. "Latter Day Pinter." *Drama Survey*, 3, No. 3 (Winter 1964), 366–77. Pinter's career to this point displays a concern with appearance vs. reality, but it also shows technical progress.

——. "The World of Harold Pinter." *Tulane Drama Review*, 6 (March 1962), 55–68. "Man vs. the System" with a "central victim-villain" conflict is proposed as Pinter's main theme as revealed through the cumulative use of symbols and dialogue.

—— and Bernard Dukore. *Twentieth Century Drama: England, Ireland, the United States.* New York: Random House, 1966.

Coleman, John. "The Road to Sidcup." *New Statesman*, 13 March 1964, p. 423. Comments on Pinter's ability to reproduce everyday language and man's propensity to degrade others in order to upgrade himself.

Conlon, Patrick O. "Social Commentary in Contemporary Great Britain as Reflected in the Plays of John Osborne, Harold Pinter, and Arnold Wesker." Diss., Northwestern, 1966.

Cook, David. "Of the Strong Breed." *Transition*, 3 (1964), 38–40. Wole Soyinka's portrayal of Nigeria is in part influenced by Pinter.

—— and Harold F. Brooks. "A Room with Three Views: Harold Pinter's *The Caretaker*." *Komos*, 1 (June 1967), 62–69.

Craig, H. A. L. "Poetry in the Theatre." *New Statesman*, 59 (12 Nov. 1960), pp. 734, 736. A discussion about the lack of verse drama in the contemporary theatre which comes to the conclusion that Pinter is one of the few artists who can still create a "mood, a pervasion of poetry."

——. "The Sound of the Words." *New Statesman*, 27 Jan. 1961, pp. 152–53. Review of the original stage production of *A Slight Ache*.

Crist, Judith. "The Agony Beneath the Skin Revealed with Surgical Skill." *New York World Journal Tribune*, 18 April 1967; rpt. in Boyum and Scott, *Film as Film*, pp. 29–31. A review of the film *Accident*, mentioning Pinter's use of language and the excellence and importance of the dialogue.

————. "Movie Dims Stage's Magic." *New York Herald Tribune*, 21 Jan. 1964, p. 12. Review of the film version of *The Caretaker*.

————. "A Mystery: Pinter on Pinter." *Look*, 24 Dec. 1968, p. 77. An interview.

Croyden, Margaret. "Pinter's Hideous Comedy." In Lahr, *A Casebook on Harold Pinter's The Homecoming*, pp. 45–56. *The Homecoming* is a combination of sexual ritual and comedy of manners in a modern form.

Curley, Daniel. "A Night in the Fun House." *Pinter's Optics*, Midwest Monographs, 1st series, No. 1 (1967), Urbana, Ill.: Depot Press, 1–2.

Cushman, Robert. "Mr. Pinter's Spoonerisms." *Observer Review*, 27 April 1975, p. 32. Review of *No Man's Land* which compares Spooner to Davies in *The Caretaker* and comments on the language of the play.

Darlington, W. A. "Enjoyable Pinter." *Daily Telegraph* (London), 19 June 1964, p. 18. Review of *The Birthday Party* revival.

————. "Mad Meg and Lodger. Play Revels in Obscurity." *Daily Telegraph* (London), 20 May 1958, p. 10. Review of the first run of *The Birthday Party*.

————. "Pinter's Play's Obscurity." *Daily Telegraph* (London), 19 Jan. 1961, p. 14. Review of the original stage production of *A Slight Ache*.

Davison, Peter. "Contemporary Drama and Popular Dramatic Forms." In *Aspects of Drama and the Theatre*. Sydney: Sydney Univ. Press, 1965. The Kathleen Robinson lecture delivered at the University of Sydney, 6 Nov. 1963, includes a discussion of language in Pinter's plays. See pp. 143–97.

Dawick, John D. "Punctuation and Patterning in *The Homecoming*." *Modern Drama*, 14 (May 1971), 37–46. Punctuation is a clue to meaning and the communication of that meaning as it cues the actors.

Dean, Michael. "Late Night Line-Up." *Listener*, 6 March 1969. An interview.

De Nitto, Dennis, and William Herman. *Film and the Critical Eye*. Riverside, N.J.: Macmillan, 1975. Includes reviews of the films *The Servant* and *The Caretaker*.

Dent, Alan. "Mr. Pinter Misses His Target." *News Chronicle* (London), 20 May 1958, p. 5. Review of the first run of *The Birthday Party*.

Diack, Phil. "A Stage Flop Is Big Hit." *Daily Herald* (London), 23 March 1960, p. 5. Review of the British television production of *The Birthday Party*.

Dias, Earl J. "The Enigmatic World of Harold Pinter." *Drama Critique*, 2 (1968), 119–24.

Dick, Kay. "Mr. Pinter and the Fearful Matter." *Texas Quarterly*, 4 (Autumn 1961), 257–65. Stresses Pinter's concern with communication.

Didion, Joan. "The Guest 'Narcoleptic Dialogue.'" *Vogue*, 1 March 1964, p. 57. Review of the film version of *The Caretaker*.

Dillon, Perry C. "The Characteristics of the French Theater of the Absurd in the Plays of Edward Albee and Harold Pinter." Diss., Univ. of Arkansas, 1968.

Dohmen, William F. "Notes on the New York Stage, 1966–67." *Dissertation Abstracts International*, 34 (1974), 5165A.

Donahue, Francis. "Anatomy of the 'New Drama.'" *Southwest Review*, 56: 269–77.

Donoghue, Denis. "London Letter: Moral West End." *Hudson Review*, 14 (Spring 1961), 93–103. Emphasizes the triangular relationships between characters in *The Room, The Dumb Waiter, The Birthday Party*, and *The Caretaker*. The general conclusion is not flattering.

Dorfman, Ariel. *El absurdo entre cuatro paredes: el teatro de Harold Pinter.* Santiago, Chile: Editorial Universitaria, S.A., 1968. Mainly a summary of other critics. Several pages are missing because of error in the printing.

Douglas, Reid. "The Failure of English Realism." *Tulane Drama Review*, 7, No. 2 (Winter 1962), 180–83.

Downer, Alan S. "Doctor's Dilemma: Notes on the New York Theatre 1966–67." *Quarterly Journal of Speech*, 53, No. 3 (1967), 213–23.

———. "Experience of Heroes: Notes on the New York Theatre." *Quarterly Journal of Speech*, 48 (Oct. 1962), 261–70. Each of the three men in *The Caretaker* deserves sympathy as an example of the character "sustained by a dream that stands between him and despair."

———. "Old, New, Borrowed, and (a Trifle) Blue: Notes on the New York Theatre 1967–68." *Quarterly Journal of Speech*, 54 (Oct. 1968), 199–211. Review of the New York production of *The Birthday Party*.

Drake, Carol Dixon. "Harold Pinter and the Problem of Verification." Thesis, Univ. of Southern California, 1964. A short study of Pinter's concept of verification as delineated in the Royal Court program notes for the performance of *The Room* and *The Dumb Waiter* and expressed in his dramas to this date.

Driver, Tom F. "On the Way to Madness." *Christian Century*, 22 Nov. 1961, pp. 1403–6. A discussion of nihilism in *The Caretaker*.

Dukore, Bernard F. "The Royal Shakespeare Company." *Educational Theatre Journal*, 22 (Dec. 1970), 412–14. Review of *Landscape* and *Silence*.

———. "The Theater of Harold Pinter." *Tulane Drama Review*, 6, No. 3 (March 1962), 43–54. Pinter's theatre is seen as "a picture of contemporary man beaten down by the social forces around him," partly based on "man's failure to communicate with other men."

———. "A Woman's Place." *Quarterly Journal of Speech*, 52, No. 3 (1967),

237–41; rpt. in Lahr, *A Casebook on Harold Pinter's The Homecoming*, pp. 109–16. Ruth's role in *The Homecoming* is described as a catalyst which brings out the animal instincts for a mating ritual among the members of the family.

Dunne, J. G. "Hauntingly Simple Denial." *National Review*, 23 Dec. 1961, p. 424. Dunne states that Pinter is "a master of vernacular" and the power of *The Caretaker* comes from its disturbing and hauntingly simple denial of Donne's line, "no man is an island."

Eder, Richard. "Losey to Film 'Remembrance.'" *New York Times*, 14 Feb. 1973, p. 24. Director Joseph Losey, who has worked with Pinter on several films, discusses Pinter's problems in transforming Proust's *A la recherche du temps perdu* from novel into screenplay, his own problems in preparing to film the work, and the keys to understanding the piece.

Eigo, J. "Pinter's Landscape." *Modern Drama*, 16 (Sept. 1973), 179–83.

Ekbom, Torston. "Pa jackt efter en identitet: Harold Pinter och den absurda traditionen." *Bonniers Literara Magasin*, 31 (1962), 809–14.

Elliott, Susan Merritt. "Fantasy Behind Play: A Study of Emotional Responses to Harold Pinter's 'The Birthday Party,' 'The Caretaker,' and 'The Homecoming,'" *Dissertation Abstracts International*, 34 (1974), 5963A.

English, Alan C. "A Descriptive Analysis of Harold Pinter's Use of Comic Elements in His Stage Plays." *Dissertation Abstracts International*, 30 (1970), 4597A–98A.

Esslin, Martin. *Absurd Drama*. London: Penguin, 1965. Discusses Pinter's plays and techniques on an individual basis and places the dramatist in the tradition of the Theatre of the Absurd.

———. "Godot and His Children: The Theater of Samuel Beckett and Harold Pinter." In Armstrong, *Experimental Drama*, pp. 128–46; rpt. in J. R. Brown, *Modern British Dramatists*, pp. 58–70. Compares Beckett and Pinter, especially in the area of language, which he finds most realistic in the latter. Decides that Pinter does not belong to the "kitchen sink" school of dramatists in his almost allegorical presentation of the human condition.

———. *Harold Pinter*. Friedrichs Dramatiker des Welttheaters, No. 38. Velber bei Hannover: Friedrich Verlag, 1967. In German. Essentially *The Peopled Wound*.

———. "Harold Pinter, un dramaturge anglais de l'absurde." *Preuves*, No. 151 (1964), 45–54. In French.

———. "The Homecoming: An Interpretation." In Lahr, *A Casebook on Harold Pinter's The Homecoming*, pp. 1–8. Repeats Esslin's earlier conclusions about *The Homecoming*.

———. *The Peopled Wound: The Work of Harold Pinter*. New York: Doubleday/Anchor, 1970; rpt. as *Pinter: A Study of His Plays*. London, 1973.

Information (some from Pinter) and background material not available elsewhere make this book both interesting and important, although the mixture of psychological and existential interpretations of the plays is not always satisfactory. Contains an excellent section on Pinter's use of language and silence.

————. "Pinter and the Absurd." *Twentieth Century*, 169 (Feb. 1961), 176–85. Pinter's poetic use of dialogue is the factor which successfully creates an Absurd realism.

————. "Pinter Translated." *Encounter*, 30, No. 3 (March 1968), 45–47.

————. *Reflections: Essays on Modern Theater.* New York: Doubleday/Anchor, 1971. Includes occasional references to Pinter in an overall view of modern theatre.

————. *The Theatre of the Absurd.* New York: Doubleday/Anchor, 1961; rev. ed., New York, 1969; London: Eyre and Spottiswoode, 1965; rev. ed., London, 1968; rev. 1974. Summarizes plays and deals with themes (menace) and techniques in general.

Evans, Gareth Lloyd. "Pinter's Black Magic." *Guardian*, 30 Sept. 1965, p. 8.

Farrington, Conor. "The Language of Drama." *Tulane Drama Review*, 5 (Dec. 1960), 65–72.

Feiffer, Jules. "What's Pinter Up To?" *New York Times*, 5 Feb. 1967, D, p. 3. The "seemingly innocent Teddy" is proposed as the "prime manipulator" in *The Homecoming*.

Feldstein, Elayne Phyllis. "The Evolution of the Characteristics of Harold Pinter." *Dissertation Abstracts International*, 34 (1974), 7748A.

————. "Radio Notes." *Observer* (London), 11 Dec. 1960, p. 26. Review of the radio version of *The Dwarfs*.

Feynman, Alberta E. "The Fetal Quality of 'Character' in Plays of the Absurd." *Modern Drama*, 9 (May 1965), 18–25. The characters in Pinter's plays are regarded as too nebulous to be true characters.

Fields, Suzanne. "Levels of Meaning in Structural Patterns of Allegory and Realism in Selected Plays of Harold Pinter." *Dissertation Abstracts International*, 32 (1972), 2087A (Catholic Univ.).

"Finger Exercise in Dread." *Time*, 18 Dec. 1964, p. 86. Review of *A Slight Ache* and *The Room*.

"First Play by Mr. Pinter. The Room Excusably Derivative." *Times* (London), 9 March 1960, p. 4. Review of *The Dumb Waiter* and *The Room*.

Fitzgerald, Marion. "Playwriting Is Agony, Says Hugh Leonard." *Irish Digest*, 79 (Jan. 1964), 34–36.

Fjelde, Rolf. "Plotting Pinter's Progress." In Lahr, *A Casebook on Harold Pinter's The Homecoming*, pp. 87–108. Tries to detail *The Birthday Party*, *The Caretaker*, and *The Homecoming* as steps in Pinter's development as seen through his imagery.

Flakes, Nanette Sue B. "Aesthetics in Modern Play Direction: Nonrealistic Drama from Pirandello to Pinter." *Dissertation Abstracts International*, 33 (1973), 896A.

Fletcher, John. "Confrontations: I. Harold Pinter, Rolland Dubillard and Eugene Ionesco." *Caliban*, 3, No. 2 (1967), 149–52.

Franzblau, Abraham N. "A Psychiatrist Looks at The Homecoming." *Saturday Review*, 8 Sept. 1967, p. 58. A psychological interpretation of *The Homecoming* (as a *ménage à trois*) which does not seem to be based on either the characters or the action of the drama.

Fraser, George Sutherland. *The Modern Writer and His World*. Revised edition. Baltimore: Penguin Books, 1964. See pp. 238–43 for discussion of Pinter.

Free, William J. "Treatment of Character in Harold Pinter's *The Homecoming*." *South Atlantic Bulletin*, 34, No. 4, 1–5.

Freedman, Morris, ed. *Essays in Modern Drama*. Boston: D. C. Heath, 1964. Includes J. R. Brown's "Mr. Pinter's Shakespeare."

———. *The Moral Impulse*. Carbondale and Edwardsville: Southern Illinois Univ. Press, 1967. See pp. 124–26.

Fricker, Robert. *Das moderne englische Drama*. Göttingen, 1964. In German.

Frisch, Jack E. "Ironic Theater: Techniques of Irony in the Plays of Samuel Beckett, Eugene Ionesco, Harold Pinter and Jean Genet." Diss., Univ. of Wisconsin, 1965. Irony in the modern theatre is directed at the audience.

Gale, Steven H. "The Films of Harold Pinter." Paper delivered at a meeting of the College English Association, San Juan, Puerto Rico, April 1973. A discussion of Pinter's techniques, with special attention to the differences between written versions and his screen adaptations.

———. *Harold Pinter: A Reference Guide*. Boston: G. K. Hall [1977].

———. "Harold Pinter: An Annotated Bibliography 1957–1971." *Bulletin of Bibliography*, 29, No. 2 (April–June 1972), 43–65. The most comprehensive bibliography published up to this time.

———. "Harold Pinter: An Overview." *Literary Half Yearly*, Jan. 1976.

———. "Harold Pinter: dramatico moderno." *Rio Piedras*, 2, No. 2 (Fall 1973). In Spanish. An overview of Pinter's place in the modern theatre, stating that Pinter cannot be categorized, as he borrows techniques from the Theatre of the Absurd and other contemporary schools of writing which best fit his talents and dramatic needs.

———. *Harold Pinter's The Birthday Party and Other Works*. New York: Simon and Schuster's Monarch Notes, 1972. An in-depth study guide to *The Birthday Party*, providing background material and an analysis of the play, as well as placing it in Pinter's canon.

———. *Harold Pinter's The Caretaker and Other Works*. New York: Simon and Schuster's Monarch Notes, in preparation. A study guide to *The*

Caretaker, providing background material and an analysis of the play, as well as placing it in Pinter's canon.

―――. *Harold Pinter's The Homecoming and Other Works*. New York: Simon and Schuster's Monarch Notes, 1971. An in-depth study guide to *The Homecoming*, providing background material and an analysis of the play, as well as placing it in Pinter's canon.

―――. "Thematic Change in the Stage Plays of Harold Pinter, 1957–1967." Diss., Univ. of Southern California, 1970. A study of Pinter's first ten years of playwrighting, tracing the movement from the simple exposure of the existence of menace and its disintegrating effect on the individual in the "comedies of menace" to the later plays which examine the source of menace (individual psychological needs) and the desperate attempts of the characters to fulfill their needs.

―――. "The Weasel Under the Cocktail Cabinet." Paper given at the College English Association, 18 April 1971, San Juan, Puerto Rico.

Gallagher, Kent G. "Harold Pinter's Dramaturgy." *Quarterly Journal of Speech*, 52, No. 3 (Oct. 1966), 242–48. The language of *The Caretaker* is an excellent example of Pinter's influence and position in the Theatre of the Absurd.

Ganz, Arthur. "A Clue to the Pinter Puzzle: The Triple Self in *The Homecoming*." *Educational Theatre Journal*, 21 (1969), 180–87.

―――. *Pinter*. Englewood Cliffs: Prentice Hall, 1972. A collection of critical essays by Lawrence Bensky ("Harold Pinter: An Interview"), Martin Esslin ("Language and Silence"), John Lahr ("Pinter and Chekhov: The Bond of Naturalism"), Valerie Minogue ("Taking Care of the Caretaker"), Ruby Cohn ("The World of Harold Pinter"), James T. Boulton ("Harold Pinter: *The Caretaker* and Other Plays"), John Russell Taylor ("A Room and Some Views: Harold Pinter"), John Pesta ("Pinter's Usurpers"), R. F. Storch ("Harold Pinter's Happy Families"), and Bert O. States ("Pinter's *Homecoming*: The Shock of Nonrecognition"). Introduced by Ganz, this volume is in the Twentieth Century Views series. All of the essays are available elsewhere.

Garber, Stephen. "Open and Closed Sequences in the Plays of Harold Pinter." *Dissertation Abstracts International*, 33 (1973), 312A.

Gascoigne, Bamber. "Cult of Personality." *Spectator*, 29 June 1962, pp. 857–58. Considers Strindberg's influence on Pinter. A review of *The Collection*.

―――. "Love in the Afternoon." *Observer* (London), 22 Sept. 1963, p. 26. Review of *The Dwarfs* and *The Lover*.

―――. "Pinter Makes It All Too Plain." *Observer* (London), 21 June 1964, p. 24. Review of *The Birthday Party* revival.

―――. "Pulling the Wool." *Spectator*, 27 Jan. 1961, p. 106. Review of original stage production of *A Slight Ache*.

Gassner, John. "Broadway in Review." *Educational Theatre Journal*, 13 (Dec. 1961), 289–97. Discussion of the use of allegory and symbol in *The Caretaker*.

————. *Dramatic Soundings*. New York: Crown, 1968. Includes "Foray Into the Absurd," pp. 503–7, which deals with *The Caretaker*. Rpt. of "Broadway in Review."

————. "Osborne and Pinter." In *The World of Contemporary Drama*. New York: American Library Association, 1965. See pp. 21–23.

Giannetti, Louis D. "The Drama of the Welfare State." Diss., Univ. of Iowa, 1967.

Gill, Brendan. "Inside the Redoubt." *New Yorker*, 15 April 1967; rpt. in Boyum and Scott, *Film as Film: Critical Responses to Film Art*, pp. 36–37. A review of the film *Accident* and Pinter's belief that "evil is an entity and that man is capable of being invaded and possessed by it."

Gillen, Francis. "'. . . Apart from the Known and the Unknown': The Unreconciled World of Harold Pinter's Characters." *Arizona Quarterly*, 26: 17–24. The major characters in *Tea Party* and *The Homecoming* are involved in the "known," physical world which they can touch, and threatened by the "unknown" world of abstractions which they can neither understand nor control.

Gilliatt, Penelope. "Achievement from a Tight-Rope." *Observer* (London), 6 June 1965, p. 25. Review of *The Homecoming*.

————. "Comedy of Menace." *Queen*, 25 May 1960, pp. 21–22. Review of *The Caretaker*.

————. "The Conversion of a Tramp." *Observer* (London), 15 March 1964, p. 24. Review of the film version of *The Caretaker*.

————. *Unholy Fools: Wits, Comics, Disturbers of the Peace*. New York: Viking, 1973. Discusses Pinter, pp. 109–12.

Gilman, Richard. *Common and Uncommon Masks*. New York: Random House, 1971. Includes discussions of *The Birthday Party*, *The Caretaker*, *The Collection*, *The Dumb Waiter*, *The Homecoming* and *The Lover*, pp. 93–113.

————. "The Pinter Puzzle." *New York Times*, 22 Jan. 1967, Sec. 2, p. 1.

————. "Pre-Vintage Pinter." *New Republic*, 21 Oct. 1968, pp. 36–38. Review of the New York production of *The Birthday Party*.

Glover, William. "Busy Playwright Lost in Creative Desert." *Durham* (N.C.) *Herald*, 21 Oct. 1973. An Associated Press interview in which Pinter discusses his feelings about his writing, at the age of 43: "my juices . . . seem to have dried up." Perhaps he has become "arid" because "I feel when writing . . . that I'm freeing myself from what I've written before. That I'm getting freer. You just end up in another trap afterwards." Though he is fond of what he has written, he would be "more economic" and "spare" if he were rewriting his plays.

————. "Pinter's Plays Reflect His Cool." *Los Angeles Times*, 14 May 1967, Calendar Section. Comments by Pinter about various plays included.

Goldman, William. *The Season: A Candid Look at Broadway*. New York: Bantam, 1970. A brilliant display of reverse snobbism. Rejects Pinter, Miller, Albee, Williams, Osborne, Arden, and Inge as being less valuable than Neil Simon because there have been more Broadway performances of Simon plays than of all these other playwrights combined (which tells us something about Broadway too). Pinter is singled out, partly because he is English, as both representative and epitome of dramatists who write meaningfully, and anti-intellectual Goldman includes amusing *parodies* of Pinter and Kenneth Tynan to prove his point.

Goldstein, Ruth M. *A Discussion Guide for the Film Pinter People*. New York: Grove Press, n.d. A twenty-three-page pamphlet which is obviously meant to advertise Grove Press products, though the guide proposes some interesting questions to be used in connection with the film (some of the questions relating techniques and concepts from the sketches to other works).

Goldstone, Herbert. "Not so Puzzling Pinter: *The Homecoming*." *Theatre Annual*, 25 (1969), 20–27. *The Homecoming* contrasts male and female attitudes toward sexuality.

Goodman, Florence. "Pinter's *The Caretaker*: The Lower Depths Descended." *Midwest Quarterly*, 5, No. 1 (Winter 1964), 117–26. Pinter as an Absurdist stresses that man's hellish condition is a result of his own humanity.

Gordon, Lois G. "Harold Pinter: Past and Present." *Kansas Quarterly*, 3, No. 2 (Spring 1971), 89–99. Pinter's characters cope with "the ordeal of ordinary experience" by attempting "the games that people play" or by abandoning themselves "to the world of fantasy and silence."

————. "Pigeonholing Pinter: A Bibliography." *Theatre Documentation*, 1, No. 1 (1968), 3–20. A fairly thorough annotated bibliography through mid-1967.

————. *Stratagems to Uncover Nakedness: The Dramas of Harold Pinter*. Columbia: Univ. of Missouri Press, 1968. Role playing, sex, etc., in Pinter's work are viewed from a Freudian viewpoint.

Gottfried, Martin. *Opening Nights*. New York, 1970. Includes a discussion of Beckett's influence on Pinter.

————. " 'The Birthday Party.' " *Women's Wear Daily*, 4 Oct. 1967, p. 44. Review of the New York production of *The Birthday Party*.

————. " 'The Lover' and 'Play.' " *Women's Wear Daily*, 6 Jan. 1964, p. 32. Review.

————. " 'The Room'—'A Slight Ache.' " *Women's Wear Daily*, 10 Dec. 1964, p. 48. Review.

————. *A Theatre Divided: The Postwar American Stage*. Boston: Little,

Brown, 1969. Examines the American theatre as a contrast between "left" (new, innovative, not seeking answers) and the "right" (establishment, demanding answers). Includes a section on Pinter as an international writer with "left" ideas expressed through acceptable "right" modes.

Gray, Wallace. "The Uses of Incongruity." *Commonweal*, 15 (Dec. 1963), 343–47. Characteristic of the Absurdists, Pinter utilizes the three kinds of incongruity ("rational and meaningful, irrational and meaningless, and irrational and apparently meaningless") to develop both the meaning and humor in his plays.

Griffiths, Gareth. "New Lines: English Theatre in the Sixties and After." *Kansas Quarterly*, 3, No. 2: 77–78.

Gross, John. "Amazing Reductions." *Encounter*, 23 (Sept. 1964), 50–52. Pinter's poetic drama is revitalizing the English theatre. Discusses *The Birthday Party*.

Guarino, Ann. "Few Happy Returns in Enigmatic 'Party.'" *New York Daily News*, 10 Dec. 1968. Review of the film version of *The Birthday Party*.

Guernsey, Otis L., Jr. *The Best Plays of 1964–1965*. New York, 1965. Pinter's plays on Broadway.

——. *The Best Plays of 1966–1967*. New York, 1967. Pinter's plays on Broadway.

Gussow, Mel. "A Conversation (Pause) with Harold Pinter." *New York Times Magazine*, 5 Dec. 1971, pp. 42 ff. An interview of interest as it deals with Pinter's latest period of creativity, beginning with a focus on *Old Times* and involving some insights into the dramatist's creative process (partially as related to his personal interests, etc.).

Habicht, Werner. "Der Dialog und das Schweigen im 'Theater des Absurden.'" *Die Neueren Sprachen*, 1967. In German.

——. "Theater der Sprache: Bemerkungen zu einigen englischen Dramen der Gegenwart." *Die Neueren Sprachen*, July 1963. In German.

Hafley, James. "The Human Image in Contemporary Art." *Kerygma*, 3 (Summer 1963), 23–24. A comparison of themes in the Theatre of the Absurd and Abstract Expressionism in art.

Hall, Rodney. "Theater in London." *Westerly*, No. 3 (Oct. 1963), 57–60. *The Birthday Party* is found to contain both the strengths and the weaknesses of serious English drama.

Hall, Stuart. "Home Sweet Home." *Encore*, 12 (July–Aug. 1965), 30–34. Review of *The Homecoming*.

Halliwell, Leslie. *The Filmgoer's Companion*. New York: Equinox, 1971. Discusses *The Pumpkin Eater*, p. 792.

Halton, Kathleen. "Pinter." *Vogue*, 150 (1 Oct. 1967), 194–95. Includes useful background material and quotations by Pinter.

Hancock, Jim R. "The Use of Time by Absurdist Playwrights: Beckett,

Ionesco, Genet, and Pinter." *Dissertation Abstracts International*, 33 (1973), 5876A.

Hare, Carl. "Creativity and Commitment in the Contemporary British Theatre." *Humanities Association Bulletin*, 16 (Spring 1965), 21–28.

Hayman, Ronald. *Harold Pinter*. Contemporary Playwrights series. London: Heinemann Educational Books, 1968; rpt. New York: Frederick Ungar. Very limited; serves only as a brief introduction.

Hays, H. R. "Transcending Naturalism." *Modern Drama*, 4 (May 1962), 27–36. The realism of Pinter's work covers the chaos which exists underneath.

Heilman, Robert B. "Demonic Strategies: *The Birthday Party* and *The Firebugs*." In *Sense and Sensibility in Twentieth-Century Writing: A Gathering in Memory of William Van O'Connor*, edited by Brom Weber. Carbondale: Southern Ill. Univ. Press, 1970. Pp. 57–74.

Henry, Patrick. "Acting the Absurd." *Drama Critique*, 6 (Winter 1963), 9–19. The actor's approach to performing a piece by Pinter.

Herin, Miriam M. "An Analysis of Harold Pinter's Use of Language as Seen in 'The Birthday Party,' 'The Caretaker,' 'The Homecoming,' and 'Old Times.'" *Dissertation Abstracts International*, 33 (1973), 1913A.

Hewes, Henry, ed. *The Best Plays of 1961–62*. New York and Toronto, 1962.

———. *The Best Plays of 1962–63*. New York and Toronto, 1963.

———. "Disobedience, Civil and Uncivil." *Saturday Review*, 28 Oct. 1967, pp. 46–47. Review of the New York production of *The Birthday Party*.

———. "Like Birthday Warmed Over." *Saturday Review*, 21 Oct. 1967, p. 50. Review of the New York production of *The Birthday Party*.

———. "Matched Pairs." *Saturday Review*, 26 Dec. 1964, p. 33. Review of *A Slight Ache* and *The Room*.

———. "Nothing Up the Sleeve." *Saturday Review*, 21 Oct. 1961, p. 34. Hewes feels there is no hidden meaning to be found in *The Caretaker*.

———. "Probing Pinter's Play." *Saturday Review*, 50 (8 April 1967), 56. An invaluable look at *The Homecoming* with comments by Pinter which are extremely important in understanding the play.

———. "Winter Pinter." *Saturday Review*, 15 Dec. 1962, p. 30. Review of *The Dumb Waiter* and *The Collection*.

Higgins, David M. "Existential Valuation in Five Contemporary Plays." *Dissertation Abstracts International*, 32 (1972), 4612A. Includes a discussion of *The Homecoming*.

Hilsky, Martin. "The Two Worlds of Harold Pinter's Plays." *Acta Universitatis Carolinae. Philologica* 3 (1969). *Prague Studies in English*, 13. Prague: Univ. Karlova, 1969. Pp. 109–15.

Hinchcliffe, Arnold P. *The Absurd*. London: Methuen, 1969. The Critical Idiom Series, Vol. V.

———. *Harold Pinter*. Twayne's English Authors series. New York: Twayne,

1967. Traces Pinter's development, concentrating on the meaning of individual plays and the use of language. Although there are some holes, it is the most complete study prior to Esslin's. Includes first printing of the revue sketch, "Special Offer."

——. "Mr. Pinter's Belinda." *Modern Drama*, Sept. 1968, pp. 173–79.

Hobson, Harold. "The Arts in Form Again." *Sunday Times* (London), 22 Jan. 1961, p. 33. Review of the original stage production of *A Slight Ache*.

——. "The Dumb Waiter. The Room." *Sunday Times* (London), 13 March, 1960, p. 25. Review.

——. "The Importance of Fantasy." *Sunday Times* (London), 22 Sept. 1963, p. 33. Review of *The Dwarfs* and *The Lover*.

——. "Life Outside London." *Sunday Times* (London), 15 June 1958, p. 11. Review of the first run of *The Birthday Party*.

——. "Old Times." *Sunday Times* (London), 6 June 1971, p. 52. Review of the play.

——. "Paradise Lost." *Sunday Times* (London), 6 July 1969. A review dealing with the theme of memory in *Landscape* and *Silence*.

——. "The Screw Turns Again." *Sunday Times* (London), 25 May 1958, p. 11. Review of the first run of *The Birthday Party*.

Hoefer, Jacqueline. "Pinter and Whiting: Two Attitudes Towards the Alienated Artist." *Modern Drama*, 4, No. 4 (Feb. 1962), 402–8. A comparison of *The Birthday Party* and Whiting's *Saint's Day* which examines the artist-vs.-society theme, concluding that where society is the victim in Whiting's drama, it becomes the villain in Pinter's.

Hollis, James R. *Harold Pinter: The Poetics of Silence.* Crosscurrents/Modern Critiques series. Carbondale: Southern Ill. Univ. Press, 1970. Another "introduction" volume mostly devoted to summaries of plot and interpretations dealing with the "linguistic and metaphoric patterns of the major plays," as well as a study of alienation and a need for but denial of transcendental experience. Purports to focus on Pinter's "relationship to and utilization of language."

Hopper, Stanley Romaine. "Irony—The Paths of the Middle." *Crosscurrents*, Winter 1962, pp. 31–40.

Houghton, Norris. *The Exploding Stage: An Introduction to Twentieth-Century Drama.* New York: Delta, 1971. A two-page summary of critical opinions regarding Pinter's work is included. Houghton thinks that *The Birthday Party* is Pinter's best play and that Pinter's dramas are fairly meaningless, though interesting in terms of technique.

Hughes, Catharine. "Broadway and The British." *Catholic World*, 212: 313–15.

——. "Pinter Is as Pinter Does." *Catholic World*, 210: 124–26.

Hunt, Joseph A. "Interaction Process Analysis of Harold Pinter's *The Home-*

coming: Toward a Phenomenological Criticism of Drama." *Dissertation Abstracts International*, 32 (1972), 4159A (New Mexico).

Hutchings, Patrick. "The Humanism of a Dumbwaiter." *Westerly*, No. 1 (1963), 56–63. A study of *The Dumb Waiter* as a play concerning alienation which is expressed in terms of a "farcical inconsequential, nightmarish" plot and dramatic enigmas.

Ibsen, Elizabeth. *Blind Man's Buff*. Diss., Universitetsbiblioteket, Bergen, 1969. Studies the theme of isolation in *The Room*, *The Birthday Party*, *The Dumb Waiter*, and *The Caretaker*.

Japa. "The Birthday Party." *Variety*, 18 Dec. 1968, p. 26. Review of the film version of *The Birthday Party*.

Jennings, Ann S. "The Reactions of London's Drama Critics to Certain Plays by Ibsen, H. Pinter, and E. Bond." *Dissertation Abstracts International*, 33 (1973), 2067A.

Jha, A. "Christopher Fry and the Theatre of the Absurd." *Indian Journal of English Studies*, 8 (March 1967), 106–23.

Jones, Paul D. "The Intruder in the Drama of Harold Pinter: A Functional Analysis." *Dissertation Abstracts International*, 32 (1972), 4758A–59A (Syracuse).

Kael, Pauline. "The Comedy of Depravity: *Accident*." In *Kiss Kiss Bang Bang*. New York: Bantam, 1971. Pp. 129–34. An interesting review of the film *Accident*, which Kael likes in spite of its faults, this selection contains an accurate discussion of Pinter's failings as a scenarist: "In movies Pinter doesn't avoid exposition—he's just no good at it."

———. *Going Steady*. New York: Bantam, 1971. Includes another disparaging review, this time of the cinematic version of *The Birthday Party* (pp. 260–61). Pinter fails because he is "the actor as dramatist" whose writing does not transfer to the screen because the magnetism of live acting becomes rigid on film.

Kahane, Eric. "Pinter et le réalisme irréel." *L'Avant-Scène*, No. 378 (15 April 1967), 9. In French. Discusses dialogue and man's isolation.

Kalem, T. E. "Is Memory a Cat or a Mouse?" *Time*, 29 Nov. 1971, pp. 70–71. A disparaging review of the New York production of *Old Times*, a "bit of a bore" that is evidence that in this treatment of memory Pinter "has mistaken a dead end for a new road."

———. "Roomer." *Time*, 12 Oct. 1970, pp. 60 ff.

Kastor, Frank. "The Theatre of Harold Pinter." Speech given at the Univ. of Southern California, 22 April 1968.

Kauffmann, Stanley. "The Birthday Party." *New Republic*, 4 Jan. 1969; rpt. in *Figures of Light: Film Criticism and Comment*. New York: Harper and Row/Colophon, 1967. Pp. 128–29. A review of the film, which Kauffmann feels is inferior to both the play and the earlier movie version of

The Caretaker, in part because *The Birthday Party* is not as strong a play and in part because Director William Friedkin is distractingly clever.

———. "The Guest." *New Republic*, 25 Jan. 1964; rpt. in *A World on Film: Criticism and Comment*. New York: Dell/Delta, 1966. Pp. 213–15. A review of the film version of *The Caretaker*, commenting on Pinter's technical artistry and drawing the conclusion that the piece is "fully revealed" as a movie.

———. "Landscape and Silence." *New Republic*, 25 April 1970, pp. 20, 31. A review.

Kaufman, M. W. "Actions That a Man Might Play: Pinter's *The Birthday Party*." *Modern Drama*, No. 16 (Sept. 1973), 167–78.

Kemper, Robert. "One Man's Family." *Christian Century*, 84 (1 March 1967), 276–77. Concerned with *The Homecoming* as a theological allegory. Unconvincing.

Kennard, Jean E. *The Literature of the Absurd*. New York: Harper, 1975.

Kennedy, Andrew. *Six Dramatists in Search of a Language*. Cambridge: Cambridge Univ. Press, 1975. Contains a heavily researched chapter on Pinter's concept of the failure of language in his creation of dialogue.

Keown, Eric. "At the Play." *Punch*, 25 Jan. 1961, p. 186. Review of the original stage production of *A Slight Ache*.

Kerr, Walter. " 'The Dumbwaiter' and 'The Collection.' " *New York Herald Tribune*, 27 Nov. 1962, p. 20. Review.

———. *God on the Gymnasium Floor, and Other Theatrical Adventures*. New York: Simon and Schuster, 1972. Includes a chapter on Pinter: "The Playwright as Existentialist," pp. 127–58. Basically a rewrite of Kerr's Columbia University pamphlet, *Harold Pinter*.

———. *Harold Pinter*. Columbia Essays on Modern Writers, No. 27. New York: Columbia Univ. Press, 1967; London, 1967. Pinter not only states existential themes, his plays "function according to existential principle," Kerr asserts.

———. "Kerr Reviews Pinter's 'Room' and 'Slight Ache.' " *New York Herald Tribune*, 10 Dec. 1964, p. 16. Review.

———. "A Pox on Shocks." *New York Times*, 15 Jan. 1967. A review of Pinter's *The Homecoming*.

———. "Put Off—Or Turned On—By Pinter." *New York Times*, 15 Oct. 1967, Sec. 2, p. 11. Offers reasons why most people would not like *The Birthday Party*. The reasons include length, lack of concrete action, a feeling that Stanley could escape if he really wanted to. Rpt. in Kerr's *Thirty Plays Hath November*.

———. "The Something That Pinter Holds Back." *New York Times*, 3 Nov. 1968, D, p. 7. Reviews of *Tea Party* and *The Basement*.

———. "Theater Is the Victim of a Plot." *New York Times*, 25 June 1967.

Kerr speaks on the theatre as mostly unchanging, though Pinter (especially in *The Homecoming*) is getting away from the conventional.

―――. *The Theatre in Spite of Itself*. New York: Simon and Schuster, 1963. Discusses *The Caretaker*, pp. 116–19. See also pp. 29–41.

―――. "The Theater: Pinter's *Homecoming*." *New York Times*, 6 Jan. 1967. An unfavorable report on *The Homecoming*.

―――. *Thirty Plays Hath November*. New York: Simon and Schuster, 1969. Includes "The Struggle to See: The Moment of Pinter," about *The Birthday Party*, pp. 41–46.

Kershaw, John. "*The Caretaker*." In *The Present Stage*. London: Collins, 1966. Pp. 70–87.

Killinger, John. *World in Collapse: The Vision of Absurd Drama*. New York: Delta, 1971. Includes a discussion of Pinter's work.

Kitchin, Laurence. *Drama in the Sixties: Form and Interpretation*. London: Faber, 1966.

―――. *Mid-Century Drama*. London, 1962. "Compressionism" is seen as Pinter's main technique in both language and dramatic situation. Mentions similarity to Chekhov. See pp. 119–22.

―――. "Realism in the English Mid-Century Drama." *World Theatre*, 14, No. 1 (Jan. 1965), 17–26. A tracing of influences on contemporary English realists, citing a mastery of experimental staging, scenery, and dialect as praiseworthy and unprecedented graces.

Klineman, Neil. "Naming of Names." In *Pinter's Optics*. Midwest Monographs. 1st series, No. 1. Urbana, Ill.: Depot, 1967. Pp. 4–5.

Knight, G. Wilson. "The Kitchen Sink: On Recent Developments in Drama." *Encounter*, 21, No. 6 (Dec. 1963), 48–54. Pinter, as a member of the "kitchen sink" school of dramatists, is depicted as trying to reestablish human values by balancing "mental discontinuities" with "objective absurdities."

Kostelanetz, Richard. *On Contemporary Literature*. New York: Avon, 1969.

Kroll, Jack. "Blood from Stones." *Newsweek*, 16 Oct. 1967, pp. 104, 106. Review of the New York production of *The Birthday Party*.

Kunkel, Francis L. "Dystopia of Harold Pinter." *Renascence*, 21 (1968), 17–20.

Lahr, John, ed. *A Casebook on Harold Pinter's The Homecoming*. New York: Grove Press, 1971. An interesting collection of essays on meaning, language, characterization, etc., by Martin Esslin ("*The Homecoming*: An Interpretation"), Irving Wardle ("The Territorial Struggle"), Margaret Croyden ("Pinter's Hideous Comedy"), John Russell Taylor ("Pinter's Game of Happy Families"), Steven M. L. Aronson ("Pinter's 'Family' and Blood Knowledge"), Rolf Fjelde ("Plotting Pinter's Progress"), Bernard Dukore ("A Woman's Place"), Augusta Walker ("Why the

Lady Does It"), and pieces by Lahr. Interviews with the director, set designer, and two actors prove surprisingly useful in insights and information.

————. "An Actor's Approach." In Lahr, *A Casebook on Harold Pinter's The Homecoming*, pp. 137–50. An interview with John Normington, Sam in *The Homecoming*.

————. "An Actor's Approach." In Lahr, *A Casebook on Harold Pinter's The Homecoming*, pp. 151–74. An interview with Paul Rogers, Max in *The Homecoming*.

————. "A Designer's Approach." In Lahr, *A Casebook on Harold Pinter's The Homecoming*, pp. 9–26. An interview with John Bury about staging *The Homecoming*.

————. "Harold Pinter." In Kostelanetz, *On Contemporary Literature*, pp. 682–89.

————. "Pinter and Chekhov: The Bond of Naturalism." *Drama Review*, 13, No. 2 (1968), 137–45. Rpt. in Lahr, *Astonish Me: Adventures in Contemporary Theatre*. New York: Viking, 1973.

————. "Pinter the Spaceman." *Evergreen Review*, No. 55 (June 1968); rpt. in Lahr, *Up Against the Fourth Wall*, pp. 175–94; rpt. in Lahr, *A Casebook on Harold Pinter's The Homecoming*, pp. 175–93. Pinter's naturalism.

————. "Pinter's Language." In Lahr, *A Casebook on Harold Pinter's The Homecoming*, pp. 123–36. Emphasis is on silence.

————. "Pinter's Room: Who's There?" *Arts Magazine*, March 1967, pp. 21–23.

————. *Up Against the Fourth Wall*. New York: Grove Press, 1969. Includes "Pinter the Spaceman" (see above).

Lambert, J. W. "Trial by Laughter." *Sunday Times* (London), 21 June 1964, p. 33. Review of *The Birthday Party* revival.

Langley, Lee. "Genius—A Change in Direction." *Daily Telegraph Magazine* (London), 23 Nov. 1973, pp. 30–36. Combination reminiscence, article, and interview, with focus on Pinter's direction of the film version of *Butley*.

Leech, Clifford. "Two Romantics: Arnold Wesker and Harold Pinter." In A. Lewis, *The Contemporary Theatre*, pp. 11–31. Leech feels that Pinter and Wesker share with Wordsworth and Coleridge and each other a similar view and approach to the inner and outer life of man.

Lesser, S. O. "Reflections on Pinter's *The Birthday Party*." *Contemporary Literature*, 13 (Winter 1972), 34–43.

————. *Tragedy*. New York: Harper and Row, 1969. Vol. I in The Critical Idiom Series. A study of tragedy which includes Pinter's work as a notable example of contemporary tragedy.

Levedova, I. "A New Hero Appears in the Theatre." *Inostrannaya Literatura*, No. 1 (Jan. 1962), 201–8. Pinter (and Osborne, Wesker, Behan, Delaney) has created a protesting plebeian hero.

Lewis, Allan. *The Contemporary Theatre*. New York: Crown, 1971.

————. "The English Theatre—Osborne, Pinter, Shaffer," In *Anthropological Essays*, by Oscar Lewis. New York: Random House, 1970. Pp. 315–35. Rpt. in A. Lewis, *The Contemporary Theatre*.

Lewis, Peter. "Fascinated by Unsatisfactory People." *Time and Tide*, 21 June 1962, pp. 16–17. *The Collection* is regarded as a typical Pinter play.

Leyburn, Ellen D. "Comedy and Tragedy Transposed." *Yale Review*, 53 (Summer 1964), 553–62.

Lockwood, Lyn. "Pinter Play's Message Is Received." *Daily Telegraph* (London), 29 March 1963, p. 16. Review of the television production of *The Lover*.

Loney, Glenn. "Broadway in Review." *Educational Theatre Journal*, 19 (Dec. 1967), 511–17. Review of the New York production of *The Birthday Party*.

Lumley, Frederick. "Harold Pinter." In *New Trends in Twentieth-Century Drama*. London: Barrie and Rockliff, 1967. Pp. 266–73.

————. *New Trends in Twentieth Century Drama: A Survey Since Ibsen and Shaw*. 3d ed. New York: Oxford, 1967.

McCarten, John. "Down, Way Down by the Seaside." *New Yorker*, 14 Oct. 1967, p. 151. Review of the New York production of *The Birthday Party*.

McCrindle, Joseph F., ed. *Behind the Scenes: Theatre and Film Interviews from the Transatlantic Review*. New York: Holt, Rinehart and Winston, 1971.

McLaughlin, J. "Harold Pinter and PBL." *America*, 118 (10 Feb. 1968), 193. A discussion of *The Dwarfs*.

MacNeice, Louis. *Varieties of Parable*. Cambridge: Cambridge Univ. Press, 1965. Pp. 121–23.

"Malice Domestic." *Newsweek*, 21 Dec. 1964, pp. 75–76. Review of *A Slight Ache* and *The Room*.

Malkin, Lawrence. "Pinter's New World." *Time*, 19 May 1975, p. 80. Review of *No Man's Land* which sees the "dark inevitability of the future . . . of death in life," as the drama's concern. The play becomes "exhilarating theatre" because it is "very funny."

Malpas, Edward. "A Critical Analysis of the Stage Plays of Harold Pinter." Diss., Univ. of Wisconsin, 1965.

Mannes, Marya. "Just Looking, Thanks." *Reporter*, 13 Oct. 1960, p. 48. "Pinter's talent lies as much in his silences as in his talk: his timing is masterly, his dialogue hypnotic in its repetition either of absurd clichés or plain human confusion."

Manvell, Roger. "The Decade of Harold Pinter." *Humanist*, 132 (April 1967), 112–15.

Marcus, Frank. "Pinter: The Pause That Refreshes." *New York Times,* 12 July 1969, D, p. 8. The use of language and non-language (especially pauses and silences) to convey meaning in *Landscape* and *Silence* is discussed in a review of the two plays.

Marowitz, Charles. "New Wave in a Dead Sea." *Quarterly Review,* 1 (Oct. 1960), 270–77. Comments on Pinter, the most important of the "New Wave" dramatists, to the effect that his poetic drama depends on symbols and "mood concept" to "bypass the cerebrum and plunge directly into the [non-Freudian] psyche."

———. "Notes on the Theater of Cruelty." *Tulane Drama Review,* 11 (Winter 1966), 152–56. Artaud's "Theatre of Cruelty" and its effect on young playwrights.

———. " 'Pinterism' Is Maximum Tension Through Minimum Information." *New York Times,* 1 Oct. 1967, pp. 36–37. Generally a character sketch of Pinter, with some relating of facts to plays, especially the early ones.

———. "Theatre Abroad." *Village Voice,* 1 Sept. 1960. Pinter is questioned about the meaning of *The Caretaker.* He claims it is "about love"—which Marowitz equates with "need."

———, Tom Milne, and Owen Hale, eds. *The Encore Reader: A Chronicle of the New Drama.* London, 1965.

——— and Simon Trussler. *Theatre at Work: Playwrights in the Modern British Theatre.* Introd. by Irving Wardle. New York, 1970. An interview.

Marshall, Norman. "The Plays of Rodney Ackland." *London Magazine,* April 1965, pp. 62–67. Ackland's plays are forerunners of Pinter's.

Mast, Gerald. "Pinter's *Homecoming.*" *Drama Survey,* 6, No. 3 (Spring 1968), 266–77.

Matthews, Honor. *The Primal Curse.* London: Chatto and Windus, 1967. See pp. 22–23, 198–201.

Melloan, George. "Pinter's Abstract Dramatic Art." *Wall Street Journal,* 18 Nov. 1971, p. 22. A review of *Old Times* which sees the play as a poetic abstract, meaning that the drama appeals to our emotions and has no meaning!

Messenger, Ann P. "Blindness and the Problem of Identity in Pinter's Plays." *Die Neueren Sprachen,* 21: 481–90.

Milne, Tom. ["*Accident*"]. *Sight and Sound,* Spring 1967, pp. 57–59; rpt. in Boyum and Scott, *Film as Film: Critical Responses to Film Art,* pp. 38–44. A review and explication of the film *Accident.*

———. "The Hidden Face of Violence." In J. R. Brown, *Modern British Dramatists,* pp. 38–46.

Minogue, Valerie. "Taking Care of *The Caretaker.*" *Twentieth Century,* 168 (Sept. 1960), 243–48. *The Caretaker* as a dramatic expression of Pinter's concepts about the evasion of communication.

Moore, Mavor. "The Decline of Words in Drama." *Canadian Literature*, 46 (1970), 11–18.

Morris, Kelly. "The Homecoming." *Tulane Drama Review*, 11, No. 2 (Winter 1966), 185–91. *The Homecoming* is seen as a sort of comedy of manners in the tradition of Ibsen and Strindberg combined with the aggressive nature of the family and a confusion of sexual roles.

Morrison, Kristin. "Pinter and the New Irony." *Quarterly Journal of Speech*, 55 (1969), 388–93.

Mortimer, John. "Now This Is What I Call Great Acting." *Evening Standard* (London), 31 May 1960, p. 12. Review of *The Caretaker*.

Muller, Robert. "Hate Yourself Though You May, You'll Enjoy These Plays." *Daily Mail* (London), 19 Jan. 1961, p. 3. Review of the original stage production of *A Slight Ache*.

Murphy, Robert P. "Non-verbal Communication and the Overlooked Action in Pinter's *The Caretaker*." *Quarterly Journal of Speech*, 58: 41–47. The actions of the characters in *The Caretaker* are as important as the dialogue in determining the meaning of the play; attention to nonverbal communication shows that Mick and Aston consciously set out to destroy Davies' psyche.

Nelson, Gerald. "Harold Pinter Goes to the Movies." *Chicago Review*, 19, No. 1 (Summer 1966), 33–43. Pinter's work in film (e.g., *The Caretaker/ The Guest*) shows both greater freedom and control of movement in creating "real human personalities."

Nelson, Hugh. "*The Homecoming*: Kith and Kin." In J. R. Brown, *Modern British Dramatists*, pp. 145–63.

"New Plays. The Word as Weapon." *Time*, 13 Oct. 1967, pp. 71–72. Review of the New York production of *The Birthday Party*.

Nightingale, Benedict. "Inaction Replay." *New Statesman*, 2 May 1975, p. 601. Review of *No Man's Land* as unsuccessful because Pinter's preoccupations have led him to repetition and "resurrecting mannerisms." The part of Spooner is more memorable than the play itself, according to the critic.

Odajima, Yushi. "Pinter Notes." *Eigo Seinen*, 115 (1969), 416–96. In Japanese.

Oliver, Edith. "The Bum in the Attic." *New Yorker*, 14 Oct. 1961, p. 162. Discusses *The Caretaker* as a non-allegorical play.

Orley, Ray. "Pinter and the Menace." *Drama Critique*, 2 (1968), 124–48.

Pálfy, István. "Modern English Drama Through Hungarian Eyes." *Hungarian Studies in English*, 5: 137–49.

Pallavincini, Roberto. "Aspetti della drammaturgia contemporanea." *Aut Aut*, No. 81 (May 1964), 68–73. In Italian. Failure to fulfill the social function of drama in terms of audience involvement.

Palmer, David S. "A Harold Pinter Checklist." *Twentieth Century Literature*, 16, No. 4 (Oct. 1970), 287–96. Beware of mistakes in citations.

Parker, R. B. "Force and Society: The Range of Kingsley Amis." *Wisconsin Studies in Contemporary Literature*, 11, No. 3 (Fall 1961), 27–38.

———. "The Theory and Theatre of the Absurd." *Queen's Quarterly*, 73 (Autumn 1966), 421–41. Pinter (Beckett, Ionesco, and Genet) never "negates negation" to conform to the theory of the Absurd advanced by Camus in *The Myth of Sisyphus*.

Pease, Nicholas B. "Role, Ritual and Game in the Plays of Harold Pinter." *Dissertation Abstracts International*, 32 (1972), 3324A (SUNY, Buffalo).

Pesta, John. "Pinter's Usurpers." *Drama Survey*, 6, No. 1 (Spring 1967), 54–65. In Pinter's dramas, from *The Room* through *The Homecoming*, man's existential security is threatened by a "usurper."

Petrulian, Catrinel. "Intre realism și absurd—Harold Pinter." *Revista de Istorie și Theorie Literara*, 21: 533–39.

Pierce, Roger. "Three Play Analyses." Diss., Univ. of Iowa, 1969.

Pinter, Harold

Plays

The Birthday Party. London: Encore, 1959; rev. in *Seven Plays of the Modern Theatre*, ed. Harold Clurman. New York: Grove, 1967.

The Birthday Party: A Play in Three Acts. London: Methuen, 1960; rev. 1962; rpt. New York: Grove, 1969.

The Birthday Party and Other Plays. London: Methuen, 1960. Includes *The Room* and *The Dumb Waiter*.

The Caretaker. London: Methuen, 1960; rev. 1962; rpt. in Hewes, *1961/62 Best Plays*; rpt. in *Modern British Drama* (orig. *The New British Drama*); recorded on Oriole Records, M.G. 20093-4.

A Slight Ache. Tomorrow. Oxford, No. 4, 1960.

A Slight Ache and Other Plays. London: Methuen, 1961; rev. 1970. The 1970 edition includes corrections (the names of the actors playing Pete and Mark in the Arts Theatre production were listed in reverse originally, and the photographer's name was misspelled). Includes *A Night Out*, *The Dwarfs*, and the revue sketches "Trouble in the Works," "The Black and White," "Request Stop," "Last to Go," and "Applicant." "The Black and White": rpt. in *The Spectator*, 205 (1 July 1960), 16, in prose; rpt. in *Flourish* (magazine of the Royal Shakespeare Theatre Club), Summer 1965; rpt. in *Transatlantic Review*, 21 (Summer 1966), 51–52. "Last to Go" recorded on *Kenneth Williams*, Decca Records, DFE 8548; also recorded on *Pieces of Eight*, Decca Records, SKL 4084.

The Birthday Party and The Room. New York: Grove, 1961, rev. 1968.

The Caretaker and The Dumb Waiter: Two Plays. New York: Grove, 1961; rev. 1965. *The Dumb Waiter*: rpt. in Cohn and Dukore, *Twentieth Cen-*

tury Drama; rpt. in New English Dramatists series, No. 3, ed. Tom Maschler, London: Penguin, 1961; rpt. in Soule, *The Theatre of the Mind.*

Three Plays: A Slight Ache, The Collection, The Dwarfs. New York: Grove, 1962; *The Collection* rpt. in Hewes, *1962/63 Best Plays.*

The Collection and The Lover. London: Methuen, 1963; rev. 1964. Also includes "The Examination" (which first appeared in *Prospect*), in prose.

"Dialogue for Three." *Stand*, 6, No. 3 (1963).

The Homecoming. London: Methuen, 1965; 2d. ed. London: Methuen, and New York: Grove, 1966; rpt. in London, 1968; rpt. in Guernsey, *The Best Plays of 1966–1967*; rpt. London: Karnac/Curwen, 1968. The Karnac/Curwen edition is limited to 200 copies signed by Pinter and Harold Cohen, who created nine lithographs for the volume. Recorded on Caedmon Records, TRS 361.

The Dwarfs and Eight Revue Sketches. New York: Dramatists Play Service, 1965. Includes the revue sketches: "Trouble in the Works," "The Black and White," "Request Stop," "Last to Go," "Applicant," "Interview," "That's All," and "That's Your Trouble."

Tea Party and Other Plays. London: Methuen, 1967. Includes *The Basement* and *Night School.*

The Lover and Other Plays. New York: Grove, 1967. Includes *Tea Party* and *The Basement.*

The Lover, Tea Party, The Basement. New York: Grove, 1967.

"Special Offer." In Hinchcliffe, *Harold Pinter*, pp. 73–74.

A Night Out, Night School, Revue Sketches: Early Plays by Harold Pinter. New York: Grove, 1968.

Three Plays: Tea Party, The Basement, and The Lover. New York: Grove, 1968.

Landscape. London: Emanuel Wax for Pendragon, 1968; rpt. in *Evergreen Review*, No. 68 (July 1969). The Pendragon publication is a limited edition, copies 1–1000 for Great Britain, 1001–2000 for the United States.

Landscape and Silence. London: Methuen, 1969; rpt. New York: Grove Press, 1970. Also includes *Night.*

Old Times. London: Methuen, 1971; and New York: Grove (Black Cat), 1971; rpt. New York: Grove (Evergreen), 1973.

Monologue. London: Covent Garden Press, 1973. Limited edition.

No Man's Land. London: Eyre Methuen, 1975; rpt. New York: Grove, 1975.

Movie scripts and sources of films representing Pinter as director or writer

The Servant, released 1962. From Robin (Sir Robert) Maugham's novel, *The Servant.* London: Falcon, 1948; rpt. New York: Harcourt Brace, 1949; rpt. London: Heinemann, 1964.

The Caretaker (*The Guest*), released 1963. Based on Pinter's original play.

The Pumpkin Eater, released 1964. From Penelope Mortimer's novel, *The Pumpkin Eater*. London: Hutchinson, 1962.

The Quiller Memorandum, released 1966. From Adam Hall's novel, *The Berlin Memorandum*. London: Collins, 1965.

Accident, released 1967. From Nicholas Mosley's novel, *Accident*. London: Hodder and Stoughton, 1965.

The Birthday Party, released 1969. Based on Pinter's original play.

The Go-Between, released 1971. From L. P. Hartley's novel, *The Go-Between*. London: Hamish and Hamilton, 1953; rpt. New York: Avon, 1968.

Five Screenplays. London: Methuen, 1971; rpt. New York: Grove Press, 1974. Includes *The Servant, The Pumpkin Eater, The Quiller Memorandum, Accident,* and *The Go-Between*.

The Homecoming, released 1973. Based on Pinter's original play.

Butley, released 1974. From Simon Gray's play, New York: Viking, 1971. Recorded on Caedmon Records, TRS 362.

Remembrance of Things Past. From Marcel Proust's novel, *A la recherche du temps perdu* (1912–1927).

The Last Tycoon. From F. Scott Fitzgerald's novel. New York: Scribner's, 1941.

Langrishe, Go Down. From the novel by Aidan Higgins. New York: Grove, 1966.

Other writings by Pinter (*see also* Additional interviews with Pinter *preceding the Index*)

"Afternoon." *Twentieth Century*, 169 (Feb. 1961), 218. A poem.

"All of That." *Times Literary Supplement*, London, 69 (11 Dec. 1970), 1436; rpt. *Vogue*, 158 (July, 1971), 98. A poem.

"Beckett." In *Beckett at Sixty: A Festschrift*. London: Calder and Boyars, 1967. P. 86. A short extract from a letter to a friend in which Pinter declares that Beckett is "far and away the finest writer working," because of his honest portrayal of life.

"Between the Lines." Speech given at the Seventh National Students Drama Festival, Bristol. In *Sunday Times* (London) 4 March 1962, p. 25. An important revelation by Pinter of his concepts of verification and the use of language and paralanguage, often for defense.

"Distressing." *New York Times*, 26 April 1970. A letter to the editor in which Pinter rejects Clive Barnes' (see above) assessment of the New York production of *Landscape* and *Silence* as being vastly inferior to the London production. Pinter replies that the Lincoln Center and director Peter Gill did not "betray" his intentions ("I totally reject this") and that the "emphasis of simplicity, economy and clarity" was "rewarding."

"Harold Pinter Replies." *New Theatre Magazine*, Jan. 1961, 8–10. An answer to the charge that he is not politically involved in his works.

"Letter to the Editor." *Sunday Times* (London), 14 Aug. 1960. Pinter's reply to Leonard Russell's criticism of the laughter evoked by *The Caretaker*: "*The Caretaker* is funny, up to a point. Beyond that point it ceases to be funny, and it was because of that point that I wrote it."

Mac. London: Emanuel Wax for Pendragon, 1968; rpt. in *Harper's Bazaar*, 102 (Nov. 1968), 234–35. A brief reminiscence of Pinter's association with the Irish actor-manager Anew McMaster. The Pendragon publication is a limited edition, copies 1–1000 for Great Britain, 1001–2000 for the United States. Also rpt. in *Good Talks: An Anthology from BBC Radio*, ed. Derwent May, 1969.

"Memories of Cricket." *Daily Telegraph Magazine*, 16 May 1969.

"New Year in the Midlands" and "Chandeliers and Shadows." *Poetry London*, 19 (Aug. 1950). Poems, concluding stanzas interchanged.

"New Year in the Midlands," "Rural Idyll," "European Revels." *Poetry London*, 20 (Nov. 1950). Poems, by "Harold Pinta."

"One a Story, Two a Death." *Poetry London*, 22 (Summer 1951). A poem.

"poem." *New York Times Magazine*, 5 Dec. 1971, p. 135. A poem.

Poems. London: Enitharmon, 1968. Includes most of Pinter's poems which have appeared in periodicals, with the exception of "Rural Idyll" and "European Revels" in *Poetry London*, No. 20 (Nov. 1950), and "One a Story, Two a Death," in *Poetry London*, No. 22 (Summer 1951), which appeared under the name of "Harold Pinta." Selected by Alan Clodd.

"Tea Party." BBC Third Programme, 1964 (read by Pinter); *Playboy*, Jan. 1965, p. 124, in prose.

The Homecoming manuscript notes and a page of the typescript. Reproduced in *London Magazine*, NS No. 100 (July–Aug. 1969), 153–54. The notes are just snips from here and there in the play; the typescript is the entrance of Ruth and Teddy.

"Two People in a Room; Playwriting." *New Yorker*, 25 Feb. 1967, pp. 34–36.

"Writing for Myself." *Twentieth Century*, 168 (Feb. 1961), 172–75. Pinter comments on the difficulties of writing stage drama, the influence of his acting career on his playwriting, the realistic/non-realistic qualities of his writing, and his refusal to write political drama.

"Writing for the Theatre." *Evergreen Review*, Aug.–Sept. 1964, pp. 80–82; rpt. in Popkin, *The New British Drama*. Contains much of the same material as "Between the Lines"; not actually written by Pinter but compiled by Findlater from the tape of an interview and reportedly considered unsatisfactory by Pinter.

Juvenile works

"James Joyce." *Hackney Downs School Magazine*, No. 160 (Christmas 1946), 32–33. An essay expressing admiration for *A Portrait of the Artist as a Young Man*, *Ulysses*, and *Finnegan's Wake*.

"Dawn." *Hackney Downs School Magazine*, No. 161 (Spring 1947), 27. A poem.
"O beloved maiden." *Hackney Downs School Magazine*, No. 162 (Summer 1947), p. 14. A poem.
"Blood Sports." *Hackney Downs School Magazine*, No. 163 (Autumn 1947), 23–24. An essay.

Translations of Pinter's Works

Czech

Navrat Domu. Trans. Milan Lukes. In *Svetlova Literatura*, No. 4 (1966). [*The Homecoming.*]
Norozeniny and *Navrat Domu*. Trans. Milan Lukes. In *Anglicke Absurdni Divaldo*. Prague: Orbis, 1966. [*The Birthday Party*; *The Homecoming*.]
Správce. Trans. Milan Lukes. Prague: Orbis, 1965. [*The Caretaker.*]

Danish

En Tur i Byen. Trans. Klaus Rifbjerg. "En Turi i Byen—Moderne Englesk Dramatik i TV og Radio." Fredensborg: Arena, 1962. [*A Night Out.*]
Vicevaerten. Trans. H. C. Branner. Fredensborg: Arena, 1961. [*The Caretaker.*]

Dutch

De Kamer, De Dienstlift, De Huisbewaarder, De Collectie, De Minnaar. Amsterdam: Uitgeverij De Bezige Bij, 1966. [*The Room*; *The Dumb Waiter*; *The Caretaker*; *The Collection*; *The Lover*.]

French

La Collection suivi de l'Amant et de Le Gardien. Trans. Eric Kahane. Paris: Gallimard, 1967. [*The Collection*; *The Lover*; *The Caretaker*.]
L'Anniversaire. Trans. Eric Kahane. Paris: Gallimard, 1968. [*The Birthday Party*.]
Le Retour. Trans. Eric Kahane. *L'Avant-Scène*, No. 378 (15 April 1967). [*The Homecoming*.]

German

Die Geburtstagsfeier, Der stumme Diener, Das Zimmer, Die Zwerge. Trans. Willy H. Thiem. Rev. ed. Hamburg: Rowohlt, 1969. [*The Birthday Party*; *The Dumb Waiter*; *The Room*; *The Dwarfs*.]
Die Heimkehr, Der Liebhaber, Die Kollektion, Teegesellschaft, Tiefparterre. Trans. Willy H. Thiem. Hamburg: Rowohlt, 1967. [*The Homecoming*; *The Lover*; *The Collection*; *The Basement*; *Tea Party*.]

Der Hausmeister, Eine Nacht ausser Haus, Abendkurs, Ein leichter Schmerz.
  Trans. Willy H. Thiem. Rev. ed. Hamburg: Rowohlt, 1969. [*The Care-
  taker; A Night Out; Night School; A Slight Ache.*]
Dramen. Trans. Renate and Martin Esslin. Hamburg: Rowohlt, 1970. Includes
  *Landschaft, Schweigen, Der Hausmeister, Eine Nacht ausser Haus,
  Abendkurs,* and *Ein leichter Schmerz.* [*Landscape; Silence; The Care-
  taker; A Night Out; Night School; A Slight Ache.*]

Hungarian

A Gondnok. Trans. Tibor Bartos. In *Mai Angol Drámák.* Budapest: Europa,
  1965. [*The Caretaker.*]

Italian

Il Gardiano e altri drammi. Trans. Elio Nissim. Milan: Bompiani, 1962. In-
  cludes *La Stanza* and *Il Calapranzi* [*The Caretaker; The Room; The
  Dumb Waiter.*]
Un leggero malessere; Una serata fuori. Trans. Laura del Bono and Elio
  Nissim. In *Teatro Uno.* Ed. L. Codignola. Turin: Einaudi, 1962. [*A
  Slight Ache; A Night Out.*]

Polish

Kochanek. Trans. B. Taborski. *Dialog,* No. 8 (1966). [*The Lover.*]
Powrot do Dumo. Trans. Adam Tarn. *Dialog,* No. 12 (1965). [*The Home-
  coming.*]
Vrodziny Stanleys. Trans. Adam Tarn. *Dialog,* No. 10 (1960). [*The Birthday
  Party.*]

Portuguese

Feliz Aniversario. Trans. Artur Ramos and Jaime Salazar Sempaio. Lisbon:
  Preto, 1967. [*The Birthday Party.*]
O Monte Cargas. Trans. Luis de Stau Moneiro. In *Tempo de Teatro,* No. 3
  (n.d.), Lisbon. [*The Dumb Waiter.*]

Serbo-Croat

Bez Pogovora. In *Avangardna Drama.* Belgrade, 1964. [*The Dumb Waiter.*]

Spanish

El Conserje. Trans. Josefina Vidal and F. M. Lorda Alaiz. In *Teatro inglés.*
  Madrid: Aguilar, 1966. [*The Caretaker.*]
El Cuidor, El Amante, El Montaplatas. Trans. Manuel Barbera. Buenos Aires:
  Nueva Vision, 1965. [*The Caretaker; The Lover; The Dumb Waiter.*]
El Portero. Trans. T. R. Trives. *Primero Acto,* Jan. 1962. [*The Caretaker.*]
La Colección; El Amante. Trans. Luis Escobar. In *Primero Acto,* No. 83
  (1967). [*The Collection; The Lover.*]

Swedish

Mathissen. Trans. Lars Goran Calsson. In *I En Akt.* Ed. Ingvar Holm. Stockholm: Aldus, 1966. [*The Dumb Waiter.*]

Turkish

Dodumgünü Partisi. Trans. Memet Fuat. Published by De Yayinevi, 1965. [*The Birthday Party.*]

Pinter, Harold, and Clive Donner. "Filming 'The Caretaker.'" *Transatlantic Review,* No. 13 (Summer 1963), 17–26; rpt. in McCrindle, *Behind the Scenes.* New York: Holt Rinehart, 1971. An interview by Kenneth Cavander.

Pinter, Harold, John Fuller, and Peter Redgrove, eds. *New Poems.* 1967; London, 1968. A P.E.N. anthology of contemporary poetry.

"Pinter Patter." *Time,* 7 Dec. 1962, p. 54. Pinter must break with his concern with the "sealed nursery–dungeon of fears" if he is to achieve true stature as a dramatic artist.

"Pinterview." *Newsweek,* 23 July 1962, p. 69. An early interview with Pinter concerning his writing.

Popkin, Henry, ed. *Modern British Drama* (orig. *The New British Drama*). New York: Grove, 1964.

Porterfield, Christopher. "Memories as Weapons." *Time,* 14 June 1971, p. 49. Review of *Old Times.*

Prentice, Penelope A. "An Analysis of Dominance and Subservience as Technique and Theme in the Plays of Harold Pinter." *Dissertation Abstracts International,* 32 (1972), 7000A (Loyola, Chicago).

Prickett, Stephen. "Three Modern English Plays." *Philologica Pragensia,* 10 (1967), 12–21.

"Profile: Playwright on His Own." *Observer,* 15 Sept. 1963, p. 13. An early biographical sketch is included in this quick summary of Pinter's playwriting and screenwriting up to *The Lover* and *The Dwarfs.*

Pugh, Marshall. "Trying to Pin Down Pinter." *Daily Mail* (London), 7 March 1964. An interview with Pinter.

"Puzzling Surrealism of the Birthday Party." *Times* (London), 20 May 1958, p. 3. Review of the first run of *The Birthday Party.*

Quigley, Austin E. "The Dynamics of Dialogue: The Plays of Harold Pinter." *Dissertation Abstracts International,* 33 (1973), 6928A. Examines Pinter's plays in a linguistic perspective to show the diversity of ways in which language can transmit information.

—————. *The Pinter Problem.* Princeton, N.J.: Princeton Univ. Press, 1975.

"The Reaction Against Realism." *Times Literary Supplement,* 30 June 1961, p. 400.

Rickert, Alfred E. "Perceiving Pinter." *English Record*, 22, No. 2 (1971), 30–35.

Robertson, Roderick. "A Theatre of the Absurd: The Passionate Equation." *Drama Survey*, 2 (June 1962), 24–43.

Robinson, Robert. "With Proper Humility." *Sunday Times* (London), 2 Aug. 1959, p. 14. Review of the radio version of *A Slight Ache*.

Roll-Hansen, Diderik. "Harold Pinter og det absurde drama." *Samtiden*, 74 (Sept. 1965), 435–40. In Norwegian. Influences on Pinter of European dramatic traditions.

Roy, Emil. *British Drama Since Shaw*. Crosscurrents/Modern Critiques series. Carbondale: Southern Ill. Univ. Press, 1972. Includes discussion of Pinter.

Rubens, Robert. "Donald McWhinnie." *Transatlantic Review*, No. 12 (Spring 1963), 34–38. An actor who has played in several of Pinter's works, Mc-Whinnie discusses Pinter's use of language.

Rusinko, Susan. "Stratagems of Language in the Poems and Plays of Harold Pinter: A Study of Text, Sub-Text and Conscious Sub-Text." *Dissertation Abstracts International*, 32 (1972), 6451A.

Russell, Leonard. Article in the *Times* (London), Aug. 1968. An open letter to Pinter regarding audience laughter at the London production of *The Caretaker*—answered by the playwright (see above).

Sainer, Arthur. "A Slight Ache." In *The Sleepwalker and the Assassin*. New York: Bridgehead Books, 1964. Pp. 99–102.

Salem, Daniel. *Harold Pinter, dramaturge de l'ambiguïté*. Paris: Denoël, 1968. In French.

Sarris, Andrew. ["*Accident*."] *Village Voice*, 18 May 1967; rpt. in Boyum and Scott, *Film as Film*, pp. 31–34. A review of the film *Accident*. The movie is too static to be successful.

———. *Confessions of a Cultist: On the Cinema, 1955–1969*. New York: Simon and Schuster, 1970. Includes "The Birthday Party," pp. 409–14.

———. ["Second Thoughts About *Accident*."] *Village Voice*, 8 June 1967; rpt. in Boyum and Scott, *Film as Film*, pp. 34–35. Decides that there is more to the movie than he first thought, though he still feels the film fails.

Schechner, Richard. "Puzzling Pinter." *Tulane Drama Review*, 11, No. 2 (Winter 1966), 176–84. Pinter's plays rely on the audience to supply the outside-world framework necessary to elicit the subtextual meanings which are conveyed through implication.

Schenker, Ueli. "Versuche zur Ordnung: Harold Pinter und sein *Caretaker*." *Neue Zürcher Zeitung*, 13 April 1969. In German.

Schiff, E. F. "Pancakes and Soapsuds: A Study of Childishness in Pinter's Plays." *Modern Drama*, June 1973, pp. 91–101.

Schlegelmilch, Wolfgang. "Der Raum des Humanen: Zu Harold Pinters *The Caretaker*." *Die Neueren Sprachen*, 13 (1964), 328–33. In German.

Schlesinger, Arthur, Jr. "*The Go-Between*." *Vogue*, 15 Sept. 1971. A review which states that Pinter's "capacity to evoke genuine mystery by words" is the reason this film is so outstanding.

Schroll, Herman T. *Harold Pinter: A Study of His Reputation, 1958–1969.* Metuchen, N.J.: Scarecrow Press, 1971. With a checklist, notable primarily for listing production reviews.

Sear, Richard. "A Play to Scorch Nerve Ends." *Daily Mirror* (London), 23 March 1960, p. 18. Review of the British television production of *The Birthday Party.*

Sharp, William L. *Language in Drama: Meanings for the Director and the Actor.* Scranton, Pa.: Chandler Pub. Co. Includes a separate chapter on Pinter.

Sheed, Wilfred. *The Morning After.* London and New York: Farrar, Straus, 1971. Discusses *The Birthday Party*, pp. 227–29.

Shorter, Eric. "Pinter Up in the World. Horrors Round the Corner." *Daily Telegraph* (London), 12 May 1961, p. 17. Review of the television production of *The Collection.*

Shulman, Milton. "Sorry, Mr. Pinter, You're Just Not Funny Enough." *Evening Standard* (London), 20 May 1958, p. 6. Review of the first run of *The Birthday Party.*

———. "Three for One Give Mr. Williams an Actor's Field Day." *Evening Standard* (London), 19 Jan. 1961, p. 14. Review of the original production of *A Slight Ache.*

Sillitoe, Alan. "Novel or Play?" *Twentieth Century*, 169 (Feb. 1961), 206–11.

Simon, John. *Movies Into Film: Film Criticism, 1967–1970.* New York: Delta Books, 1971. Includes a review of *Accident* (pp. 337–42) in a chapter on "Pseudo-Art" which says some very unflattering things about Pinter's technique.

———. "Pinter, Boy Soprano." *Commonweal*, 27 Oct. 1967, pp. 122–23. Review of the New York production of *The Birthday Party.*

———. "Theatre Chronicle." *Hudson Review*, 14 (1961), 586–92. *The Caretaker* is seen as an almost complete failure in this review.

Singh, Mohindar. "Harold Pinter: A Reappraisal." *Indian Journal of English Studies*, 10 (1969), 81–95.

Sinko, Gregorz. "Atara i Mloda Anglia." *Dialogue*, 60, No. 4 (April 1961), 97–99. In Polish. Claims that the early plays are in the tradition of Kafka.

Smallwood, Clyde G. "Harold Pinter." In *Elements of Existentialist Philosophy in the Theatre of the Absurd.* Dubuque, Iowa: William C. Brown, 1966. Pp. 140–45.

Smith, Cecil. "Pinter: The Compulsion of Playwriting." *Los Angeles Times*, 3 Dec. 1967, Calendar Section, pp. 1 and 19. Pinter discusses his playwriting.

———. "Pinter's The Homecoming Opens." *Los Angeles Times*, 7 Dec. 1967.

A review of *The Homecoming*, including an interpretation of the characters.

Smith, Frederik N. "Uncertainty in Pinter: *The Dwarfs.*" *Theatre Annual*, 26 (1970), 81–96.

Smith, R. D. "Back to the Text." In Brown and Harris, *Contemporary Theatre*, pp. 117–37.

Soule, George. *The Theatre of the Mind*. Englewood Cliffs, N.J.: Prentice-Hall, 1974. Includes *The Dumb Waiter* in an anthology emphasizing the visual, theatrical aspects of drama.

Spanos, William V. "Modern Drama and the Aristotelian Tradition: The Formal Imperatives of Absurd Time." *Contemporary Literature*, 12: 345–72.

Spark, Muriel. "An Experiment in Gluttony." *Observer* (London), 13 Aug. 1961, p. 19. Review of *The Dumb Waiter* television production.

Sprague, Claire. "Possible or Necessary?" *New Theatre Magazine*, 8, No. 1 (Autumn 1967), 36–37.

Starkman, Alfred. "Schweigen—wörtlich genommen." *Die Welt*, 16 July 1969, p. 7. In German.

States, Bert O. "The Case for Plot in Modern Drama." *Hudson Review*, 20 (Spring 1967), 49–61. Attacks Pinter's formlessness and lack of linear plot (in answer to John Russell Brown's "Mr. Pinter's Shakespeare"; see above).

———. *Irony and Drama: A Poetics*. Ithaca, N.Y.: Cornell Univ. Press, 1971.

———. "Pinter's *Homecoming*: The Shock of Nonrecognition." *Hudson Review*, 21 (Aug. 1968), 474–86; rpt. Ganz, *Pinter*.

Stein, Karen F. "Metaphysical Silence in Absurd Drama." *Modern Drama*, 13, No. 4 (Feb. 1971), 423–31.

Storch, R. F. "Harold Pinter's Happy Families." *Massachusetts Review*, 8 (Aug. 1967), 703–12; rpt. Ganz, *Pinter*.

Streiker, Lowell D. "Pinter: Artificer of Menacing Meaninglessness." *Christian Century*, 13 Dec. 1967, p. 1604. Review of the New York production of *The Birthday Party*.

Styan, J. L. *The Dark Comedy: The Development of Modern Comic Tragedy*. 2d ed. Cambridge: Cambridge Univ. Press, 1968. Includes "After 'Godot': Ionesco, Genet, and Pinter," pp. 234–50.

———. "The Published Play After 1956: II." *British Book News*, No. 301 (Sept. 1965), 601–605. Pinter (drama of the Absurd) and Arden (new realism) are the most exciting of the new British dramatists.

———. "Television Drama." In Brown and Harris, *Contemporary Theatre*, pp. 185–204.

Supple, Barry. "Pinter's Homecoming." *Jewish Chronicle*, 25 June 1965, pp. 7, 31.

Sutherland, Jack. "Brilliant, Despairing Pinter." *Daily Worker* (London), 20 June 1964, p. 3. Review of *The Birthday Party* revival.

Sykes, Alrene. *Harold Pinter*. St. Lucia: Univ. of Queensland Press, and New York: Humanities Press, 1970. A good examination of theatrical techniques, but limited in interpretations.

———. "Harold Pinter's Dwarfs." *Komos*, 1 (June 1967), 70–75.

———. Introduction to *The Caretaker*. Sydney, 1965.

"Talk of the Town." *New Yorker*, 25 Feb. 1967. An interview with Pinter.

Talley, Mary E. "The Relationship of Theme and Technique in Plays of Harold Pinter." *Dissertation Abstracts International*, 33 (1973), 1744A–45A.

Taubman, Howard. "Harold Pinter: His 'Dumbwaiter' and 'Collection' Arrive." *New York Times*, 27 Nov. 1962, p. 44. Review.

———. "A Leap Forward (Pinter Makes Progress in Caretakers)." *New York Times*, 15 Oct. 1961. Comment on Pinter's rapid progression in ability from *The Birthday Party* to *The Caretaker*.

———. "Shared Quicksand (Our Reality Is Infirm, Says Pinter, as His Plays Probe Silence)." *New York Times*, 9 Dec. 1962. Comment on Pinter's style, especially in *The Caretaker* and *The Dumb Waiter*; *The Collection* is mentioned. A short passage contrasts Pinter and Robert Bolt.

———. "The Theater: Two Early Pinter Dramas." *New York Times*, 10 Dec. 1964, p. 62. Review of *A Slight Ache* and *The Room*.

Taylor, John Russell. "*Accident*." *Sight and Sound*, Autumn 1966, pp. 179–84. A review of the film *Accident*.

———. *Anger and After: A Guide to New British Drama*. London: Methuen, 1962; rev. 1969. Published in America under the title *The Angry Theatre*. New York: Hill and Wang; rev. 1969. Includes an important chapter on Pinter as a writer whose "unique eminence" entitles him to be studied by himself. A study of each play through *Landscape* which includes a discussion of Pinter's techniques (especially in relation to "casting doubt upon everything by matching each apparently clear and unequivocal statement with an equally clear and unequivocal statement of its contrary") which concludes that Pinter's work is the "most 'musical,'" [i.e., poetic], "of the new British drama."

———. "British Drama of the 50's." *World Theatre*, 11 (Autumn 1962), 241–54; rpt. in Kostelanetz, *On Contemporary Literature*, pp. 90–96. Pinter is studied among the "non-realists" as one of the most interesting writers (along with Arden) in English—part of "an explosion" of activity in the English theatre.

———. *Harold Pinter*. Longmans' Writers and Their Work series, No. 212. London: Longmans Green, 1969. The study traces Pinter's development (up to and including *Landscape*, *Silence*, and *Night*) from the comedies of menace to the questions of identity and verification explored in the later plays.

———. "A Pinter Power Struggle." *Plays and Players*, 12 (Aug. 1965) 34–35. Review of *The Homecoming*.

———. "Pinter's Game of Happy Families." In Lahr, *Casebook on Harold Pinter's The Homecoming*, pp. 57–66. Essentially *The Homecoming* section from *Anger and After*.

———. "Rags to Riches." *Plays and Players*, 11 (Aug. 1964), 28–29. Review of *The Birthday Party* revival.

———. "The Servant." *Sight and Sound*, Winter 1963–64, pp. 38–39. A review of the film.

———. "*Tea Party* and *The Basement*." *Plays and Players*, 18 (Nov. 1970), 36–39. Review.

Thompson, Harry. "Harold Pinter Replies." *New Theatre Magazine*, Vol. 2, No. 2 (1961). Interview.

Thornton, Peter C. "Blindness and the Confrontation with Death: Three Plays by Harold Pinter." *Die Neueren Sprachen*, 17 (May 1968), 213–23.

Towey, Denis J. "Form and Content in Selected Plays of Harold Pinter." *Dissertation Abstracts International*, 33 (1973), 3609A.

Trewin, John Courtenay. "Between the Lines." *Illustrated London Times*, 240 (30 June 1962), 1058. *The Collection*, a "full-hearted bore," is another instance of Pinter's persistence in failure.

———. "Cutting It Short." *Illustrated London News*, 4 Feb. 1961, p. 192. Review of the original stage production of *A Slight Ache*.

———. *Drama in Britain*. London, 1965.

———. "Four in Hand." *Illustrated London News*, 236 (14 May 1960), 850. Characterization is cited as a major reason for Pinter's success.

———. "The World of the Theatre. After the Party." *Illustrated London News*, 31 May 1958, p. 932. Review of the first run of *The Birthday Party*.

Trilling, Ossia. "The New English Realism." *Tulane Drama Review*, 7, No. 2 (Winter 1962), 184–93. Pinter follows the tradition begun with Osborne's *Look Back in Anger* in hostility toward the English institution of class structure and living under the modern world's threat of nuclear annihilation.

———. "The Young British Drama." *Modern Drama*, 3 (May 1960), 168. Theatres and their productions in England.

Tutaev, David. "The Theater of the Absurd . . . How Absurd?" *Gambit*, No. 2 (n.d.), 68–70. Looks at the Theatre of the Absurd as an expression of modern Romanticism which will die out.

Tynan, Kathleen. "In Search of Harold Pinter." *Evening Standard* (London), Part 1, 25 April 1968; Part 2, 26 April 1968. An interview with Pinter.

Tynan, Kenneth. "At the Theatre. Eastern Approaches." *Observer* (London), 25 May 1958, p. 15. Review of the first run of *The Birthday Party*.

————. "Let Coward Flinch." *Observer* (London), 22 Jan. 1961, p. 30. Review of the original production of *A Slight Ache*.

————. *Right and Left*. London: Longmans, 1967. A discussion of modern drama.

————. *Tynan on Theater*. London, 1964. A discussion of modern drama.

————. "A Verbal Wizard in the Suburbs." *Observer* (London), 5 June 1960, p. 16. Review of *The Caretaker*.

Uhlmann, Wilfred. "Neurotische Konflikte und triebsgesteuertes Sozialverhalten in den Stücken Harold Pinters." *Literatur in Wissenschaft und Unterricht*, 5: 299–312.

Vamos, Laszlo, and Gyorgy Lengyel. "Laszlo Vamos and Gyorgy Lengyel." *Transatlantic Review*, No. 18 (Spring 1965), 107–15. Hungarian reaction to Pinter—alien.

Vidan, Ivo. "Komedija nespokpjstava: a forum report." *Zagreb*, 9 (1963), 462–73.

von Rosador, Kurt Tetzeli. "Pinter's Dramatic Method: *Kullus, The Examination, The Basement*." *Modern Drama*, 14, No. 2 (Sept. 1971), 195–204. Reexamines the similarities in treating the subject of dominance in these three works in terms of "(1) the use of the door, (2) the adaption of the intruder to the room and its furniture, and (3) the lapse into silence as an instrument to circumvent the owner's privileged position."

Wade, David. "New Poetry in Pinter." *Times* (London), 26 April 1968, p. 9. Review of the radio version of *Landscape*.

Wagner, Marlene S. "The Game-Play in Twentieth-Century Absurdist Drama: Studies in a Dramatic Technique." *Dissertation Abstracts International*, 32 (1972), 4637A.

Walker, Augusta. "Messages from Pinter." *Modern Drama*, 10, No. 1 (May 1967), 1–10. Divides Pinter's work into allegories about life and cosmic concerns on the one hand and an examination of the drives within relationships between individuals.

————. "Why the Lady Does It." In Lahr, *Casebook on Harold Pinter's The Homecoming*, p. 117–22. Concludes that Ruth is needed.

Wardle, Irving. "A Director's Approach." In Lahr, *Casebook on Harold Pinter's The Homecoming*, pp. 9–25. An interview with Peter Hall about staging *The Homecoming*.

————. "Holding up the Mirror." *Twentieth Century*, 173 (Autumn 1964), 34–43. The action of contemporary British drama on English audiences and their reactions to it (nullifying the shock).

————. "Laughter in the Wilderness." *Observer* (London), 24 June 1962, p. 23. Review of *The Collection*.

————. "New Waves on the British Stage." *Twentieth Century*, 172 (1963), 57–65. Pinter has succeeded where his imitators have not in surviving the fads in taste of the English theatre.

————. "No Man's Land." *Times* (London), 25 April 1975, p. 13. A review which concludes that *No Man's Land* "makes its effects with total confidence: the objection is that effect has been raised into a first priority." Wardle is impressed by the use of language of the play (in spite of its being in part "pastiche Eliot" combined with an "insistent" Beckettian presence), but feels that the work fails to "locate spiritual malaise in some concrete image."

————. "Pinter Propriety." *Times* (London), 18 Sept. 1970. A review of *Tea Party* and *The Basement* which are both "concerned with the experience of invasion." Generally approving, Wardle does feel that there are some problems in transferring the works from the medium of television to the stage and that the cyclical ending of *The Basement* is not prepared for.

————. "Revolt Against the West End." *Horizon*, 5 (Jan. 1963), 26–33. Pinter's poetic drama is part of the challenge to conservative audiences put forth by the English Stage Company.

————. "The Territorial Struggle." In Lahr, *Casebook on Harold Pinter's The Homecoming*, pp. 37–44. Applies the idea of ethnology to Pinter's plays.

————. "There's Music in That Room." *Encore*, 7 (1960), 32–34. Pinter's symbolic *The Caretaker* creates the formal quality of music similar to Chekhov.

Warner, John M. "The Epistemological Quest in Pinter's *The Homecoming*." *Contemporary Literature*, 2 (Summer 1970), 340–53. In *The Homecoming* Pinter explores the "epistemological possibilities" open to man "in his efforts to overcome his crippling alienation from his own self."

Wasson, Richard. "Mime and Dream." In *Pinter's Optics*, Midwest Monographs, 1st series, No. 1. Urbana, Ill.: Depot, 1967, pp. 7–8.

Watts, Richard, Jr. "An Adventure in Early Pinter." *New York Post*, 5 Oct. 1967, p. 55. Review of the New York production of *The Birthday Party*.

————. "Two Remarkable Plays by Pinter." *New York Post*, 10 Dec. 1964, p. 46. Review of *A Slight Ache* and *The Room*.

Weales, Gerald. "Pinter at Work." *Commonweal*, 6 Dec. 1968, pp. 350–51. Review of *The Tea Party* and *The Basement*.

Welland, Dennis. "Some Post-War Experiments in Poetic Drama." In Armstrong, *Experimental Drama*.

Wellwarth, George. *The Theater of Protest and Paradox*. New York: New York Univ. Press, 1964; rev. 1971. Pinter's "Comedy of Allusiveness" is reminiscent of the French *avant-garde*. By the time he had written *The Lover*, Pinter had established himself as "the most promising of England's young playwrights" with his "most original mind" and willingness to "experiment with new dramatic forms and techniques."

West, Anthony. "The Birthday Party, 'Theatre at Its Very Best.'" *Vogue*, 1

Nov. 1967, p. 134. Review of the New York production of *The Birthday Party*.

Williams, Raymond. "*The Birthday Party*: Harold Pinter." In *Drama from Ibsen to Brecht*. London: Chatto and Windus, 1968. Pp. 322–25.

————. "New English Drama." *Twentieth Century*, 170 (1961), 169–80; rpt. in J. R. Brown, *Modern British Dramatists*, pp. 26–37. An overview which mentions Pinter.

Wilsher, Peter. "What Happened in Leeds?" *Sunday Times* (London), 17 June 1962, p. 44. Review of the radio version of *The Collection*.

Winegarten, Renee. "The Anglo-Jewish Dramatist in Search of His Soul." *Midstream*, 12 (Oct. 1966), 40–52.

Winsten, Archer. "Reviewing Stand." *New York Post*, 21 Jan. 1964, p. 44. Review of the film version of *The Caretaker*.

————. "A New Wave Rules Britannia." *Theatre Arts*, 45 (Oct. 1961), 17–19. A brief survey of the English theatre in the early sixties.

Worsley, T. C. "The Arts and Entertainment: A New Dramatist or Two." *New Statesman*, 31 May 1958, pp. 692, 694. An early estimation of Pinter as an offbeat comic writer who shows potential, though an excess of symbolism is the major fault of *The Birthday Party*.

Wray, Phoebe. "Pinter's Dialogue: The Play on Words." *Modern Drama*, 13, No. 4 (Feb. 1971), 418–22.

Zimmerman, Paul D. "Theatre in the Camera." *Newsweek*, 3 Dec. 1973, pp. 61–62. A review of the film version of *The Homecoming*, stating that it is even better than the original stage play.

Zolotow, Maurice. "Young Man with Scorn." *New York Times*, 17 Sept. 1961. A sketch of Pinter's character and an extended biography, with synopses of plays *The Birthday Party*, *The Dumb Waiter*, *The Caretaker*, and *The Collection*.

Selected reviews of Pinter plays not included above

The Basement
  New York Times, 16 Oct. 1968, p. 40.
  Time, 25 Oct. 1968, p. 69.
  New Yorker, 26 Oct. 1968, pp. 140–41.
  Newsweek, 28 Oct. 1968, p. 135.
  Nation, 207 (4 Nov. 1968), 477.
  Vogue, Dec. 1968, p. 170.
  Commonweal, 89 (6 Dec. 1968), 350–51.
The Birthday Party
  Spectator, 200 (30 May 1958), 687.
  New Statesman, 55 (31 May 1958), 692; 58 (12 Dec. 1959), 836.

Encore, July–Aug. 1958, pp. 39–40.

Saturday Review, 26 Aug. 1961, p. 26; 21 Oct. 1967, p. 50; 28 Oct. 1967, pp. 46–47.

Christian Science Monitor, 24 June 1964, p. 6.

New York Times, 1 Oct. 1967, sec. 2, p. 1; 4 Oct. 1967, p. 40; 15 Oct. 1967, sec. 2, p. 1; 17 Jan. 1968, p. 39.

Time, 13 Oct. 1967, pp. 71–72.

New Yorker, 14 Oct. 1967, p. 151.

Newsweek, 16 Oct. 1967, p. 104.

New Republic, 21 Oct. 1967, pp. 36–38.

Nation, 205 (23 Oct. 1967), 412–14.

Commonweal, 77 (27 Oct. 1967), 122–23.

America, 117 (28 Oct. 1967), 487; 118 (6 Jan. 1968), 10–12.

Vogue, 1 Nov. 1967, p. 134.

Christian Century, 74 (13 Dec. 1967), 1604.

New Theatre Magazine, Jan. 1969, p. 28.

The *Caretaker*

Spectator, 204 (10 Jan. 1960), 835; (6 May 1960), 661.

Illustrated London News, 236 (4 May 1960), 850.

New Statesman, 59 (7 May 1960), 666.

New Yorker, 9 July 1960, pp. 60–61; 14 Oct. 1961, p. 162.

Reporter, 13 Oct. 1960, p. 48.

Hudson Review, 14 (Spring 1961), 94–95; (Winter 1961/62), 590.

New York Times, 4 Oct. 1961, p. 42; 15 Oct. 1961, sec. 2, p. 1.

Time, 13 Oct. 1961, p. 58.

Newsweek, 16 Oct. 1961, p. 101.

Nation, 193 (21 Oct. 1961), 276.

Saturday Review, 23 Oct. 1961, p. 34.

New Republic, 23 Oct. 1961, pp. 29–30.

Commonweal, 75 (27 Oct. 1961), 122–23; 77 (28 Dec. 1962), 366.

Life, 17 Nov. 1961, pp. 195–96.

Christian Century, 78 (22 Nov. 1961), 1403–6.

America, 106 (9 Dec. 1961), 376.

National Review, 11 (16 Dec. 1961), 414.

Educational Theater Journal, 13 (Dec. 1961), 294–96.

Theatre Arts, Dec. 1961, p. 12.

New Theatre Magazine, July 1969, 29–30.

The *Collection*

Spectator, 208 (29 June 1962), 857.

Illustrated London News, 240 (30 June 1962), 1058.

New York Times, 27 Nov. 1962, p. 44; 9 Dec. 1962, sec. 2, p. 5.

Time, 7 Dec. 1962, p. 73.

New Yorker, 8 Dec. 1962, pp. 148–50.

Nation, 195 (15 Dec. 1962), 430.
Saturday Review, 15 Dec. 1962, p. 30.
Commonweal, 77 (28 Dec. 1962), 367.
Theatre Arts, Jan. 1963, pp. 10–11.

The Dumb Waiter
New Statesman, 59 (30 Jan. 1960), 150.
Illustrated London News, 236 (6 Feb. 1960), 226.
New York Times, 27 Nov. 1962, p. 44; 9 Dec. 1962, sec. 1, p. 5.
Time, 7 Dec. 1962, pp. 72–73.
New Yorker, 8 Dec. 1962, pp. 148–50.
Nation, 195 (15 Dec. 1962), 429–30.
Saturday Review, 15 Dec. 1962, p. 30.
Commonweal, 77 (28 Dec. 1962), 367.
Theatre Arts, Jan. 1963, pp. 10–11.

The Dwarfs
Theatre Arts, Jan. 1963, pp. 10–11.
New York Times, 29 Jan. 1968, p. 63.
America, 118 (10 Feb. 1968), 193.

The Homecoming
Guardian, 27 March 1965; 4 June 1965.
Daily Express, 3 April 1965.
Manchester Evening News, 3 April 1965.
New York Times, 4 June 1965, p. 38.
New Statesman, 69 (11 June 1965), 928.
Spectator, 11 June 1965, pp. 755, 758.
New Republic, 26 June 1965, pp. 29–30; 28 Jan. 1967, pp. 35–36.
New Yorker, 31 July 1965, p. 50; 14 Jan. 1967, p. 48.
Christian Century, 82 (8 Sept. 1965), 1096–97; 84 (1 March 1967), 267.
Vogue, 15 Sept. 1965, p. 75; 1 March 1967, p. 110.
Time, 89 (13 Jan. 1967), 43.
Newsweek, 69 (16 Jan. 1967), 93.
Saturday Review, 50 (21 Jan. 1967), 51.
Nation, 204 (23 Jan. 1967), 122.
Commonweal, 85 (27 Jan. 1967), 459.
Reporter, 36 (23 Feb. 1967), 46.
Life, 62 (3 March 1967), 6.
America, 116 (11 March 1967), 353.
National Review, 19 (21 March 1967), 316.
Hudson Review, 20 (Spring 1967), 105–107.
Commentary, 43 (June 1967), 73–74.

Landscape
Time, 94 (18 July 1969), 67.
Catholic World, 210 (Dec. 1969), 124–26.

New Yorker, 46 (11 April 1970), 84.
Saturday Review, 53 (25 April 1970), 16.
New Republic, 162 (25 April 1970), 20+.
The Lover
  Spectator, 211 (27 Sept. 1963), 386.
  New Yorker, 39 (11 Jan. 1964), 69–70.
  Saturday Review, 47 (17 Jan. 1964), 25.
  Time, 83 (17 Jan. 1964), 64.
  Commonweal, 79 (24 Jan. 1964), 484–85.
  Nation, 198 (27 Jan. 1964), 106.
  New Republic, 150 (1 Feb. 1964), 28.
  Vogue, 143 (15 Feb. 1964), 22.
A Night Out
  The Times (London), 2 March 1960, Sec. C, p. 13; 25 April 1960, Sec. C,
      p. 16.
Night School
  The Times (London), 22 July 1960, p. 16, A.
Old Times
  Newsweek, 77 (14 June 1971), 70.
  Time, 97 (14 June 1971), 76.
  Nation, 212 (28 June 1971), 829–30.
  Vogue, 158 (Aug. 1971), 71.
  Life, 71 (17 Sept. 1971), 16.
The Room
  Spectator, 204 (29 Jan. 1960), 138.
  Illustrated London News, 236 (6 Feb. 1960), 226.
  Time, 84 (18 Dec. 1964), 86; 18 July 1969, p. 67.
  New Yorker, 40 (19 Dec. 1964), 68.
  Newsweek, 64 (21 Dec. 1964), 75–76.
  Saturday Review, 47 (26 Dec. 1964), 33.
  Nation, 199 (28 Dec. 1964), 522–24.
  Vogue, 145 (1 Feb. 1965), 98.
  Commonweal, 82 (30 April 1965), 193.
  New York Times, 17 June 1965, p. 24; 13 July 1969, sec. 2, p. 8.
Silence
  Time, 94 (18 July 1969), 67.
  Catholic World, 210 (Dec. 1969), 124–26.
  New Yorker, 46 (11 April 1970), 84.
  Saturday Review, 53 (25 April 1970), 16.
  New Republic, 162 (25 April 1970), 20+.
A Slight Ache
  Spectator, 206 (27 Jan. 1961), 106.
  New York Times, 10 Dec. 1964, p. 62; 17 June 1965, p. 24.

Time, 84 (18 Dec. 1964), 86.
New Yorker, 40 (19 Dec. 1964), 68.
Newsweek, 64 (21 Dec. 1964), 75–6.
Saturday Review, 47 (26 Dec. 1964), 33.
Nation, 199 (28 Dec. 1964), 522–24.
Vogue, 145 (1 Feb. 1965), 98.
Commonweal, 82 (30 April 1965), 194.

Tea Party
    The Times (London), 5 Jan. 1965, Sec. G, p. 11; 26 March 1965, Sec. A,
        p. 15.
    New York Times, 16 Oct. 1968, p. 40.
    Time, 92 (25 Oct. 1968), 69.
    New Yorker, 44 (26 Oct. 1968), 140–41.
    Newsweek, 72 (28 Oct. 1968), 135.
    Nation, 207 (4 Nov. 1968), 477.
    Commonweal, 89 (6 Dec. 1968), 350–51.
    America, 119 (9 Nov. 1968), 447.
    Vogue, 152 (Dec. 1968), 170.

Selected reviews of Pinter films

Accident
    New York Times, 18 April 1967, p. 33; 30 April 1967, sec. 2, p. 1; 7 May
        1967, sec. 2, p. 1.
    Life, 21 April 1967, p. 12.
    Time, 21 April 1967, p. 101.
    New Yorker, 22 April 1967, pp. 150–51.
    Newsweek, 24 April 1967, p. 96.
    Commonweal, 28 April 1967, pp. 177–78.
    Saturday Review, 29 April 1967, p. 47.
    Nation, 204 (15 May 1967), 638.
    Esquire, June 1967, pp. 110–11.
    Vogue, 149 (June 1967), 77.
    New Republic, 3 June 1967, pp. 36–41.
    Christian Century, 84 (7 June 1967), 754–55.

The Birthday Party
    New Republic, 4 Jan. 1967, p. 34.
    Saturday Review, 7 Dec. 1968, p. 68.
    New York Times, 10 Dec. 1968, p. 54.
    New Yorker, 21 Dec. 1968, pp. 90–91; 13 Feb. 1971, p. 52.
    Newsweek, 23 Dec. 1968, pp. 89–90.
    Vogue, 1 Jan. 1969, p. 66.

Nation, 6 Jan. 1969, pp. 29–30.
Commonweal, 7 Feb. 1969, p. 591.
Holiday, March 1969, p. 30.
Time, 22 Feb. 1971, p. 52.
The Caretaker (*The Guest*)
    Town, Dec. 1963.
    Films and Filming, 4 Jan. 1964, pp. 24–25.
    New York Times, 21 Jan. 1964, p. 25.
    New Statesman, 13 March 1964, p. 423.
    The Observer, 15 March 1964, p. 24.
    The Sunday Times, 15 March 1964, p. 33.
    Spectator, 20 March 1964, p. 381.

The Go-Between
    New York Times, 30 July 1971, p. 21.
    Time, 9 Aug. 1971, pp. 44–45.
    New York Times, 11 Aug. 1971, p. 44; 12 Sept. 1971; 19 Sept. 1971.
    Film Quarterly, 25 (Spring 1972), 37–41.

Pinter People
    Christian Science Monitor, 4 April 1969, p. 6.
    New York Times, 7 April 1969, p. 86.

The Pumpkin Eater
    New York Times, 10 Nov. 1964, p. 58; 15 Nov. 1964, sec. 2, p. 1.
    Life, 13 Nov. 1964, p. 15.
    Time, 13 Nov. 1964, p. 125.
    New Yorker, 14 Nov. 1964, p. 148a.
    New York Times, 15 Nov. 1964, sec. 2, p. 1.
    Newsweek, 16 Nov. 1964, p. 102.
    Saturday Review, 21 Nov. 1964, p. 34.
    Commonweal, 27 Nov. 1964, p. 332.
    New Republic, 19 Dec. 1964, pp. 28–29.
    Vogue, 1 Jan. 1965, p. 66.

The Quiller Memorandum
    New York Times, 16 Dec. 1966, sec. 16, p. 59.
    Time, 23 Dec. 1966, p. 75.
    Newsweek, 26 Dec. 1966, p. 72.
    New Republic, 14 Jan. 1967, p. 42.
    Life, 27 Jan. 1967, p. 15.
    Commonweal, 3 Feb. 1967, p. 489.
    America, 4 Feb. 1967, p. 194.

The Servant
    The Observer, 17 Nov. 1963.
    New Yorker, 30 Nov. 1963, p. 207.

Sight and Sound, Winter 1963/64, pp. 38–39.
Saturday Review, 14 March 1964, p. 12.
New York Times, 17 March 1964, p. 30; 29 March 1964, sec. 2, p. 1.
Commonweal, 20 March 1964, p. 751.
Time, 20 March 1964, pp. 94a–94b.
New Republic, 21 March 1964, pp. 27–28.
Newsweek, 23 March 1964, pp. 95–96.
Nation, 6 April 1964, pp. 354–55.

Additional interviews with Pinter

Interview with John Sherwood. BBC European Service. In The Rising Generation series, 3 March 1960.*

Interview with Hallam Tennyson. BBC General Overseas Service. 7 Aug. 1960.*

Interview with Kenneth Tynan. BBC Home Service. Recorded 19 Aug. 1960, broadcast 28 Oct. 1960.*

Interview with Carl Wildman and Donald McWhinnie. BBC Network Three. In the Talking of Theatre series, 7 March 1961.

Interview with Laurence Kitchin and Paul Mayersberg. BBC Third Programme. "New Comment," 10 Oct. 1963.

Interview with John Kershaw. ITV. 1964.

Interview with John Russell Taylor. *Sight and Sound*, Autumn 1966.

Interview in "The Actor," a CBS Television special, 1968.

Interview with Joan Bakewell, BBC 2 TV. 11 Sept. 1969.

*Denotes duplicated manuscript exists.

Index